Childhood Adversity

PSYCHOLOGICAL PERSPECTIVES FROM SOUTH AFRICAN RESEARCH

EDITED BY

Andrew Dawes and David Donald

David Philip

CAPE TOWN & JOHANNESBURG

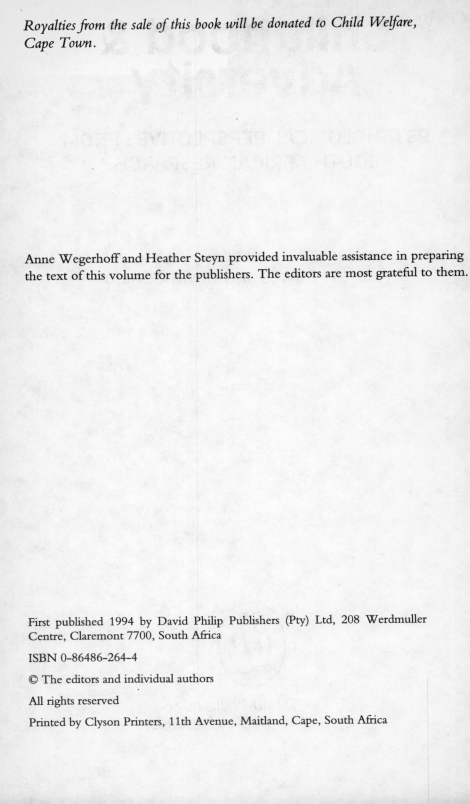

Royalties from the sale of this book will be donated to Child Welfare, Cape Town.

Anne Wegerhoff and Heather Steyn provided invaluable assistance in preparing the text of this volume for the publishers. The editors are most grateful to them.

First published 1994 by David Philip Publishers (Pty) Ltd, 208 Werdmuller Centre, Claremont 7700, South Africa

ISBN 0-86486-264-4

Printed by Clyson Printers, 11th Avenue, Maitland, Cape, South Africa

Contents

Contributors

SHIRLEY BERGER is a clinical psychologist with the Department of Psychiatry at the University of Cape Town.

KEVIN CONNOLLY is Professor and Head of the Department of Psychology at the University of Sheffield, England.

ANDREW DAWES is an Associate Professor in the Department of Psychology at the University of Cape Town.

DAVID DONALD is Professor of Educational Psychology in the School of Education at the University of Cape Town.

DON FOSTER is a Professor in the Department of Psychology at the University of Cape Town.

DAVID GILMOUR is a Senior Lecturer in the School of Education at the University of Cape Town.

RAOUL GRIESEL is Professor and Head of the Institute of Behavioural Sciences at the University of South Africa.

JAVE KVALSVIG is Head of the Child Development Programme of the Human Sciences Research Council in Durban.

ANN LEVETT is an Associate Professor in the Department of Psychology at the University of Cape Town.

CHRISTINE LIDDELL is a Senior Lecturer in the Psychology Department at the University of Ulster at Coleraine, Northern Ireland. She is also a Senior Researcher with the Early Education Unit of the Human Sciences Research Council in Johannesburg.

PUMLA QOTYANA is a field worker with the Child Development Programme of the Human Sciences Research Council in Durban.

LINDA RICHTER is Professor in the Division of Community Pediatrics in the Department of Pediatrics and Child Health at the University of the Witwatersrand.

BRIAN ROBERTSON is Professor and Head of the Department of Psychiatry at the University of Cape Town.

AGNES SHABALALA is a field worker with the Early Education Unit of the Human Sciences Research Council in Johannesburg.

CRAIN SOUDIEN is a Lecturer in the School of Education at the University of Cape Town.

JILL SWART-KRUGER is a lecturer in the Department of Social Anthropology at the University of South Africa.

Foreword

The protracted birth process of a new South African society offers an appropriate opportunity for reflecting on childhood as a developmental phase, and on the impact of adversity on the quality of childhood. The history of South Africa is as much about racial prejudice, discrimination and underdevelopment of the majority of the total population as it is about the systematic neglect reflected by the horrific statistics reported by the *Race Relations Survey* (and much more by what remains unreported and unacknowledged) about unrecorded births, illnesses, deaths, lost opportunities for child development and so on.

It could thus be said that our history has been characterised by our failure as a nation to nurture our children. It comes as no surprise that we are reaping the bitter fruits of that historical failure. Current concern about 'the marginalised youth' or 'the lost generation' is a belated response to a problem which has been evolving since the 1970s and which adults have been ignoring all along. But even more disconcerting is the tendency of significant opinion-formers to blame the young people alone for the situation they find themselves in. The solutions proposed to deal with the problem also indicate a lack of understanding of the nature of the problem and its origins. Proposals for militarisation programmes or calls for community service for the youth are likely to complicate an already complicated problem area.

A report by the Community Agency for Social Enquiry, *Growing Up Tough – A Survey of South African Youth, 1993,* suggests that what is needed is nurturance and support for the youth, and not further demands for their service. They have served South Africa for too long as activists, comrades, 'boys on the border', and so on. As Gill Straker aptly concluded in her book *Faces in the Revolution*: 'In the final analysis, it will be the degree to which proper nurturance and care of all South African children is provided, and the degree to which they are socialised toward tolerance, that will determine the extent to which South African youth can be transformed from faces in a revolution to whole persons in a peaceful world.'

This new book, *Childhood and Adversity,* tackles research questions from the perspective of psychologists. It provides a useful overview of the experience of childhood in the context of adversity whilst exploring methodological issues around research into childhood. It is an overdue contribution because academics, and specifically psychologists, have been slow to acknowledge disadvantaged children, let alone tackle the problems they face.

The book is also an important milestone in collaborative inter-disciplinary research. The strengths of anthropologists, psychiatrists, psychologists and educationists have been brought to bear on this effort. Childhood is a complex developmental phenomenon with a multiplicity of problems. It is only through a holistic approach that we can begin to unravel some of these complexities.

As Dr David Hamburg, President of Carnegie Corporation, has noted: 'In health, education, and in the social environment, we humans have been doing a lot of damage to our children – inadvertently for the most part, and with regret – but serious damage nonetheless. Yet there is good reason for hope.'

Hope is the touchword in this book. By understanding childhood in South Africa, we can contribute towards halting the historical theft of hope which Monica Wilson referred to in her anthropological research. South Africa and its children need a large dose of hope to face the future with greater confidence.

Dr M. A. Ramphele
Deputy Vice-Chancellor
University of Cape Town

1

Understanding the Psychological Consequences of Adversity

ANDREW DAWES AND DAVID DONALD

This chapter has two aims. The first is to outline the material and ideological context of childhood adversity in South Africa. The second is to discuss the way in which epistemological frameworks shape our knowledge of the psychological consequences of adversity. We note key structural features of South African society which contribute to the hardships experienced by most of the nation's children. Thereafter we discuss reasons for the relative lack of psychological research on disadvantaged children in this context. Finally we point to the importance of the ecocultural context and the child's active engagement in the developmental challenges presented by adverse environments.

Research on child development in high-risk environments has historically been driven mostly by positivistic forms of inquiry. Recently the dominance of this paradigm has been challenged by an approach to psychological knowledge broadly known as social constructivism. Examples of both orientations appear in this volume. The latter in particular has alerted us to the importance of questioning the universality of psychological responses to adversity. The perspective we shall be taking here is that the child is as much a cultural-historical construct as it is an object of absolutist scientific study. For this reason, both orientations to the study of child development are important.

The South African Context

The Situation of South African Children and Contributions to This Volume

Adversity during childhood is produced by a range of circumstances. On the one hand there are clearly structural causes which include poverty and political oppression, and on the other there are circumstances which arise in interpersonal contexts, such as the family, or through accident and illness. By the standards of those modern societies within which most psychological knowledge has been generated, the majority of South African children can be considered to be grossly disadvantaged and as being at risk for less than optimal psychological development. This is mainly due to structurally generated conditions of disadvantage.

These children are predominantly black[1] and live in a society in which barriers to social and economic advancement have been part of the racist structure of apartheid. Thus, simply being black rather than white predisposes them to experiencing a range of adverse life conditions which would not have arisen had the children's genes for skin colour been different. There is also a range of other major life struggles that are generated within the interpersonal realm to which all South African children may be subject. These include such risks as being subjected to sexual or physical abuse, experiencing the distress of divorce, and living with parental psychiatric illness or alcoholism. While the primary site of these adversities is usually the family or the school, it is clear that the risks of being exposed to them are higher in poor communities where adult coping is frequently stretched to the limit.

An examination of some salient statistics provides a context for understanding the structural aspects of adversity for South African children. For a variety of reasons, South African population statistics are not entirely reliable. Information compiled by the South African Institute of Race Relations (SAIRR) is, however, widely recognised as being a reasonably comprehensive and balanced source of this type of data. According to the Institute, the South African population (including the so-called homelands) is in the region of 38 million (SAIRR 1992). The breakdown by race is: African 76%; white 13%; coloured 9%; and Indian 3%. Of the total population, 47% is under 19 years of age with 40% of the African children being under 14 years of age.

The historical situation of apartheid has ensured that 86% of the land is under white ownership or control. While the issue of land reform is on the current agenda for social transformation, the gross maldistribution of land in the past has resulted in severe overcrowding in those areas designated for occupation by African people. The continuing migration to the cities, following the removal of restrictions on the mobility of African people, has caused great pressure on the urban housing situation. This affects children in a variety of ways. Of the population 59% is now urbanised, and it is estimated that 7 million urban dwellers are informal settlers (squatters). The Urban Foundation (SAIRR 1992) expects the urbanisation rate during the next decade to reach 300 000 per annum. Thus, both now and to an increasing extent, substantial numbers of children are being reared in these large informal settlements which are impoverished, overcrowded, and dangerous, lack basic services such as electricity and proper sanitation, and are inadequately provided with health and educational facilities. Such settle-

[1]Following the system used in the recent report of the National Education Policy Investigation (NEPI 1993) which, because of the sensitivity of the issue, was based on considerable debate and consultation, the following terms will be used consistently throughout the text: *black* – referring to the general disenfranchised majority in South Africa; *African* – referring specifically to black Africans; *white; coloured;* and *Indian*. Although all such racially constructed terms are offensive and are recognised and rejected as such by the editors and authors of this volume, it is nevertheless necessary to use such terms in so far as they reflect the past history and reality of the divisions and social structures created by apartheid.

ments are high-risk environments for the generation of child health problems, exposure to political, criminal and domestic violence, and pervasive social and educational problems (Wilson and Ramphele 1989).

By contrast, being born white in South Africa has tended to ensure a range of advantages. These are closely linked to the provision of material well-being. Currently it is estimated that 5% of the population (overwhelmingly white) controls 88% of the wealth (*The Economist*, 29 February 1992), while 45% of the population (overwhelmingly black) exists below the 'minimum living level' (SAIRR 1992). All the literature on risk factors for psychological development acknowledges that growing up in poverty is the single most powerful and multifaceted negative influence on psychological development.

Being born white also increases the child's chances of survival. On average 50/1000 South African children did not survive infancy in 1989. For white children the mortality rate was 9.3/1000 but for blacks it was 60.6/1000. In rural areas the death rate for African infants is far higher and comparable with the poorest nations in the world (Wilson and Ramphele 1989). After the child has survived, the chances are high that it will further suffer nutritional deficits and increased health hazards during childhood. There is no question that the poverty and disadvantage generated through these macro structural forces have both broad and direct influences on development (Anastasi 1958).

The impact of poverty on particular aspects of development is taken up in several chapters in this volume. Richter (Chapter 2) reviews research evidence on the influence of poverty on family caretaking patterns within a general synergistic framework. Liddell and colleagues (Chapter 3) demonstrate the effects of a range of developmentally significant interactional experiences of young children in a variety of impoverished yet differently constituted environments. In particular their concern is with the notion of 'culture' as an independent variable in developmental research, and the problems presented by its unconsidered use. Richter and Griesel (Chapter 4) explicate the complex relationship that binds poverty, malnutrition and psychological development. Kvalsvig and Connolly (Chapter 5) show how a particular health factor – parasitic infection – which is associated with poverty and lack of sanitation impacts on cognitive performance and the development of pro-social behaviours. Swart-Kruger and Donald (Chapter 6) focus on street children and how much this phenomenon has to do with survival in the poverty of rapidly urbanising environments. Finally, Donald (Chapter 8) illustrates the interaction of poverty, health and inadequate educational facilities in the creation and perpetuation of disability and special educational need.

The extent, nature and form of formal educational provision is a further structural feature of any society that influences development. Within the policy of apartheid the delivery of education in South Africa has been the responsibility of a complex and uncoordinated arrangement of 18 different education departments basically divided across racial lines (Donald and Csapo 1989). The damage that has been created through the inequalities, hegemonic distortions and bureaucratic wastage of this system is at last beginning to be articulated and recognised (Nasson and Samuel 1990; Nkomo 1990). It is clear that the roots of this damage are deep and pervasive. Despite current commitments to the reconstruction of education the process will inevitably be slow and imperfect (Department of National Education 1991; National Education Policy Investigation 1993). It will be long before the majority of South Africa's children can escape the developmental disadvantages inherent in the existing situation.

The most basic structural factor underlying this situation has been the unequal distribution of resources in education. In 1990 there were 9.6 million school pupils in South Africa, of whom 79.2% were African. The Institute of Race Relations (1992) reports that the per capita spending on this group was, at this stage, one quarter of what it was for white children (9.6% of the school population) – this being a substantial improvement on the spending ratio of 1:18 that had existed in 1969. The effects of such gross and sustained under-resourcing of African education have been both cumulative and acute. This has resulted in overcrowded classrooms, lack of teaching and learning materials, underqualified teachers, excessively high pupil–teacher ratios, and lack of specialist and support services (Donald 1989). This in turn has led to a situation where failure rates in the first two years of school are distressingly high (Taylor 1989). There is also a consistent drop-out from schooling, with a particularly disturbing rate of 25% of enrolment in the first year (SAIRR 1992). Of those who finally reach Standard 10, less than half qualify with a matriculation certificate (37% in 1990). It is further estimated that one-fifth of the population over the age of 16 has never attended school and that basic literacy runs at between 50 and 60% of the population (*The Economist*, 29 February 1992).

Why so many African children in the African education systems drop out of school has been insufficiently researched. Researchers generally acknowledge that drop-out is determined by a number of factors (Trueba, Spindler and Spindler 1989). Those structural factors mentioned above that create an inadequate and inferior educational environment for African students unquestionably play their part. In particular the lack of specialised services or any meaningful support for those who experience difficulties of learning is bound to contribute to the high failure and drop-out rate (Donald, Chapter 8). However, it is likely that the single most influential factor is poverty. Frequently parents cannot afford the costs of schooling and children are required to leave school in order to help support their families (Gordon 1987). Reynolds (1989) notes the withdrawal of girls in their early teens from school in order to take care of younger siblings while parents work. No doubt there are other such factors underlying this phenomenon. Given the extent of the problem and its impact on the educational development of large numbers of children, it is important to improve our understanding of why some drop out and others do not.

The school experience has profound effects on psychological development. Both Gilmour and Soudien (Chapter 7) and Donald (Chapter 8) discuss the complex of factors through which the educational system in South Africa itself ironically constitutes a source of adversity for the majority of children. Gilmour and Soudien develop a general argument based on a distinction between equality and equity in education. They argue that the macro structural factors that define inequality need to be seen as interacting with the micro processes that operate in the schools themselves. Donald emphasises the importance of a cyclical and interactional conceptual framework in understanding the creation and reproduction of special educational need.

A further consequence of apartheid and poverty has been their influence on the ability of families to serve as adequate support structures for the nurturance and development of children. Increasingly, failures of this type have led to the production of street children. Swart-Kruger and Donald (Chapter 6) address some of the roots of this problem and examine the coping patterns of South African children who have this path to survival thrust upon them.

Poverty, familial strain, educational deficit and illnesses such as malnutrition all increase the risk of psychological disorder and handicap in children. These occur in most developing societies but, with the particular stresses associated with South Africa's history of apartheid, one of the questions it is appropriate to ask is whether higher rates of childhood psychopathology can be expected in this country. However, this is not a simple matter to resolve. Robertson and Berger (Chapter 9) indicate the paucity of research in this area and some of the complexities associated with the estimation of the incidence of psychopathology in South African children.

Similarly, growing up under conditions of violence constitutes a developmental risk, and rates of violence in South Africa are amongst the highest in the world. Political violence has been a common feature of South African life for many years. While this is a structurally generated form of adversity, it also takes profoundly personal forms and is responsible for the generation of widespread fear, hatred and despair. This political violence is compounded by criminal and domestic violence which is also rife in poor areas (Dawes 1990; Marks and Andersson 1990). According to the government's 1992 figures, South Africa (excluding the 'homelands') has 20 000 murders per year – an average of 55 murders per day (1:1000 of population) (*Cape Times,* 17 March 1993 report on Parliament). Dawes (Chapters 10 and 11) considers the available research evidence and complexities in teasing out the psychological consequences of political violence. Questions are raised in relation to common misconceptions of this subject and in relation to the appropriateness of prevailing research paradigms for addressing this problem.

Regarding sexual violence, 24 812 rapes were reported in 1992 (*Cape Times* 17 March 1993). It is estimated that only one in twenty rapes is reported (Vogelman 1990), and on this basis it is likely that about 480 000 rapes actually occur in South Africa each year. Sexual abuse during childhood, a related and similarly common and under-reported phenomenon, is more directly the concern of a volume such as this. Levett (Chapter 13) addresses this issue and the important task of unravelling the emotive from the real in defining the origins and the psychological effects of child sexual abuse in a complex society such as South Africa.

Finally, the very fact of a legacy of racism in South African society continues to ensure insults at the personal level to South African children. Foster (Chapter 12) discusses the development of racial orientations in children. He also considers how growing up in a racist society might be damaging to children's psychological development. Foster's analysis of the research evidence shows that this question is not answered simply. His work is important in demystifying this emotive subject.

Chapter 14 draws the threads together. *Inter alia*, the relationship between research and intervention – ultimately the most urgent need of all – is discussed as an issue, and possible ways of moving forward in the study of child development under conditions of adversity are suggested.

It is perhaps surprising that this is the first volume of its kind to address the psychological consequences of adversity in South Africa. Previous publications such as the pioneering volume of Burman and Reynolds (1986) included a range of material but its focus was not on specifically psychological studies. Reynold's (1989) study of children in Crossroads comes closer to the work considered in the present volume. Conducted by an anthropologist rather than a psychologist, it focuses on one community and is a good example of the application of ethnographic anthropological techniques to an understanding of the way children living in informal settlements see their worlds. But why is it that apart from studies of the effects of malnutrition on development (Chapter 4), there has been so little work conducted specifically by psychologists on disadvantaged children in South Africa?

Psychology and Psychological Research in South Africa

William Kessen (1983) suggested that the issues we address as human scientists are deeply influenced by the social and political milieu we inhabit. The history of psychological research in South Africa, in particular that which has focused on children, provides evidence in support of his contention. Despite the vast majority of South African children being disadvantaged by western standards, an examination of research publications indicates that the developmental issues facing this sector have, with few exceptions, hardly begun to be examined (Liddell and Kvalsvig 1990). As in the rest of the world, the bulk of South African psychological research has been skewed away from examining the developmental consequences of living under disadvantaged circumstances. A survey by Mauer, Marais and Prinsloo (1991) has revealed that publications on developmental issues over the five years prior to 1991 constituted only about 10% of all psychological research published in South Africa over that period. They also note that journal articles in the area constituted only 7% of all articles published over the period.

The relative lack of attention devoted to researching these issues reflects badly on the South African psychological research community. The reasons for this are complex, but in all probability a significant influence has been that apartheid policy has 'normalised' the racist and exploitative structure of the society (Dawes 1985). The worlds of the disenfranchised and the rulers, from whom the ranks of professional psychologists have mostly been drawn, have been separated by government policy. Psychological services for blacks remain very poor, and contact with their developmental problems has thus been uncommon for white psychologists (Donald and Csapo 1989; Robertson and Berger, Chapter 9).

In segregating the society and the education system, and in making virtually no provision for psychological services to the most disadvantaged sector, the state virtually ensured that consciousness of the developmental problems of the population remained racially compartmentalised. One small example is the way state-funded agencies like the National Institute of Personnel Research and the Human Sciences Research Council (and their predecessors) focused considerable attention during the 1950s and 1960s on the development of tests of intelligence, aptitude and ability to assist in the educational and career placement of white children. No comparable measures were constructed for other children. However, a considerable amount of attention was given to the design of selection batteries for African labourers for the mining community and other industrial sectors. This suggested that there was a role for psychology in the promotion of the productivity of African people, if not in the promotion of their well-being and life chances (Bulhan 1981).

The organised profession of psychology has itself a deeply racist past (Louw 1987; Foster, Nicholas and Dawes 1993). In the 1960s, the then prime minister, Dr Verwoerd (himself a psychologist), encouraged the racial segregation of scientific societies including the South African Psychological Association. The latter split into two associations, one for whites only, and the other open to all (Louw 1987). The racially segregated association, the Psychological Institute of the Republic of South Africa, actively supported apartheid policy until its demise some ten years ago. Its president during the latter part of the 1960s was also the head of the Human Sciences Research Council – the statutory body charged with the administration and execution of state-funded psychological research. It is small wonder then that this body did not proceed to stimulate work on the problems with which we are concerned here until many years later.

In addition, very few psychologists are drawn from working class communities (Nicholas and Cooper 1990; PASA 1989). At one time, the only significant psychological work on the situation of the South African oppressed produced by a black South African psychologist was that generated by Manganyi (1973). However, since the middle of the 1980s increasing numbers of black psychologists have graduated and have begun to contribute significantly to debates on the role of psychology in South Africa (Nicholas and Cooper 1990).

The notorious Extension of Universities Act of 1959, which saw to the racial segregation of university education, is also likely to have played a role in limiting opportunities for graduate training among those drawn from black communities. It reinforced the concentration of intellectual and financial resources within the more established white institutions which, until recently, provided most training in research psychology. The training in these institutions has been characteristically Euro-American in orientation, and the job opportunities for professional research psychologists are limited to a small number of university positions and government-financed research institutions such as the HSRC. These are all in their way consequences of the structural and ideological elements of the policy of apartheid.

A final point to note is that the psychological profession itself, probably because of the ideological socialisation of its members, has failed to place human rights abuses under apartheid on the psychological agenda (Dawes 1985; 1992). This has been left to a few individuals and organisations who have been openly opposed to apartheid, and has led to ongoing tensions and divisions in organised psychology (Foster, Nicholas and Dawes, 1993). Examples are the Psychology and Apartheid Committee (Nicholas and Cooper 1990), and the Organisation for Appropriate Social Services in South Africa (OASSSA) (Swartz, Gibson and Swartz 1990). Both these groups stimulated therapeutic and research work on South African children affected by political repression.

As we enter a period of political transformation it has become particularly urgent to redress the psychological profession's history of neglect of poor black children. South Africa is faced with a rising population of young people – sometimes referred to as a 'lost generation' – who are poorly educated, who are socialised in a violent environment, and whose families are often too caught up in the stresses of poverty and survival to offer what western middle-class society would call a normal childhood. Regardless of the appropriateness of the term 'lost generation', and the manipulative uses to which it has been put, it does capture something of the situation of these young people (Straker 1989; Dawes, Chapter 11). If mental health workers are to play a meaningful role in the transformation of these conditions, then we need to improve our understanding of the psychological consequences of the adversities facing the majority of South Africa's children. Without knowledge of what constitutes adversity in these communities (for adversity is a social construct), and without knowledge of the conditions and processes that promote psychological resilience and coping, we will not be able to develop effective interventions to reduce, if not prevent, some of the casualties of adversity. This raises the thorny issue of the relationship between an academic discipline and the context within which it operates.

The Issue of Relevance

Strümpfer (1981) and Holdstock (1981) were amongst the first to raise concerns about the relevance of South African psychology to its context. Since about 1985 this debate has been taken further, the central point being to question whether psychology should become more relevant in researching those issues that confront the majority of South Africans (Dawes 1986; Mauer 1987; Mauer, Marais and Prinsloo 1991; Gilbert 1989; Retief 1989). While not always specifically stated, a particular dichotomy appears in some of the discourse on relevance. Essentially this asserts that relevant research is inevitably less rigorous and of a lower scientific standard than that which has no public service agenda (pure research) – the latter is seen as worthy of being labelled excellent while the former is not. We reject this dichotomy as false and hope to show within this volume that relevance does not preclude excellence.

Frequently, behind the notion of excellence lies the idea that research can and should be neutral and value-free (Biesheuwel 1987). Again, we maintain that no researcher, particularly in the human sciences, can avoid reflecting one or other value position – although this is often neither admitted nor even understood (Dawes 1985). Relevant research differs only in that it is explicit about its value position. It is not neutral. It adopts a moral orientation to the issues that need to be researched but seeks answers that are real and not necessarily those that public opinion would want.

Thus the decision to focus psychological research on children's ways of dealing with adversity reflects an ideological and moral decision as much as it reflects an interest in psychological processes. Children's responses to the circumstances we call adverse are complex and there is much that we do not understand about how they cope with hardship. How best to study these children, and what theoretical frames of reference are appropriate, are further issues that must be confronted.

Frameworks for Understanding Developmental Processes

Any account of psychological development has to formulate an understanding of the relationship between those factors which contribute to the emergence of particular psychological characteristics. It requires the conceptualisation of the relationships between the various components and levels of functioning of the individual human subject (intra-individual factors) and his or her environment (inter-individual and contextual factors). The intra-individual factors include the biological, structural and maturational processes, which are universal features of the developing human organism and which set the limits of human performance, intellectual understanding and emotional functioning. However, the existence of these features should not lead us to assume a universal, decontextualised model of child development. As we shall argue, the study of the child in and as a part of the social context is crucial for our understanding of children's functioning and development.

Most obviously, this context includes the physical elements of the environment such as the sort of house the person inhabits, the sanitation system, the cultural artefacts and the characteristics of the region. The environment also embraces social features which have a fundamental influence in people's lives. These include not only inter-individual relationships but also forms of language use, values and conventional social practices, as well as systems of economy, government and other elements of the state apparatus which regulate society.

Also, each society will have certain dominant and subsidiary (usually competing) ideologies which are inserted into everyday as well as official discourse and are visible both in people's practices and expressed beliefs. This discourse serves to affirm and perpetuate certain truths and falsehoods about such things as the social good, power relations, the nature of children, and the naturalness of certain social arrangements such as the family and particular gender roles. Ultimately ideology serves to mystify the manner in which social and economic arrangements operate by presenting them as natural and inevitable. It is through the social institutions such as the family and educational structures that ideologies are perpetuated and so shape the development of human consciousness.

The inter-relationship of some of these factors may be illustrated within one case example which reflects a typical adverse life situation for many thousands of South African children. The child concerned was referred for remedial help to a student special educationist as part of her training at the University of Cape Town during 1992.

Themba is an 11-year-old, Xhosa-speaking boy who is one of 45 other children in the third year of school in a state primary school in Khayelitsha – a large, peri-urban settlement outside Cape Town. His personal history indicates that his birth and early development were normal but that at 6 years of age he sustained a head injury in a pedestrian traffic accident. He was hospitalised for a week and discharged without further follow-up. His mother is 29 years old, unmarried and has four children. She is unemployed but runs an informal second-hand clothing trade between Khayelitsha and the Transkei. Because his mother is often away, drinks heavily and keeps very erratic hours, Themba stays with his grandmother in her two-roomed, corrugated-iron shack in Khayelitsha. Grandmother exists on her pension and some erratic support from her adult children but has to cope with up to 16 grandchildren living with her at any one time. She reports that Themba's mother seldom visits and that when she does she gets impatient, shouts at him and hits him.

Scholastically, Themba has spent six years at school having had to repeat each of the first three classes. His scholastic performance is poor all round and he is finding it particularly difficult to cope with English reading and spelling when he has not mastered the basics in his own language. He is restless, easily distracted, frequently aggressive and is avoided by other children in the class. His teacher has too many children in her class to give him extra attention and she believes he is 'just a lazy, no-good child' who needs more disciplining. Because of a lack of services, no formal psychological or scholastic assessment has been done. No special classes or programmes are available for such children in Khayelitsha.

This is an illustration of the complex interaction of contextual, inter-individual and intra-individual factors shaping this child's personal and scholastic experience – and no doubt his life's future path. Structurally it is not difficult to identify poverty, lack of adequate health care, unemployment, inadequate housing, an overcrowded classroom, an educationally indefensible language curriculum, lack of specialised educational services and an underqualified teacher. The child's absent father, his mother's punitive relationship with him, his poor peer relationships and the teacher's lack of understanding of him are apparent as negative inter-individual factors. They are ameliorated only by his grandmother's caring and the fortuitous intervention of the special education student. Intra-individually, his possibly limited intellectual ability and tendency to impulsivity finally complicate the picture. Cumulatively the story is a bleak one and has been told many times in South Africa before. One does not have to be a psychologist to understand its tragedy or to know that, had this child been born white, the story would have been very different. Nevertheless, what is missing is an understanding of how the structural conditions impact on the inter- and intra-individual factors and vice versa; which factors compound the problem; and most important, how this child constructs his sense of self and social identity in such a context.

If we are to contribute anything further to understanding such problems it is our task to construct models that explain, at a psychological level, how the various strands in the web interact and contribute to the child's developmental trajectory. Before we can deal with these models we need to consider how the child is subject to ideological construction.

The Ideological Dimension and the Construction of Childhood

Around the mid-1970s, the field of developmental psychology began to be examined more critically than was previously the case. A central issue which has been associated with these debates concerns the nature of childhood and the question of how we can deal with the problem of different definitions of childhood. Kessen's (1983) seminal papers on this matter brought about a greater awareness among psychologists that childhood was both a sociocultural and an historical phenomenon. Different historical periods, cultures and classes have had different ideas about the duration of the period called childhood, the nature of children's emotional vulnerabilities, their needs, their rights and their duties. The childhood of modern industrial 'first world' society did not exist prior to the twentieth century, and for the majority of the children in the world – those of the 'third world' – childhood implies a very different status from that which is regarded as right and proper in modern Euro-American society. So to talk of what is 'normal for children' or of the expected psychological characteristics of a particular age group is to ignore the fact that beyond biological dimensions, the state of childhood is not natural but social, and that it is deeply influenced by the sociocultural practices which provide a framework for psychological development.

This is particularly evident in South Africa where the statutes which lay down the rights of the child, and the duties of the state and parents towards the child, reflect an intertwining of apartheid discrimination and historical and cultural practice. While the notion of 'cultures' in South Africa as crystallised and unchanging entities has been strongly and appropriately criticised (Boonzaier and Sharp 1988; Said 1991), it is nonetheless important to recognise that there are varieties of childhood in South Africa. Some of the variation has been structurally the result of apartheid; but some has its roots in historical conventions which were a product of other sets of social and political relations in our past.

An example of the construction of difference under apartheid appears in the Child Care Act 74 formulated as late as 1983. This and other welfare-related statutes determine that the state is only liable for the support of African children up until the age of 16 years whereas for other children it is 18. Where support is paid (including cases of handicap), it differs according to race, with African children receiving the least. Burman (1988) notes, when referring to other legislation, that the social pensions of African persons may be reduced if they have their own children between 16 and 18 years of age living with them. Unlike their white age counterparts, these African children are seen as being old enough to work and to contribute to the household income; therefore the state has less of a responsibility to contribute to their aged parents' income. A consequence of this is that once African children reach 16 there is the pressure – and associated risk – of having to leave the home of their pensioner parents so that the latter may avoid losing some of their income. These points show that the law contains an underlying assumption that in some senses African children end their childhoods before the rest. This is despite the fact that all people only reach full legal majority at 21 years of age.

The age at which a person becomes criminally responsible is nevertheless 14 years for all South Africans (Burman 1988). This in itself reflects a set of beliefs about the age of 'maturity' which contradicts other legislation. It is interesting that in southern African preliterate societies, legal responsibility was also not attained until puberty had been reached (Bennett 1991). However, while legal responsibility coincided with the initiation ceremony at puberty for men, this was not so for women, who remained legal minors. Many of these status distinctions remain in contemporary African customary law. This reflects the entrenchment of historical practices and images of childhood and women largely derived from the practices of rural people of the nineteenth century. As Bennett notes, this body of our law is highly conservative and generally works for the benefit of male adults. He comments on the failure to alter this system over the years:

> The courts are empowered by the so-called repugnancy proviso to delete or amend any rule of customary law that is contrary to the principles of public policy or natural justice. The fact that they have not invoked this proviso for the past forty years has been commended as an enlightened sympathy for cultural relativism. It could equally be interpreted as a symptom of neglect... As a result of this neglect, South African customary law is now at variance with contemporary social conditions. (1991:v)

Thus South African customary law contains images of childhood and accepted practices in relation to children which have not shifted with societal and historical change and which are also at variance with the current civil law. One aspect of customary law which reflects this and which can lead to serious problems in female-headed single parent or migrant families is that in customary practice a woman may not discipline her male child once he has been initiated. This is because he has become an adult male and his mother is technically a minor. As Burman (1988:168) puts it: 'heads of households are often legally responsible for "adults" whom they cannot control but whom the civil law defines as "children" under their control'. Clearly this situation is not inevitable, but in conservative communities it can certainly arise.

What we have illustrated here is that in South Africa, as in other countries with a mix of classes and cultures, there is both commonality and divergence in the way childhood is construed. This has implications for how we theorise the psychological effects of adversity. The way in which people (and children) appraise events influences how they deal with them. Thus, if a person becomes a man at 15 and regards himself as such, what does this mean in terms of his construction of self and his appraisal of a hardship? His response would surely be different from one who is held to be a child and apprehends the events 'as a child'.

But what about the 'norms' of development – the typical behaviour we expect for different developmental or age levels? These would suggest that there is a degree of universality in psychological development and functioning. Part of the business of the science of human development has been to construct these norms of behaviour which have played a major role in the regulation of modern childhood (Rose 1990). The psychodynamic theory of Erikson for instance leads us to expect the adolescent to go through a series of identity experiments, which are evident in behaviour characterised by intense and shifting affiliations. But if childhood ends at puberty, then it is quite possible for the psychological constitution of the period we call adolescence to be very different.

Diversity in the construal of childhood, therefore, creates problems at the level of description – the normative level. This is not so much a problem when we talk of the biological parameters and norms of development and the fact that certain organic and morphological structures must mature before certain performances are possible. But beyond these universals, constructing norms of psychological development becomes a problem because the 'child' for whom the norms are constructed is not only a natural object, but also a social and historical subject. Norms of conduct and notions of what is valued performance are inevitably social and ideological constructs – that is, products of culture (Rose 1990). Without understanding cultural constructs and practices and how they influence development we cannot understand development itself, and any 'norms' of development – universal or otherwise – must take this into account.

An Ecocultural Framework and Research Approach

Several overarching schemes have been produced which suggest the variables we should consider, and which posit the relationships between these various elements of the child's ecocultural context and developmental outcome. The framework introduced by Segall, Dasen, Berry and Poortinga (1990) has been developed for deployment in cross-cultural research, while those of Lerner (1986) and Bronfenbrenner (1986) have been constructed in order to facilitate theoretical understanding and research more broadly.

Segall and colleagues link a set of background variables, which includes the physical ecology and resource base of an area in which people live, and its sociopolitical and cultural context, to the processes and forms of biological and cultural adaptation which are developed in response. These are the sociocultural and organismic characteristics of communities which have evolved in a certain way due to the adaptive strategies they have employed. They are also reflected in specific patterns of socialisation and child treatment.

Thus certain practices or values about children would emerge as a response to the demands of the environment. As Scheper-Hughes (1987) and Kagitçibasi (1992) have noted, children in the rural, underdeveloped world are valued in part as contributors to the family's economy as workers, while in modern societies they carry primarily affectional value and virtually no productive value. These differences reflect varying images of childhood.

Segall and colleagues also identify a series of 'process variables' which operate at the level of the group and the individual. For example, at the group level (e.g. a society), processes such as cultural transmission take a form determined by the cultural practices of that group. Thus, certain values common to the society regarding the degree of independence desirable in a child or how a child should be disciplined would be transmitted through specific, culturally determined child-rearing practices.

Other factors associated with the child's ecocultural niche which influence caretaking practices have been identified by Weisner (1989) in his work on socialisation in different societies. They include sources of child stimulation, the nature of family relationships, the available caretakers, household composition, and the degree of flexibility or rigidity in the value system which will influence the caretaker's capacity to adjust to new demands.

Within the realm of cognition, Dasen has shown that where certain forms of reasoning and competence are not valued in a particular society, not surprisingly the children will score poorly on tasks that involve such reasoning. Also, he has shown that some communities have definitions of intelligence which embody social and intellectual components. He refers to the Baoule people of the Ivory Coast, who define intelligence as including a willingness to help and carry out tasks in an obliging and effective manner. There is thus 'coherence between parental ethnotheories and the daily activities of children' (Segal *et al.* 1990:153) – ethnotheories being indigenous ideas or beliefs about such things as children's needs.

Such examples of cultural transmission and practice, particularly when they occur in non-western, usually ex-colonised people, are frequently labelled as the 'traditional' practices of such-and-such a group. This implies something fixed and natural about the people in question, and is frequently represented as such (Spiegel and Boonzaier 1988). Here again we have an example of the operation of ideology, which can enter our discourse as social scientists. There is no understanding of the fact that these practices, while often ritualised, ingrained and resistant to change, nevertheless have their roots in the processes of adaptation to ecological, political and economic forces. As these forces change, adaptation itself imposes its own change on the very practices that have been labelled as traditional and immutable. The force of economic adaptation, for instance, is well illustrated by Kagitçibasi (1992) in her account of changes in traditional relationship patterns and the status of women and children in poor but recently urbanised Turkish families.

While the framework of Segall and colleagues is useful in pointing to some of the essential variables which influence cultural adaptation, its usage is limited by its reliance on an essentially mechanistic approach to the development of cultural forms. It does not deal with the processes involved in change, as Lerner (see below) attempts to explain, and it says little about the active agentic aspects of the child in its own development.

The family is a key site of social transmission, but there is a range of other social sites which children and their families occupy. Adversities directly affecting the child may arise within the family itself, or in other contexts where the child spends time such as the school. Also, family members other than the child may experience adversities in contexts which the child does not enter, such as the workplace. Each of these settings requires adaptations which are themselves sites of cultural and ideological transmission. How do we begin to separate out the influences on the child's development of these different settings, and demonstrate more precisely how they influence both family functioning and the child's development?

Using Bronfenbrenner's (1986) formulation, research which investigates the influence on development of environmental factors external to the family can employ one of three models. First, *mesosystemic* research models investigate the effects of events occurring in one setting on the child's functioning in another setting. An example would be the way in which the child's distressed response to racism at school is dealt with at home. What does this do to the family's reaction and the processes which are mobilised (or fail to be mobilised), and which determine the psychological outcome for the child and other family members?

Second, *exosystemic* research examines the influence of events occurring in settings which the child does not occupy, but which are occupied by other family members. An example would be the impact of a parent becoming unemployed. This could produce strains within the family, leading to the child's exposure to increased domestic conflict. It might lead to certain political attitudes being expressed which could influence the child's attitude formation, or it might lead to a change in standard of living which could affect the child's level of nutrition and potential survival. The effects of all these would depend in turn on the level of development of the child's physical, emotional and cognitive capacities.

The third research approach identified by Bronfenbrenner is called the *chronosystem* model. Here the ontogenetic changes occurring with maturation over time are examined in relation to changes in the environment over the same period. Thus a normative change in the child, such as the onset of puberty, would ordinarily affect family relations. If these changes occur in a context of changing sexual mores in the wider society, say towards more liberal attitudes to teenage sexuality, there would be different effects in families which occupy a cultural niche that prohibits teenage sexual relationships and those which do not.

Another chronosystem effect could be illustrated by different cohorts of adolescents in South Africa, one of which has been directly exposed to political violence while others have not been exposed in the same way. This non-normative external event would have different consequences for the development of a range of psychological characteristics during adolescence, which would be likely to differ in the two groups. For example, Braungart and Braungart (1986) have shown that exposure to major political events during adolescence, such as the 1976 rebellion in South African schools, is likely to have shaped the attitudes and political consciousness of this cohort of youth in ways which render them very different from their parents who did not undergo these formative experiences (Dawes 1990). This may in turn promote intrafamilial conflict as values between the older and younger generations clash (Chikane 1986). Equally, those white South African children of the same age who were not part of this action would not have developed politically in the same way or have experienced similar intergenerational conflict.

Probabilistic Epigenesis

The effects of the mesosystemic, exosystemic and chronosystemic forces may influence the child in ways that are more *or* less direct. Bronfenbrenner's position is thus complemented by that of Anastasi (1958), who showed that the environment has broad or narrow effects on development. Broad effects are those which impact on the individual in such a manner that a wide range of functioning is affected while narrow effects impact on a more limited area of development. The effects depend also on the developmental level of the child at the time and the particular aspects of psychological functioning which are sensitive to that particular form of environmental influence (Lerner 1986).

Lerner (1986:175) calls for a more contextually based developmental science and has proposed a 'dynamic-interactional model of individual–context relations'. This attempts to bring these complex factors together in what is called a probabilistic epigenetic conception of development. Here the multiplicity of factors both intrinsic and extrinsic to the organism and the complexities of their interaction are recognised. Developmental outcomes are thus always 'probabilistic' rather than definite. The more complex and global the aspect of psychological functioning, the less likely we are to be able to predict the outcome (see also Magnusson 1992).

An essential component of this framework is its emphasis on the child's level of development in a specific domain of psychological functioning, such as language. Another essential determinant of development, frequently not recognised by models of this type, is the child's active contribution through its engagement (internally) with itself and its social and physical world (Schneirla 1957). For example, Reynolds (1989) discusses how squatter children learn certain principles of mechanics – without any formal educational mediation – through their construction of cars made of discarded wire and tin cans.

Lerner's model also observes that development has discontinuous features (e.g. stages). These are defined by characteristic psychological processes that determine the possibilities of the child's action or thought at a particular stage. Conversely, continuous aspects of development refer to psychological processes that operate in an unchanging manner across the life span, such as processes of social learning (Bandura 1973). Both these concepts are useful when considering the effects of a particular adverse situation on the child's functioning (see for example Chapter 10).

An additional and important feature of Lerner's framework is his reference to Werner's orthogenetic principle, which posits that development moves from a global and undifferentiated state to one of differentiated and hierarchical integration. At early stages of development when structures and functions are less specialised and not clearly linked in functionally coherent and more complex units, the child's response to particular forms of adversity will differ markedly both in extent and type from when it is more mature. Thus a four-month-old baby would be likely to be affected across a broad range of areas of functioning (probably permanently) if it was severely malnourished for a period of time. A 10-year-old would not be likely to be affected in the same way or to the same extent at its more differentiated level of neurological development. On the other hand the older child could be severely traumatised by continuous anticipation of violent attack because of the signification of such events, while the baby would not because its level of cognitive and emotional development could not articulate this.

These contributions provide a metatheory of the developmental process. This is a framework which we can use to integrate the very complex determinants of development which proceed as the child engages with the ecocultural context he or she inhabits. It is also a framework within which theories of specific aspects of development such as cognition or personality can be elaborated, and then brought together in a more holistic account.

The framework is particularly useful when discussing development in adverse circumstances because it reminds us to be cautious about the conclusions we reach about the short- and long-term consequences of adversity for development. It also alerts us to the factors we should consider when planning research. As Bronfenbrenner (1986) notes, ideally one should be able to examine a specific form of adversity, over a period of time, on the psychology of a child who is at a particular developmental level and who occupies a specific context (e.g. a recently urbanised family in a squatter community). The processes of child-rearing and other factors such as cultural prescriptions on violence towards women and understandings of the roles of men and women are also essential to incorporate. Unfortunately few studies approach this level of sophistication, and in South Africa they are in their infancy. Elsewhere they have been conducted and have contributed a great deal to our understanding of risk factors in development (e.g. Rutter 1985; Werner and Smith 1983; Magnusson 1992).

Positivism and Constructivism

The dominant approach to the study of children's psychological reactions to adversity is exemplified by the work of Rutter, which falls within the neo-positivist research tradition. Positivist orientations to developmental psychology hold that it is possible to build up knowledge of development which is objective, ahistorical and therefore cumulative (Gergen 1979). Positivism nurtures a particular view of psychological science as being concerned with the quantification, description and explanation of the relationships between separate variables which, through the application of controls and the use of statistical tests of probability, are tested for their effects on development. Several of the contributions in this volume illustrate this approach to research.

As Walkerdine (1984:154) puts it, in positivist research 'the "developing child" is an object premised on the location of certain capacities within the child and therefore within the domain of psychology. Other features are thereby externalised as aspects of the social domain which influence or affect the pattern of development.'

Aside from the research prescriptions of positivist science, perhaps its most crucial feature is that, for the purposes of research and theoretical conceptualisation, the child is seen as ontologically separate from its social context. They are regarded as two distinct realities, about each of which universal truths may be sought.

However, the research process can be seen as involving choices of strategy designed to obtain answers to specific questions one has asked rather than being a search for 'ultimate truths', whatever these might be (Du Preez, in press). From this perspective positivist approaches have adopted a research strategy that provides answers to specific types of questions about development. This strategy is no more than a useful but specific set of lenses which frames questions and methods in particular ways. It is, for example, appropriate if one's question is to establish the characteristics of groups under various conditions so that one can make general, probabilistic statements as to what is likely to happen to children under the influence of such conditions.

However, are children simply objects being influenced by the forces of nature? According to Wartofsky (1983), the answer is no. Childhood is more of a social-historical phenomenon than it is a natural phenomenon. Although under some circumstances it is appropriate to study the child from a positivist perspective, work at this level, Wartofsky argues, will not help us address a range of important psychological questions. The assumption that there *is* a natural truth leads to a quest for the discovery of the natural elements underlying developmental functioning. This is what the positivist quest strives to do. The problem arises when children are *only* construed as natural objects.

Wartofsky, Ingleby (1986) and others argue that this is a fundamental error. Children are also social, agentic beings and we need to develop theoretical and research strategies in order to deal with these features of humanity. When prescriptions for research and theories of child development ignore this and become established, they enter the ideological order of the research community. At the popular level they enter society and play a role in reproducing children in the image of the theory (Rose 1990). An example of this is the way Piagetian cognitive stage 'norms' have been taken up by educators. This has resulted in the level of the educational material and teachers' expectations of children being shaped to fit these supposedly 'natural' age bands and stages of development (Walkerdine 1984). If a generation of children are educated in this way, then they will certainly have learned to perform within the 'natural' progression of Piagetian stages. Ironically this merely illustrates their agentic capacity rather than the 'naturalness' of the stages (Light 1986). It is this sort of problem that leads some to argue the importance of trying to sort out scientific 'facts' from evaluative statements, and what is 'natural' about development from what is cultural in respect of children's functioning (Woodhead 1991). Others would argue that once the child is born, this is simply an impossible task. Beyond the biological parameters of development, the child is an essentially social agent and there is no psychological skeleton to be stripped bare (Riley 1983; Walkerdine 1984).

This emphasis on the social nature of childhood and the child's psychological make-up has led to challenges to the positivist perspective. These have been emerging since the 1970s, and have become much more prominent in the last six to ten years. Broadly, one can label these as constructivist (or constructionist) approaches to psychology and development. They have their roots within interpretative approaches to psychological functioning such as ethnomethodology, symbolic interactionism, and (more recently) studies of the social role of language in the construction of sign systems and meaning (Parker 1990; Burman 1992). Constructivist approaches to development, such as those of the Soviet social-historical school of Vygotsky (1978) and Luria (1976), have also been influential, as have certain applications of psychoanalytic theory (e.g. Hollway

1989). A central feature of the last-mentioned theory is that it deals with the way people approach the world in terms of its representation as an internalised system of signs having emotional significance for the person concerned. Several of the authors in this volume draw on constructivist ideas (Levett in particular) because they see them as central to understanding how children's socially constructed subjectivity influences their responses to adversity.

What is social constructivism as applied to psychological inquiry? Gergen (1985:266) states it in broad terms: 'Social constructionist inquiry is principally concerned with explicating the processes by which people come to describe, explain or otherwise account for the world (including themselves) in which they live.' Elsewhere he notes the particular way in which the idea of human agency or activity is seen from this perspective. It is very different from that employed by neo-positivist scholars such as Rutter (1985). 'The terms in which the world is understood are social artefacts, products of historically situated interchanges among people... The process of understanding is not automatically driven by the forces of nature, but is the result of an active, co-operative enterprise of persons in relationship.' (Gergen 1985:267)

The key ideas here are that knowledge, including psychological theory, is a cultural artefact and historical product; that the production of human knowledge is a social enterprise; and that this occurs 'in relationship'. This last point is different from the common psychological idea of 'interaction', which presupposes a mechanical relationship between separate variables, actors or objects. Being 'in relationship' suggests rather that the ontological distinction between individuals and their contexts is dissolved since the contexts themselves are largely defined through socially structured relationships. In this sense, they do not simply 'interact' like the separate physical forces of Cartesian science. Constructivism therefore holds that what is most important about human action is meaning and how it is communicated; that the assignment of meaning to action is mediated and constructed socially; and, finally, that we are born into a world of given and evolving sign or meaning relationships (culture). Human development involves the appropriation of these interpersonal processes and knowledge.

Regarding methodology, Rizzo, Corsaro and Bates (1992) explore the implications of constructivist principles for developmental research. Thus:

1. The researcher must accept the subjective nature of action and take into account its meaning and functional significance to the research subject.

2. Human behaviour should be studied as an act of communication. Within this it is essential to understand the relation between behaviour and context as that context is understood by the subject.

3. People should be studied in context without controls and with a tolerance for uncertainty. 'To achieve an accurate understanding of human action psychologists must observe, analyse and interpret the practical, everyday activities of people along with a detailed study of the ecological conditions in which these actions are embedded.'

4. A reflexive stance by the scientist is necessary in that he or she must understand the effects of his or her presence on the setting under investigation.

Rizzo and colleagues differ from some other constructivists in that they argue that this approach complements rather than replaces the positivist orientation. In many ways their orientation is an elaboration of established qualitative approaches.

A more radical version of the constructivist approach, which questions the fundamentals of all positivist psychological knowledge, is exemplified in the collections of work produced by Henriques, Hollway, Urwin, Venn and Walkerdine (1984) and Parker and Shotter (1990). One of the important contributions of these scholars has been to deconstruct the productions of psychologists to reveal the manner in which ideology enters statements of scientific fact. Ideology masquerades as fact in much psychological writing. An example is in specifications of what children do or do not 'need' for their psychological development (Woodhead 1991). Thus the analysis of how psychological discourse about development is constructed is essential in unmasking false assumptions and propositions about children's psychological functioning.

There is no doubt that constructivism has important contributions to make to the study of development − particularly to those aspects concerned with the development of children's understanding of self and society, and to the construction of individual subjectivity. However, constructivist orientations do run the risk of ignoring or reducing the role of biological maturational forces, which are still fundamental to the process of the construction of subjectivity during development. Unless warily approached, this can lead to problems when we attempt to formulate a constructivist understanding of developmental processes under conditions of adversity. The problem may, however, be avoided. Henriques and colleagues (1984), for example, recognise the importance of biological forces and, indeed, usefully show how biological processes themselves are subject to the influence of forces in the social and economic environment.

A central contribution of constructivism is the rejection of any notion of a decontextualised psychological subject. This is because there is no possibility of maintaining the social–individual divide. As Henriques and colleagues say (1984:24), we cannot assume that 'the individual and the social are commensurate notions'. Thus they reject the idea of a unitary psychological being as independent of its social context. The influence of the social or the biological on the individual is always in relational terms rather than in terms which reinforce a subject–object dualism. Clearly such an epistemology is very different from that proposed by positivists.

Nonetheless, our view is that human subjectivity must be seen as being both biologically *and* socially constructed. In this we adopt a stance known as complementarism (Deveraux 1980), which suggests that it is useful to employ different epistemological perspectives simultaneously. Complementarism assumes that there is evidence for each perspective, and each may illuminate the phenomenon we are studying usefully without forcing a resolution of the individual–social conundrum. Complementarism also recognises that while it is necessary to accommodate the general relativism of context, it is also necessary to assert that certain structural universals are relatively context-independent and can therefore be examined across differing contexts (Swartz 1989). Thus, certain consistencies *do* occur in children's development across differing contexts, and biological shifts that occur with maturation *do* make for different forms of consciousness.

The Notion of Adversity and the Problem of Relativism

It is well recognised that the structural forces and material adversities outlined at the beginning of this chapter are powerful in shaping children's psycho-social, emotional and cognitive functioning, as well as their life chances (Bronfenbrenner 1986; Goodyer 1990; Richter 1990). Nevertheless, the notion of adversity is itself problematic and it is important to explore why this is so.

Although conceptions of the effects of adversity on the psychological development of children has largely been produced in the industrial 'first world', the majority of children and adults inhabit the underdeveloped world. Such communities have a variety of interpretations of what is good and bad for children, and these are sometimes at variance with notions of adversity in North America and Europe. Most South African children form part of that majority.

Terms such as adversity and optimal development are thus not neutral, but are socially constructed, and the standards employed in modern psychological discourse about child development are in fact minority standards (James and Prout 1990; Ennew and Milne 1989). Any notion of adversity is necessarily framed with reference to a value statement on life circumstances and the desirability or otherwise of a certain developmental outcome.

All developmentalists today would accept the presence of some diversity in communities' views regarding the norms of development. However, most would also argue that there is sufficient evidence to suggest that certain forms of environmental insult do compromise development and that this is not a matter for debate. Thus the degree to which developmental psychologists endorse the notion of cultural relativism with regard to psychological processes is variable (Miller 1989; Bronfenbrenner, Kessel, Kessen and White 1986; Heelas 1984; Krausz and Meiland 1982). The problem for many is that the more radical cultural-relativist approaches of theorists such as Kessen (1983) can lead to a denial of any significant level of psychic unity in the human community. This can lead to a sort of psychological apartheid based on cultural difference.

Swartz (1989) notes that the issue of culture and relativism in South African psychology and psychiatry is an area fraught with conceptual and ideological problems. In particular this is due to the dominance of essentialist views of culture, which nest easily with apartheid ideology. While we cannot debate the complex range of issues pertaining to cultural relativism here, some comments are appropriate.

All cultures have views on what is normal for children at different points in their lives. What we do not often realise is that knowledge derived from psychology itself can become part of that order – for example, categorical statements about children's inherent 'needs' (Woodhead 1991). If statements about children's needs are based on research conducted with American or British children, then the claim about what children 'universally' need is no more than a reflection of particular cultural orders. Thus while a statement about the child's needs may be correct for some children, it may not necessarily be correct for all children.

Edelstein (1983) sees the main advantage of relativism as being its critical function in contributing to the removal of false reifications such as the above. Its main disadvantage is that its inevitable consequence is to espouse the view that there is *no* ultimate reality – each historical period or culture has its own equally valid reality.

As Du Preez (in press:10) puts it: 'relativism is a good strategy for undermining dogmatism but it is an incoherent epistemological position. Apart from the contradiction of maintaining the exclusive truth of relativism, the relativist is soon forced to choose between truths' – particularly where the morality of social practices is concerned.

Despite this view, Edelstein (1983:51) goes on to point to an ethical advantage:

> awareness of the cultural and historical relativity of social science methodologies and findings, and of the truth criteria and validity claims of scientific propositions, is bound to corrode the link between scientific descriptions and the prescriptive deductions leading to their application in practical intervention... If you doubt the universality of the knowledge, how can you prescribe a treatment or give advice or propose what is best for children's development? This makes relativism ethically compelling.

(Again, this is particularly true where simplistic or hegemonic cross-cultural prescriptions are concerned.) So, given the relativist argument, is it true that the child is not able to be researched in some non-transient sense? What is clearly correct is that conceptions of 'the child' and developmental regularities (norms), which are *not* bound by biological limitations, do change across social contexts and through history. There is thus empirical support for relativism at the level of norms of behaviour, norms of child care and so on. But we are not only concerned with norms; we are concerned with developmental processes, and here we perhaps need to rely on a more fundamentalist strategy (Du Preez, in press).

Edelstein (1983:53) believes that we have to separate process from norm if we are to have at least minimal frameworks for explaining how psychological development occurs. He proposes research programmes to 're-establish developmental regularities while taking into account performance conditions due to time and space and context'.

What does this imply? First, the developmentally relevant structures of society *must* be taken into account. Second, data on culturally specific aspects of child development (descriptive data, ideas about adversity, etc.) would need to be incorporated into a theory of social evolution. Linked into this would have to be a theory of child development as a phenomenon in social evolution (i.e. a theory of how childhood changes as societies evolve). If we put these together, then particular processes would emerge as universal patterns across societies and cultures – patterns of which there is indeed already evidence (Miller 1989). Effectively what this does is to leave the possibility of a theory of the developmental process intact while contextualising the content and norms of behaviour.

What still remains, however, is the moral issue. Wartofsky (1983), in response to Edelstein, argues that since psychology is a social practice, developmentalists have a moral responsibility to define what is good or bad for child development. We cannot talk about 'development' unless we have a notion of what counts as developmental progress – rather than just change. We agree with this position. Walking is a more developed point in life than crawling and enables the solution of a wider range of problems. At the psychological level, we believe that more powerful choices are possible if the individual has a wider range of physical and mental tools at his or her disposal. These tools differ in quantity and quality with development. Equally, communities and societies may differ in the sorts of tools best suited to the survival tasks which confront them. Whether one or other society is the best is not a psychological matter but a question of values. What constrains or facilitates the power of the individual to adapt either self or society in optimal terms *is,* however, a psychological matter.

Finally, relativism also contains the risk of allowing one to remain neutral about conditions of life which, from one's own moral position, are repugnant. In this volume, we are *not* neutral about the conditions of life that have been created under apartheid, gendered power relations and poverty. As Richter (1990:2) has put it, there 'is no question of the immorality of conditions that make children suffer' or that these conditions are less than optimal for child development. Nevertheless, what is at stake psychologically is just *how* these conditions affect development and through what *processes* the relationship occurs. Ultimately, therefore, we return to Edelstein's position. We believe this does not preclude a moral stand, provided that stand is prepared to examine its own assumptions, and provided that an understanding of psychological processes is acknowledged as the ultimate aim of psychological studies of development in different contexts.

Conclusion

While we do not accept the notion of the universal normative child, we do assert that there is considerable evidence, from a number of societies, which has been able to identify a range of life circumstances that influence developmental processes in particular ways and that pose risks to development. Children's life circumstances *can* restrict the optimal development of their adaptive powers and hence their ability to engage actively in the world. By the same token, it is clear that children who are given opportunities to extend their powers are able to apprehend a wider range of physical, cognitive and social challenges than would otherwise be the case. The assumption that runs through this is that the notion of adaptive power may indeed have universal significance and may therefore be asserted as a legitimate developmental goal across contexts. Within this it is crucial to understand that the opportunities which facilitate or restrict this power are profoundly determined by the structural, cultural and social dimensions of context – the contents of this volume being an explicit illustration of this. The notion of adaptive power, therefore, is as much an assertion of the active, agentic child as a force in its own development, as it is an assertion of the social forces that interact with, and thus shape and are shaped by, that very capacity for adaptation.

Beyond this we also accept the need to search for universal developmental processes that are superordinate to cultural differences. Thus, the real impact of major developmental theories such as those of Piaget, Vygotsky and Bruner lies in their focus on, and search for, universal *process* explanations. Although some normative aspects of, in particular, Piaget's theory have been shown to be culture and context dependent (Light 1986), and although these theories do come from differing ontological and epistemological positions (Moll 1989), notions such as the complementary action of assimilation and accommodation in the process of equilibration (Piaget 1953), the process of social mediation through the zone of proximal development (Vygotsky 1978), and the process of active, strategic transformation of information emphasised by Bruner (1964) have all had a significant impact on our understanding of the constructive nature of cognitive development in any context.

As we have argued, the sort of life chances one wishes to promote for children is a complex moral and ideological matter. Nevertheless, how they can best be promoted may still be informed by developmental psychology. Certainly, with the absence of certainty in this post-modern, deconstructed period of history, some faith is required in order to maintain the possibility that psychological knowledge can make a contribution to the understanding and amelioration of adversity. However, as long as it is cautious and not grandiose in its claims, a relevant developmental psychology can help to clarify those conditions that limit children's power to adapt, and it can help to understand the processes by which this occurs. Only through this understanding can it strive to alter the conditions that restrict children in their development. It is this that adds the psychological content to a moral project.

References

Anastasi, A. (1958). Heredity and environment and the question 'how'? *Psychological Review, 65,* 197–208.

Bandura, A. (1973). *Aggression: A Social Learning Analysis.* Englewood Cliffs N.J.: Prentice Hall.

Bennett, T. W. A. (1991). *A Sourcebook of African Customary Law for Southern Africa.* Cape Town: Juta.

Biesheuwel, S. (1987). Psychology: science and politics. Theoretical developments and applications in a plural society. *South African Journal of Psychology, 17,* 1–8.

Braungart, R. G. and Braungart, M. M. (1986). Life course and generational politics. *Annual Review of Sociology, 12,* 205–231.

Bronfenbrenner, U. (1986). Ecology of the family as a context for human development: Research perspectives. *Developmental Psychology, 22*(6), 723–742.

Bronfenbrenner, U., Kessel, F. S., Kessen, W. and White, S. (1986). Toward a critical social history of developmental psychology. A propaedeutic discussion. *American Psychologist, 41*(11), 1218-1230.

Bruner, J. (1964). The course of cognitive growth. *American Psychologist, 19,* 1–15.

Boonzaaier, E. and Sharp, J. (1988). *South African Keywords. The Uses and Abuses of Political Concepts.* Cape Town: David Philip.

Bulhan, H. A. (1981). Psychological research in Africa. *Race and Class, 32,* 25–41.

Burman, E. (1992). Feminism and discourse in developmental psychology: Power, subjectivity and interpretation. *Feminism and Psychology, 2*(1), 45-59.

Burman, S. (1988). Defining children. In Boonzaaier, E. and Sharp, J. (1988). *South African keywords. The Uses and Abuses of Political Concepts.* Cape Town: David Philip.

Burman, S. and Reynolds, P. (eds) (1986). *Growing Up in a Divided Society. Contexts of Childhood in South Africa.* Johannesburg: Ravan Press.

Chikane, F. (1986). The effects of township unrest on children. In S. Burman and P. Reynolds (eds), *Growing Up in a Divided Society. Contexts of Childhood in South Africa*. Johannesburg: Ravan Press.

Dawes, A. (1985). Politics and mental health: The position of clinical psychology in South Africa. *South African Journal of Psychology, 15*, 55–61.

Dawes, A. (1986). The notion of relevant psychology with particular reference to Africanist pragmatic initiatives. *Psychology in Society, 5*, 28–48.

Dawes, A. (1990). The effects of political violence on children: A consideration of South African and related studies. *International Journal of Psychology, 25*, 13–31.

Dawes, A. (1992). Mental health in South Africa. *South African Journal of Psychology, 22*, 28–33.

Department of National Education. (1991). *Education Renewal Strategy: Discussion Document*. Pretoria: Department of National Education.

Deveraux, G. (1980). *Basic Problems of Ethnopsychiatry*. Chicago: University of Chicago Press.

Donald, D. (1989). *Applied Child Psychology in South African Society: Purposes, Problems and Paradigm Shifts*. Inaugural lecture. Pietermaritzburg: University of Natal Press.

Donald, D. and Csapo, M. (1989). School psychology in South Africa. In P. Saigh and T. Oakland (eds), *International Perspectives on Psychology in the Schools*. Hillside, N.J.: Lawrence Erlbaum.

Du Preez, P. (in press). Reason which cannot be reasoned with: What is public debate and how does it change? To appear in R. Dalitz, E. Krabbe and P. Smit (eds), *Empirical Logic and Public Debate*. Groningen: Wolters-Noordholt.

Edelstein, W. (1983). Cultural constraints on development and the vicissitudes of progress. In F. S. Kessel and A. W. Siegel (eds), *The Child and Other Cultural Inventions*. New York: Praeger.

Ennew, J. and Milne, B. (1989). *The Next Generation. Lives of Third World Children*. London: Zed Books.

Foster, D., Nicholas, L. and Dawes, A. (1993). Psychology in South Africa: A reply to Raubenheimer. *The Psychologist, 6*(4), 172–174.

Gergen, K. (1979). The positivist image in social psychological theory. In A. R. Buss (ed.), *Psychology in Social Context*. New York: John Wiley.

Gergen, K. (1985). The social constructionist movement in modern psychology. *American Psychologist, 40*(3), 266–275.

Gilbert, A. J. (1989). Things fall apart? Psychological theory in the context of rapid social change. *South African Journal of Psychology, 19*, 91–100.

Goodyer, I. M. (1990). *Life Experiences, Development and Childhood Psychopathology*. Chichester: Wiley.

Gordon, A. (1987). *Another Mielie in the Bag*. Pretoria: Human Sciences Research Council.

Heelas, P. (1984). Emotions across cultures: Objectivity and cultural divergence. In S. C. Brown (ed.), *Objectivity and Cultural Divergence*. Cambridge: The Royal Institute of Philosophy.

Henriques, J., Hollway, W., Urwin, C., Venn, C. and Walkerdine, V. (1984). *Changing the Subject: Psychology, Social Regulation and Subjectivity*. London: Methuen.

Holdstock, T. L. (1981). Psychology in South Africa belongs to the colonial era. Arrogance or ignorance? *South African Journal of Psychology, 11*, 123–129.

Hollway, W. (1989). *Subjectivity and Method in Psychology*. London: Sage.

Ingleby, D. (1986). Development in social context. In M. Richards and P. Light (eds), *Children of Social Worlds. Development in Context*. Cambridge: Polity Press.

James, A. and Prout, A. (1990). *Constructing and Reconstructing Childhood. Contemporary Issues in the Sociological Study of the Child*. London: The Falmer Press.

Kagitçibasi, C. (1992). Family and human development in cross-cultural perspective: The case of the Turkish enrichment programme. Paper delivered at the XVth International School Psychology Colloquium, Istanbul.

Kessen, W. (1983). The child and other cultural inventions. In F. S. Kessel and A. W. Siegel (eds), *The Child and Other Cultural Inventions*. New York: Praeger.

Krausz, M. and Meiland, J. W. (1982). *Relativism, Cognitive and Moral*. South Bend, Indiana: University of Notre Dame Press.

Lerner, R. M. (1986). *Concepts and Theories of Human Development*. New York: Random House.

Liddell, C. and Kvalsvig, J. (1990). Science and social accountability: Issues related to South African developmental psychology. *South African Journal of Psychology, 20*, 1–9.

Light, P. (1986). Context, conservation and conversation. In M. Richards and P. Light (eds), *Children of Social Worlds: Development in Social Context*. Cambridge: Polity Press.

Louw, J. (1987). From separation to division. The origins of two psychological associations in South Africa. *Journal of the History of the Behavioural Sciences, 23*, 341–352.

Luria, A. R. (1976). *Cognitive Development: Its Cultural and Social Foundations*. Cambridge, Mass.: Harvard University Press.

Magnusson, D. (1992). Individual development: A longitudinal perspective. *European Journal of Personality, 6*, 119–138.

Manganyi, N. C. (1973). *Being Black in the World*. Johannesburg: SPROCAS/Ravan.

Marks, S. and Andersson, N. (1990). The epidemiology and culture of violence. In N. C. Manganyi and A. du Toit (eds), *Political Violence and the Struggle in South Africa*. London: Macmillan.

Mauer, K. F. (1987). Laporello is on his knees. In search of relevance in South African psychology. *South African Journal of Psychology, 17*, 83–92.

Mauer, K. F., Marais, H. C., and Prinsloo, R. J. (1991). Psychology: The high road or the low road? *South African Journal of Psychology, 21*(2), 90–96.

Miller, R. (1989). Critical psychology: A territorial imperative. *Psychology in Society, 12*, 3–32.

Moll, I. (1989). Roots and disputes of cognitive developmental conceptions of teaching. *South African Journal of Education, 9*, 714–721.

Nasson, B. and Samuel, J. (eds) (1990). *Education: From Poverty to Liberty*. Cape Town: David Philip.

National Education Policy Investigation (NEPI). (1993). *The Framework Report and Final Report Summaries*. Cape Town: Oxford University Press.

Nicholas, L. J. and Cooper, S. (1990). *Psychology and Apartheid*. Johannesburg: Vision/Madiba.

Nkomo, M. (ed) (1990). *Pedagogy of Domination: Towards a Democratic Education in South Africa*. Trenton, N.J.: Africa World Press.

Parker, I. (1990). Discourse: Definitions and contradictions. *Philosophical Psychology, 3*(2), 189–205.

Parker, I. and Shotter, J. (1990). *Deconstructing Social Psychology*. London: Routledge.

Piaget, J. (1953). *The Origin of Intelligence in the Child*. London: Routledge and Kegan Paul.

Psychological Association of South Africa (PASA) (1989). *Mental Health in South Africa*. Report by the Council Committee on Mental Health: Pretoria, PASA.

Retief, A. (1989). The debate about the relevance of South African psychology – A metatheoretical imperative. *South African Journal of Psychology, 19*, 75–83.

Reynolds, P. (1989). *Childhood in Crossroads. Cognition and Society in South Africa*. Cape Town: David Philip.

Richter, L. M. (1990). *Wretched Childhoods: The Challenge to Psychological Theory and Practice*. Inaugural lecture, University of South Africa, Pretoria.

Riley, D. (1983). *War in the Nursery. Theories of the Child and Mother*. London: Virago.

Rizzo, T. A., Corsaro, W. A., and Bates, J. E. (1992). Ethnographic methods and interpretive analysis: Expanding the methodological options of psychologists. *Developmental Review, 12*, 101–123.

Rose, N. (1990). *Governing the Soul. The Shaping of the Private Self*. London: Routledge.

Rutter, M. (1985). Resilience in the face of adversity. Protective factors and resistance to psychological disorder. *British Journal of Psychiatry, 147*, 598–611.

Said, E. (1991). *Identity, Authority and Freedom: The Potentate and the Traveller*. 31st T.B. Davie Memorial Lecture, University of Cape Town.

Scheper-Hughes, N. (1987). The cultural politics of child survival. In N. Scheper-Hughes (ed.), *Child Survival: Anthropological Perspectives on Treatment and Maltreatment*. Dordrecht: Reidel.

Schneirla, T. C. (1957). The concept of development in comparative psychology. In D. B. Harris (ed.), *The Concept of Development*. Minneapolis: University of Minnesota Press.

Segall, M. H., Dasen, P. R., Berry J. W., and Poortinga, Y. H. (1990). *Human Behaviour in Global Perspective. An Introduction to Cross-Cultural Psychology*. New York: Pergamon.

South African Institute of Race Relations. (1992). *Race Relations Survey 1991/92*. Braamfontein: SAIRR.

Spiegel, A. and Boonzaier, E. (1988). Promoting tradition: Images of the South African past. In E. Boonzaier and J. Sharp (eds), *South African Keywords. The Uses and Abuses of Political Concepts*. Cape Town: David Philip.

Straker, G. (1989). From victim to villain: A slight of speech? Media representation of township youth. *South African Journal of Psychology, 19*(1), 20–27.

Strümpfer, D. J. W. (1981). Towards a more socially responsive psychology. *South African Journal of Psychology, 11*, 18–28.

Swartz, L. (1989). Aspects of culture in South African psychiatry. Unpublished PhD thesis, University of Cape Town, South Africa.

Swartz, L., Gibson, K. and Swartz, S. (1990). State violence in South Africa and the development of a progressive psychology. In N. C. Manganyi and A. du Toit (eds), *Political Violence and the Struggle in South Africa*. London: Macmillan.

Taylor, N. (1989). *Falling at the First Hurdle*. Research report No. 1, Education Policy Unit, University of the Witwatersrand.

Trueba, H., Spindler, G. and Spindler, L. (eds) (1989). *What Do Anthropologists Have to Say About Dropouts?* London: The Falmer Press.

Vogelman, L. (1990). Violent crime: Rape. In B. McKendrick and W. Hoffman (eds), *People and Violence in South Africa*. Cape Town: Oxford University Press.

Vygotsky, L. S. (1978). *Mind in Society. The Development of Higher Mental Processes*. Cambridge, Mass.: Harvard University Press.

Walkerdine, V. (1984). Developmental psychology and the child centered pedagogy: The insertion of Piaget into early education. In J. Henriques, W. Hollway, C. Urwin, C. Venn, and V. Walkerdine (eds), *Changing the Subject: Psychology, Social Regulation and Subjectivity*. London: Methuen.

Wartofsky, M. (1983). The child's construction of the world and the world's construction of the child. From historical epistemology to historical psychology. In F. S. Kessel and A. W. Siegel (eds), *The Child and Other Cultural Inventions*. New York: Praeger.

Weisner, T. (1989). An ecocultural model and activity setting model of socialisation. Presented at the Ethnography of Childhood Conference, Victoria Falls, Zimbabwe.

Werner, E. E. and Smith, R. S. (1983). *Vulnerable but Invincible. A Longitudinal Study of Resilient Children and Youth*. New York: McGraw Hill.

Wilson, F. and Ramphele, M. (1989). *Uprooting Poverty: The South African Challenge*. Cape Town: David Philip.

Woodhead, M. (1991). Psychology and the cultural construction of children's needs. In M. Woodhead, P. Light and R. Carr (eds), *Growing Up in a Changing Society*. London: Routledge and the Open University.

2
Economic Stress and Its Influence on the Family and Caretaking Patterns
LINDA RICHTER

Introduction

Longitudinal birth cohort studies have stressed that many biological risk factors for children are only realised as negative developmental outcomes when they are combined with the kind of persistently poor environmental conditions that occur with chronic poverty (Werner 1985). Similarly, a consistent theme that will be further developed in Chapter 4 is that the influence of poor growth on psychological development is inseparable from the impact of poverty and deprivation. The notion that economic stress generally is harmful to children's psychological development is implicit in both these conclusions. There is a great deal of social scientific information to support this, some of which will be reviewed in this chapter. However, the major focus will be on the mechanisms and processes by which poor economic and social conditions come to have adverse effects on children.

Economic stress is a pervasive feature of southern African life. Information from a Worldwatch Institute Report (Gauthier 1990) indicates that sub-Saharan Africa has the highest share of the population (62%) living in absolute poverty of all continents. Latin America follows with 35% of the population living in such conditions. In 1980, 61% of Africans in South Africa were estimated to be living below the Minimum Living Level and in the so-called homelands 81% were reported to be living in dire poverty (Wilson and Ramphele 1989). In South Africa we have to confront not only the material poverty of large numbers of people but also the fact that their impoverishment has been exacerbated by the deliberate political policy of apartheid.

In conditions such as these, there is what Unicef has called the silent emergency of 40 000 children suffering or dying each day from preventable and treatable causes (Korbin 1992). We know that being poor for a child means being at risk for developing both physical and psychological problems. Over the last two decades in the social sciences, theories have been developed and studies conducted which take account of the human ecology of childhood. These new directions have helped to clarify some of the processes involved when children succumb to the risks of poverty or, alternatively, are protected from them.

Economic Stress: Conceptualisation, Definition and Measurement

Poverty

What is meant by terms such as economic stress, poverty and low socio-economic or social status? Each of these terms is complex and tied to different referents in the social and economic domains. Sociologists frequently make a distinction between three dimensions of poverty – absolute poverty, relative poverty and subjective poverty (Haralambos 1985). The term 'absolute poverty' is intended to focus on the material dimension of economic insufficiency. It has its origins in the subsistence concept articulated by Rowntree at the beginning of this century. According to this view, households are in poverty when their income is inadequate to meet the basic costs for healthy survival and decency. It is clear that there is nothing simple or straightforward about this concept – it refers to households rather than families or individuals, it assumes standards for judging wise and careful spending, and it implies that there is some agreed-upon notion of decency. The fact that it is a highly contentious issue is illustrated by the existence of at least five measures for estimating poverty in South Africa. These include the Poverty Datum Line (PDL) and the Minimum Living Level (MLL).

Relative poverty is based on the social and economic stratification of capitalist societies in which it is generally accepted that people in the society will differ with respect to their access to educational and occupational opportunities; essentially it is a concept of inequality. Available economic resources determine power and prestige. According to one particular coefficient, South Africa has the highest measure of inequality of 57 countries for which data are available (Wilson and Ramphele 1989). As Tulkin (1972) put it, the poor are less than poor. They are poor while others are rich.

Subjective poverty refers to several things. Amongst others, it refers to the feeling of being poor, particularly in relation to those who are not poor, to the sense of being socially denigrated for being poor, as well as to the sense of insecurity which accompanies the lack of money (Fried 1982). Garbarino argues that the phenomenology of poverty is 'dominated by the experience of deprivation and exacerbated by widespread promulgation of highly monetarised affluence as the standard' (1992:231). Hamburg points out that poverty is partly a matter of income and partly a matter of human dignity. 'It is one thing', he said, 'to have a very low income but to be treated with respect by your compatriots; it is quite another matter to have a very low income and to be harshly depreciated by more powerful compatriots' (quoted in Wilson and Ramphele 1989:5).

Another common distinction is the one made between chronic or endemic poverty and transitory or event-related poverty. Substantial numbers of children in developed countries are estimated to experience poverty for at least some period in their lives (Miller, Kolvin and Fells 1985). For example, approximately one-third of all children in the United States are calculated to live in poverty for at least one year of their lives. On the other hand, endemic or chronic poverty is far more common and affects the majority of children in developing countries. Poverty is not therefore an isolated or singular condition – certainly not a distinct event or a phenomenon that can be treated as a unitary variable in empirical studies (Baumeister, Kupstas and Klindworth 1991). Chronic poverty is a multi-dimensional process incorporating a conglomerate of stressful conditions as well as compensatory social adaptations. Most authors emphasise the subjective or psychosocial implications of poverty – the restrictions it places on access to social institutions and services, the constrictions of life choices, and the subjection of the individual to control by others (McLoyd 1990b). It is through this emphasis that common conceptual ground can be found between the concepts of poverty and of socio-economic status (SES) and social class.

Socio-economic Status and Social Class

Both social class and SES are heuristic concepts indicating the significant hierarchical differentiations within a society (Hess 1970). As Hess points out, to designate the social status of people is to identify, in general terms, the social and economic context in which they normally operate and to indicate, also in general terms, the experiences they are likely to encounter. As with poverty, social class is not a unitary variable, despite the fact that it is often treated as such.

Many measures and methods have been used to try to assess the SES of families. Most of them incorporate some combination of education, occupation, income and residential location (Gottfried 1985; Osborn 1987). The majority of the definitional and measurement controversies arise out of divergent views regarding the essential nature of social stratification. At one extreme is an emphasis upon the social and psychological dimensions, particularly those associated with prestige, power and access. At the other extreme, stress is placed on economic circumstances and resources represented mainly by income (Hess 1970). These problems of definition and measurement spill over into research on how SES or poverty affects the behaviour of either parents or children. In most studies, comments Hess, there is insufficient clarity and specificity about the nature of the socio-economic stratifications used as independent variables.

It is also clear that the socio-structural foundations of a society will influence the way in which components of SES affect people at the psychological level. For example, low income is a better predictor of child developmental deficits and pathology in the United States than in other countries because, argues Garbarino (1992), social policies in the US tend to exaggerate (rather than minimise) the impact of family income on access to human services. In contrast, Heyneman (1976) has suggested that the influence of SES on children's psychological performance may be weaker in less developed countries, although it is not entirely clear why this should be so. One possibility is that the relationships between the components of SES measures (education, occupation, income, location) vary between developed and less developed countries. In South Africa, for example, Prinsloo (1984) has noted that for most black workers, education does not significantly affect income. Higher educational levels give access to marginally higher wages but do not protect workers from low wages.

Despite these problems, SES has been found to be a potent and meaningful variable in psychological research (Gottfried 1985). Nonetheless, there is, as Block (1971) puts it, a need to 'psychologise' the notion of social class. Block sees SES as an atheoretical and conceptually unwieldy notion – one that has only been tolerated because it 'works' by lacing together an extensive network of influences. However, from a social scientific point of view it is a poor and confused indicator of several rather different determinants of behaviour and seldom reveals anything of the psychological meaning of behaviour (Clarke-Stewart 1988).

Poverty and Child Outcomes

In 1972, Rutter summarised a large quantity of child development research from the previous decade by concluding that there had simply been an accumulation of evidence showing the extent to which deprivation and disadvantage can impede children's psychological development. The positive correlations between SES and development have remained the strongest and most widely reported relationships in child development research (Sameroff and Chandler 1975). For the rest of this chapter, the terms SES and poverty will be used to describe specific social and economic states. Although the use of these terms may seem inconsistent, this is largely so (in addition to the conceptual problems outlined above) because they have been kept in agreement with the meaning intended by the authors cited.

From the moment of conception onwards, SES creates a funnel of causality. It begins with children from low SES backgrounds having a greater number of perinatal complications than their counterparts from the higher classes (Gray, Dean and Lowrie 1988) and it continues throughout childhood through the intrinsic link between biological and social stresses (Kopp 1990). It culminates with working-class youth's greater risk for conduct disorders and arrest for infringements of the law (Rutter 1985). Information collected by the Children's Defense Fund in the United States in 1986 (Garmezy 1991) indicates that in comparison with better-off groups, children who live in poverty in the United States are, amongst other things, three times as likely to have their mother die in childbirth, twice as likely to suffer one or more disabilities, and three times as likely to be in foster care or die of child abuse.

However, it would be 'both inaccurate and overly simplistic to assume that poverty is the singular and most immediate cause for health and developmental problems. The tie that binds is not always direct, nor is the connection one of inevitable certainty' (Baumeister, Kupstas and Klindworth 1991:474). Somehow the balance has to be found between this conviction and the proof that of all factors that underlie the developmental problems of children, the most profound and pervasive exacerbating factor is poverty (Halpern 1990).

'Culture of Poverty' and 'Poverty of Culture'

Two popular misconstructions have dogged attempts to understand the processes by which poverty undermines children's intellectual, social and emotional development. The first is the idea that the state of poverty constitutes a sub-culture which determines behaviour transgenerationally, and the second is the opinion that certain cultures or classes are impoverished in terms of the stimulation and values they offer children.

Poverty as Culture. The idea of equating poverty with a culture was first formulated by Oscar Lewis in 1959. The main tenet of this view is that poverty is primarily due to the behaviour, attitudes and values of the poor. Furthermore it is argued that poverty and dependency are transmitted intergenerationally by parents who do not inculcate in their children the traits of autonomy, independence and ambition (McLoyd 1990b). Schiller (1980) has argued that there are two perspectives on the causes of poverty; one is the 'restricted opportunity' point of view while the other, the notion of the 'flawed character', is the basis of culture of poverty theories. In the latter there is the conviction that ample opportunities are given to the poor but that they do not take advantage of them because of their supposed present-time orientation, fatalism and feelings of inferiority.

In contrast to culture of poverty theories, the standpoint of 'restricted opportunity' orientations is that poor people fail to achieve or escape from poverty because of structural barriers or prejudices which inhibit their access to the job market. From this perspective the lifestyle of the poor, rather than causing their own condition of poverty, is a direct effect of their impoverished condition. For example, Hess (1970) points out that there are a number of common social and psychological concomitants of low socio-economic status. As a response to these common elements, adaptations in the form of a pseudo-culture may arise out of attempts to deal with a hostile and depriving environment. Some of the common elements of such a culture listed by Hess are:

1. The very limited extent to which individuals are able to exercise power in the society, through their status, prestige or affiliation with institutions or organisations. For example, poor people are more likely to be arrested without justification.

2. A vulnerability to disaster which is compounded by a lack of financial reserves. For example, the poor are least likely to be given advance warning of job terminations. Hess (1970) claims that in these conditions, life is lived on the edge of incipient tragedy, which people are powerless to avert.

3. A restricted range of alternatives of action including, for example, restricted medical services and educational opportunities.

The perception that personal relationships are structured in terms of power, low self-esteem and a sense of passivity and hostility can all be interpreted as responses and adaptations to the social concomitants of poverty.

Cultural Deprivation. A number of terms (cultural deprivation, cultural disadvantage, culturally different) arose during the 1960s to describe the view that certain cultures and classes provided insufficient and inappropriate experiences for young children to enable them to cope with the demands of a modern technological society (Reschly 1986). Apart from the fact that, like the culture of poverty theories, these views imply a negative categorisation of poor people, they are also fundamentally ethnocentric. For example, in the same year that Soweto schoolchildren challenged the education system and the state, Groenewald (1976:1) argued that the intellectual growth of African children was handicapped by their cultural milieu. Specifically, he claimed that their restricted learning environment gave rise to 'a defective orientation towards activities requiring intellectual effort' and an 'ineffective ability for dissociation at the cognitive level'.

There is currently a widespread rejection of the idea that western middle-class behaviour or values are the universal standard for optimum development of children (Tulkin 1972). Cultural relativism, particularly with respect to black Americans, has been articulated by Ogbu (1981:417) who argued that 'child rearing techniques serve only as a mechanism for inculcating and acquiring certain culturally defined instrumental competencies'. However, the issue of cultural relativism is complex (see also Dawes and Donald, Chapter 1). Criticism of working-class attitudes or behaviour, or of the attributes of any minority group, is often taken to be disparagement, which undermines self-esteem and political manoeuvres. Because of this, many people have taken to championing a 'non-evaluative' kind of social and cultural relativism (Zigler 1985). This stance is not without its critics. In the first place it is challenged by those who argue that 'the doctrine of cultural relativism has a hollow ring for people for whom the harsh realities of survival include famine, disease, oppression and exploita-tion' (Miller 1989:3). It is also challenged by those who argue that it denies the existence in children of basic, universal needs for human growth (Zigler 1985).

However, it is quite clear that poor or minority environments do not involve anything like stimulus deprivation. An example of the way in which this con-tention has been refuted is contained in Pamela Reynolds's observations of chil-dren in Crossroads (1989). She maintains that the ingenuity and variety of chil-dren's play cautions against placing too great an emphasis in accounts of cogni-tive development on the simplicity of dwellings and lack of possessions. Reschly (1986) and others have argued that poor children, rather than being culturally deprived, are insufficiently exposed to structural learning situations which pre-pare them for later school achievement.

It is important to note that several authors have criticised early childhood interventions, like Head Start, for being based on assumptions about the 'cycle of poverty' – 'that is, poor parenting produces children with social and intellec-tual deficits who, unable to perform well in school and on the job, will them-selves experience poverty, leading again to high risk births and inappropriate parenting' (Oyemade 1985:591). In the main, however, such criticisms emanate from a concern that there is too little focus in statements about poverty on 'the total environmental structure that disenfranchises, alienates and disaffects' (Tulkin 1972:331).

Mediators Between Social Conditions and Children's Behaviour

In order to produce statements about the effects of poverty on children's behaviour we need to expose the assumptions usually made about the existence and operation of mediators between social conditions and children's develop-ment. Hess (1970) has summarised the processes thus far set forward as links between social structures and behaviour:

1. A functional relationship is posited to exist between economic activities and child-rearing practices. As illustration of this link, Hess (1970) quotes the

1959 study by Barry, Bacon and Child of 104 societies. This study found that in line with expected adult behaviour and group survival, societies based on agriculture and animal husbandry tended to place a premium on obedience to age and experience as well as conformity to accepted routines. In contrast, hunting and fishing societies, which would obviously benefit from innovation, tended to stress initiative, individualism and creativity in their young members.

2. Following Mead and others who see the self arising in interaction with society, an awareness may develop in children of their relative social position and prestige in the social hierarchy.

3. Social conditions may lead to children being deprived of essential experience. This is the central mediating process hypothesised within deficit theory, which holds that differences in intellectual performance between social groups can largely be attributed to the lack of stimulation of cognitive processes provided in the poor family.

4. Another route of transmission has been proposed as occurring through traditional cultural and religious values, which are thought to give rise to different types of child-rearing practices.

5. According to Bernstein (1960) and others, the child is thought to be socialised into particular modes of thought and behaviour through child-rearing styles which correspond to parental experiences of social conditions. Hess (1970:472) gives the example that a child of low social class is not taught to be passive; 'rather, the unpredictability of his life and the lack of orderly contingencies in his experience with his environment induces caution and apathy'.

We can also distinguish different forms of relationship between child and social conditions in terms of the child's direct experience of the social and economic world on the one hand, and contact between child and the environment as mediated through parents and other significant people in the child's life, on the other. Much more attention has been given to the latter than the former process. According to Vygotsky (1978) and others, contact between a child and the world is always mediated even if the mediation is not immediate but occurs through individually historic encounters which have become internalised.

In contrast, Hess (1970:464) cautions that we may underestimate the extent to which 'diffuse but direct experience with the environment through interaction with peers, television, newspapers, popular music, observations of life in the community, awareness of social and economic inequality and other points of contact directly shapes the child's cognitive and behavioural strategies and resources'. For example, there are wide variations, structured by social class parameters, in the way that children learn to perceive the environment and its rewards for achievement, initiative and so on.

Rutter (1985) has made the same point. He notes that numerous studies have shown that children with behaviour and learning problems are more likely to come from families which are disadvantaged, and that it is widely assumed that such family environments cause psychiatric or educational disturbance. In contrast, he argues, the association between maladjustment and disadvantaged background may equally be due to the operation of a third common variable in the equation – that of poverty. The great weakness of the argument for parent-mediated experiences lies in the fact that it implicitly places the responsibility for poor outcomes on the poor parents themselves (Halpern 1990). Inevitably, this approach has focused on deficits in parental skills and knowledge, which are then presumed to be in need of remediation through parent training (Oyemade 1985). Perhaps most unfortunate about the emphasis on parenting as forming the connection between children and socio-economic deprivation is the fact that it minimises the direct impact of poverty on children by denying them such things as adequate housing, medical care, nutrition and safe environments in which to play (Halpern 1990). Parents are thus easily blamed for what are, at root, matters of political and economic design.

On a theoretical level, Hess (1970:458) has pointed out that approaches which emphasise the role of parents often convey a 'concept of adult life as a relatively monolithic structure of norms and sanctions with immense power to impress its expectations upon the developing child'. Instead, the notion of stable adult cultural norms only really applies to isolated sub-groups in society and it is a difficult concept to apply in a modern, complex, differentiated and pluralistic society. Under these conditions, there are usually several intersecting socialising units, including the family, school and neighbourhood. Hess also claims that the multiplicity of norms made available in this network diffuses the impact of any single socialising unit. It is precisely this diffusion of influence which makes possible the kind of experiences hypothesised to occur in the lives of resilient children.

Studies in the 1960s and 1970s led to the view that there was a direct connection between the deficient performance of poor children in intelligence tests and in school and the behaviour of their parents. Working-class parental behaviour was generally characterised as lacking in appropriate teaching strategies, responsiveness to child behaviour and particular verbal focusing characteristics. Instead these parents were described as directive, dominating and cognitively undemanding in interaction with their children (Freeburg and Payne 1967). However, all of these studies faced a number of methodological problems, notably the following: a lack of specificity between particular family structures, cultures and classes; the use of assessment techniques, such as observations in university laboratories, which often discriminate against working-class families; the fact that complex constructs like maternal responsiveness and sensitivity were seldom operationalised; and a largely unidirectional (parent→child) interpretation of effects (Clarke-Stewart 1988). This last bias has changed somewhat as psychologists have begun to recognise the effects which children have on their parents' behaviour (Bell 1968).

The parenting styles described above were considered to be part of the value orientation of the poor and were largely derived from questionnaire studies of parents' reports of their values about children and child-rearing behaviour, as well as parents' reports of their behaviour in interaction with children (Hess 1970). However, the reported relationships between children's performance and parental behaviour cannot be accepted uncritically. Firstly, there is a great deal of evidence to suggest that bias against children from lower socio-economic groups pervades the educational system. Also, poor children are not inducted into the 'hidden curriculum' of the middle-class orientation to the educational establishment, and the procedures for assessment have been criticised for being biased, in terms of both the tests used and insensitive tester attitudes (Reschly 1986).

Finally, there is much to suggest that poor parents do not rear their children the way they do because they believe in, or value, the correctness of their behaviour; but rather because their circumstances frequently leave them few options, economically or personally.

Poverty and Family Life

In South Africa, at least, it is impossible to discuss any particular feature of poverty and its effects on the lives of people without the discussion moving into the area where poverty, culture and population group membership overlap. There have been few studies of the structure and functioning of poor families in South Africa, although a considerable amount of work has been done on changes in black family life as Africans have moved away from traditional practices governing social relationships, including marriage and child care (Marks and Rathbone 1983). These changes have taken place both in an artificial way in adaptation to apartheid laws and spontaneously in response to urbanisation and modernisation.

Throughout southern Africa there is a concern about family life and its role in the care of children (LeVine and LeVine 1981). As Uzoka (1980) puts it, the seat of responsibility for child-rearing is currently somewhat uncertain. Nonetheless, what follows is a description of those features of family life amongst the poor, including the majority of black South Africans, believed to have either direct or indirect effects on children's development.

The environments in which most economically deprived children grow are frequently prejudicial to optimal physical and psychological development. These conditions are often deep-rooted, enduring and intergenerational (Baumeister, Kupstas and Klindworth 1985; Dowdney, Skuse, Heptinstall, Puckering and Zur-Szpiro 1987). Many urban black townships are ghettos in which civil strife, violence and crime intrude daily in the lives of children (Mtshali 1988; Straker 1992). In rural areas, migrant labour and the resultant poverty have created what Thomas (1988) called a relentless cynical synergism which dissolves the bonds of community, dismembers families, and depletes the physical and psychic resources of individuals.

Garbarino (1985:125) and other adherents of an ecological approach have suggested that 'neighbourhoods' are one of the principal niches for children's development, in which 'conditions of life either collaborate to bolster parents or conspire to compound their deficiencies and vulnerabilities'. Thus, the impact of poverty on children is likely to vary depending on the nature of the neighbourhood in which they live (Gross and Monteiro 1989; Korbin 1992). In the Pretoria area, for example, more 'street children' come from the surrounding peri-urban slums like Winterveldt than from the established residential areas of Mamelodi and Atteridgeville, even though comparable levels of poverty exist in parts of these townships.

Crowded dwellings and large family size are typical features of poor families. In South Africa, a mean household density (people per room) of two-plus in black areas is not uncommon (Richter 1989). Although living in crowded conditions is not pleasant (Duckitt 1983), neither family size nor household crowding has been consistently associated with adverse effects on children (Gordon 1986; Mednick, Baker and Hocevar 1985). For example, Richter and Griesel (1986a) reported that of a large number of factors including household density and family size considered in their study, only SES showed significant relationships with children's performance on psychological tests and with school achievement. Moreover, it has been reported that many people consider overcrowded living conditions preferable to being divided as families under a migrant labour system (Hewatt, Lee, Nyakaza, Olver and Tyeko 1984).

Single parenthood, the absence of fathers from the home, and female-headed households are also common amongst poor black families in South Africa (Richter and Griesel 1986b). Households without fathers have been a consistent feature of South African life ever since the imposition of taxes forced rural men into urban employment (Liddell, Kvalsvig, Shabalala and Masilela 1991). However, the effects of migrant labour and influx control laws (Wilson 1972) have been compounded by a social trend towards late marriage, if marriage at all. Gulbrandsen (1986) has described a pattern of fluctuating premarital unions often leading to women with one or two small children receiving no financial or social support from the children's fathers. It is a complex situation, but several authors have attributed a major part of this trend to a strategy by women for retaining financial and personal independence (Gulbrandsen 1986; Van der Vliet 1984).

While a number of structural constraints may have made marriage more difficult and less rewarding (Simkins 1986), single parenthood creates ambiguity around the issue of responsibility and liability for children's care. Numbers of technically illegitimate children are estimated to be around 70% among women aged 20–35 years (Van der Vliet 1984). In such cases, women, with the help of relatives, lovers, older children and neighbourhood groups, take full responsibility for both the financial and personal needs of their children (Clark 1987). One adaptation to this situation has been the increase in female-headed households, which are estimated to comprise more than a third of households in metropolitan areas and 60% in rural districts (Simkins 1986). The extent to which families are broken up is illustrated by figures quoted by Simkins: approximately one-third of husbands live away from their wives and nearly 20% of children under the age of 15 years live apart from their mothers.

It should be borne in mind that, amongst poverty-stricken families, the distinction between married, single and separated marital status very seldom has much meaning (Parker, Piotrowski and Peay 1987). Nonetheless there is a substantial body of psychological research (mainly conducted in developed societies) which links psychopathology and underachievement with troubled family relationships (Moilanen and Rantakallio 1988; Pillay 1987; Wadsworth 1986). As in large families (Wagner, Schubert and Schubert 1985), single mothers have been reported to stress obedience in their children and tend to enforce it with corporal punishment (Segal 1985). Consistent with this is the finding that single mothers are at significant risk for child abuse, particularly if they are poor (Gelles 1992).

In South Africa, Cock and Emdon (1987) have recorded that the number of black working women increased by more than 50% between 1973 and 1981 and that the situation of working mothers makes alternative child care a major problem. At the time of writing, they estimated that nearly 20 000 Soweto preschool children were in the care of childminders and that most of the women taking on this role were old, sick and with few household facilities. While the extended family is still the main form of child care for most black children, about half are cared for outside of the family circle and many from a very early age. On the basis of their study in Soweto, Cock, Emdon and Klugman (1984) suggested that around 50% of working women may be returning to work when their babies are less than six months old. In the same vein, Brazelton (1988) chided America for lacking the commitment to support working mothers and pointed out that in the United States half of all parents do not have adequate day care available to them.

In the United States, the proportion of teen births rose between 15% and 61% in the thirty years from 1960. Furthermore, reports Osofsky (1990), the vast majority of these births (80%) are unplanned and unwanted. In South Africa, in 1989, pregnancies amongst teenage girls were estimated to run at about 14% of all black births (Boult and Cunningham 1991). Here, as elsewhere, the young mother is very often a schoolgirl and not in any position to support either herself or her baby. Moreover, although the mechanisms are not clear, research generally suggests that children born to teenage mothers show poor social and intellectual competence as compared with children born to older mothers (Hechtman, 1989; Roosa, Fitzgerald and Carlson 1982). When the caregiving styles or behaviour of poor or low SES parents are discussed, seldom can the effects of poverty or class be separated from the structural and functional features of family and child-care conditions described above.

Poverty and Child Care

As indicated, financially impoverished environments place children at risk for a number of intellectual and behavioural problems (Baumeister, Kupstas and Klindworth 1991; Garmezy 1991; Toomey and Christie 1990). Child abuse and neglect have also been reported to occur more often amongst low-SES parents, who are particularly vulnerable to the emotional stresses associated with poverty (Gelles 1992; Trickett, Aber, Carlson and Cicchetti 1991). Although the bulk of this research is American or European in origin and local contexts must always be considered, several reasons have been proposed for this supposed transmission of risk.

It has been claimed that indicators of psychopathology and underachievement are biased against lower-class and minority children, thus inflating the incidence of disorders amongst this group and artificially strengthening the relationship between social class and maladjustment (Freeberg and Payne 1967). In the case of child abuse and neglect, for example, a labelling bias has been shown to exist which makes poor families more likely to be identified, whether correctly or not (Gelles 1992). While such biases undoubtedly exist, there is no doubt that the relationship between social class and psychopathology nonetheless holds (see also Robertson and Berger, Chapter 9).

Earlier theories maintained that low-SES parents in industrialised societies socialised their children into a particular value system and promoted behaviour which was at odds with adjustment and achievement in mainstream society. For example, reviews prior to 1970 concurred in asserting that middle-class mothers expected more of their children, in comparison with low-SES mothers, in the areas of their children's independent behaviour and achievement (Hess 1970).

It is assumed that parents hold tacit theories of child development and child-rearing which reflect a cultural image of the ideal child (Hundeide 1984). This view is believed to account for many of the child-rearing differences reported between cultural and socio-economic class groups. For example, African child-rearing is widely believed to be characterised by compliance and obedience which is enforced through corporal punishment (Cox 1971; Opolot 1982). Welch (1978) has challenged these findings and has claimed that there is in fact little support for differences in childhood socialisation patterns and that there is less divergence between African and non-African societies than is commonly believed. Other authors have not challenged the findings but rather the interpretations placed upon them. For example, Munroe and Munroe (1972) have suggested that an emphasis on compliance may well be a concomitant of children's expected participation in the economic activities of a household.

Hess (1970:457) and others have pointed to the inherent methodological weakness of studies which emphasise the central tendency of class or cultural behaviour while at the same time diminishing variability within those groups. They present, argues Hess, 'a profile of a social class group that portrays each social class as distinct in values, attitudes and behaviours when, in fact, the original data very often shows a high degree of similarity between the groups, and a distribution of characteristics that clearly overlap class lines'. In this way, concludes Hess, a number of caricatures of social class and cultural group behaviour have appeared in the literature, which are simplistic and misleading.

There is widespread agreement in the portrayal of the middle-class mother as more attentive and more responsive to her children than low-SES mothers. The middle-class mother is also described as being more aware of her children's feelings and their perspectives on the activities in which they are engaged (Ricciuti 1977). In contrast to the theory described above, Hess (1970:480) offers an analysis of working-class parental behaviour which is based on their presumed adaptation to the social structure in which they live. He argues that 'It is not that they do not wish to perform adequately as mothers or that they prefer punishment as a control strategy... They lack alternatives in their own exchanges with the institutions of the community ... and they are poorly motivated to seek other techniques because there is little reason to expect reward.'

However, the emphasis in more recent writings has shifted and has stressed that poverty affects child-rearing by diminishing the capacity for supportive, consistent and child-centred parenting (McLoyd 1990b; Halpern 1990). The major mediating link between economic hardship and parenting is psychological distress originating from endemic adversity and negative life events. According to McLoyd (1990b), such distress could account for all the reported features of low-SES parenting – a diminished expression of affection, a diminished responsiveness to socio-emotional needs explicitly expressed by a child, a tendency to issue commands without explanation, a greater use of physical punishment, and a lowered likelihood of rewarding a child verbally. However, in addition, over-stressed, poor parents may also adversely influence their children in indirect ways through the communication of their despondency and despair (McLoyd and Wilson 1990). This should not be taken to suggest that all low-SES parents respond in these ways. Nevertheless the stress of poverty plays a major role in directly undermining the quality of child care (Goodyer 1988; Hundeide 1984). Garbarino (1992) has drawn attention to the fact that as the costs of survival rise, children increasingly become a financial burden, especially for people with already few material resources. It costs a great deal to raise a child as well as costing parents, especially single mothers, through lost income often needed to support other children and dependants.

Although there has been a substantial amount of work on stress in response to negative life events, Fried (1982) claims that, relatively speaking, the kind of endemic chronic stress associated with persistent economic scarcity has been neglected by researchers. He argues that endemic stress, from a psychological point of view, includes feelings of resignation and is linked to a sense of helplessness and hopelessness as well as a decline in the individual's sense of self-esteem. He concludes that endemic stress may result in a pervasive low-level depression.

South African studies confirm high stress levels and low life satisfaction amongst economically impoverished groups. Møller, Schlemmer and Strijdom (1984) found that the most demoralised group of people they interviewed in South Africa were shack dwellers. They concluded that, besides a low cash income, the poor residential environment of squatter settlements was also highly related to life dissatisfaction.

Parental stress is believed to be capable of affecting children's behaviour through a number of routes, including the parent's own depressive state. In addition, negative attributions about children are a corollary of the emotional reactions to stressful life circumstances – as stress increases, child characteristics and behaviour may be perceived in an increasingly negative light (Belle 1990). In a North American observational study, Conger, McCarty, Yang, Lahey and Kropp (1984) found that demographic conditions accounted for 53% of the variance in mothers' psychological characteristics and 37% of the variance in positive and negative behaviours towards young children. In contrast, maternal psychological characteristics only accounted for 15% of the variance in maternal behaviour. Therefore it would appear that maternal psychological characteristics are in large part determined by external life conditions, which in turn influence mothers' behaviour with their children.

Goodyer (1990) contends that a decade of research has shown that two areas make women vulnerable to parenting difficulties: firstly, the kinds of structural factors referred to above and, secondly, functional factors including a lack of social and emotional support. It is generally accepted that social support can buffer individuals against the negative consequences of stressful circumstances (Winnubst, Buunk and Marcelissen 1988). It is probably the cumulative balance between stress and support that determines individual differences in parental care (Vondra and Toth 1989).

In the ecology of human development, families do not exist as separate units but are closely linked into wider social environments. Social support networks have been posited to be one of the dimensions in which families, and individual parents, vary in their capacity to cope with adversity. For example, Giovannoni and Billingsley (1970) found that women from impoverished families who were neglectful were generally estranged from social networks. Studies of child abuse have also highlighted the critical role played by social isolation in creating a situation conducive to parental loss of control (Gelles 1992; Trickett, Aber, Carlson and Cicchetti 1991).

Social support networks are thought to affect parental behaviour through at least three paths of influence. The first is through the provision of emotional support, the second through the exercise of social controls over parenting styles, and the third through the provision of models of parenting and social behaviour (Cochran and Brassard 1979). However, social support networks in very impoverished communities often mean survival. For example, Stack (1974) and Wilsworth (1980) in South Africa have described the way in which people in poor areas manage to maintain their dwellings and avoid periodic starvation through access to mutually cooperative social networks. Where economically stressed families and individuals live in isolation from each other, their social impoverishment is likely to exacerbate their economic impoverishment.

Parenting and Emotions

Halpern (1990) has posed the question of why poverty affects parenting and child care so much. He lists the following possibilities: first, that the presence of poverty increases the likelihood that other personal and situational determinants of parenting will act as risk rather than protective factors; second, that poverty exerts a negatively potentiating effect on other risk factors; third, that poverty has intrinsic risks such as overcrowding and poor nutrition; and lastly, that poverty and its associated stresses may denude available sources of social support. However, the possibility also exists that parenting is an emotionally driven activity and that the emotional states necessary for its optimal expression are the ones most affected by the stresses of poverty (Richter 1990).

Dix (1991) has recently developed a model of parenting in which he proposes that positive emotional states are vital to effective parenting. Drawing on evidence which indicates that neglectful mothers are uninvolved, emotionally unavailable and indifferent to their parenting tasks, Dix has suggested that distressed mothers, overwhelmed by immediate life tasks, may suppress or never activate the child-rearing emotions necessary for effective parenting. In parenting, argues Dix, emotions must be empathic and organised to a large extent around concerns and outcomes relevant to children's well-being and development. When invested in the interests of children, emotions organise sensitive, responsive parenting. Such emotional states promote vigilance to the needs of the child, patience and the willingness to teach, comfort and encourage children.

Wahler and Dumas (1989) have given an account of how they believe the affective states of troubled mothers may adversely impact on children's adjustment. In order for appropriate parental responses to occur, they argue that immediate cues from the child's behaviour should optimally exert a maximal effect on parenting. However, when parents are distracted by economic pressures, marital strife and similar problems they are likely to be less responsive to the child's needs. The effects of such parental states on children probably operate through disruptions in the attachment system (Ainsworth, Bell and Stayton 1974).

A number of studies have documented that poverty, unemployment and economic loss cause depression in parents. This decreases their emotional availability and responsiveness to young children (Toomey and Christie 1990) and also to adolescents (Lempers, Clark-Lempers and Simons 1989). McLoyd (1990b) has pointed to a growing body of data, mostly from mothers of infants and preschoolers, which directly ties parental punitiveness, inconsistency and unresponsiveness to negative emotional states in the parent. In South Africa, Cleaver and Botha (1989) found that 74% of the urban black women they interviewed had negative or ambivalent feelings towards their babies. Most of these women found the lack of involvement on the part of the father, both financially and personally, to be the most upsetting part of motherhood.

The incidence of depression amongst young women is high, reaching as much as 40% among non-working mothers of preschool children (Puckering 1989). Mothers report that it is hard to be nurturant, patient and involved when feeling depressed. It has been suggested that the category of people most vulnerable to depression and other forms of psychological distress are those that are simultaneously single, isolated, exposed to burdensome parental obligations and, according to McLoyd (1990b), most serious of all, poor (Kamwendo, Vaughan and O'Dowd 1987). Children who are reared by depressed mothers are estimated to suffer an increase in risk for psychopathology by a factor of two or three (Dodge 1990). Although it is not at all clear that the effects on children of maternal depression are direct, depressed mothers have been reported to be withdrawn, inappropriate and passive in interactions with their children, as well as less able to establish and maintain positive interactions. Even very young infants have been demonstrated to be sensitive to maternal depressed moods and to be less contingently responsive to such mothers (Zekosi, O'Hara and Wills 1987). Finally, Rutter (1990) has pointed out that there are a number of ways in which parental depression may affect children. These include a reduction in parental sensitivity and responsivity to children's needs and the inappropriate use of children as sources of comfort. However, he stresses that it is equally likely that the parenting difficulties stem from the same social and economic adversities that create an increased risk for depression in women.

Economic Stress and Parenting: A Wider Perspective

In this chapter it has been argued that 'different levels of socio-economic status offer children experiences which are both different and unequal with respect to the resources and rewards of the society' (Hess 1970:457). According to Hess, social class differences in behaviour have to be understood, first, as the effects of the fixed structural features of a social system (prestige, power, access to information, etc.) and, second, in terms of other environmental and personal features which respond to the socio-economic environment (stress, social support networks, etc.).

However, despite this close association, neither low SES nor poverty nor deprivation has been shown to have an inevitably negative effect on children's development. Variations in social cohesion, family stability and the personal resources of parents (Belsky 1984) lead to a wide variety of children's outcomes including excellent adjustment and achievement. There are differences in the intellectual performance and social competence of low-SES children, which are determined by, amongst other things, child temperament, parental education, social networks and maternal attitudes, thus challenging the supposition that poor socio-economic homes are homogeneous (Ricciuti 1977).

This is best illustrated by the work on the HOME (Home Observation for the Measurement of the Environment) Scales over the last two decades. These studies have shown that socio-economic status is less consistently related to children's developmental status than are specific, measurable aspects of the home environment, known collectively as the micro-environment (Bradley and Caldwell 1977). Irrespective of social class, the best predictors of children's developmental outcomes have been shown to be the quality of the learning experiences available to the child (e.g. availability of play materials) and the mother's deliberate efforts to support advances in her child's development (Bradley, Caldwell, Rock, Ramey *et al.* 1989; Richter and Grieve 1991).

A consciousness on the part of parents of the importance of their behaviour to children's development as well as a belief in their capacity to fulfil their children's physical and emotional needs has been found in several studies to be the axis around which optimum child care takes place (Roosa, Fitzgerald and Carlson 1982; Tinsley and Holtgrave 1989). These mental states are in turn a reflection of the wider social relationships in which parents participate. Instead of a strong sense of internality and child-centredness, external pressures may become so great that parents project, instead, their own state of dejection onto their children.

We are only beginning to unravel the complexities of the way in which aspects of parenting become internalised within self-structures of even very young children (Richter 1990). That poverty poses the most severe risk to parenting, and therefore to children's development, is without doubt. However, despite long-standing hardship and stressful life events, many parents manage to rear their children in ways that seem to protect their children and render them, if not invulnerable, then at least resilient in the face of adversity.

Individual Resilience and Protective Factors

A number of protective factors for children have been identified, including a sociable personality, a stable family, and personal relationships with supportive adults outside of the family (Garmezy 1991; Werner 1985). On the child's part, sociability is stressed, and the ability of some children to elicit a supportive social network is thought to be the key to their resilience (Kimchi and Schaffner 1990). In terms of the family, Werner (1985) found that parents of resilient children were supportive of their children, set rules and routines for behaviour in the home, and acted in ways to promote the stability and cohesion of the family.

Osborn (1990) points out that while the inner character of resilient children may be of theoretical interest, it is the enabling external and environmental factors which foster and support resilience that are open to intervention. In general, he maintains on the basis of the Bristol longitudinal study that a critical element of childhood resilience could be attributed to an all-pervading parental attitude of interest in and devotion towards the child. However, it may be that such a parental attitude is only likely to survive when stresses associated with economic hardship are mitigated by compensatory positive influences, like supportive family and friends and a good marital relationship.

At least some of the personal capacities identified in the parents of resilient children include a belief in the meaning of their lives and that of their community (Antonovsky and Sourani 1988), as well as a sense of pride in themselves and personal integrity. Halpern (1990) speculates that these inner resources may themselves be the product of the parents' internalised experiences of devoted and concerned care by adults during their own childhood (Richter 1990). As Rutter (1989) and others concede, it may be that certain kinds of experiences, particularly those that occur in long-term positive emotional engagements with caring adults, are essential aspects of human development. Individuals deprived of such experiences may be very much more vulnerable to the effects of adversity and to parenting difficulties when faced with hardship than their more fortunate counterparts.

Rutter (1985) has challenged much of the research on the effects of deprivation and adversity on young children. He has persistently asserted that negative effects on children are primarily the result of continuing currently stressful events that happen to have lasted for most of the child's life. This is the assertion of the cumulative deficit hypothesis, namely that negative effects on children persist because key elements of the environment often remain unchanged. On a policy level, apart from trying to prevent adversity from marring the lives of young children, every effort has also to be made to give children living in poverty a chance to break out of the cycle of hardship.

Directions for Future Research

We have not yet answered the questions about the connections between social systems and growth, learning and development posed by Hess in 1970. Specifically, he urged the development of an adequate theory of the social and cultural effects on behaviour. 'A theory of the influence of social class and ethnicity should be derived from a comprehensive analysis of the points of contact and exchange between the external environment and human development and behaviour, rather than upon a body of research which deals in false dichotomies for the sake of methodological and conceptual convenience' (1970:531).

Apart from theory, we need studies which are methodologically equipped to answer the complex questions posed by the issues raised in this chapter. Clearly we need prospective, longitudinal and multivariate designs (Garmezy 1983). We also need new and improved methods of data collection. As Clarke-Stewart (1988:69) puts it: 'What we should strive for now are measures that not only are replicable across time and place, that reflect the qualities they claim to, and can be used to triangulate constructs, but measures that yield information that is psychologically meaningful – to researchers and to parents and children.'

In no area is this more important than in research amongst minority groups and those who suffer economic hardship. McLoyd (1990a) has stated that researchers have frequently been self-serving and opportunistic in their interactions with these groups of people. She claims that they have frequently distanced themselves from the social problems of the poor and have also been unwilling to contribute to efforts to improve social and economic conditions. She advises that considerable financial and human resources will have to be invested in research programmes to bridge what she calls 'the chasms between researchers and minority participants created by cultural and class differences' (1990a:265).

We also need psychologically valid procedures for assessing the developmental status of poor and minority children. As Pamela Reynolds (1989) notes in the context of South Africa, our current psychological measures are biased against these groups. Without any suitable substitutes we cannot provide proper services or advocacy for these children. Also, we need better indicators of the effects of important constancies and changes in the social climate of childhood (Brim 1975). Research which can influence health, welfare and education policy seems, at this time in the history of South Africa, the most important contribution social scientists can make. Particular areas of need include research on the best ways of providing quality day care, promoting family cohesion under conditions of hardship, and models for intervention programmes that extend beyond parent and child education. It is clear that one of the best ways to intervene is to help children's natural caregivers and to support the ecological system in which they are embedded.

Several audits of early interventions, like Head Start, have indicated that the real advantage of these programmes may lie outside the direct involvement of children in educational or compensatory activities (Gallagher 1991). For parents, involvement may extend far beyond child-care information or enrolment in support groups (Parker, Piotrowski and Peay 1987). In the process of their participation, poor or minority parents may acquire a host of skills and experiences which could be important for their empowerment – practice in negotiating with institutions, experiences of leadership, and making decisions in important areas of their lives (Washington 1985). All these aspects should help to provide support for parents living in economically stressed environments.

All research in this field should be singular in its purpose – to create for young children those conditions in childhood which the whole history of social psychological studies has confirmed to be essential to human development: 'Defenceless as babies are, they have mothers at their command, families to protect the mothers, societies to support the structure of families and traditions to give a cultural continuity to systems of child care and training. All this is necessary for the human infant to evolve humanly, for his environment must provide the outer continuity which permits the child to develop his capacities in distinct steps and to unify them.' (Erikson, 1964:113)

References

Ainsworth, M., Bell, S. and Stayton, D. (1974). Infant–mother attachment and social development: Socialisation as a product of reciprocal responsiveness to signals. In M. P. M. Richards (ed), *The Integration of a Child into a Social World*. Cambridge: Cambridge University Press.

Antonovsky, A. and Sourani, T. (1988). Family sense of coherence and family adaptation. *Journal of Marriage and the Family, 50,* 79–92.

Baumeister, A., Kupstas, F. and Klindworth, L. (1991). The new morbidity: A national plan of action. *American Behavioral Scientist, 34,* 468–500.

Bell, R. (1968). A reinterpretation of the direction of effects in studies of socialisation. *Psychological Review, 75,* 81–95.

Belle, D. (1990). Poverty and women's mental health. *American Psychologist, 45,* 385–389.

Belsky, J. (1984). The determinants of parenting: A process model. *Child Development, 55,* 83–96.

Bernstein, B. (1960). Language and social class. *British Journal of Sociology, 11,* 271–276.

Block, J. (1971). *Lives through Time*. Berkeley: Bancroft.

Boult, B. and Cunningham, P. (1991). Black teenage pregnancy in Port Elizabeth. *Early Child Development and Care, 75,* 1–70.

Bradley, R. and Caldwell, B. (1977). Home observations for measurement of the environment: A validation study of screening efficiency. *American Journal of Mental Deficiency, 81,* 416–420.

Bradley, R., Caldwell, B., Rock, S., Ramey, C., Barnard, K., Gray, C., Hammond, M., Mitchell, S., Gottfried, A., Siegel, L. and Johnson, D. (1989). Home environment and cognitive development in the first three years of life: A collaborative study involving six sites and three ethnic groups in North America. *Developmental Psychology, 25,* 217–235.

Brazelton, T. (1988). Stress for families today. *Infant Mental Health Journal, 9,* 65–71.

Brim, O. (1975). Macro-structural influences on child development and the need for childhood social indicators. *American Journal of Orthopsychiatry, 45,* 516–524.

Clark, P. (1987). A home-based study of social interaction with the pre-school child in a sample of KwaMashu homes. University of Natal: Unpublished research report.

Clarke-Stewart, K. (1988). Parents' effects on children's development: A decade of progress? *Journal of Applied Developmental Psychology, 9,* 41–84.

Cleaver, G. and Botha (1989). Experiences of motherhood amongst a group of Tswana mothers. Paper presented at the Seventh National Congress of the Psychological Association of South Africa, Durban.

Cochran, M. and Brassard, J. (1979). Child development and personal social networks. *Child Development, 50,* 601–616.

Cock, J. and Emdon, E. (1987). 'Let me make history please': The story of Johanna Masilela, child-minder. In B. Bozzoli (ed.), *Class, Community and Conflict: South African Perspectives*. Johannesburg: Ravan Press.

Cock, J., Emdon, E. and Klugman, B. (1984). Child care and the working mother: A sociological investigation of a sample of urban African women. Paper presented at the Second Carnegie Inquiry into Poverty and Development in Southern Africa, Paper number 115. Cape Town.

Conger, R., McCarty, J., Yang, R., Lahey, B. and Kropp, J. (1984). Perception of child, child-rearing values and emotional distress as mediating links between environmental stressors and observed maternal behavior. *Child Development, 55,* 2234–2247.

Cox, A., Puckering, C., Pound, A. and Mills, M. (1987). The impact of maternal depression in young children. *Journal of Child Psychology and Psychiatry, 28,* 917–928.

Cox, D. (1971). Child rearing and child care in Ethiopia. *Journal of Social Psychology, 85,* 3–5.

Dix, T. (1991). The affective organisation of parenting: Adaptive and maladaptive processes. *Psychological Bulletin, 110,* 3–25.

Dodge, K. (1990). Developmental psychopathology in children of depressed mothers. *Developmental Psychology, 26,* 3–6.

Dowdney, L., Skuse, D., Heptinstall, E., Puckering, C. and Zur-Szpiro, S. (1987). Growth retardation and developmental delay amongst inner-city children. *Journal of Child Psychology and Psychiatry, 28,* 529–541.

Duckitt, J. (1983). Household crowding and psychological well-being in a South African Coloured community. *Journal of Social Psychology, 121,* 231–238.

Erikson, E. (1964). Human strength and the cycle of generation. In *Insight and Responsibility.* New York: Norton Press.

Freeberg, N. and Payne, D. (1967). Parental influence on cognitive development in early childhood: A review. *Child Development, 38,* 65–87.

Fried, M. (1982). Endemic stress: The psychology of resignation and the politics of scarcity. *American Journal of Orthopsychiatry, 52,* 4–19.

Gallagher, J. (1991). Longitudinal interventions: Virtues and limitations. *American Behavioral Scientist, 34,* 431–439.

Garbarino, J. (1985). Habitats for children: An ecological perspective. In J. Wohlwill and W. Van Vliet (eds), *Habitats for Children: The Impact of Density.* New Jersey: Lawrence Erlbaum.

Garbarino, J. (1992). The meaning of poverty in the world of children. *American Behavioral Scientist, 35,* 220–237.

Garmezy, N. (1983). Stressors of childhood. In N. Garmezy and M. Rutter (eds), *Stress, Coping and Development in Children.* New York: McGraw Hill.

Garmezy, N. (1991). Resiliency and vulnerability to adverse developmental outcomes associated with poverty. *American Behavioral Scientist, 34,* 416–430.

Gauthier, P. (1990). Children of the world and the role of educator. In M. Mitchell, C. Tobin, J. Johncox and R. Rocco (eds), *Proceedings of the XII World Congress of the International Association of Workers for Troubled Children and Youth.* Albion, Michigan: Starr Commonwealth Institute Press.

Gelles, R. (1992). Poverty and violence towards children. *American Behavioral Scientist, 35,* 258–274.

Giovannoni, J. and Billingsley, A. (1970). Child neglect among the poor: A study of parental adequacy in families of three ethnic groups. *Child Welfare, 49,* 169–204.

Goodyer, I. (1988). Stress in childhood and adolescence. In S. Fisher and J. Reason (eds), *Handbook of Life Stress, Cognition and Health.* New York: John Wiley.

Goodyer, I. (1990). Family relationships, life events and psychopathology. *Journal of Child Psychology and Psychiatry, 31,* 1161–1192.

Gordon, A. (1986). Black education in South Africa: Psychological and sociological correlates of achievement. In L. Ekstrand (ed.), *Ethnic Minorities and Immigrants in a Cross-Cultural Perspective,* 240–255. Lisse: Swets and Zeitlinger.

Gottfried, A. (1985). Measures of socio-economic status in child development research: Data and recommendations. *Merrill-Palmer Quarterly, 31,* 85–92.

Gray, J., Dean, R. and Lowrie, R. (1988). Relationship between socio-economic status and perinatal complications. *Journal of Clinical Child Psychology, 17,* 352–358.

Groenewald, F. (1976). *Aspects of the Traditional Culture of the Black Child Which Hamper the Actualisation of His Intelligence: A Cultural-Educational Exploratory Study.* Pretoria: Human Sciences Research Council No. 0–54.

Gross, R. and Monteiro, C. (1989). Urban nutrition in developing countries: Some issues to learn. *Food and Nutrition Bulletin, 11,* 14–20.

Gulbrandsen, D. (1986). To marry or not to marry: Marital strategies and sexual relations in a Tswana society. *Ethnos, 1,* 7–28.

Halpern, R. (1990). Poverty and early childhood parenting: Toward a framework for intervention. *American Journal of Orthopsychiatry, 60,* 6–18.

Haralambos, M. (1985). *Sociology: Themes and Perspectives*. London: Richard Clay.

Hechtman, L. (1989). Teenage mothers and their children: Risks and problems, a review. *Canadian Journal of Psychiatry*.

Hess, R.D. (1970). Social class and ethnic influences upon socialization. In P.H. Mussen (ed.), *Carmichael's Manual of Child Psychology*. New York: John Wiley and Sons.

Hewatt, G.,·Lee, T., Nyakaza, N., Olver, C. and Tyeko, B. (1984). An exploratory study of over-crowding and health issues at Old Crossroads. Paper presented at the Second Carnegie Inquiry into Poverty and Development in Southern Africa, Paper number 14. Cape Town.

Heyneman, S. (1976). A brief note on the relationship between socio-economic status and test performance among Ugandan primary school children. *Comparative Education Review, 20*, 42–47.

Hundeide, K. (1984). The indigenous approach to early deprivation and development: A rationale for intervention. Paper prepared for Unicef meeting, New York.

Kamwendo, A., Vaughan, M. and O'Dowd, T. (1987). Maternal depression and the preschool child. *Early Child Development and Care, 27*, 31–42.

Kimchi, J. and Schaffner, B. (1990). Childhood protective factors and stress risk. In L. Arnold (ed.), *Childhood Stress*. New York: John Wiley.

Kopp, C. (1990). Risks in infancy: Appraising the research. *Merrill-Palmer Quarterly, 36*, 117–140.

Korbin, J. (1992). Introduction: Child poverty in the United States. *American Behavioral Scientist, 35*, 213–219.

Lempers, J., Clark-Lempers, D., and Simons, R. (1989). Economic hardship, parenting and distress in adolescence. *Child Development, 60*, 25–39.

LeVine, S. and LeVine, R. (1981). Child abuse and neglect in sub-Saharan Africa. In J. Korbin (ed.), *Child Abuse and Neglect: Cross-Cultural Perspectives*. Berkeley: University of California Press.

Liddell, C., Kvalsvig, J., Shabalala, A. and Masilela, P. (1991). Historical perspectives on South African childhood. *International Journal of Behavioral Development, 14*, 1–19.

McLoyd, V. (1990a). Minority children: Introduction to the Special Issue. *Child Development, 61*, 263–266.

McLoyd, V. (1990b). The impact of economic hardship on black families and children: Psychological distress, parenting and socioemotional development. *Child Development, 61*, 311–246.

McLoyd, V. and Wilson, L. (1990). Maternal behaviour, social support, and economic conditions as predictors of distress in children. In V. McLoyd and C. Flanagan (eds), *Economic Stress: Effects on Family Life and Child Development*. San Francisco: Jossey-Bass.

Marks, S. and Rathbone, R. (1983). The history of the family in Africa: Introduction. *Journal of African History, 24*, 145–161.

Mednick, B., Baker, R. and Hocevar, D. (1985). Family size and birth order correlates of intellectual, psychosocial, and physical growth. *Merrill-Palmer Quarterly, 31*, 67–84.

Miller, F., Kolvin, I. and Fells, H. (1985). Becoming deprived: A cross-generation study in the Newcastle-upon-Tyne 1000-family survey. In A. Nicol (ed.), *Longitudinal Studies in Child Psychology and Psychiatry: Practical Lessons from Research Experience*. New York: John Wiley.

Miller, R. (1989). Critical psychology: A territorial imperative. *Psychology in Society, 12*, 3–18.

Moilanen, I. and Rantakallio, P. (1988). The single parent family and the child's mental health. *Social Science and Medicine, 27*, 181–186.

Møller, V., Schlemmer, L. and Strijdom, H. (1984). Poverty and quality of life among blacks in South Africa. Second Carnegie Inquiry into Poverty and Development in Southern Africa, Paper number 6. Cape Town.

Mtshali, M. (1988). *Give Us a Break: Diaries of a Group of Soweto Children*. Johannesburg: Skotaville.

Munroe, R. and Munroe, R. (1972). Obedience among children in an East African society. *Journal of Cross-Cultural Psychology, 3*, 395–399.

Ogbu, J. (1981). Origins of human competence: A cultural ecological perspective. *Child Development, 52*, 413–429.

Opolot, J. (1982). Ethnicity and child-rearing practices. *Journal of Social Psychology, 116*, 155–162.

Osborn, A. (1987). Assessing the socio-economic status of families. *Sociology, 21*, 429–448.

Osborn, A. (1990). Resilient children: A longitudinal study of high achieving socially disadvantaged children. *Early Child Development and Care, 62,* 23–47.

Osofsky, J. (1990). Risk and protective factors for teenage mothers and their infants. *SRCD Newsletter,* Winter, 1–2.

Oyemade, U. (1985). The rationale for Head Start as a vehicle for the upward mobility of minority families: A minority perspective. *American Journal of Orthopsychiatry, 55,* 591–602.

Parker, F., Piotrowski and Peay (1987). Head Start as a social support for mothers: The psychological benefits of involvement. *American Journal of Orthopsychiatry, 57,* 220–245.

Pillay, A. (1987). Psychological disturbances in children of single parents. *Psychological Reports, 61,* 803–806.

Prinsloo, J. (1984). A description of income, expenditure and earning patterns from households in Cape Town and Durban. Second Carnegie Inquiry into Poverty and Development in Southern Africa. Paper number 16. Cape Town.

Puckering, C. (1989). Annotation: Maternal depression. *Journal of Child Psychology and Psychiatry, 30,* 807–817.

Reschly, D. (1986). Economic and cultural factors in childhood exceptionality. In R. Brown and C. Reynolds (eds), *Psychological Perspectives on Childhood Exceptionality.* New York: John Wiley.

Reynolds, P. (1989). *Childhood in Crossroads: Cognition and Society in South Africa.* Cape Town: David Philip.

Ricciuti, H. (1977). Adverse social and biological influences on early development. In H. McGurk (ed.), *Ecological Factors in Human Development.* Amsterdam: North Holland.

Richter, L. and Griesel, R. (1986a). The psychological development and scholastic achievement of black children in the context of their social backgrounds. Paper presented at the Human Sciences Research Council Advanced Seminar on Research with regard to the Psychological and Educational Evaluation of Children. Pretoria.

Richter, L. and Griesel, R. (1986b). Family life in urban black townships: Possible consequences for child development. Paper presented at the Fourth National Conference of the Psychological Association of South Africa. Johannesburg.

Richter, L. (1989). Household density, family size, and the growth and development of black children: A cross-sectional study from infancy to middle childhood. *South African Journal of Psychology, 19,* 191–198.

Richter, L. (1990). *Wretched Childhoods: The Challenge to Psychological Theory and Practice.* University of South Africa: Inaugural Lecture.

Richter, L. and Grieve, K. (1991). Home environment and cognitive development of black infants in impoverished South African families. *Infant Mental Health Journal, 12,* 88–102.

Roosa, M., Fitzgerald, H. and Carlson, N. (1982). Teenage parenting and child development: A literature review. *Infant Mental Health Journal, 3,* 4–18.

Rutter, M. (1972). *Maternal Deprivation Reassessed.* Harmondsworth: Penguin.

Rutter, M. (1985). Family and school influences: Meanings, mechanisms and implications. In A. Nicol (ed.), *Longitudinal Studies in Child Psychology and Psychiatry: Practical Lessons from Research Experience.* New York: John Wiley.

Rutter, M. (1989). Pathways from childhood to adult life. *Journal of Child Psychology and Psychiatry, 30,* 23–51.

Rutter, M. (1990). Commentary: Some focus and process considerations regarding effects of parental depression on children. *Developmental Psychology, 26,* 60–67.

Sameroff, A. and Chandler, M. (1975). Reproductive risk and the continuum of caretaking casualty. In F. Horowitz, M. Hetherington, S. Scarr-Salapatek and G. Siegel (eds), *Review of Child Development Research,* Volume 4. Chicago: University of Chicago Press.

Schiller, B. (1980). *The Economics of Poverty and Discrimination.* Englewood Cliffs, N.J.: Prentice-Hall, Inc.

Segal, M. (1985). A study of maternal beliefs and values within the context of an intervention program. In I. Sigel (ed.), *Parental Belief Systems: The Psychological Consequences for Children.* Hillsdale, N.J.: Lawrence Erlbaum.

Simkins, C. (1986). Household composition and structure in South Africa. In S. Burman and P. Reynolds (eds), *Growing Up in a Divided Society: The Contexts of Childhood in South Africa.* Johannesburg: Ravan Press.

Stack, C. (1974). *All Our Kin: Strategies for Survival in a Black Community*. New York: Harper and Row.

Straker, G. (1992). *Faces in the Revolution: The Psychological Effects of Violence on Township Youth in South Africa*. Cape Town: David Philip.

Thomas, T. (1988). The psychosocial pathology of the homelands. Paper presented at the Conference of the Organisation for Appropriate Social Services in South Africa. University of the Western Cape.

Tinsley, B. and Holtgrave, D. (1989). Maternal health locus of control beliefs, utilisation of childhood preventive health services, and infant health. *Journal of Developmental and Behavioral Pediatrics, 10,* 236–241.

Toomey, B. and Christie, D. (1990). Social stressors in childhood: Poverty, discrimination and catastrophic events. In L. Arnold (ed.), *Childhood Stress*. New York: John Wiley.

Trickett, P., Aber, J., Carlson, V. and Cicchetti, D. (1991). Relationship of socio-economic status to the etiology and developmental sequelae of physical child abuse. *Developmental Psychology, 27,* 148–158.

Tulkin, S. (1972). An analysis of the concept of cultural deprivation. *Developmental Psychology, 6,* 326–339.

Uzoka, A. (1980). The African child and the dilemma of changing family functions: A psychological perspective. *African Social Research, 30,* 851–867.

Van der Vliet, V. (1984). Staying single: A strategy against poverty? Second Carnegie Inquiry into Poverty and Development in Southern Africa, Paper number 116. Cape Town.

Vondra, J. and Toth, S. (1989). Ecological perspectives on child maltreatment: Research and intervention. *Early Child Development and Care, 42,* 11–29.

Vygotsky, L. (1978). *Mind in Society: The Development of Higher Psychological Processes*. Cambridge, Mass.: Harvard University Press.

Wadsworth, M. (1986). Evidence from three birth cohort studies for long-term and cross-generational effects on the development of children. In M. Richards and P. Light (eds), *Children of Social Worlds: Development in a Social Context*. Cambridge: Polity Press.

Wagner, M., Schubert, H. and Schubert, D. (1985). Family size effects: A review. *Journal of Genetic Psychology, 146,* 65–78.

Wahler, R. and Dumas, J. (1989). Attentional problems in dysfunctional mother–child interactions: An interbehavioural model. *Psychological Bulletin, 105,* 116–130.

Washington, V. (1985). Head Start: How appropriate for minority families in the 1980s? *American Journal of Orthopsychiatry, 55,* 577–590.

Welch, M. (1978). Childhood socialisation differences in African and non-African societies. *Journal of Social Psychology, 106,* 11–15.

Werner, E. (1985). Stress and protective factors in children's lives. In A. Nicol (ed.), *Longitudinal Studies in Child Psychology and Psychiatry: Practical Lessons from Research Experience*. New York: John Wiley.

Wilson, F. (1972). *Migrant Labour in South Africa*. Johannesburg: SACC and SPRO-CAS.

Wilson, F. and Ramphele, M. (1989). *Uprooting Poverty: The South African Challenge*. Cape Town: David Philip.

Wilsworth, M. (1980). Transcending the culture of poverty in a black South African township. Grahamstown: Rhodes University, Unpublished Master's Thesis.

Winnubst, J., Buunk, B. and Marcelissen, F. (1988). Social support and stress: Perspectives and processes. In S. Fisher and J. Reason (eds), *Handbook of Life Stress, Cognition and Health*. New York: John Wiley.

Zekosi, E., O'Hara, M. and Wills, K. (1987). The effects of maternal mood on mother–infant interaction. *Journal of Abnormal Child Psychology, 15,* 361–378.

Zigler, E. (1985). Assessing Head Start at 20: An invited commentary. *American Journal of Orthopsychiatry, 55,* 603–609.

3

Defining the Cultural Context of Children's Everyday Experiences in the Year Before School[1]

CHRISTINE LIDDELL, JANE KVALSVIG, AGNES SHABALALA AND PUMLA QOTYANA

Defining Cultural Context

One of the underlying assumptions of cross-cultural psychology is that 'cultures' represent homogeneous and, at least to some extent, distinct units that can be meaningfully compared. This assumption has been challenged at a number of levels in recent years (e.g. Cowlishaw 1986; Weisner 1981).

A common concept used to discriminate *between* cultural groups is ethnicity. However, Burdette (1988) reports that contemporary Zambians distinguish themselves on the basis of region rather than ethnicity. Similarly, Cowlishaw (1986) and Keefe (1988) question the degree to which Australian Aborigines who have lived in urban areas for many years can be meaningfully defined as Aboriginal rather than as urban Australian. In the South African context, Sharp (1980) questions the degree to which ethnicity persists as a meaningful discriminatory construct. Felgate (1982), too, discusses the degree to which different communities of Thonga from northern Natal varied from one another, depending on factors such as local ecology, subsistence modes, and patterns of social organisation.

Within individual cultures, rural–urban markers are commonly used to make distinctions between groups. Here, too, some debate exists about construct validity (Graves and Graves 1978; Weisner 1981). In the South African context, Reynolds (1989) reports that the rural–urban divide has given way to a division based on socio-economic status, particularly in terms of differences in family life, household organisation and child behaviour.

The assumption that cultural divisions can be made on the basis of concepts such as ethnicity or degree of urbanisation is an important one for empirical examination. To the extent that cross-cultural investigators compare groups according to such fixed and relatively clear-cut constructs, difficulties may arise when studying groups undergoing rapid change along a number of dimensions

[1]Financial assistance from the following institutions is gratefully acknowledged: Human Sciences Research Council; Anglo American and De Beers Chairman's Fund; Johannesburg Chamber of Industries; First National Bank.

simultaneously. In many instances, cultural transformations involve a number of *concurrent* changes, e.g. migrations across rural–urban and geographic boundaries, combined with intermarriage between cultural groups, changes in subsistence mode, etc. Without a *simultaneous* investigation of a number of different dimensions of change, it remains difficult to isolate the most salient aspects of culture, and cross-cultural psychology runs the risk of focusing on inappropriate or simplistic constructs that may have limited predictive power.

The problem is not merely of academic relevance. If cultural groups are being distinguished along simplistic dimensions of limited validity, then the discipline may be misrepresenting the communities it seeks to promote an understanding of, by failing to grapple with the complexity and richness of cultural transformation (Keefe 1988).

Dimensions of Culture in a Broader Descriptive Framework

This chapter illustrates the usefulness of methods located within the positivist research tradition in teasing out the relative influence of a range of ecocultural factors on the everyday behaviour, social interactions and activities of eighty 5-year-old children from four different South African communities. These children could be grouped according to three different cultural descriptors: first, ethnicity, defined in terms of the two linguistic groups from which children were drawn (Sotho and Nguni); second, urbanicity, with two of the groups living in deep rural areas, and two being second-generation urban; and third, in terms of the four individual communities from which children came (Mamelodi township near Johannesburg, Umlazi township near Durban, Nqabeni near the Transkei border, and Jane Furse in the so-called homeland of Lebowa). In terms of the children's everyday behaviours, domestic routines, interaction patterns and so on, the question we addressed was: Which cultural descriptor is best? Are children most accurately grouped according to their ethnic group, or their experience of urban life, or their residence in a particular local community?

However, cultural descriptors such as ethnicity and urbanicity should ideally be examined in a broad analytical framework and not in isolation. For example, urbanicity may often be confounded with socio-economic status or educational level, and it is only by examining these in conjunction with one another that a better understanding of their effects on children's behaviour can be achieved.

For the purposes of the present study, then, the three cultural variables were evaluated in statistical models that also incorporated measures of socio-economic status (SES), household size, and household reliance on subsistence agriculture. SES is considered by many developmental psychologists to be one of the overarching factors which enable one to predict child outcome variables such as school performance (Edelstein 1983; Tizard, Blatchford, Burke, Farquhar and Plewis 1988), social competence (Rubin, Maioni and Hornung 1976), and language use (Brice-Heath 1986). Household size has been reported as a consistent factor in predicting children's performance in South African (Richter 1989), other African (Durojaiye 1980; Munroe and Munroe 1971), and western communities (Bryant 1985; Osborn and Milbank 1987). Also, the degree to which families rely on subsistence agriculture has been reported as salient for children's everyday patterns of behaviour in non-western samples (Berry 1976; Weisner 1981). The children studied here varied considerably in terms of the degree to which their households relied on food from the land; surprisingly, this included 20% of the urban families studied.

This chapter therefore compares the predictive validity of three cultural descriptors (ethnicity, degree of urbanicity, and individual community) in *conjunction* with factors pertaining to the child's household (SES, household size, and reliance on subsistence agriculture). Though such multifactorial designs are reasonably common in studies of European children (e.g. Bradley and Caldwell 1984), they are rare in non-western research.

Data Collection

Full details of methodology are described in Liddell, Kvalsvig, Shabalala and Qotyana (1991). Eighty children of average age 63 months (standard deviation = 4.14) were studied, with 20 (10 boys and 10 girls) being selected from each of four study sites. These sites were based in Mamelodi (urban), Umlazi (urban), Nqabeni (rural), and Lebowa (rural). Hence 40 children were studied in urban and 40 in rural settings. Of the children 52 were from Nguni families, and 28 from Sotho families.

Children were observed during daylight hours by the third and fourth authors, who were fully conversant with the language and customs of the families. No attempt was made to constrain the spontaneous activities of the focal children or their families. In other words, the observer followed the child wherever his or her routines of daily activity led.

Observations were coded in terms of pre-defined categories of behaviour, details of which can be found in Liddell and colleagues (1991b). Codings of the child's behaviour were made every 30 seconds, marked by a hand-held electronic bleeper, and each observation session lasted for two hours. In total, 12 hours of data were collected for each child (1440 thirty-second samples).

Once all observational data had been collected on an individual child, a biographical questionnaire was completed for each household. Items pertaining to type of dwelling, number of books, toys and magazines in the home, water supply, and degree of reliance on subsistence economy were completed by the observer independent of the primary caretaker, and were based on her 16–20 hours of observation of the household. Items pertaining to household size, levels of education in the family, age of primary caretaker, and relationship of primary caretaker to child (mother or non-mother) were completed with the assistance of the primary caretaker.

Evaluating Cultural Descriptors Empirically

Multiple regression models are particularly well suited to the comparative evaluation of different variables and their effects on any one behaviour (see Cohen and Cohen 1983). This is because multiple regression can provide information on how much of the variance in a dependent variable (e.g. time spent alone) can be explained by a given independent variable (e.g. ethnicity), once

Table 1. R-squared values for models containing SES, household size, reliance on subsistence economy, and either 4 places, rural–urban, or ethnicity markers

Model containing SES, size, subsistence plus:	4 Places	Rural–urban	Ethnicity
Interaction patterns			
Solitary	19.36*	17.16*	11.88*
Cooperative	14.07*	13.56*	2.92*
Interaction with adults	0.00	0.00	3.91
Interaction with children	30.91*	20.24*	15.17*
Language use			
Total speech	10.78*	7.78	0.00
Commands from adults	4.28	3.84	2.87
Commands to adults	0.00	0.91	6.06
Commands between children	2.92	3.07	2.58
Information from adults	2.32	1.63	11.73
Information to adults	13.07	6.67	0.00
Information between children	23.88	13.96	12.80
Activities			
Acrobatic play	0.00	0.00	0.84
Domestic/agricultural chores	6.92	7.81	0.00
Draw/scribble	8.37	8.39	8.02
School- or literacy-related	27.29*	23.30*	21.42*
Simple manipulation objects	23.33*	30.84*	10.04*
Fantasy play	0.00	0.00	3.90
Fight	16.63*	21.49*	11.97*
Game	11.80*	20.43*	9.75*
Unoccupied	5.26	13.56*	4.91

$*p <= 0.05$

the effects of other, often highly correlated independent variables (such as SES) have been removed.

To take the example referred to earlier, let us assume that most children from urban areas come from families that are better off financially than children from rural areas. If we find differences between these two groups of children, it would be reasonable to enquire whether the differences were largely attributable to different poverty levels or to other dimensions of urbanicity. A multiple regression model allows the effect of SES to be removed before the remaining effect related to *other* aspects of urbanicity is examined. In this way, a more precise pattern of correlations can be built up.

In the present case, three separate regression analyses were run for each of 20 dependent variables. All three analyses contained SES, household size, and reliance on subsistence agriculture as independent variables. The models differed only in terms of which of the three cultural descriptors was also incorporated. When different models are examined in this way, comparisons are made between resultant R-squareds for each model. The R-squared values indicate the percentage of variance in children's behaviour that can be explained by a particular model. Obviously, the model that explains the highest percentage of variance is the best (i.e. contains the most meaningful set of descriptors). The results of this set of comparisons are contained in Table 1.

Of the 20 categories examined, the model containing markers for four different places predicted significant amounts of variance most often (for 10 of 20 dependent variables), followed by a rural–urban marker (9 of 20 categories), followed by ethnicity (8 categories). On average, the model with markers for four places predicted 12% of variance in children's behaviour, with a rural–urban marker 11%, and with an ethnicity marker 7% of the variance.

On the basis of a relatively small sample size (n=80), and on the similar performance of models containing four levels of place and two levels of urbanicity, the law of parsimony pointed to the rural (n=40) versus urban (n=40) model, as opposed to the four-place model (n=20 in each), as the more suitable model for these data.

But it must be remembered that the model containing a rural–urban marker also contained three other independent variables, viz SES, household size, and

Table 2. Predictive power of the four selected independent variables across all categories: *F* values.

Category	SES	House-hold size	Reliance on sub-sistence	Urban vs rural
Solitary	1.43	4.62	2.15	8.02★
Cooperative	3.22	2.55	0.03	7.46★
Interaction with adults	0.40	0.23	1.08	0.19
Interaction with children	0.21	7.84★	0.90	10.02★
Total speech	1.17	1.20	0.01	6.60★
Commands from adults	2.13	1.69	1.95	.0.59
Commands to adults	0.93	3.00	0.01	0.61
Commands between children	0.03	0.11	4.22★	1.50
Information from adults	0.19	4.74★	0.00	0.04
Information to adults	0.65	1.92	0.36	5.29★
Information between children	1.26	6.15★	0.35	5.81★
Acrobatic	0.91	0.04	0.29	0.69
Chores	1.60	0.02	0.30	7.07★
Draw/scribble	6.21★	0.00	2.68	0.51
School/literacy	9.19★	4.11★	7.28★	1.35
Simple manipulation	7.87★	0.06	1.41	20.97★
Fantasy	0.86	1.15	1.61	0.00
Fight	0.01	1.28	0.26	18.60★
Game	5.07★	0.08	1.33	12.66★
Unoccupied	1.12	2.99	0.75	8.39

★*p* <=0.05

reliance on subsistence agriculture. The next question to be addressed is, Which
of the four explained most variance in the model? To do this we must examine
the *F* and *p* values of the four independent variables separately, and establish
which of them is significant. Table 2 contains this information.

The rural–urban marker explains significant proportions of variance in 9 of
20 categories, *even after* the effects of SES, household size, and reliance on subsistence agriculture have been removed. In other words, it comprises an extremely
powerful predictor, over and above the other variables previously examined in
the model.

Why should urban and rural children differ so much in terms of their patterns
of everyday behaviour? The degree to which urban and rural children differed
in terms of biographical data was examined at this point, to establish whether

Table 3. Biographical data and rural–urban differences: Kruskal–Wallis test for
categorical data (KW values), and simple regression analyses (F values) for other
data.

Category	Rural–urban difference F & KW values	Details		
Household characteristics				
% dwellings man-made (KW)	48.07*	Rural	73%	Urban 0%
% homes with no running water (KW)	63.31*	Rural	100%	Urban 22%
X no. books observed in home (KW)	6.53*	Rural	2	Urban 5
X no. newspapers/magazines (KW)	15.10*	Rural	1	Urban 5
X no. toys observed in home (KW)	5.35*	Rural	3	Urban 5
% families relying on daily subsistence agriculture (KW)	21.15*	Rural	75%	Urban 5%
X household size (F)	2.87	Rural	7	Urban 7
No. workers per household (F)	4.10*	Rural	1	Urban 2
Highest education in household (F)	27.24*	Rural	5 yrs*	Urban 9 yrs
Socio-economic status[1] (F)	20.48*	Rural	52	Urban 128
Characteristics of primary caretaker				
% children cared for by mother (KW)	1.92	Rural	57%	Urban 63%
Caretaker's age (F)	2.08	Rural	40 yrs	Urban 35 yrs
Caretaker's years education (F)	6.56*	Rural	3 yrs	Urban 5 yrs

*$p <= 0.05$

1. SES was a composite score derived according to the following formula:
   $(a \times 10) + (b \times 100) + (c \times 10)$ where
   a = highest education in household expressed in years
   b = ratio of workers per household
   c = highest level of employment in family. Scored as 1 for pensions or sale of subsistence goods only; 2 for unskilled manual work; 3 for semi-skilled work; 4 for professional work.

significant differences in behaviour were also reflected in different home circumstances. A Kruskal–Wallis test for significance was conducted on categorical data, and a simple regression on ordinal data. Results are contained in Table 3.

Urban and rural children differed in 10 of 13 biographical categories. Provision of basic amenities differed in a predictable manner. For example, rural children more often lived in home-made dwellings, and were never observed in households containing running water. However, urban and rural children did not differ in the size of the households they lived in, which in all cases tended to be overcrowded (7 members per household) when rated in terms of international standards (see Loo and Ong 1984). Urban children were more likely to have access to books, newspapers, magazines and toys. The greater availability of these resource materials may have reflected more optimal environments for urban children.

The households of rural children relied more substantially on subsistence agriculture, and contained fewer workers. The overall socio-economic score indicated greater poverty amongst rural households when compared with their urban counterparts.

In terms of educational attainment, the highest level of education evident in a household and the level of education attained by the child's primary caretaker were likely to be greater in urban areas. Children in urban areas were as likely as those in rural areas to be looked after by their mother, and the average age of caregiver was the same for rural and urban groups.

Taken overall, rural–urban differences in biographical data were substantial. They were evident in measures of physical environment, educational achievement in the household, and socio-economic status. The fact that 9 of 20 behaviours evidenced significant rural–urban differences, even though this variable was examined last in the regression model, seems hardly surprising. Although researchers such as Graves and Graves (1978) and Wesiner (1981) have questioned the usefulness of rural–urban markers, it appears that urban and rural children in South Africa inhabit very different environments, and that this is reflected in many of their everyday activities and interactions in the year before school.

Ethnicity versus Urbanicity versus Community

The fact that a model containing an urban–rural marker was selected for analysis here, in spite of the fact that a marker denoting four unique places was more successful overall, merits consideration. As previously discussed, the more parsimonious model was selected on the grounds of a small sample size. Nevertheless, the degree to which the urban–rural grouping masks important and highly significant differences between the four places is noteworthy in itself. It suggests that communities vary considerably from one another, though not entirely in terms of more overarching factors such as urbanicity.

The finding is an important one for several reasons. First, it provides clear evidence of the degree to which broader descriptors may obfuscate the precise roots of difference. As in Weisner, Gallimore and Tharp's (1982) study of Native Hawaiian children, there was considerable variation between children in the same community, which meant that global divisions on the basis of factors such as SES and urbanicity were rarely able to explain more than a quarter of the variance in children's behaviour. Second, the finding points to the critical importance of including more than two samples in any comparison that ranks groups along an independent variable of interest. This has also been noted by Fischer (1986), but is rarely adhered to in cross-cultural studies (Berry 1976).

To the extent that communities comprise unique settings for children, over and above more general conceptual divisions of ethnicity or urbanisation, it may be important for cross-cultural psychologists to focus more frequently on community comparisons, as opposed to broader cross-cultural comparisons. As Preston-Whyte and Miller (1987) have argued for anthropology, the horizons of our disciplines may have to shrink from a science of universal laws to the more mundane but equally challenging level of understanding local dramas.

That ethnicity proved of relatively little significance in explaining differences between children corroborates the work of South African anthropologists such as Sharp (1980). Clearly, ethnicity is of less salience than degree of urbanisation, at least in terms of children's everyday lives. The absence of marked ethnic differences may be explained by the fact that Nguni and Sotho children lived in ethnically diverse communities. The degree to which this may minimise the effect of ethnicity has been commented on by previous researchers (e.g. Weisner 1981). By contrast, a study in which two different ethnic groups of San were found to be markedly different in terms of children's activities and social interaction patterns focused on a study site where the two ethnic groups lived in separate compounds, rarely intermingled, and had never intermarried (Liddell 1988). To the extent that groups of different ethnic origin live together in cohesive communities, the effects of ethnicity on children's play and other activities may be considerably reduced. This does not mean, however, that ethnic identity is never salient in these communities. At some stage it does become meaningful in constructing certain activities (see Foster, Chapter 12). Even then, though, it is unclear to what extent this becomes reflected in different patterns of everyday *behaviour* among children and adults who claim different ethnic origins.

Interpreting the Selected Model

The predictive model incorporating SES, household size, reliance on subsistence agriculture and urbanicity explained significant proportions of variance in most areas of social interaction and activity, but was of little predictive validity for language use. Details about significant differences for all categories of behaviour are contained in Table 4.

Socio-economic Status

Contrary to Reynolds's speculations about SES and South African children, levels of poverty had surprisingly little effect on children's behaviour, being of significance in only 4 of 20 categories. If we bear in mind the considerable salience of SES as a predictor in other studies of children's development and behaviour, this finding merited further consideration. The most obvious reason for the lack of SES differences probably lay in the fact that the entire cohort of

Table 4. Details of significant differences in the regression model containing SES, household size, subsistence, and rural–urban markers: means and standard deviations for rural/urban differences.

Category	Effect of increased SES[1]
School/literacy activities	Increased
Simple manipulation of objects	Decreased
Game	Increased

Category	Effect of increased household size[1]
Interactions between children	Increased
Information exchange between children	Increased
Information exchange with adults	Decreased
School/literacy activities	Decreased

Category	Rural		Urban	
Solitary	54.61	(24.34)	38.36	(17.42)
Cooperative	6.38	(7.33)	13.98	(10.54)
Interaction with children	45.46	(35.10)	65.16	(25.18)
Information between children	34.42	(10.24)	36.99	(8.77)
Simple manipulation objects	49.92	(11.05)	31.57	(13.50)
School-/literacy-related	2.21	(2.73)	3.70	(3.35)
Game	2.94	(3.72)	10.19	(7.91)
Fight	0.85	(0.94)	2.17	(1.80)
Unoccupied	0.08	(0.22)	0.53	(0.84)

1. SES and household size were treated as continuous variables in the regression analyses, i.e. categorical means were not the unit for significance testing.

80 children were living in socio-economically deprived circumstances, when compared with children in the western world. Whilst there may have been substantial variation in SES score within the group, this did not alter the fact that all children came from poor families. In that the sample was randomly selected, this socio-economic skew represents the reality of black South Africa, and calls into question the degree to which the spread of SES is sufficiently broad for local psychologists to achieve a realistic understanding of its potential significance for young children. Nevertheless, the fact that families with lower SES scores had children who engaged in fewer school- or literacy-related activities, fewer games, and more simple manipulation of objects, suggests that where SES could be isolated as a significant factor, lower scores were associated with less optimal patterns of child behaviour.

Household Size

This affected 4 of the 20 behaviour categories, which seemed a relatively small number bearing in mind, first, that households varied widely in size (range

2–19) and, second, that other researchers have reported on the salience of household size for children's behaviour and developmental status. One possible explanation for the absence of size effects lay in the fact that almost all the households were overcrowded. Homes never exceeded more than 5 rooms and housed an average of 7 people. In the light of the fact that thresholds for crowding are thought to exist, beyond which additional levels of crowding have little further effect, household size may have represented a saturated variable in the present sample.

Interactions between children were more likely to occur as household size increased, as was the exchange of information between children. Information from adults was less likely to occur as household size increased, suggesting that adults might be less available to children, but that other children were more so in larger households.

Less time was spent in school- or literacy-related activities by children in larger households, which may imply an environment less oriented to school-preparedness. Taken in conjunction with the fact that children in large households relied more on other children, rather than adults, for interaction and information, these data may be suggestive of larger households providing (in terms of western values) less optimal environments for preschool-aged children. With this sort of background, the children enter school and confront the tasks associated with the school environment, with minimal prior orientation.

Reliance on Subsistence Economy

This varied greatly, with 31% of families practising regular subsistence agriculture, 26% practising some, and 43% none. If one bears in mind the degree to which this factor has been associated with differences in psychological performance (Berry 1976), it might have had an important role in the model. However, it proved a significant factor for children in only 2 of 20 categories. In addition, school- and literacy-related activities were less frequent as homes relied more on subsistence agriculture, and (less understandably) commands between children occurred less often. By commands we mean instructions given in an authoritative manner.

Urban–rural differences

In terms of interaction patterns, rural children were more inclined to be solitary, and less inclined to engage in co-operative interaction. One possible explanation was that there may have been fewer interaction partners available in rural settings. But household size did not differ for rural and urban children, which made this unlikely. During observational data collection, additional information was collected every fifth minute on the number of adults and children within a three-metre radius of the focal child, and this was analysed to further explore the possibility of differential availability.

Results indicated no significant rural–urban differences for adults or children in proximity to focal children (F (79) < 0.00, $p < = 1.00$ and F (79) $= 1.54$, $p < = 0.22$ respectively). Hence, the tendency for rural children to be alone more often, and in co-operative interaction less often than urban children, may reflect a real difference in levels of sociability, rather than a mere difference in the availability of interaction partners.

Urban–rural differences were found in the exchange of information, with rural children exchanging information with other children less often, and receiving information from adults more often than urban children. Taken in conjunction with the fact that they interacted more often with adults than did urban children, these data suggest that rural children may have closer links with the adult world than their urban counterparts.

The data on commands issued by adults and children evidenced no rural–urban difference. This calls into question the assumption that rural African families are more authoritarian than urban families (Klingelhofer 1971). As data in Table 5 illustrate, neither urban nor rural environments appeared notably authoritarian, but instead were relatively well balanced in terms of command–information ratios. Adults certainly issued more commands to children than vice versa and had a higher command–information ratio than was evident in speech between children (also reported for European children by Tizard *et al.* 1988), but they were equally likely to provide children with information as they were to direct them. Children also passed information to adults almost as often as they received it. Wells (1981) reports that 27% of 5-year-old British children's speech was in the form of controlling statements. The comparative figure for the present sample is 30%, further reflecting the fact that speech was not used excessively for directive purposes.

Table 5. Command and information patterns in language use: means and standard deviations for rural and urban samples.

Category	Rural	Urban
Commands given by adults	4.90	5.02
	(4.85)	(5.02)
Commands from child to adults	0.64	1.00
	(0.99)	(1.10)
Commands between children	14.55	18.20
	(5.25)	(6.84)
Information given by adults	6.58	5.41
	(5.14)	(3.81)
Information from child to adults	5.15	3.80
	(5.09)	(2.82)
Information between children	34.42	36.99
	(10.24)	(8.77)

There was, therefore, little evidence of an authority-based structure of communication for either rural or urban children. These are important data comprising the first quantitative analyses of command and information rates in African children's language exchanges. They provide little evidence for either a *general* pattern of authoritative interactions or a greater degree of authoritarianism in rural as opposed to urban settings.

In terms of activities, rural children spent significantly more time in simple manipulation of objects than urban children. This suggests that rural children were more likely to use objects for their own sake without a transformation of the objects into tools for games, fantasy or work. The predominance of simple object manipulation in rural children (which occupied them for almost 50% of the time) may thus reflect a more limited degree of flexibility in resource utilisation.

The fact that rural children spent less time in chores than urban children was surprising, in the light of previous research reporting the reverse (Weisner 1981). It should be noted that rural children lived in households where water had to be drawn from outdoors, and where reliance on subsistence agriculture was greater — two important sources of domestic work which children may be called on to assist with. In an attempt to understand the finding, we examined the mean length of time a chore took to complete in urban and rural areas, the possibility being that urban chores were more time-consuming. However, the urban–rural difference was not significant (F (79) = 1.45, p< = 0.23).

Household circumstances provided little in the way of data that could explain the difference. As indicated in Table 3, urban and rural households were of similar size and had similar ratios of workers to household size. In other words, the demands for assistance around the home were likely to have been similar.

A final explanation was sought in the fact that food production in urban areas took place in the garden, where children would be immediately available to assist. In rural areas, fields were often some distance (as much as 8 kilometres) from the homestead, and preschool-aged children were not frequently taken there to assist. If assistance with chores that were specifically related to reliance on subsistence was the main source of the urban–rural difference, then one could predict that this difference would be greatest in the households relying regularly on subsistence, i.e. there would be a significant interaction effect for chores between the urban–rural marker and degree of reliance on subsistence agriculture. A regression analysis in which the two independent variables were entered as main effects before the interaction effect was examined indicated no significant interaction (F (3,76) = 2.95, p < = 0.09).

At this stage, therefore, we are unable to offer any explanation for the fact that urban children are involved in more chores than their rural counterparts, although it is unlikely to be the result of urban chores taking longer, or of urban households having fewer adults available for chores, or of urban children being more likely to be used for gardening around the home. However, the data provide no evidence that urbanisation results in children performing fewer chores and thus developing more marginal roles in the subsistence-related activities of their families.

That rural children were observed fighting less often than urban children correlated strongly with the fact that their communities had been involved in less community violence than their urban counterparts (Liddell, Kvalsvig, Qotyana and Shabalala 1991). Fry (1988) also reports this correlation for Zapotec children in Mexico. Finally, rural children spent more time unoccupied than did urban children, although the overall amount of time spent unoccupied was less than

1% in both groups, suggesting that the difference may have been relatively unimportant in terms of overall differences in activity.

Summary of the Model

Taken as a whole, the model predicted significant amounts of variance in most of the social interaction and activity categories, and could be regarded as a useful predictive model for these. Nevertheless, it is worth noting that the amounts of variance explained by the model were, at best, considerably lower than those reported from similar models (which included SES, ethnicity and crowding variables) for North American children (Bradley and Caldwell 1984). In terms of language use the model proved notably unsuccessful in predicting variance.

One may conclude from this that, while western and non-western children share certain similarities in terms of the home factors that affect their behaviour and experiences, these similarities are somewhat limited. Factors such as crowding, SES and ethnicity are less powerful in predicting the African children's behaviour in the present study. As previously discussed, this is probably attributable at least in part to the fact that SES and crowding were already saturated variables; i.e. these variables did not discriminate much between the individual children studied. They were all very poor and their housing conditions were, with few exceptions, similarly crowded. However, in selecting a random sample of these African children, it remains true that the poor predictive validity of the variables is a reflection of their limited ability to explain the children's activity in the everyday world. This does not mean of course that these variables have no effect on the children's behaviour. They clearly do, but in terms of the variables considered in this research their relative influence in determining the children's behaviour was not as powerful as expected. Nevertheless, the study corroborates that of Bradley and Caldwell (1984) for North American children, and Weisner and colleagues (1982) for Native Hawaiian children, in finding that within-group variations were often of greater magnitude than between-group variations (see, for example, the large standard deviations in Tables 4 and 5). This finding offers an important caution against attempting to characterise (or caricature) groups on the basis of dimensions such as ethnicity, SES and urbanicity. These are categories invented by experimenters and may bear little resemblance to the categories employed by the communities themselves to guide their everyday activity.

Conclusions

As detailed earlier, global predictors such as SES, household size and ethnicity have been of great value in explaining western children's behaviour. This chapter has assessed the predictive validity of these, using data from young African children growing up in the very different circumstances of South Africa. Whilst they continue to have significance, their validity is much reduced. Clearly, our sample is not easily compared with western children in terms of the factors that prevail on their everyday patterns of behaviour, social interaction and activity. Of course, part of the explanation for this lies in the fact that variables such as

SES and household density are not sufficiently spread – children were all poor, and all lived in crowded conditions. Given more equable opportunities, the salience of these predictors might be expected to change substantially. However, data presented here offer a contemporary assessment of 'predictors from the West' for children living under the vicissitudes of apartheid, and highlight the need for more culture-specific descriptors that can better explain variation.

The children could not be grouped satisfactorily in terms of the combined effects of poverty, crowding in the home, household reliance on subsistence agriculture, and urbanicity. Despite this, high standard deviations give testament to the fact that the sample did vary greatly in terms of everyday experiences and activities. What is evident is that the descriptors offered us by western psychology are unsatisfactory in explaining this variety.

References

Berry, J. W. (1976). *Human Ecology and Cognitive Style*. New York: Sage.

Bradley, R. H. and Caldwell, B. M. (1984). 174 children: A study of the relationship between home environment and cognitive development during the first 5 years. In A. W. Gottfried (ed.), *Home Environment and Early Cognitive Development*. Orlando: Academic Press.

Brice-Heath, S. B. (1986). What no bedtime story means: Narrative skills at home and school. In B. B. Schieffelin and E. Ochs (eds), *Language Socialization across Cultures*. Cambridge: Cambridge University Press.

Bryant, P. (1985). Parents, children and cognitive development. In R. Hinde, A. Perret-Clermont, and J. Stevenson-Hinde (eds), *Social Relationships and Cognitive Development*. Oxford: Clarendon Press.

Burdette, M. M. (1988). *Zambia: Between Two Worlds*. Boulder: Westview Press.

Cohen, J. and Cohen, P. (1983). *Applied Multiple Regression/Correlation Analysis for the Behavioral Sciences*. Hillsdale, N.J.: Erlbaum.

Cowlishaw, G. K. (1986). Aborigines and anthropologists. *Australian Aboriginal Studies, 1*, 2–12.

Durojaiye, M. O. A. (1980). *The Contribution of African Universities to the Reform of Education, Notably As It Concerns Research on the Development of the African Child*. Paris: UNESCO Press.

Edelstein, W. (1983). Cultural constraints on development and the vicissitudes of progress. In F. S. Kessel and A. W. Siegel (eds), *The Child and Other Cultural Inventions*. New York: Praeger.

Felgate, W. S. (1982). *The Tembe Thonga of Natal and Mozambique – An Ecological Approach*. Occasional Publication No. 1. Durban, South Africa: University of Natal Press.

Fischer, M. M. J. (1986). Ethnicity and the post-modern arts of memory. In J. Clifford and G. E. Marcus (eds), *Writing Culture: The Poetics and Politics of Ethnography*. Berkeley: University of California Press.

Fry, D. (1988). Intercommunity differences in aggression among Zapotec children. *Child Development, 59*, 1008–1019.

Graves, T. D. and Graves, N. B. (1978). Evolving strategies in the study of cultural change. In G. D. Spindler (ed), *The Making of Psychological Anthropology*. Berkeley: University of California Press.

Keefe, K. (1988). Aboriginality: Resistance and persistence. *Australian Aboriginal Studies, 1*, 67–81.

Klingelhofer, E. L. (1971). What Tanzanian secondary school students plan to teach their children. *Journal of Cross-Cultural Psychology, 2* (2), 189–195.

Liddell, C. (1988). The social interaction and activity patterns of children from two San groups living as refugees on a Namibian military base. *Journal of Cross-Cultural Psychology, 19* (3), 341–360.

Liddell, C., Kvalsvig, J., Qotyana, P. and Shabalala, A. (In press *a*). Community violence and levels of aggression in young South African children. *International Journal of Behavioral Development*.

Liddell, C., Kvalsvig, J., Strydom, N., Shabalala, A. and Qotyana, P. (In press *b*). An observational study of 5-year-old South African children in the year before school. *International Journal of*

Behavioral Development.

Loo, C. and Ong, P. (1984). Crowding perceptions, attitudes, and consequences among the Chinese. *Environment and Behavior, 16,* 55–87.

Munroe, R. H. and Munroe, R. L. (1971). Household density and infant care in an East African society. *Journal of Social Psychology, 83,* 3–13.

Osborn, A. F. and Milbank, J. E. (1987). *The Effects of Early Education.* Oxford: Clarendon Press.

Preston-Whyte, E. and Miller, R. (1987). Coping with ethnography: The construction and interpretation of an ethnographic text. *African Studies, 46* (1), 1–32.

Reynolds, P. (1989). *Childhood in Crossroads.* Cape Town: David Philip.

Richter, L. M. (1989). Household density, family size, and the growth and development of black children – a cross-sectional study from infancy to middle childhood. *South African Journal of Psychology, 19* (4), 191–197.

Rubin, K. H., Maioni, T. L. and Hornung, M. (1976). Free play behaviors in middle- and lower-class preschoolers: Parten and Piaget revisited. *Child Development, 47,* 414–419.

Sharp, J. (1980). Can we study ethnicity? A critique of fields of study in South African anthropology. *Social Dynamics, 6* (1), 1–6.

Tizard, B., Blatchford, P., Burke, J., Farquhar, C. and Plewis, I. (1988). *Young Children at School in the Inner City.* Hove: Lawrence Erlbaum Associates.

Weisner, T. S. (1981). Cities, stress and children: a review of some cross-cultural questions. In R. H. Munroe, R. L. Munroe and B. B. Whiting (eds), *Handbook of Cross-Cultural Development.* New York: Garland STPM Press.

Weisner, T. S., Gallimore, R. and Tharp, R. G. (1982). Concordance between ethnographer and folk perspectives: observed performance and self-description of sibling caretaker roles. *Human Organization, 41* (3), 237–244.

Wells, G. (1981). *Learning through Interaction.* Cambridge: Cambridge University Press.

4

Malnutrition, Low Birth Weight and Related Influences on Psychological Development

LINDA RICHTER AND RAOUL GRIESEL

Introduction

Undernutrition, as assessed by low birth weight and inadequate growth, is the focus of this chapter. It deals with moderate to severe undernutrition, which is often referred to as malnutrition. There are, however, other nutritional deficiencies — specifically micro-nutrient deficiencies — a few of which are as prevalent as general undernutrition in developing countries. Some of these nutritional deficiencies have devastating effects on children's capacities. Iodine deficiency, for example, is still the main cause of mental retardation in children throughout the world, and vitamin A deficiency is the most common cause of irreversible loss of sight amongst children in developing countries. Such deficiencies, however, will not be dealt with here.

According to a report by the World Food Council in 1975, up to a third of the world's children die from malnutrition and related diseases before their fifth birthday. Of those who survive, 25–50% are nevertheless likely to experience moderate to severe protein-energy malnutrition during their early childhood (Riopelle 1982). Iron deficiency is the most prevalent of all nutritional deficiencies, iron being necessary for the ability of the blood to carry oxygen for vital organ functions. On the basis of the limits of normality of haemoglobin for different age groups proposed by the World Health Organisation, it is estimated that 51% of preschool and 38% of schoolchildren in developing countries suffer from iron-deficiency anaemia (UN ACC/SCN 1991). By estimation, more than five million South African children between the ages of 5 and 14 years could be affected by iron deficiency. Most experts in this field agree that there is a strong negative relationship between iron-deficiency anaemia, cognitive functioning and educational outcomes (Fairchild, Haas and Habicht 1989). However, the precise mechanisms of the effect are poorly understood. As in most work on low birth weight and undernutrition, a common complicating theme emerges. This may be summarised as follows: Amongst children in developing societies the effects of nutritional deficiencies cannot be isolated from a variety of other socio-economic, environmental and psychosocial stresses which act in concert with one another in ways that compound and obscure the influence of individual factors. In particular, apart from specific aetiological agents, inadequate growth amongst infants and children and the effects of poor growth on child development are rooted in poverty and deprivation.

GROWTH AS AN INDEX OF ENVIRONMENTAL ADEQUACY AND INDIVIDUAL WELL-BEING

Growth is a proxy, rather than a direct, measure of nutritional adequacy. For example, foetal undernutrition is inferred from a low birth weight for gestational age, and low weight and height relative to reference values in young children are assumed to be the consequence primarily of undernutrition. Thus growth is taken to be a key indicator of the adequacy of the nurturing qualities of environments for children's development.

The use of growth as an indicator in this way is supported by biological correspondences between nutrition and growth, and also by findings which show that growth is related to socio-economic status. The incidence of all perinatal complications, including low birth weight, show significant associations with socio-economic measures (Gray, Dean and Lowrie 1988; Kopp 1990). Throughout the world newborns, infants and children from higher socio-economic levels are heavier and taller than their less privileged counterparts at all ages (Baumeister, Kupstas and Klindworth 1991; Meredith 1984). Socio-economic status (SES) does, of course, have a ceiling effect on growth, and above this threshold a relationship between the two measures is no longer found (Christiansen, Mora and Herrera 1975).

As well as being an indicator of environmental adequacy, growth is also used as an indicator of current and future individual well-being. For example, an infant's birth weight is regarded as one of the most important prognostic indicators of later growth and development. Mortality and morbidity rates are highest for infants with a birth weight less than 2500 g (Rip, Keen and Kibel 1986), and the rate of major birth defects is five times greater amongst babies in this range of birth weight than for babies of normal weight (Mili, Edmonds, Khoury and McClearn 1991). Low-birth-weight infants are unanimously considered to be at risk for developmental problems of all kinds – intellectual, emotional and behavioural (Kopp 1983).

Amongst young children, poor growth has been associated with later lower levels of measured IQ (Humphreys, Davey and Park 1985) and, throughout the preschool years, generally positive correlations are found between measures of growth (height, weight and head circumference) and measures of cognitive development (Ernhart and Marler 1987). Thus, poor growth is both an outcome of earlier influences on development and, at the same time, a determinant of future outcomes.

Low Birth Weight

Internationally, normal birth weight is accepted as being in the region of 3300 g (Keller 1981) with 2500 g or below referred to as low birth weight (LBW) and 1500 g or below as very low birth weight (VLBW). Low birth weight may be attributed to prematurity or dysmaturity. Premature or preterm babies are those whose weights are appropriate for their gestational age, but who are immature because they have been born before 37 of the normal 40 weeks of gestation. Dysmature babies have retarded growth; i.e. they are small for their respective gestational ages. Small-for-gestational-age (SGA) babies are those whose birthweights are either below the 10th percentile for their respective week of gestation or below 2 standard deviations from the mean for gestation (Lester 1979). These babies are considered to have been foetally malnourished.

Although both prematurity and dysmaturity result in an increased proportion of neonatal and later developmental problems, the distinction between the two conditions is important. Firstly, different aetiological factors are involved, with SGA babies being more common in poor communities. Low birth weight has been found to have a greater impact on children's development in such situations. Secondly, the two groups of LBW babies have different outcomes. There are indications that SGA babies may be more seriously impaired than preterm babies, and that their impairments may be discernible for longer periods of time into childhood and adolescence. For example, SGA babies are more likely than preterms to remain small throughout the pre-adolescent period (Riopelle 1982). It should be noted, however, that most studies of LBW do not make this distinction, and this seriously limits the specificity of research findings. In addition, little research (and few longitudinal studies) have been conducted in developing countries, where the majority of LBW babies are born and where there is a multitude of concurrent adverse influences that are likely to compound the effects of low birth weight.

Low-birth-weight infants comprise less than 2–3% of all live births in Europe and the United States of America, whereas the proportion of LBW ranges from 13% to 43% amongst poor communities in many developing countries (Lester 1979). In a study of LBW African babies in Soweto, Stein and Ellis (1974) found that 73% were small for their gestational ages. They concluded that these children had suffered intrauterine growth retardation and that the most significant causes were multiple pregnancies, poor socio-economic conditions and maternal undernutrition. In comparison, the percentage of LBW among white babies in South Africa has been reported to vary between 4% and 14% (Zille 1986).

Determinants of Low Birth Weight

As indicated earlier, not all low birth weight can be taken as indicative of prenatal undernutrition. Foetal undernutrition is inferred from SGA status and the diagnosis is supported by associated clinical signs, such as dry peeling skin and a generally wasted appearance. When other abnormalities are ruled out (such as genetic defects, chronic infections, or toxic agents which reduce the growth potential of the foetus), the most probable cause of LBW is a reduced supply of nutrients to the foetus (Lester 1979).

Maternal undernutrition is one of the primary causes of foetal undernutrition and therefore of low birth weight. Birth weight is accepted by the World Health Organisation as an indicator of maternal nutritional status (1981). The influence of the mother's nutritional status on the foetus may be direct or indirect through effects on placental development and function (Lester 1979). For many years it was believed that the foetus would be able to extract whatever nutrients it required from the mother, even if maternal health suffered as a result. However, it is now known that the mother and foetus are, in a sense, competitors for available nutrients and that if a woman is undernourished it is highly likely that her unborn child will suffer the same deprivation (Riopelle 1982).

From a broader perspective, prenatal undernutrition and associated LBW cannot be separated from a variety of other factors that might affect the pregnancy and birth conditions of women in poor communities. Lack of adequate prenatal care and a poor reproductive history (multiple, closely spaced or problematical pregnancies) are often also associated with maternal undernutrition and LBW (Lester 1979). In developing countries, specific maternal risk factors associated with LBW include age (above 40 years or below 17 years), short stature (<140 cm), a history of chronic infectious disease, a short inter-pregnancy interval (<6 months), and pregnancy complications (including oedema, high blood pressure and urine positive for protein) (Husaini, Husaini and Sulaiman 1986). In other words, a number of factors identified as increasing the risk of LBW are related to income or socio-economic status (Kopp 1990). Birch and Gussow put it this way: 'The poor woman having a baby may be at risk because of her age, her nutritional status, her probable poor growth, her excessive exposure to infection in the community that she inhabits, her poor housing and her inadequate medical supervision, as well as because of complex interactions between these and other potentially adverse influences' (1970: 175).

In several North American studies, LBW has been shown to be predominantly associated with smoking, being single, receiving no prenatal care, and being black (Boone 1985; Giblin, Poland, Waller and Ager 1988), which are also related to socio-economic status. One recent study, while controlling for differences in race, health habits and prior complications of pregnancy, found a six-fold increase in the risk of LBW in association with financial problems during the current pregnancy (Binsacca, Ellis, Martin and Petitti 1987). In South Africa lack of antenatal care is very strongly associated with LBW. For example, one report from Bloemfontein indicated that only 2 of 50 mothers who delivered a baby weighing less than 1000 g had received any form of antenatal care (Zille 1986). This does not mean, of course, that lack of antenatal care is directly or causally related to LBW. It may simply indicate that lack of antenatal care and low birth weight are concurrent expressions of the same complex of social and economic deprivation.

Low socio-economic status women report high levels of stressful life events (Dohrenwend 1973), and several studies have examined the relationships between stress and perinatal outcome. High levels of psychosocial stress have been found to increase the risk of pregnancy complications generally, and of preterm delivery specifically (Levin and DeFrank 1988) although no direct link has been established between measured life stress and LBW.

Consequences of Low Birth Weight
The mortality and morbidity of LBW and VLBW babies have changed

dramatically over the last thirty years, as medical advances have occurred in peri-natal and neonatal care. For example, as a group, with all weights averaged together, preterm infants of this generation show less serious developmental sequelae and higher intelligence test scores in childhood than samples of children studied a generation ago (Kopp 1983). However, mortality and residual impair-ment increase with decreasing birth weight. While there is wide variation between countries and even between centres of health care, only 50–75% of babies weighing less than 1500 g at birth have been reported to survive the neonatal period, and just 30–50% have been judged to be developing normally by middle childhood (Jones, Cummins and Davies 1979; Steiner, Sanders, Phillips and Naddock 1980). Taken as a group, surviving VLBW children have been found to have lower IQs, to be more likely to perform poorly at school, and to show signs of emotional disturbance, as compared with controls (Lloyd 1984). Some studies have shown that learning difficulties persist into adolescence amongst about 20% of VLBW children (Francis-Williams and Davies 1974).

During the neonatal period and early infancy, LBW babies have been found to show deficits in basic reflexes, muscle tone, spontaneous movements and visual orientation. Their performance on standardised measures of infant devel-opment has also been shown to be poorer than that of larger infants. In addition, LBW babies have been observed to be apathetic, under-demanding and un-responsive to environmental stimulation, as well as irritable when aroused (Brazelton, Tronick, Lechtig, Lasky and Klein 1977; Zeskind and Ramey 1978).

Early differences in performance between LBW babies and those of normal weight tend to disappear with time, particularly when there is a highly support-ive caregiving environment. Nevertheless, reviews of studies on the outcome of LBW indicate general agreement that severe handicapping conditions occur in approximately 10–15% of children (Kopp 1983) with environmental factors con-tributing substantial individual differences. The handicaps which have been found include visual and auditory impairments, spasticity, and learning prob-lems.

The development of LBW infants is thought to be influenced by three major groups of factors: the history, personal characteristics and social context of care-givers, the constitution and temperament of the child, and the nature and extent of medical complications. Longitudinal investigations, such as Emily Werner's birth cohort study (1985) on the Hawaiian island of Kauai, in which children were followed from birth to adulthood, show that perinatal complications (including LBW) were consistently related to later physical and psychological development only when combined with poor environmental circumstances, such as chronic poverty. One of the most critical components of the caregiving context that has been identified is the ongoing interaction between a child and his or her caregivers. For example, Bradley, Caldwell, Rock, Casey and Nelson (1987) found that the most efficient predictor of the cognitive development of LBW infants at 18 months of age was a measure of characteristics of the child's home experience, including the variety of stimulation available to the child and the organisation of the home environment.

In addition to differences in caretaking environments, the incidence of developmental problems in LBW children is believed to be due also to the greater sensitivity of such children to environmental insufficiencies (Escalona 1987). Thus, LBW status may render children constitutionally more vulnerable to negative environmental experiences and so compound their problems.

Further, it has been observed that LBW status affects interaction with caregivers. Preterm babies have, for example, been called 'unreadable' for caregivers (McGehee and Eckerman 1983). That is, their erratic movements and unstable behaviour states make it difficult for caregivers to predict the infant's behaviour and to establish smooth and mutually satisfying interactions. LBW infants are often perceived by caregivers to be more difficult to care for and less rewarding because they do not contribute as much as normal weight babies to the adult–child interactions (Brown and Bakeman 1980). On the basis of such findings, it has been argued that LBW babies may elicit less optimal care from caregivers than normal weight babies, and that this may exacerbate the effects of prenatal undernutrition. As Lester (1979: 389) puts it: 'A poorly organized infant who has difficulty interacting with the environment and is a poor elicitor of maternal response from a caregiver who is already stressed and nutritionally depleted, may not receive the kind of caregiving necessary for his or her recovery.'

Low Birth Weight: Conclusions

Foetally malnourished infants are almost always simultaneously exposed to multiple other biological, economic, social and familial risks for normal development. Many of these risks exert synergistic, rather than independent, effects on children. That is, there is either a compounding or a diluting effect of various factors in interaction with one another. Thus, a general conclusion about biological risk, including LBW, is that effects can be ameliorated by a supportive and stimulating caregiving environment or exacerbated by a deprived and stressed environment. There is great individual variation in the developmental outcome of LBW children but most studies find substantial differences in performance between groups of socio-economically advantaged and disadvantaged children. Newman (1987:135) has argued that this variation is not 'relatable only to ethnicity, socio-economic status or marital status, or to the social or biological factors that characterise those at risk for LBW itself, but rather to adult commitment to the child'. While this is a conclusion shared by others (e.g. Rickel and Allen 1987), adult commitment to the optimal care of a child is not simply a matter of motivation. The way in which the adequacy of child care is also influenced by structural socio-economic factors as well as interpersonal and individual factors is dealt with in more detail in the sections below and in Chapter 2.

Growth of Infants and Children

In less developed countries the growth of infants begins to falter around the sixth month of life in comparison with growth patterns of children in the United Kingdom and the United States (Waterlow, Ashworth and Griffiths 1980). At about the age of 5 years, growth rates begin to normalise but inadequate height continues into adolescence and adulthood as evidence of the deprivation experienced at earlier ages (Waterlow 1978).

In South Africa, Hansen (1984), in a review of over thirty studies, has concluded that approximately one-third of all African, coloured and Indian children below the age of 14 years have been shown to be underweight and stunted for their age. In addition, Wagstaff and Geefhuysen (1974) have reported a very high incidence of malnutrition amongst hospitalised children. In a survey of over 1500 paediatric patients, they found that only 9% of the children reached or exceeded the 3rd percentile for weight.

However, such figures are not necessarily stable and may be influenced by concurrent contextual factors. For example, in 1977 Richardson reported a drop in the prevalence of underweight in South Africa. Nearly ten years later she observed that although the fall in underweight had been sustained after 1975, by 1985 the prevalence had increased again. This she attributed to the drought and to other economic constraints characterising that period (Richardson 1986). Thus, monitoring the growth of young children is an important aspect of health and social surveillance in developing countries and among poor communities who are particularly vulnerable to such economic fluctuations.

Types of Malnutrition

In the past a distinction was made between two main types of malnutrition in young children: marasmus and kwashiorkor. Marasmus was assumed to be due to a reduction in total food supply and also to be characterised by poor growth from birth. On the other hand, kwashiorkor was assumed to be due to a high-starch, low-protein diet and to be characterised by normal growth for the first 6–8 months of life followed by a sharp decline during the second year. This distinction is now regarded as an oversimplification of the dietary aetiology of malnutrition. It is current practice to speak only of different degrees of protein-energy malnutrition. It is, however, customary to make a distinction between wasting, which refers to a normal or near-normal height-for-age (HFA) but a low weight-for-age (WFA), and stunting, which refers to a low HFA. When underweight children receive compensatory feeding they usually show rapid catch-up weight gain. However, the degree of stunting of a child remains the same – or becomes worse as children get older. Wasting is thus taken to be indicative of acute nutritional deprivation, whereas stunting is believed to reflect chronic undernutrition.

Various classification systems have been proposed to describe different kinds and levels of severity of malnutrition. For example, according to the Wellcome Classification (1970), the term 'marasmus' is applied to children who are less than 60% of WFA with no oedema, while the diagnosis of marasmic kwashiorkor is applied to children whose weight is less than 60% of WFA with oedema. The term 'kwashiorkor' is applied to children who have oedema and are between 60% and 80% of WFA. Children who are between 60% and 80% WFA with no oedema are called undernourished children. Another widely used classification system (Gomez, Galvan, Frenk, Munoz, Chavez and Vasquez 1956) proposes a way of assessing the severity of malnutrition based on international growth standards. A weight of 76–90% WFA is called first-degree malnutrition, 61–75% WFA is called second-degree malnutrition, and third-degree malnutrition occurs when weight falls below 60% WFA.

Malnutrition is a difficult concept to operationalise because it refers to input (food eaten), but the most practical measure of it is output (growth and health). Thus, the criteria for malnutrition are inferential (Klein, Irwin, Engle and Yarbrough 1977). A substantial part of the debate about malnutrition in the international and local literature has been concerned with what the appropriate measures and standards of normal growth should be and the implications of this for assessing malnutrition. For example, Cameron (1986) has advocated that local standards for growth should be developed in South Africa for each of the major population groups, but that such local standards should not be seen as an acceptance of any differences between groups in terms of growth potential. This is a complex issue because differences between populations in growth patterns are due to both genetic and environmental factors, and these are difficult to separate (Tanner 1976). Further, Richardson (1973) has claimed that it is unjustifiable and unrealistic to inflate estimates of the degree of malnutrition in South Africa by the use of North American growth standards. On the other hand, Coovadia, Adhikari and Mthethwa (1977) have claimed that analyses of multiple growth measures (height, weight and head circumference) indicate that the Harvard standards are, in fact, appropriate for South African children.

At a symposium in 1979 at the Institute of Child Health at the University of Cape Town, consensus was reached among a group of professionals working in the field of child health in South Africa that the National Center for Health Statistics (NCHS) growth standards (Hamill, Drizd, Johnson, Reed and Roche 1977) should be used in South Africa for monitoring the growth of infants and children. This decision acknowledged the equal growth potential of all children, regardless of the extent to which that potential may be thwarted in any particular circumstance, and advocated growth potential as the ideal standard against which the growth of individual children all over the world should be assessed.

However, further controversy exists around whether there are necessarily negative consequences to being small. For example, Walker, Jones, Walker and Tshabalala (1983) have argued, with reference to differences in growth rates of children in South Africa, that slower growth does not necessarily prejudice health or well-being. As Habicht, Meyers and Brownie (1982) put it, one can classify a child as growing less well than some percentile of the healthy population, but one cannot easily ascertain the point at which the child's growth is unhealthy. Thus, while large numbers of poor children in South Africa are small, some experts question whether this inadequate growth, by North American standards, has any direct implications for health or development. This issue will be taken up below where data indicating that being small and poor may well compromise psychological development and performance will be presented.

Determinants of Malnutrition

It has long been recognised that the syndrome of malnutrition does not exist in isolation. Malnutrition is inseparable from poverty, and within that context a variety of social, economic, medical and psychological factors affects the total well-being of children. Thus, a range of concurrent factors may interact with poor growth to co-determine health and development outcomes for individual children (Pollitt 1969).

For example, there is a growth–health interaction referred to as the malnutrition–infection complex (see Kvalsvig and Connolly, Chapter 5). Infections adversely affect nutritional status while nutritional status affects vulnerability to, and the severity of, infections. In conditions of poverty, people are often simultaneously exposed to a number of infectious conditions and to inadequate food intake. This double hazard particularly affects infants and preschool children because they have immature immune systems and high nutritional demands for growth. Most infections result in a measurable but temporary decline in nutritional status. In normal circumstances, a good diet during illness and the recovery period can ensure that infections do not adversely affect growth over a longer term. However, under conditions of dietary inadequacy, recovery is often incomplete, resulting in both impaired growth and increased vulnerability to subsequent infections arising from depression of the immune system. This effect becomes circular, causing a progressive decline in health (UN ACC/SCN 1990:29).

In cases such as famine, war or widespread social deprivation, the primary determinant of malnutrition is the general inadequacy of the food supply. Secondary determinants of malnutrition, however, are more socially and contextually specific. That is, adequate food may not be consumed by an individual child for a variety of particular economic, social or psychological reasons (Sims, Paolucci and Morris 1972). For example, in many Asian and Latin American countries, female children are more at risk for the development of malnutrition than males (Wray and Aguirre 1969). This is the result of a variety of beliefs, values and child-care practices concerned with a child's sex, which mediate between the child and the food specifically available to her in the household. Equally, in underdeveloped and disadvantaged communities, where large numbers of people are impoverished, undernourished children can be precipitated into states of florid malnutrition by any number of unfortunate circumstances, such as loss of a breadwinner, birth of another child, infection, and so on. (It is interesting to note that the term 'kwashiorkor' was coined specifically to describe the condition of a young child displaced by the birth of a younger sibling.) In South Africa, as in most other developing countries, childhood malnutrition is a problem in disadvantaged and underdeveloped rural and urban communities. A critical problem in slums and shantytowns is its relation to social disorganisation and lack of health and welfare support services, like child care (Gross and Monteiro 1989).

In general, risk factors for malnutrition can be identified at the community, family and individual levels.

Community: Risk factors at the community level include political structures and government policy. For example, influx control in South Africa created a risk factor for malnutrition through its devastating effect on family life and systems of care for young children. However, community risks also include such things as geographic proneness to disaster (such as droughts and floods), poor food availability (due, for example, to the collapse of subsistence farming), endemic infections, inadequate or insufficient housing, poor water supplies, poor employment opportunities, inadequate health services, and poor quality of education. These community risks can be countered, to some extent, by positive government policies. For example, some developing countries like Chile and Cuba have very low rates of malnutrition because of a record of sustained government support for health and social services.

Family: Risks for childhood malnutrition in the family and household include low caregiver income and education, vulnerable family structure (such as single female-headed households, a large number of which occur in South Africa), poor housing and sanitation, and large family size. Recently urbanised poor families in squatter communities are particularly at risk.

Individual: Risks at the individual level include child spacing, age of the mother, birth weight, multiple births, father absence, physical or mental handicaps in the child, abrupt weaning, an inadequate or poorly structured diet, lack of immunisation, and infections.

Children become malnourished as a result of a long chain of personal and social vulnerabilities in the families and people responsible for their care. Inevitably, child malnutrition is linked to community and family impoverishment and disorganisation, frequently as a result of societal oppression, marginalisation and exploitation.

Consequences of Poor Growth

The immediate effects of acute protein-energy malnutrition on infants and young children are symptoms of apathy, withdrawal, irritability, monotonous crying, a reduction in activity level, a low responsivity to environmental stimuli, and poor attention (Pollitt and Thompson 1977). Recovery from malnutrition is first signalled by increased alertness and social responsiveness (Galler 1984).

However, the question which bedevils researchers and practitioners concerns the possible long-term, rather than immediate, effects of experiencing an episode of clinical malnutrition. Research on this question is complicated by embedded control problems, or the inability to isolate the effects of malnutrition from the effects of deprivation in general, and the inability to control adequately the effects of other concurrent variables (Barrett 1984; Warren 1973). In particular, it is difficult to find control groups of children from the same communities who have not themselves suffered some degree of undernutrition. It is equally difficult to match children adequately on the range of social and personal variables which influence children's development – such as structural features of the household, father presence, and degree of maternal social support. Other factors that are also difficult to control are the influence of separation from caregivers, of hospitalisation and illness, as well as the timing, duration and severity of the episode of malnutrition. Further conceptual problems that arise in research on the psychological sequelae of malnutrition include the definition and measurement of mental and social development, particularly in contexts where standardised psychological tests have to be adapted to local conditions (Wig, Mehta and Verma 1981).

At one stage it was believed that animal experiments could be used to model 'pure' states of undernutrition, without the confounding influence of social variables, but this has proved otherwise (Crnic 1984). All the ways of inducing a state of malnutrition in young animals (for example, creating artificially large groups of offspring, malnourishing the mother, or reducing suckling by separating the mother from her young for various periods) also affect the social organisation of the animals. As an example, undernourished dam rats spend more time suckling their litter than do well-nourished controls, with the effect that some nutritional and social compensation is introduced into the situation (Fleischer and Turkewitz 1984). Nonetheless, animal experiments have been useful in the development of more complex models and in producing results which have helped to confirm findings from studies of human malnutrition. For present purposes the most important conclusions are, firstly, that apart from direct individual effects on the offspring, malnutrition also affects the physical and behavioural properties of the young as a stimulator of maternal caretaking, and secondly, that some types of induced malnutrition produce direct energy changes in the mother and thus affect the quality of care she is able to give her young.

Despite the general complexity of research on the medium- and long-term effects of malnutrition on young children, the following general conclusions can be drawn:

1. Stunted children, as a result of malnutrition, tend to come from the lowest socio-economic groups in the society and also tend to perform less well on a variety of psychological and scholastic indicators than children of average height (Pollitt and Lewis 1980; Pollitt and Thompson 1977).

At least two studies in South Africa have confirmed this general proposition. In 1987, Wagstaff, Reinach, Richardson, Mkhasibe and De Vries reported their findings from 1407 lower-primary schoolchildren in Soweto. They found that approximately 14% of the children were stunted (HFA below 90% of the NCHS median) and that there was a significantly higher failure rate amongst stunted children than with children of normal height. Griesel, Richter and Belciug (1990) assessed nearly 1500 African children between the ages of 3 and 14 years (of whom about one-third fell below 80% expected WFA) on electroencephalographic (EEG) measures, psychological tests and school performance. They found that the undernourished children showed a small but consistent retardation of electrocerebral maturity across the whole age range studied. On the other measures, including scholastic achievement as measured by place in class, the undernourished group performed consistently worse than children of normal WFA.

2. The importance of the social context of undernutrition has been consistently demonstrated in studies, which show that, amongst undernourished children in developing communities, socio-economic status measures correlate with both growth and cognitive measures, and that socio-economic factors may be as important as nutritional factors in determining cognitive and school performance (Bogin and MacVean 1983).

The fact that sex differences are often found in studies of malnutrition effects is also taken to indicate that social factors mediate the relationship between performance measures and malnutrition (Klein, Kagan, Freeman, Yarbrough and Habicht 1972). However, the most critical evidence for the importance of social factors is that middle-class children with organic illnesses which result in under-nutrition (such as cystic fibrosis and various intestinal diseases) do not show poor developmental outcomes, whereas malnourished children in economically impoverished communities generally show marked negative effects (Barrett and Frank 1987).

Thus, researchers no longer attempt an artificial separation between the mal-nourished child and the context in which that malnutrition occurs – and in which the child is likely to remain. Both nutrition and social circumstances, in the years following recovery, determine, together with nutritional and psycho-social antecedents of malnutrition, the magnitude of the psychological impair-ments associated with severe clinical malnutrition in early childhood.

3. Protein-energy malnutrition, occurring as it does in the context of nega-tive environmental factors, is likely to result in psychological deficits, both intel-lectual and social, which could be permanent if no comprehensive effort is made to provide the child with remedial intervention (Pollitt and Lewis 1980). This issue has generated extensive controversy and debate.

In part, the controversy has arisen from the inseparability of direct from indi-rect environmental effects. However, in 1974, the World Health Organisation concluded that there was very little evidence showing that malnutrition directly damages mental development but that it was certain that malnutrition did have damaging effects in interaction with negative antecedent and consequent envi-ronmental factors.

There have been countless studies, both in southern Africa and elsewhere, which have a bearing on this issue. As Brozek (1980) remarks, Africa was the site of the earliest research on the psychological sequelae of malnutrition and South Africa has remained an important source of accounts of the concomitants of malnutrition and its long-term effects on young children (Griesel and Richter 1987). There have been three groups of researchers in South Africa whose work on this subject has had a significant impact on the international scene. Probably most important is the work of Stoch, Smythe, Moodie and Bradshaw (1982) who, in 1955, began a longitudinal study of 20 infants and a matched control group whom they managed to follow up for 20 years. Their main findings were that the malnourished group showed striking intellectual deficits which, in time, became increasingly apparent. Although these authors acknowledge the difficul-ties involved in separating environmental from nutritional factors in the poor performance of their sample, they argue that the lower head circumference and high incidence of EEG abnormalities in the previously malnourished group sug-gest that they had sustained some organic damage during their malnutrition episode.

In contrast, Moodie, Bowie, Mann and Hansen (1980) conducted a 15-year follow-up study of 123 children compared with their siblings. They concluded that growth retardation after kwashiorkor was largely reversible and that, as a group, the ex-patients were educationally and occupationally no different from their siblings or peers from the community in which they had been reared.

While the Stoch study emphasised the poor prognosis attached to early malnu-trition, Moodie and colleagues found that late onset patients had lower IQ scores and showed poorer school performance than those with an early episode of malnutrition.

Bartel, Griesel and others (Bartel 1980) studied 30 children who, four to ten years previously, had been hospitalised for malnutrition. They assessed the chil-dren's current status on both EEG and psychomotor measures. The children's performance was compared with three other groups: siblings nearest in age to the malnourished child, yardmates, and white children from good socio-economic circumstances. In general, few significant differences between the groups were found, and the authors concluded that one explanation for the findings was that whatever deficits the previously malnourished children might have had, had been overcome by the time of the follow-up assessment.

Well-controlled studies, for example the INCAP study in Guatemala, which has involved evaluation, follow-up and supplementation in whole villages and which has controlled for socio-economic status and social deprivation as mea-sured by family functioning, have nonetheless found that intellectual perfor-mance is significantly affected by malnutrition. On the basis of these findings, INCAP researchers dismiss the possibility that family functioning or SES level alone can explain lower test performance amongst previously malnourished chil-dren (Klein *et al.* 1977).

Winick and Coombs (1972) concluded that, even if malnutrition is not the sole cause of the impairment, the complex of social ills encompassing severe malnutrition does affect learning ability and, given the continuation of social and material deprivation, this appears to be permanent. One of the most recent and comprehensive long-term studies is that of Galler and her co-workers in Barbados (see Galler, Ramsey, Solimano, Lowell, and Mason 1983; Galler and Ramsey 1989). They assessed 129 children who had been malnourished up to ten years previously, on a variety of intellectual, neurological and scholastic indi-cators, as well as a comparison group matched for age, sex and socio-economic status. In a comprehensive review, Galler (1984) concluded that deficits associat-ed with early moderate-to-severe malnutrition persist at least to adolescence, and are most noticeable in attention deficits and emotional instability. These are more subtle and perhaps more pervasive disturbances of function than the cog-nitive and psychomotor indices measured in earlier studies.

4. There has been a general shift in emphasis in the research on the effects of malnutrition from an exclusive focus on cognition to the inclusion of emotional, motivational and social functions. Numerous lines of evidence suggest that affec-tive and social behaviours are the ones most severely affected by malnutrition and that they also appear to improve most through remedial intervention (Barrett and Frank 1987).

Animal studies have indicated that malnourished individuals show reductions in exploratory behaviour, attentiveness and persistence in problem-solving tasks, as well as heightened emotionality, fearfulness about new situations, and irri-tability (Cowley and Griesel 1964). These observations have also been made of malnourished children. Barrett and others conclude that the effects of malnutrition on children are mediated by changes in social behaviours, as well as by changes in stress tolerance and coping (Barrett and Frank 1987). In line with the findings of Galler and colleagues (1984), Barrett concludes that early malnutrition has long-term and adverse consequences for social and emotional development, with attention, social responsiveness and emotional adjustment being significantly affected.

5. Children who have experienced moderate-to-severe malnutrition in infancy may be partly rehabilitated by remedial nutritional and psychological programmes, the principle being that the more extensive and comprehensive the programme, the more successful is the rehabilitation (Pollitt 1987; Pollitt and Lewis 1980).

Several studies have shown that dietary intervention alone is not very effective, with little gain being shown on measures of cognitive development by children receiving supplementation (Palmer and Barba 1981). Similarly, nutrition education programmes directed to the mothers of children admitted for treatment for malnutrition also tend to show few positive benefits for children. Richter-Strydom, Griesel and Glatthaar (1985) followed up 21 children and a matched control group, three years after a malnutrition episode. The mothers of the index group had received a comprehensive programme of nutrition education, while the control group mothers had received only home visits. No statistically significant differences were found between the physical growth or measured psychological functioning of the children whose mothers had received nutrition education and those whose mothers had not.

It is currently accepted that nutritional supplementation is in itself insufficient to bring malnourished children back to normal levels of development. It is equally important, maintain Carson and Greeley (1988), to enrich the immediate social milieu through persistent and appropriate stimulation of the child, physically, mentally, socially and emotionally, in order to reverse the usually deleterious developmental consequences associated with malnutrition.

Theories of Malnutrition Effects

Several theories have been advanced regarding the mechanisms of the effect of malnutrition on development and behaviour. What has been called 'the main effects' model postulates that malnutrition involves a direct biochemical insult to the central nervous system, which is particularly damaging because malnutrition usually occurs during a period of very rapid brain growth (Lester 1976). Pollitt (1987) has been especially critical of this point of view, arguing that it is reductionist and ignores the social context, a context which may exacerbate or reduce the deleterious effects of malnutrition itself. There has, in general, been a tendency to move away from theories which maintain a direct causal relationship between early malnutrition, altered brain functioning and intellectual performance, towards more systemic analyses of the ways in which nutritional and social experiences interact to affect outcome (Dasen and Super 1988).

There are basically two views about the interaction between nutrition and social experience, neither view being entirely independent of the other. According to the one view, malnourished infants and young children demonstrate what Levitsky and Barnes (1972), in their animal work, called 'functional isolation'. That is, the individual withdraws from interaction with the social and material environment, thus isolating himself or herself from learning experiences. With regard to malnourished children, it has been argued that apathetic and withdrawn infants fail to elicit optimal levels of encouragement, stimulation and reinforcement from their caregivers (Super, Clement, Vuori, Christiansen, Mora and Herrera 1981). Another point of view emphasises the disturbing effects that the symptoms of malnutrition have on the caregiver–child relationship as a whole system. This perspective will be described in more detail in the following sections.

GROWTH AND DEVELOPMENT IN THE MICRO-ENVIRONMENT

In the previous sections two points have been stressed. First, it has proved practically impossible to separate specific effects of malnutrition from the influence of other aspects of material and social deprivation. Second, the processes by which malnutrition exerts adverse effects on children's development are inextricably tied up with non-nutritional factors. There are clearly community and family differences between children who become malnourished and those who do not; and between children who attain complete or near-complete recovery and those who remain handicapped by their experience of malnutrition for a significant portion of their lives (Barrett and Frank 1987; Zeitlin, Ghassemi and Mansour 1990).

The effects of poverty on parenting and child-rearing have been dealt with more generally in Chapter 2. In this section, we will draw attention more specifically to those studies which have identified aspects of the home environment and caretaking patterns among very poor communities that relate to both aetiology and recovery from protein-energy malnutrition.

The Home Environment and Caretaking Practices

Several studies have confirmed Ricciuti's observation (1977) that the environments of low-SES homes in the third world are not as homogeneous as it was once thought. For example, Bradley and colleagues (1989) have demonstrated that families within any given SES group differ widely in terms of the kinds and amount of stimulation provided to children in the home environment. In South Africa, Richter and Grieve (1991) studied the qualities of the home environments of 305 African infants. Amongst other things, they found that the mental development of infants correlated with measures of the intentions and actions of caregivers to stimulate their children's development as well as with measures of the organisation of the physical environment. Within the generally poor group of township families studied, SES was found to have only a small effect on caregiver behaviour and on the physical characteristics of the home, as well as on mental and motor development. It was primarily the caregiver's (mostly the mother's) active structuring of her infant's experiences through the ways in which she patterned her interactions with her child and the ways in which she arranged the child's environmental experiences, which was found to have important implications for cognitive development.

These aspects of the home environment and of caretaking practices are known as the micro-environment of the child. The micro-environment of young children, or the 'developmental niche' as it is referred to by Super (1989), constitutes the proximal, day-by-day experience of young children, to which socio-economic variables are only distally related.

Many studies of malnutrition in young children have identified disturbances of the home environment and in caretaking practices that appear to be closely related to the child's condition and to recovery. Some of the structural features of the home environment frequently associated with malnutrition are single parenthood, desertion by the father, family disorganisation, low levels of maternal social support, care of the child by people other than the parents, and secondary or even tertiary economic dependence of the malnourished child on income-earning adults other than the child's own parents. Trudy Thomas, working in the Ciskei in South Africa, has persistently drawn attention to the family as the nexus of the problem of malnutrition. She has argued that the main determinant of protein-energy malnutrition is disorganisation of home and family life as this occurs under conditions of poverty (1981).

Similarly, Dixon, Le Vine and Brazelton (1982), in a Kenyan study, reported that a common risk factor for malnutrition was an alteration in the usual attachment of the child to a primary caregiver. 'At some time', they say, 'societal, familial, individual and economic events combined to produce this "bonding failure", with nutritional failure as a secondary event' (1982: 680). They go on to suggest that the malnutrition of these children should be conceptualised as a 'disorder of attachment', in the same way that failure to thrive as well as abuse and neglect has been conceptualised in the West. From this point of view, the growth failure of infants and young children is seen to be the result of 'psycho-nutritional deprivation'.

Mother–Child Interaction

How poverty and disorganised and disrupted family life exert their effects on young children is mainly through the way caretaker–child interactions are affected. In the only prospective study of malnutrition yet conducted, Cravioto and Delicardie (1976), working in Mexico, described features of mother–child interaction which preceded the onset of protein-energy malnutrition and appeared to be causally related to it. Specifically, they concluded that a low level of home stimulation and a passive, traditional mother, unaware of the needs of her child and responding in a minimal way as if unable to decode the infant's signals, are characteristic features of the poor micro-environment that lead to clinical malnutrition.

Rossetti-Ferreira (1978) first formally articulated the view that the behavioural features of malnourished children, together with the depleting effects of grinding poverty, create circumstances in which normal mothering is difficult to maintain. She suggested that a cycle of interactional deprivation is created through both the unavailability of the caregiver and the undernourished child's loss of interest in the social environment.

Dysfunctional interactions between malnourished children and their mothers have now been documented in a number of studies. Cravioto and Delicardie (1976) described the mothers in their study as being less interested in their children's performance, less responsive, less sensitive to their children's needs, less verbally communicative, and less emotionally involved with their children than control mothers. Valenzuela (1990) reported disturbed attachments, as measured in Ainsworth's 'strange situation', between malnourished children and their caregivers. Richter, Bac and Hay (1990) showed, in an 18-month follow-up study of 26 malnourished children and their matched controls in South Africa, that attachment status was significantly related to the rate of catch-up growth displayed by malnourished infants after discharge from a treatment unit.

As Galler and colleagues (1984) note, observations of dysfunctional patterns of infant care and mother–child interaction in malnutrition go beyond the idea that such patterns are merely associated with protein-energy malnutrition. It is now being maintained that these child-care characteristics may be significantly involved in the aetiology of malnutrition. Hepner and Maiden (1977) argue that not only may inadequate care precipitate malnutrition but, in reverse, adequate 'mothering' may be protective of a child under the combined stresses of rapid growth and low-quality nutrient intake.

Various views have been expressed about the origin of these 'inadequacies' in the care of malnourished children, all of which have important implications for models of intervention. First, there is what might be called the 'lack of affection' hypothesis exemplified in the views of Shorter (1977). He argued that the expression of affection towards infants was dependent upon the existence in the particular society of a philosophy of 'maternal sentiment'. He suggests that such a sentiment only appeared in Europe in the late nineteenth century among the upper classes and that it has only gradually and incompletely spread elsewhere. Contentious as this specific hypothesis is, it does relate to views that childhood is not an ahistorical phenomenon (Kessen 1983).

Second, there is the idea that poor women, or specifically women whose children become malnourished, are ignorant of appropriate child-care techniques. While most intervention models are based on this supposition there is very little evidence to support this contention (Pollitt 1973). Richter and Mphelo (1991) have recently criticised this model, arguing that it demeans women who already feel helpless and hopeless about their situations.

Third, a number of anthropologists have drawn attention to child-care practices which they have termed 'benign neglect'. For example, Cassidy (1980) has described a number of specific cultural practices of which malnutrition is an indirect, often accidental effect – such as limiting the protein intake of toddlers, or encouraging independence in young children by letting weanlings compete with siblings for food.

Scheper-Hughes (1985) has described another form of benign neglect, expressed in maternal detachment from infants judged too weak to survive. In her study of women in a Brazilian shantytown, she found that an infant's survival was highly dependent on the mother's perception of the child's constitu-

tion and temperament as one fit for the uphill struggle in life under those conditions. Quieter and slower babies tended to be handled with less affection. In a
study amongst the Maasai in Kenya, De Vries (1987) found that it was the tem-
peramentally 'difficult' children who seemed best able to survive in the harsh
environment inhabited by these people – unlike in the West, where tempera-
mentally 'easy' babies have been found to have an adaptive advantage.

In our own work, we have pursued the idea that maternal emotional state is
critical to the disturbance in child care so often evident amongst malnourished
children. What seems to have been ignored in earlier writing is the obvious fact
that the social and material conditions invariably associated with malnutrition are
also the social and material conditions most likely to give rise to depression in
women and to what Polansky, Borgman and De Saix (1972) call an 'apathy–
futility' syndrome.

Disturbances of Affect in Malnutrition

It is well known that malnutrition disturbs the emotional and social functions
of infants and young children. However, less often has the disturbed caregiving
behaviour of the mothers of malnourished children been described from the
same perspective, despite a great deal of direct and indirect evidence for the idea
of disturbed motivational and emotional states in mothers of malnourished children. For example, Kerr, Bogues and Kerr (1978) reported that the mothers of
malnourished children they studied were depressed and socially isolated, and had
low self-esteem and low energy levels. Richter and Mphelo (1991) reported
clinical levels of depression in nearly 70% of the mothers of malnourished children admitted to a rehabilitation unit in South Africa. Salt, Galler and Ramsey
(1988) reported both low morale and depression in mothers of malnourished
children. The authors argue that while these maternal states may well result from
the stresses of caring for a sick and irritable child, such maternal emotional states
nonetheless exacerbate the impact of malnutrition on children by modifying
maternal responsiveness in child-care encounters.

In addition, accounts of the interpersonal behaviour of mothers with malnourished children indicate some similarities with those of depressed mothers,
particularly in terms of their watchfulness, inactivity and low levels of expres-
siveness (Alvarez, Wurgaft and Wilder 1982; Kamwendo, Vaughan and
O'Dowd 1987). Epidemiological studies have also shown that mothers of preschoolers, particularly those who lack social support and have increased stresses,
experience high levels of depression. For example, Puckering (1989) concludes
that depression occurs in 20–30% of mothers of preschool children. In South
Africa, Cleaver and Botha (1989) reported that 74% of the African women they
studied experienced negative or ambivalent feelings towards their young babies
– primarily related to lack of support or involvement by the child's father.

Thus it is possible, although not yet certain, that depression in mothers may
precipitate detached, or what some call neglectful, caretaking and thus a full-
blown episode of protein-energy malnutrition. If this is so, depressed states in
mothers have important consequences for the recovery and rehabilitation of
young malnourished children. It is well documented that depressed mothers dis-

play atypical parenting and that they are less successful in eliciting positive emotional states in their infants (Field, Healy, Goldstein and Guthertz 1990). For a
malnourished child, maternal depression may create a further environmental disability which, conjointly with other adverse conditions, may hamper full recovery of the developmental course.

This focus has facilitated a breaking down of the conceptual barrier between
protein-energy malnutrition and non-organic failure-to-thrive. Several authors
have drawn attention to the similarities between the two conditions (Barrett and
Frank 1987; Dixon *et al*. 1982). Maintaining that they are distinct has the effect
of diminishing important dimensions common to both. For example, the division tends to obscure the important role that socio-economic conditions play in
failure-to-thrive, which occurs predominantly amongst stressed and disorganised
lower-class families in the West (Black and Dubowitz 1991). However, it also
obscures the psychological, interpersonal and intrafamilial dimensions of protein-
energy malnutrition. Feeding and eating are not merely physical or mechanical
activities, especially for infants and young children. Many years ago, Widdowson (1951) documented the way in which caregiver handling and child mental
state seriously modified growth rates in orphanage children. While this is a principle well accepted in the field of failure-to-thrive and in the development of
therapeutic models to deal with that condition, it is, as yet, disappointingly
absent from rehabilitation models for work with malnourished children.

TRANSACTIONAL MODELS OF UNDERNUTRITION

We now have several complex models for conceptualising both normal and
disturbed development, including Bronfenbrenner's (1977) 'ecological model',
the notion of the 'developmental niche' as a concept for organising information
about the micro-environments of children (Super 1989), and the 'new morbidity', an integrated, multivariate perspective on why and how biomedical, environmental and psychological factors affect children's health and well-being
(Baumeister *et al*. 1991). A variety of 'transactional models' which attempt to
integrate economic, cultural, social, familial and psychological influences on the
course and outcome of development have also been proposed (e.g. Sameroff and
Chandler 1975). These models have three common elements. The first is the
concept of synergy, which implies that forces at different levels (e.g. at the
socio-economic and psychological) may merge to exacerbate, modulate or
decrease their combined individual effects on development. The second is the
assumed link between the society, its institutions and conditions of life, and the
behaviour of adults who act as the socialising agents of children. The third is the
self-righting tendencies which operate in human development and which provide the impetus for recovery from exposure to adverse effects.

Many developmental theorists stress the pervasive and powerful influence of
socio-economic variables on children's development. However, conceptual
problems inhere in linking socio-economic forces to children's day-to-day
experiences in the home (see Chapter 2). Generally, it is thought that high risk
environments, like those associated with poverty, inhibit or complicate (rather

than facilitate) healthy development. Such environments uncover and magnify both the child's and the parent's vulnerabilities, and reduce the supports that could enable parent and child to overcome weaknesses or recover from deficits (Solnit 1984).

On the basis of theoretical advances made in some of these models we propose that a transactional model of protein-energy malnutrition includes, at least, the following levels of factor which operate in environments of poverty:

- riskful physical environments
- poor parental education and unemployment
- fragmented family life, unstable and disrupted child-care practices
- economic and psychological dependency
- high levels of life stress and social isolation
- poor parental morale and emotional withdrawal
- infant vulnerabilities (e.g. temperament, illness, sex)
- difficulties in caregiving.

Malnutrition itself is thus an expression of failure in child care in a poverty situation. We speculate that children may become malnourished as a result of forces operating at any of the proposed levels. However, we consider that the prognosis of any particular child worsens as the aetiological factors included at more levels become compounded. For example, a child who develops protein-energy malnutrition as a result of the combined forces of undernutrition in a poverty situation and persistent exposure to infections is likely to have a better prognosis than a child whose condition is the result of the combined forces of these factors together with poor parental morale and difficulties in caregiving.

Any model of the effects of malnutrition on children's development has to include an appreciation of the importance of the continuity of care and what Saco-Pollitt, Pollitt and Greenfield (1985) call the 'cumulative deficit hypothesis'. By this term these authors indicate the increasingly negative effects engendered by the continuity of a child's exposure to an environment that does not meet its physical and psychological needs. Prolonged exposure to adverse environments which offer few opportunities for recovery diverts the trajectory of growth and development further and further from the standard. As Birns and Noyes (1984) observe, it is not single events or experiences which produce healthy or pathological development. Long-term positive human relationships and the provision of stable, healthy environments for children are the most important determinants that we know of for normal human development.

CONCLUSION

On the basis of the material presented in this chapter, it is clear that simplistic or one-dimensional comparisons of the psychological performance of low birth weight or malnourished children with control groups are not likely to have much place in future research. In order to extend current knowledge, a lead should be taken from transactional models which stress context, synergy and resilience. On the basis of these models, future studies should concentrate on the social context of poor growth and particularly on the micro-environment of child care, the nature of synergistic interactions between factors involved in poor growth as it occurs as part of generalised conditions of deprivation, as well as individual resilience and its relationship to protective factors nested in the social environment.

Prospective, longitudinal studies are best suited, as designs, to addressing many of these issues, but in South Africa these would also need to be based on an appreciation of the total ecology of childhood deprivation in this country. On a more specific level, there is an urgent need for research directed at designing intervention, as well as on specific goals for children, communities and families.

Perhaps most important is the need for collaborative research between social scientists and health and education professional which aims to prioritise, develop and apply indicators of childhoods well-being. These goals and tools are necessary for conducting the kind of social surveillance essential for monitoring the developmental states of young children and the conditions of their care. Part of our health and welfare brief should comprise ongoing audits of our policies and practices in regard to children, as well as of the effects of our actions on children's health and well-being.

References

Alvarez, M., Wurgaft, F. and Wilder, H. (1982). Non verbal language in mothers with malnourished infants: A pilot study. *Social Science and Medicine, 16,* 1365–1369.

Barrett, D. (1984). Methodological requirements for conceptually valid research studies on the behavioral effects of malnutrition. In J. Galler (ed.), *Nutrition and Behavior,* Volume 5. New York: Plenum Press.

Barrett, D. and Frank, D. (1987). *The Effects of Undernutrition on Children's Behavior.* New York: Gordon and Breach.

Bartel, P. (1980). Findings of EEG and psychomotor studies on malnourished children. In R.D. Griesel (ed.), *Malnutrition in Southern Africa.* Pretoria: University of South Africa.

Baumeister, A., Kupstas, F. and Klindworth, L. (1991). The new morbidity: A national plan of action. *American Behavioral Scientist, 34,* 468–500.

Binsacca, D., Ellis, J., Martin, D. and Petitti, D. (1987). Factors associated with low birth weight in an inner city: The role of financial problems. *American Journal of Public Health, 77,* 505–506.

Birch, H. and Gussow, G. (1970). *Disadvantaged Children.* New York: Grune and Stratton.

Birns, B. and Noyes, D. (1984). Child nutrition: The role of theory in the world of politics. *International Journal of Mental Health, 12,* 22–42.

Black, M. and Dubowitz, H. (1991). Failure-to-thrive: Lessons from animal models and developing countries. *Journal of Developmental and Behavioral Pediatrics, 12,* 259–274.

Bogin, B. and MacVean, R. (1983). The relationship of socio-economic status and sex to body size, skeletal maturation and cognitive status of Guatemalan City school children. *Child Development, 54,* 115–128.

Boone, M. (1985). Social and cultural factors in the etiology of low birth weight among disadvantaged blacks. *Social Science and Medicine, 20,* 1001–1011.

Bradley, R., Caldwell, B., Rock, S., Casey, P. and Nelson, J. (1987). The early development of low birth weight infants: Relationship to health, family status, family context, family processes, and parenting. *International Journal of Behavioral Development, 10,* 301–318.

Bradley, R., Caldwell, B., Rock, S., Ramey, C., Barnard, K., Gray, C., Hammond, M., Mitchell, S., Gottfried, A., Siegel, L. and Johnson, D. (1989). Home environment and cognitive development in the first 3 years of life: A collaborative study involving six sites and three ethnic groups in North America. *Developmental Psychology, 25,* 217–235.

Brazelton, T., Tronick, E., Lechtig, A., Lasky, R. and Klein, R. (1977). The behavior of nutritionally deprived Guatemalan infants. *Developmental Medicine and Child Neurology, 19*, 364–372.

Bronfenbrenner, U. (1977). Toward an experimental ecology of human development. *American Psychologist, 32*, 513–531.

Brown, J. and Bakeman, R. (1980). Relationships of human mothers with their infants during the first year of life: Effects of prematurity. In R. Bell and W. Smotherman (eds), *Maternal Influences and Human Behavior*. New York: Spectrum.

Brozek, J. (1980). Malnutrition research around the world: Recent developments. In R.D. Griesel (ed.), *Malnutrition in Southern Africa*. Pretoria: University of South Africa.

Cameron, N. (1986). Standards for human growth: Their construction and use. *South African Medical Journal, 70*, 422–425.

Carson, D. and Greeley, S. (1988). Not by bread alone: Reversing the effects of childhood malnutrition. *Early Child Development and Care, 30*, 117–131.

Cassidy, C. (1980). Benign neglect and toddler malnutrition. In L. Greene and F. Johnson (eds), *Social and Biological Predictors of Nutritional Status, Physical Growth and Neurological Development*. New York: Academic Press.

Christiansen, N., Mora, J. and Herrera, M. (1975). Family social characteristics related to physical growth of young children. *British Journal of Preventive and Social Medicine, 29*, 121–130.

Cleaver, G. and Botha, A. (1989). Experiences of motherhood amongst a group of Tswana mothers. Paper presented at the 7th National Conference of the Psychological Association of South Africa, Durban.

Coovadia, H., Adhikari, M., and Mthethwa, D. (1977). Physical growth of Negro children in the Durban area. *Tropical and Geographical Medicine, 30*, 373–378.

Cowley, J. and Griesel, R. (1964). Low protein diet and emotionality in the albino rat. *Journal of Genetic Psychology, 104*, 89–98.

Cravioto, J. and Delicardie, E. (1976). Microenvironmental factors in severe protein-calorie malnutrition. In N. Scrimshaw and M. Behar (eds), *Nutrition and Agricultural Development*. New York: Plenum.

Crnic, L. (1984). Nutrition and mental development. *American Journal of Mental Deficiency, 88*, 526–533.

Dasen, P. and Super, C. (1988). The usefulness of a cross-cultural approach in studies of malnutrition and psychological development. In P. Dasen, J. Berry and N. Sartorius (eds), *Health and Cross-Cultural Psychology: Toward Applications*. New Delhi: Sage.

De Vries, M. (1987). Cry babies, culture and catastrophe: Infant temperament among the Masai. In N. Scheper-Hughes (ed.), *Child Survival: Anthropological Perspectives on the Treatment and Maltreatment of Children*. Dordrecht: D. Reidel Publishing Co.

Dixon, S., Le Vine, R. and Brazelton, T. (1982). Malnutrition: A closer look at the problem in an East African village. *Developmental Medicine and Child Neurology, 24*, 670–685.

Dohrenwend, B. (1973). Social status and stressful life events. *Journal of Personality and Social Psychology, 28*, 225–235.

Ernhart, C. and Marler, M. (1987). Size and cognitive development in early preschool years. *Psychological Reports, 61*, 103–106.

Escalona, S. (1987). *Critical Issues in the Early Development of Premature Infants*. London: Yale.

Fairchild, M., Haas, J. and Habicht, J. (1989). Iron deficiency and behavior: Criteria for testing causality. *American Journal of Clinical Nutrition, 50*, 566–574.

Field, T., Healy, B., Goldstein, S. and Guthertz, M. (1990). Behavior-state matching and synchrony in mother–infant interactions of nondepressed versus depressed dyads. *Developmental Psychology, 26*, 7–14.

Fleischer, S. and Turkewitz, G. (1984). The use of animals for understanding the effects of malnutrition on human behavior: Models vs a comparative approach. In J. Galler (ed.), *Nutrition and Behavior*, Volume 5. New York: Plenum Press.

Francis-Williams, J. and Davies, P. (1974). Very low birth weight and later intelligence. *Developmental Medicine and Child Neurology, 16*, 709–728.

Galler, J. (1984). Behavioral consequences of malnutrition in early life. In J. Galler (ed.), *Nutrition and Behavior*, Volume 5. New York: Plenum Press.

Galler, J. and Ramsey, F. (1989). A follow-up study of the influence of early malnutrition on development: Behavior at home and at school. *Journal of the American Academy of Child and Adolescent Psychiatry, 28,* 254–261.

Galler, J., Ramsey, F., Solimano, G., Lowell, W. and Mason, E. (1983). The influence of early malnutrition on subsequent behavioral development I: Degree of impairment in intellectual performance. *Journal of the American Academy of Child Psychiatry, 22,* 8–15.

Galler, J., Ricciuti, H., Crawford, M. and Kucharski, L. (1984). The role of the mother-infant interaction in nutritional disorders. In J. Galler (ed.), *Nutrition and Behavior.* New York: Plenum Press.

Giblin, P., Poland, M., Waller, J. and Ager, J. (1988). Correlates of neonatal morbidity: Maternal characteristics and family resources. *Journal of Genetic Psychology, 149,* 527–533.

Gomez, F., Galvan, R., Frenk, S., Munoz, J., Chavez, R. and Vasquez, J. (1956). Mortality in second and third degree malnutrition. *Journal of Tropical Pediatrics, 2,* 77–83.

Gray, J., Dean, R. and Lowrie, R. (1988). Relationship between socio-economic status and perinatal complications. *Journal of Clinical Child Psychology, 17,* 352–358.

Griesel, R. and Richter, L. (1987). Psychosocial studies of malnutrition in South Africa. In G. Bourne (ed.), *World Review of Nutrition and Dietetics.* Basel: Karger.

Griesel, R., Richter, L. and Belciug, M. (1990). Electro-encephalography and performance in a poorly nourished South African population. *South African Medical Journal, 78,* 539–543.

Gross, R. and Monteiro, C. (1989). Urban nutrition in developing countries: Some lessons to learn. *Food and Nutrition Bulletin, 11,* 14–20.

Habicht, J., Meyers, L. and Brownie, C. (1982). Indicators for identifying and counting the improperly nourished. *American Journal of Clinical Nutrition, 35,* 1241–1254.

Hamill, P., Drizd, T., Johnson, C., Reed, R. and Roche, A. (1977). *NCHS Growth Curves for Children Birth – 18 Years.* National Center for Health Statistics, U.S. Department of Health, Education and Welfare.

Hansen, J. (1984). Food and nutrition policy with relation to poverty: The child malnutrition problem in South Africa. Second Carnegie Inquiry into Poverty and Development in Southern Africa, Paper No. 205, Cape Town.

Hepner, R. and Maiden, N. (1977). Growth rate, nutrient intake and 'mothering' as determinants of malnutrition in disadvantaged children. *Nutrition Reviews, 29,* 219–223.

Humphreys, L., Davey, T. and Park, R. (1985). Longitudinal correlation analysis of standing height and intelligence. *Child Development, 56,* 1465–1478.

Husaini, Y., Husaini, M. and Sulaiman, Z. (1986). Maternal malnutrition, outcome of pregnancy, and a simple tool to identify women at risk. *Food and Nutrition Bulletin, 8,* 71–76.

Jones, R., Cummins, M. and Davies, P. (1979). Infants of very low birth weight: A 15-year analysis. *Lancet,* 1332–1335.

Kamwendo, A., Vaughan, M. and O'Dowd, T. (1987). Maternal depression and the preschool child. *Early Child Development and Care, 27,* 31–42.

Keller, A. (1981). Epidemiological characteristics of preterm birth. In S. Friedman and M. Sigman (eds), *Preterm Birth and Psychological Development.* New York: Academic Press.

Kerr, M., Bogues, J. and Kerr, D. (1978). Psychological function of mothers of malnourished children. *Pediatrics, 62,* 778–784.

Kessen, W. (1983). The child and other cultural inventions. In F.S. Kessel and A. W. Siegel (eds), *The Child and Other Cultural Inventions.* New York: Praeger.

Klein, R., Irwin, M., Engle, P. and Yarbrough, C. (1977). Malnutrition and mental development in rural Guatemala. In N. Warren (ed.), *Advances in Cross-Cultural Psychology.* New York: Academic Press.

Klein, R, Kagan, J., Freeman, H., Yarbrough, C. and Habicht, J. (1972). Is big smart? The relation of growth to cognition. *Journal of Health and Social Behaviour, 13,* 219–225.

Kopp, C. (1983). Risk factors in development. In M. Haith and J. Campos (eds), *Infancy and Developmental Psychobiology,* Volume II: *Handbook of Child Psychology,* 4th edition. New York: John Wiley.

Kopp, C. (1990). Risks in infancy: Appraising the research. *Merrill-Palmer Quarterly, 36,* 117–140.

Lester, B (1976). Psychological and central nervous system consequences of protein-calorie malnutrition: A review of research findings and some implications. *Interamerican Journal of Psychology*, *10*, 17–31.

Lester, B. (1979). A synergistic process approach to the study of prenatal malnutrition. *International Journal of Behavioral Development*, *2*, 377–393.

Levin, J. and DeFrank, R. (1988). Maternal stress and pregnancy outcomes: A review of the psychosocial literature. *Journal of Psychosomatic Obstetrics and Gynaecology*, *9*, 3–16.

Levitsky, D. and Barnes, R. (1972). Nutritional and environmental interactions in the behavioral development of the rat: Long-term effects. *Science*, *176*, 68–71.

Lloyd, B. (1984). Outcome of very low birth weight babies from Wolverhampton. *Lancet*, 739–741.

McGehee, L. and Eckerman, C. (1983). The preterm infant as a social partner: Responsive but unreadable. *Infant Behavior and Development*, *6*, 461–470.

Meredith, H. (1984). Body size of infants and children around the world in relation to economic status. In H. Reese (ed.), *Advances in Child Development and Behavior*, Volume 18. New York: Academic Press.

Mili, F., Edmonds, L., Khoury, M. and McClearn, A. (1991). Prevalence of birth defects among low-birth-weight infants: A population study. *American Journal of Diseases in Children*, *145*, 1313–1318.

Moodie, A., Bowie, M., Mann, M. and Hansen, J. (1980). A prospective 15-year follow-up study of kwashiorkor patients. Part II: Social circumstances, educational attainment and social adjustment. *South African Medical Journal*, *58*, 677–681.

Newman, L. (1987). Fitness and survival. In N. Scheper-Hughes (ed.), *Child Survival: Anthropological Perspectives on the Treatment and Maltreatment of Children*. Dordrecht: D. Reidel Publishing Co.

Palmer, C. and Barba, C. (1981). Mental development after dietary intervention: A study of Philippine children. *Journal of Cross-Cultural Psychology*, *12*, 480–488.

Polansky, N., Borgman, R. and De Saix, C. (1972). *Roots of Futility*. San Francisco: Jossey-Bass.

Pollitt, E. (1969). Ecology, malnutrition and mental development. *Psychosomatic Medicine*, *31*, 193–200.

Pollitt, E. (1973). Behavior of the infant in causation of nutritional marasmus. *American Journal of Clinical Nutrition*, *26*, 264–270.

Pollitt, E. (1987). A critical view of three decades of research on the effects of chronic energy malnutrition on behavioral development. In B. Schurch and N. Scrimshaw (eds), *Chronic Energy Deficiency: Consequences and Related Issues*. Guatemala City: International Dietary Energy Consultancy Group.

Pollitt, E. and Lewis, N. (1980). Nutrition and educational achievement. Part I: Malnutrition and behavioral test indicators. *Food and Nutrition Bulletin*, *2*, 32–35.

Pollitt, E. and Thompson, C. (1977). Protein-calorie malnutrition and behavior: A view from psychology. In R. Wurtman and J. Wurtman (eds), *Nutrition and the Brain*, Volume 2: *Control of Feeding Behavior and Biology of the Brain in Protein-Calorie Malnutrition*. New York: Raven Press.

Puckering, C. (1989). Annotation: Maternal depression. *Journal of Child Psychology and Psychiatry*, *30*, 807–817.

Ricciuti, H. (1977). Adverse social and biological influences on early development. In H. McGurk (ed.), *Ecological Factors in Human Development*. Amsterdam: North Holland.

Richardson, B. (1973). Growth standards: An appraisal with special reference to growth in South African Bantu and White preschool children. *South African Medical Journal*, *23*, 699–701.

Richardson, B. (1977). Underweight – Nutritional risk? *South African Medical Journal*, *51*, 42–48.

Richardson, B. (1986). Changes in anthropometric measurements of South African children: A cause for concern. *South African Medical Journal*, *69*, 11–12.

Richter, L., Bac, M. and Hay, I. (1990). Psychological aspects of the health care of young children. *South African Family Practice*, *11*, 490–497.

Richter, L. and Grieve, K. (1991). Home environment and cognitive development of black infants in impoverished South African families. *Infant Mental Health Journal*, *12*, 88–102.

Richter, L. and Mphelo, M. (1991). Enhancing mother–child relationships in undernutrition. Paper presented at the 7th Health Priorities Conference: Urbanisation and Child Health, Cape

Town.

Richter-Strydom, L., Griesel, R. and Glatthaar, I. (1985). Effects of a nutrition education programme on the psychological performance of malnourished children: A 3-year follow-up study. *South African Medical Journal, 68,* 659–662.

Rickel, A. and Allen, L. (1987). *Preventing Maladjustment from Infancy through Adolescence*. California: Sage.

Riopelle, A. (1982). Protein deprivation and offspring behaviour. In H. Fitzgerald, J. Mullins and P. Gage (eds), *Child Nurturance,* Volume 3. New York: Plenum Press.

Rip, M., Keen, C. and Kibel, M. (1986). A medical geography of perinatal mortality in metropolitan Cape Town. *South African Medical Journal, 70,* 399–403.

Rossetti-Ferreira, M. (1978). Malnutrition and mother–infant asynchrony: Slow mental development. *International Journal of Behavioral Development, 1,* 207–219.

Saco-Pollitt, C., Pollitt, E. and Greenfield, D. (1985). The cumulative deficit hypothesis in the light of cross-cultural evidence. *International Journal of Behavioral Development, 8,* 75–97.

Salt, P., Galler, J. and Ramsey, F. (1988). The influence of early malnutrition on subsequent behavioural development: VII. The effects of maternal depressive symptoms. *Journal of Developmental and Behavioral Pediatrics, 9,* 1–5.

Sameroff, A. and Chandler, M. (1975). Reproductive risk and the continuum of caretaking casualty. In F. Horowitz, M. Hetherington, S. Scarr-Salapatek and G. Siegel (eds), *Review of Child Development Research,* Volume 4. Chicago: University of Chicago Press.

Scheper-Hughes, N. (1985). Culture, scarcity and maternal thinking: Maternal detachment and infant survival in a Brazilian shantytown. *Ethos, 13,* 291–317.

Shorter, E. (1977). Maternal sentiment and death in childbirth: A new agenda for psychomedical history. In P. Branca (ed.), *The Medicine Show: Patients, Physicians and the Perplexities of the Health Revolution in Modern Society.* New York: Science History Press.

Sims, L., Paolucci, B. and Morris, P. (1972). A theoretical model for the study of nutritional status: An ecosystem approach. *Ecology of Food and Nutrition, 1,* 197–205.

Solnit, A. (1984). Keynote address: Theoretical and practical aspects of risk and vulnerability in infancy. *Child Abuse and Neglect, 8,* 133–144.

Stein, H. and Ellis, U. (1974). The low birthweight African baby. *Archives of Diseases of Childhood, 49,* 156–158.

Steiner, E., Sanders, E., Phillips, E. and Naddock, C. (1980). Very low birth weight children at school age: Comparison of neonatal management methods. *British Medical Journal, 281,* 1237–1240.

Stoch, M., Smythe, P., Moodie, A. and Bradshaw, D. (1982). Psychosocial outcome and CT findings after gross undernourishment in infancy: A 20-year developmental study. *Developmental Medicine and Child Neurology, 24,* 419–436.

Super, C. (1989). The cultural regulation of infant and child activities. In B. Schurch and N. Scrimshaw (eds), *Activity, Energy Expenditure and Energy Requirements of Infants and Children.* Cambridge, Mass.: International Dietary Energy Consultancy Group.

Super, C., Clement, J., Vuori, L., Christiansen, N., Mora, J. and Herrera, M. (1981). Infant and caretaker behavior as mediators of nutritional and social intervention in the Barrios of Bogota. In T. Field, A. Sostek, P. Vietze and P. Leiderman (eds) (1981). *Culture and Early Interactions.* Hillsdale, New Jersey: Lawrence Erlbaum.

Tanner, J. (1976). Population differences in body size, shape and growth: A 1976 view. *Archives of Diseases of Childhood, 51,* 1–2.

Thomas, G. (1981). The social background of childhood nutrition in the Ciskei. *Social Science and Medicine, 15,* 551–555.

UN ACC/SCN (1990). United Nations Administrative Committee on Coordination – Subcommittee on Nutrition. *SCN News,* No. 6.

UN ACC/SCN (1991). United Nations Administrative Committee on Coordination – Subcommittee on Nutrition. *SCN News,* No. 7.

Valenzuela, M. (1990). Attachment in chronically underweight young children. *Child Development, 61,* 1984–1996.

Wagstaff, L. and Geefhuysen, J. (1974). Incidence and spectrum of malnutrition in paediatric hospital wards. *South African Medical Journal, 48,* 2595–2598.

Wagstaff, L., Reinach, S., Richardson, B., Mkhasibe, C. and De Vries, G. (1987). Anthropometrically determined nutritional status and the school performance of black urban primary school children. *Human Nutrition: Clinical Nutrition, 41C,* 277–286.

Walker, A., Jones, J., Walker, B. and Tshabalala, E. (1983). When is slower growth noxious? What young are malnourished? *South African Journal of Science, 79,* 351.

Warren, N. (1973). Malnutrition and mental development. *Psychological Bulletin, 80,* 324–328.

Waterlow, J. (1978). Some aspects of childhood malnutrition: Classification, long-term effects, experimental analogies. *Australian and New Zealand Journal of Medicine, 5,* 87–96.

Waterlow, J., Ashworth, A. and Griffiths, M. (1980). Faltering in infant growth in less-developed countries. *Lancet,* 1176–1178.

Wellcome Trust Working Party (1970). Classification of infantile malnutrition. *Lancet, 2,* 302–303.

Werner, E. (1985). Stress and protective factors in children's lives. In A. Nicol (ed.), *Longitudinal Studies in Child Psychology and Psychiatry: Practical Lessons from Research Experience.* New York: John Wiley.

Widdowson, E. (1951). Mental contentment and physical growth. *Lancet, 1,* 1316–1318.

Wig, N., Mehta, S. and Verma, S. (1981). Methodological shortcomings of previous studies on malnutrition and mental development. *Race, 8,* 25–36.

Winick, M. and Coombs, J. (1972). Nutrition, environment and behavioral development. *Annual Review of Medicine, 23,* 149–160.

World Health Organisation (1974). Malnutrition and mental development. *WHO Chronicle, 28,* 95–102

World Health Organisation (1981). *Development of indicators for monitoring progress towards health for all by the year 2000: 'Health for All' Series, No. 4.* Geneva: WHO.

Wray, J. and Aguirre, H. (1969). Protein-calorie malnutrition in Candaria, Colombia: Prevalence, social and demographic causal factors. *Journal of Tropical Pediatrics, 15,* 76–98.

Zeitlin, M., Ghassemi, H. and Mansour, M. (1990). *Positive Deviance in Child Nutrition – With Emphasis on Psychosocial and Behavioral Aspects and Implications for Development.* Japan: The United Nations University.

Zeskind, P. and Ramey, C. (1978). Fetal malnutrition: An experimental study of its consequences on infant development in two caregiving environments. *Child Development, 49,* 1155–1162.

Zille, H. (1986). Beginning life in an apartheid society: Childbirth in South Africa. In S. Burman and P. Reynolds (eds), *Growing Up in a Divided Society: The Contexts of Childhood in South Africa.* Johannesburg: Ravan Press.

5

Health and Psychological Development among Children in Poor Communities[1]

JANE KVALSVIG AND KEVIN CONNOLLY

Introduction

The health of children in poor communities is influenced by many factors, some of which are biological while others are more social in nature. The web of factors is complex. Nutritional deficits, infections, socio-economic and environmental conditions, and behavioural variables affect and are in turn affected by each other. Protein-energy malnutrition and specific nutrient deficiencies have relatively well-documented deleterious effects on behaviour and psychological functioning and ultimately on educational achievements and the capacity to cope with and adapt to the environment (Barrett and Frank 1987; Hetzel 1989; Pollitt and Leibel 1982). A striking illustration of the complexity of the interaction between biological and social variables is the fact that maternal education is the best single predictor we have of child health in the less developed countries (World Bank 1991; Young, Edmonston and Andes 1983).

Infections may influence children's psychological development, either directly or indirectly, by causing nutritional deficits. The frequent respiratory and digestive tract infections which are common among children living in poor communities cause loss of appetite and malabsorption of nutrients and hence malnutrition (Smith, Lehman, Coakley, Spooner and Alpers 1991; Brown 1991; Stephenson 1989; Stephenson, Latham, Kurz, Kinoti and Brigham 1989). In this chapter we shall consider a set of infections endemic to many poor communities in South Africa, namely parasite infections – in particular the helminthiases. We shall be concerned especially with the ways in which children act to become infected with these organisms as well as with how they react to infection.

Risk Factors

A very high proportion of children living under poor social and economic conditions in South Africa are believed to harbour one or more species of para-

[1]Financial assistance from the following institutions is gratefully acknowledged: Human Sciences Research Council; South African Medical Research Council; Janssen Pharmaceutic; Smith-Kline Beecham.

site (Evans, Du Preez, Maziya, Van der Merwe and Schutte 1987). These are especially prevalent in areas of high population density where clean water supplies and adequate sanitation are minimal. The spectrum of endemic parasite infections varies with climatic conditions and population density. Schistosome infections are endemic to warm, low-lying areas but are rarely found in areas where frost occurs because the intermediate snail host cannot establish breeding populations in cold climates. For example, the most common helminth infections in Natal are schistosomes (bilharzia), *Ascaris lumbricoides* (roundworm) and *Trichuris trichiura* (whipworm) while hookworm (*Necator americanus*) is significantly less common. Protozoan infections, notably *Giardia lamblia* and *Entamoeba histolytica*, are also found in many of the same areas. All of these have different characteristics: schistosomes for instance are blood parasites which need water to complete their life cycle. The other species referred to are gut parasites, transmitted from person to person, ingested by mouth in most cases or penetrating the skin, usually through the sole of the foot in the case of hookworm. What is common to all of them is transmission in the environment by means of excreta. In this way the life cycle is completed and the infection is transmitted to other humans. They all thrive, therefore, in similar circumstances – in communities which lack adequate sewage disposal. In the South African context this usually means black peri-urban and rural settlements where there is little or no sanitation provision; schools and crèches lacking adequate toilet facilities are prime transmission sites.

Preschool-age children in such environments are particularly vulnerable to soil-transmitted parasites. This is because the children rarely have shoes to wear and they play on ground that is polluted with animal and human excreta. From this, larvae enter the child's body by penetrating the skin, or the child ingests eggs from the hands or on contaminated food (Reinthaler, Mascher, Klem and Sixl 1988). However, behavioural changes in the host account for the observation that the prevalence of water-transmitted infections increases over that of

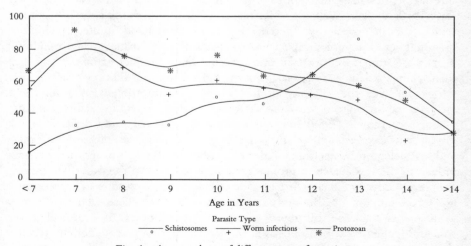

Fig. 1. Age prevalence of different types of parasites

soil-transmitted infections after early childhood. For example, areas where schistosomiasis is endemic tend to be warmer, and older children in these areas commonly play in contaminated rivers and dams. Thus, many protozoan and worm infections which are soil-transmitted are more prevalent in younger children, whereas schistosome infections are more frequently found in older children. This transition is illustrated in Figure 1, which represents data from a parasite survey of 280 KwaZulu primary schoolchildren in the Valley of a Thousand Hills area.

Within this general pattern, different parasite species have different transmission characteristics. *Schistosoma haematobium* (urinary bilharzia) is more prevalent among younger children than *Schistosoma mansoni* (bowel bilharzia) but it continues into adulthood less commonly than *S. mansoni*. Similarly, children tend to be infected by *Ascaris* at a younger age than *Trichuris,* and the age prevalence peaks and tails off earlier in *Ascaris* than in *Trichuris*. These differences in age distribution are probably a function of ease of transmission, acquired immunity, longevity within the host, and changes in children's behaviour as they grow older.

Predisposition to parasite infection is also related to the characteristics of the child. There is evidence of age-related acquisition of immunity in endemic areas, and certain children acquire immunity more easily than others (Butterworth *et al.* 1987). From a behavioural standpoint a significant variable is the selective exposure factor. More vigorous children tend to be at greater risk of infection because of their more frequent and prolonged play in polluted streams during hot summer weather (Kvalsvig and Schutte 1986; Kvalsvig 1988). If the schistosome infection then leads to energy depletion, it is difficult to detect a fundamental difference in activity level between infected children and those more passive individuals who spend less time playing in the rivers.

Under complex conditions of this kind, the design of any investigation becomes especially important. Many studies of the impact of parasite infections have employed a descriptive cross-sectional design in which the selective exposure factor may mask deleterious effects. In South Africa in the late 1960s and early 1970s Walker, Walker and Richardson (1970) undertook a series of studies which failed to reveal any difference between infected and uninfected children on a number of physiological, anthropometric and performance measures. However, these studies did not take into account that a number of infections other than schistosomiasis were prevalent in the same areas, nor did they examine in a satisfactory way the intensity of the schistosome infections. Either of these factors would serve to obscure the detection of effects due to the schistosomiasis.

Further, Tanner (1989) has noted that cross-sectional study designs cannot satisfactorily take account of the fact that most schistosome infections are mild and that deleterious effects might also be masked by the high proportion of individuals in the low infection group. Treatment studies, on the other hand, have been more effective in showing up deleterious effects. In studies of schistosomiasis which employ a before-and-after treatment design, where each child serves as his or her own control, improvements in physical fitness have been demonstrated (Stephenson *et al.* 1989), as have increases in spontaneous activity (Kvalsvig 1988).

Parasite Infections and Schooling

The risk of failure in the first year of primary school is very high among KwaZulu schoolchildren. According to Taylor (1989) approximately one in four children entering the first grade does not proceed to the second grade in the following year. Of course, many factors unrelated to the health of the child contribute to such failure but it cannot be ignored that most children entering school harbour multiple parasite infections, and it is important to understand the nature and extent of any handicap this may impose on them.

There are a number of routes through which parasite disease might affect a child's functional capacity, the most obvious being through effects on nutrition. There is evidence indicating that parasite infections cause malabsorption of nutrients and in some cases loss of appetite (Crompton 1986; Stephenson 1987). This raises the question whether it is more cost-effective in endemic areas to introduce mass treatment programmes for parasite infections or school-feeding schemes. Which of these will have the greater benefit for the affected children? Thus, establishing the direction and nature of any causal link between malnutrition and infection and understanding the processes involved may well have important 'real life' consequences for millions of children.

Although it is not yet clearly established, there is some evidence indicating that parasite infections may impair mental development. To probe the relationship between trichuriasis and behavioural development, Callendar, Grantham-McGregor, Walker and Cooper (1992) examined 19 children aged between 3 and 6 years who presented with the trichuris dysentery syndrome. The children showed deficits initially on each of the four sub-scales of the Griffiths test and, following a series of treatments with anthelmintic drugs over the course of a year, they improved significantly on the locomotor development sub-scale relative to matched but uninfected controls. Nutritional status (weight-for-height and height-for-age) also improved significantly during the year. The existence of some connection between parasitic disease and mental function has been known or suspected for a number of years. Castle, Clarke and Hendrikz (1974), working with a small sample of children infected with schistosomes, reported 'mental fatigue' in these children which affected their accuracy and speed of performance on Thurstone's tests of primary mental abilities. Haycock and Schutte (1983) investigating children in KwaZulu reported that parasite infection, in this case schistosomiasis, was associated with poor progress through school. Nokes, Grantham-McGregor, Sawyer, Cooper and Bundy (1992) report correlations between the prevalence of *T. trichiura, A. lumbricoides, N. americanus* and school performance in a population of poor Jamaican children, and a similar relationship between average worm burden and school performance measured by the class stream into which the teachers placed the children. Streaming itself is a very crude measure of school performance, and these correlations are not necessarily indicative of a causal relationship – each of the variables being a co-variate of other factors such as socio-economic status. However, the relationship is suggestive and it does indicate the need for further investigations employing stronger designs.

In South Africa, poor performance by children on an attentional task has been found to be associated with parasite status, and more severely infected children were found to perform an information-processing task less efficiently than less severely infected children (Kvalsvig, Cooppan and Connolly 1991). Impaired efficiency in elementary cognitive processes may be an important route whereby parasitic disease affects mental functions, their development and their expression in educational contexts. Further evidence which supports this view in relation to memory has recently been reported (Nokes, Grantham-McGregor, Sawyer, Cooper and Bundy 1992).

Kvalsvig and colleagues (1991) found that, relative to their age, children who were undernourished and infected with parasite species were in lower school grades than children suffering from neither condition. In addition, children with the poorest nutritional status and more severe infections had the lowest educational attainment. It is not yet clear whether relatively poor cognitive functioning and poor educational attainment can be considered as direct outcomes of factors known to compromise children's health. Along with poor nutrition and parasitic infections these children also tend to come from households where standards of hygiene are low and where adverse social conditions such as alcoholism and violence often disrupt their lives. Such circumstances are also likely to have deleterious effects on educational attainment and on various aspects of psychological development. Nevertheless, difficult as it is, the more stringent research objective of establishing whether a causal connection exists between parasite infections and a child's intellectual and behavioural development has important practical implications for intervention programmes aimed at raising educational achievement and improving the quality of life of children living in adverse circumstances.

Researchers in South Africa and elsewhere are inevitably faced with these complex questions. In order to generate more useful and testable hypotheses, not only will more stringent research strategies need to be developed but current theories – about such concepts as resilience in children and the factors which afford protection against adverse environments – will need to be drawn upon. For example, Horowitz's structural-behavioural model (Horowitz 1989), which was developed for the purpose of investigating the effects of nutritional deficits on child development, has useful elements that may be more broadly applied. Thus, in this model, organismic characteristics may be conceptualised on a continuum ranging from vulnerability to invulnerability with respect to disruption of a particular aspect of child development – such as language. Environmental factors may similarly be placed on a continuum from facilitative through to non-facilitative. The language development of an organismically resilient child may proceed well even in a non-facilitative environment. On the other hand, language development in organismically vulnerable children may differ markedly between facilitative and non-facilitative environments.

In terms of research design, the multiplicity of confounding factors present in human environments needs, in particular, to be taken into account. Studies of adverse conditions often involve high intercorrelations between several relevant variables. For example, age and level of education are usually highly correlated and may be confounded. However, this situation can be avoided by drawing the sample from either age group or educational level, depending on the hypothesis under investigation. In general, high intercorrelations between variables, termed multicollinearity, can cause high standard errors and unstable estimates in multi-variate analyses. One way to avoid this is to create a new variable which is a composite of several intercorrelated variables (Edwards 1985). For example, measures of sociability in children such as talkativeness, co-operative behaviour and social play are intercorrelated, and the construction of a composite index – in order to assess, say, the effects of parasite infection on this cluster of children's behaviours – would avoid some of the above problems.

The validity of process measures, such as cognitive tasks, in the immediate local context is another important consideration. Donaldson (1978) and others have alerted us to the fact that children frequently have a different understanding of task demands from those intended by the examiner. Also, there is ample evidence that children in different cultures respond differently to a standard test (Church and Katigbak 1988). Similarly, consideration must be given to outcome measures. Those which have obvious practical significance such as educational achievement, failure rates, drop-out rates and individual educational trajectories are likely to have a greater impact on policy-makers than measures which do not have such clearly defined outcome implications.

Some of these conceptual and operational difficulties can be illustrated by considering a study that we have recently carried out with preschool children. Preschool education is now commonly available in many developed countries, and a widely held view is that it is valuable in helping children acquire a range of skills, both social and cognitive, that are required for the child to operate in the formal education system. Our concern is whether parasitic infection has any detectable and significant effects on behaviours related to school readiness. The details of this work as well as the data collected will be published elsewhere. What follows is a general account of the investigation and the broad findings.

KwaZulu Crèche Study

Using direct observational methods to measure and record behaviour in an intervention study, we obtained data on children aged between 4 and 6 years attending informal crèches in two areas of KwaZulu where parasite infections are highly endemic. These informal crèches are established by the community and are not subject to regulation or supervision by any government agency. The two locations differ in respect of climate and altitude, one being on the coast in the Mtwalume area, the other inland at Nqabeni, which is at a much higher altitude. There are differences between the two areas in terms of species and intensity of infections (see Figure 2).

The areas also differ in other respects. Mtwalume is on an access route connecting industrial centres such as Port Shepstone and Umkomaas, whereas Nqabeni is not within easy daily commuting distance from its nearest industrial centre, Port Shepstone. The socio-economic circumstances of the two areas were found to be different, with 49.7% of the adult population in employment at Mtwalume as opposed to 14.5% at Nqabeni. The population density at Mtwalume is higher, particularly in these areas close to the motorway

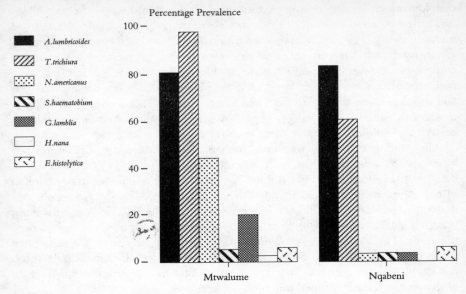

Fig. 2. Parasite infections in two areas of KwaZulu.

(Mtwalume: 334 people per square kilometre; Nqabeni: 214 people per square kilometre). Functional literacy (6 years of schooling) has been estimated at 53% of the adult population in Mtwalume as against 30% at Nqabeni (personal communication, D. Krige, from the 1985 census statistics). Neither area has any sanitation provision but the tribal authorities in both areas have announced that fines will be levied for households without pit latrines. This will be difficult to enforce because many households in both areas are without the means to build the latrines themselves or to pay others to build them.

The sample was composed of children aged between 4 and 6 years in the 16 crèches visited. Meetings were held with parents to explain the purpose of the project and to discuss information on treatment and control of parasite infections. In general, parents were well aware of worm infections and concerned about the effects which these have on their children's health and activity. In a prior study conducted at Nqabeni to document the perceptions of women regarding worm infections of the children in their care, respondents identified several different species of parasites and gave clear and accurate descriptions of the symptoms displayed by affected children, emphasising the pain and misery of those children who were severely infected (Kvalsvig, Preston-Whyte and Mtsali 1990). By contrast, transmission of the infections was poorly understood. Medical personnel at a clinic in the Mtwalume area recalled two deaths of young children during the previous year from inappropriate home medication for worm infections, poignantly underscoring the urgent need for information and assistance in this community.

Parental consent for participation in the study was obtained in all cases. The children were tested for parasites by a medical team on two occasions in the first half of the year before treatment and on two occasions in the second half of the year following treatment. The behaviour of the children was observed during normal crèche activities by a team of specially trained research assistants. Details were recorded on a checklist every 30 seconds during 16–20 observation periods each of 15 minutes duration. Inter-observer reliability checks were conducted before the start of the observations and twice during the data collection period. Agreement was over 75% on all categories on each occasion. Observation periods were spread over at least four days and were always more than an hour apart. The team making the behaviour observations were not aware of the infection status of the subjects throughout the study period. Before the mid-year holidays a medical team toured the crèches treating the children, each child being given treatment specific to his or her parasite infection. In most cases this was a single paediatric dose of a broad spectrum anthelmintic drug, Albendazole, but children with severe infections or schistosomiasis, which requires a different treatment, were treated appropriately.

During the three months following the mid-year holiday break, the psychologists repeated the series of observations on the children, using the same schedule as before. Subsequently, the children were treated again by the medical team for any remaining or new infections.

The Measures

Details of data collection methods will be published elsewhere. What follows here is an account of the principles involved in preparing the data for analysis and the main findings.

Three types of measures were obtained from each child: infection status before and after treatment, behavioural status before and after treatment, and quality of crèche care. The data on several species of parasite were converted to give an index score of parasite load for each child according to a formula devel-

Table 1. PATH score: An index of total parasite load

Species	Weight
G. lamblia	1
H. nana	
N. americanus	
Taenia spp	2
E. histolytica	
T. trichiura	
A. lumbricoides	3
S. haematobium	
S. mansoni	
S. mattheii	
Additional weight for intensity	1

oped in previous work with primary schoolchildren (Kvalsvig *et al*. 1991). There
are advantages in using an index score to describe parasite load. Each child is
typically infected with several parasite species, some of which have low prevalence rates or very skewed distributions. Such data are consequently unsuitable
for use in regression analyses without transformation. In this study, therefore,
the number of species, intensity within species, and the estimated relative patho-
genicity between species were all represented in an index that gives weight to
these different aspects of parasite infection within a single variable (see Table 1).

A composite measure of behaviour was obtained for each child, composed of
the percentage of time spent being active, sociable and vocal and displaying positive affect (see Tables 2 and 3).

Table 2. Brief definitions of behaviour categories.

Concentration	Three levels: attention focused on one activity; divided between two activities; divided among more than two activities, or no focus of attention.
Interaction	All interaction with others.
Activity	Four levels of activity: immobile, stationary, mobile, energetic.
Emotion	Observable emotion at the time of the bleeper, recorded on a 5-point scale from intense negative (crying, screaming) through to intense positive (laughing), with 3 as neutral.
Social play	Fantasy play, games and informal social play.
Co-operation	Active co-operation as in turn-taking, rule-following, role-playing, and singing, dancing or chanting in unison.
Speech	The focal child was involved in speech interchanges, either as a speaker or as a listener.

Table 3. The behaviour index. (Percentage time spent in each sub-category,
weighted, summed & standardised to a mean of 50 and standard deviation of 10.)

Pattern	
Concentration	(Level 1 x .03) + (Level 2 x .02) + (Level 3 x .01)
Interaction	(Interaction x .02) + (Solitary x .01)
Activity	(Level 1 x .01) + (Level 2 x .02) + (Level 3 x .03) + (Level 4 x .04)
Emotion	(Level 1 x .01) + (Level 2 x .02) + (Level 3 x .03) + (Level 4 x .04) + (Level 5 x .05)
Social play	All
Co-operation	All
Speech	All
POSITIVE BEHAVIOUR	Concentration + Interaction + Activity + Affect + Social Play + Co-operation + Speech

Note: Concentration and Emotion were based on all intervals in which the child was
observed, but all other categories were based only on free activity time, i.e. time not
structured by adults.

In the choice of these aspects of behaviour, the assumption was made that in order to integrate well into a school class, a reasonable degree of energy, an ability to concentrate and social competence are important. These we refer to as positive behaviour (see Table 3). Once again, a composite measure has certain advantages over a series of variables treated separately, at least initially. It is entirely conceivable that different children will react to a stressor in quite different ways: one might become quiet and passive, another irritable and socially difficult, and a third tearful. By grouping measures it is possible to contrast those children who appear to be generally unaffected with children who, relative to their peers, are not coping with everyday crèche activities.

General measures of the quality of care afforded by the crèche were made by assessing each crèche on four broad dimensions: buildings, play and educational materials available, staffing, and hygiene and provision of nutrition. A questionnaire was developed to obtain this information (Table 4). For each crèche, scores along the four dimensions were obtained and the crèches classified on this basis.[2]

Table 4. Questionnaire on crèche characteristics.

---

1. Name of Crèche:
2. Number of children generally present:
3. Number of staff generally present:
4. Building: mud walls/earth floor/ concrete walls/concrete floor
5. Toilet facilities: water closet/pit latrine/ none
6. Water supply: piped/tank/carried to crèche
7. Furniture: little/adequate/well furnished
8. Decoration (drawings/picture): none/little/good
9. What is a typical lunch for the children? Is the amount adequate?
10. Toys, Materials, Apparatus:
    Is there a toybox at the crèche? yes/no
    Availability of toys? few/adequate/plenty
    Do the staff use waste to make toys and play materials? yes/no
    Availability of books and pictures? none/few/adequate/plenty
    Are there drawing/writing materials available? none/few/adequate/plenty
    Is there apparatus for outdoor play? yes/no. If 'yes', what types?
11. Educational component: Please describe briefly the educational component of crèche activity. Does this form a large, average or small part of the children's day?
12. Please describe briefly the general organisation of the day. Is there a pattern which is normally followed? Please give a rough indication of time in various activities: e.g. free play, story/rhyme, maintenance, education, etc.
13. Please give a summary rating on the following. Tick best description:
     (a) Hygiene: low   average   good
     (b) Nutrition: low   average   good
     (c) Education   low   average   good
     (d) General level of involvement of children: passive/average/lively and vigorous

---

2. More information on this can be obtained from the authors.

Parasite and Behavioural Status with Respect to the Crèche Environment

A series of preliminary analyses was conducted to determine the relationship between pairs of factors before the final statistical models were selected. It was found that the mean and variance of behaviour scores differed considerably from crèche to crèche. The ratings of crèche standards of hygiene and nutrition correlated significantly with the composite positive behaviour score (rho = 0.21, p < = 0.01), whereas there was no correlation between the parasite index and behaviour scores (rho = 0.03, p < = 0.77). This indicated that crèche quality was an overriding factor in relation to the behaviours measured. In a multivariate analysis utilising two levels of crèche quality (high and low) and two levels of parasite status (heavy and light infection), the model was statistically significant (F = 3.87, p < = 0.0076, r^2 = 0.056201). Only the crèche quality reached the 5% level of significance in predicting the behaviour score (F = 7.46, p < = 0.0072), while the parasite index fell outside this criterion (F = 0.40, p < = 0.5306).

Differences in Behaviour Scores Following Treatment

As expected, there was an overall drop in the intensity and prevalence of

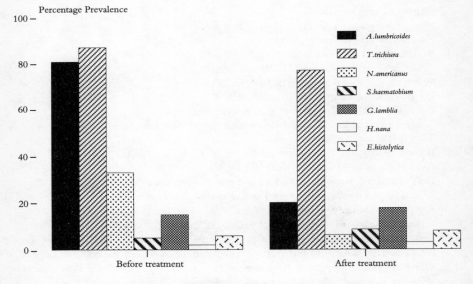

Fig. 3. Parasite prevalence before and after treatment

parasitic infection following treatment. As is evident in Figure 3, the prevalence of *Ascaris* dropped more markedly than did that of *Trichuris*. Also noteworthy is the increase in the number of cases of schistosomiasis. Given that the study sites are in areas of high endemicity, it is not surprising that following treatment there was still evidence of infection in the majority of the children.

The pre- and post-treatment behaviour scores were compared and a difference score obtained. This difference score did not correlate with the crèche quality score across the children overall. There was, however, a high and significant negative correlation (−0.75) between the difference score and the pre-treatment measures of behaviour, indicating that the principal effects of reducing the parasite burden are on those children whose behaviour was sub-optimal, defined in relation to the sample mean, at the outset. To explore this further, the children were grouped into four sets in respect of their position relative to the sample's mean.

(a) Low sub-optimal: children whose behaviour scores were more than 1 standard deviation below the sample mean.

(b) Sub-optimal: children whose behaviour scores fell within 1 standard deviation below the mean.

(c) Satisfactory: children whose behaviour scores were between the sample mean and 1 standard deviation above it.

(d) Optimal: children whose behaviour scores were more than 1 standard deviation above the sample mean.

We then tested the hypothesis that the differences in behaviour were related to the change in parasite status within the four groups. The model was significant ($F = 7.00$, $p < = 0.0001$, $r^2 = 0.320133$) in predicting behavioural improvement, and the post-treatment improvement in parasite score was significant: $F = 13.36$, $p < = 0.0001$.

Conclusions

The main finding which emerges from the investigation is that treatment for parasitic infection does have an effect on children's behaviour. The effect is strongest in those children who were relatively inactive or socially isolated before treatment or both. Although there was no indication from this particular analysis that the parasite infections affected the children's behaviour in the initial phase of the study, the analysis of post-treatment changes did reveal evidence of deleterious effects. It was possible for this pattern to emerge because the complexity of the extraneous factors was contained through using each child as his or her own control. Thus, the magnitude of reduction in intensity following treatment predicted the size of change in the behaviour index. This finding, linking parasite status to behavioural changes in young children, indicates the importance of treating these conditions and maintaining treatment because of residual infection and re-infection.

In our view, these findings indicate the importance of chemotherapy targeted at preschool children, many of whom can be reached and treated by means of the crèche service. Freeing these children of parasites and maintaining a regular de-worming programme are likely to have consequences for the effectiveness of preschool and school programmes. Nevertheless, although the problem can be addressed by medication in the short term, re-infection remains a factor in the environments described here. Ultimately the environment itself must be changed. While there are no easy solutions to the provision and maintenance of clean water supplies and sanitation in areas where housing is scattered, the problem is exacerbated by having different administrative authorities responsible for services in adjacent areas of Natal and KwaZulu. A lot more could be done to improve the health of KwaZulu children if this division did not exist. The fact remains that the transmission of parasite infections does not take place in communities where there is satisfactory disposal of faeces. Bundy (1989) makes the point that even if satisfactory sanitation is difficult to achieve and the benefits take years to become apparent, this does not constitute an excuse for abandoning the attempt.

The quality of crèche care, defined in terms of the nutritional and hygiene practices adopted, emerged as the single most important factor associated with high behaviour scores prior to drug treatment. Arguably, good quality crèche care serves as a protective factor for children whose health is threatened. This finding requires more detailed investigation since crèche quality may not be wholly independent of health status. However, it does suggest that crèches provide a route for improving conditions for these children and they may serve to cushion some of the effects of chronic ill health in early childhood.

The crèche attended, infection status and the characteristic behaviour of the children observed in this study were all relevant factors in the analyses. This emphasises the need for careful research design in the complex circumstances pertaining to studies of this type. Stratification of the sample, the use of before-and-after treatment measures, and the composite behaviour and infection indices all helped to manage the complexity and to clarify the issues. The children entered the study with varying degrees of behavioural competence, and later changes in behaviour following treatment were superimposed on this. Modern statistical packages have made available a variety of multivariate analytic techniques for the analysis of data of this kind. The analyses described above illustrate, but by no means exhaust, the range and flexibility of multivariate techniques that can be used by psychologists working in primary health contexts.

The children we worked with had fallen prey primarily to organisms which they encountered through living in a polluted environment – polluted because adequate sanitation was not provided. Approximately 10% of the sample became infected with water-borne schistosomes during the study period, indicating that as the children become older, more independent and ranged further, they would be vulnerable to new health threats. Simultaneously, the demands made upon them would be likely to change. In the crèche setting, the behavioural demands are largely social: to participate and co-operate in games and play, and to speak out and sing in formal and informal activities – with some introductory, formal educational exercises in some of the crèches. In the more structured school environment, the introduction to literacy and numeracy would be much more cognitively challenging and would occur at a time when many of the children would be coping with new infections. It is not difficult to imagine that children who have not coped adequately in the crèche environment would face a more testing battle to meet these new demands and should be protected from the frequent infections which would make this task significantly more difficult. The challenge is one of creating and maintaining suitable environments for these children, and this, in turn, raises a number of complex theoretical, methodological and public policy questions. We need to understand the processes whereby ill health, caused by conditions such as parasite infection, affects development, both physical and psychological, so that limited resources can be most effectively utilised to improve the lives of these children. Developing the means of measuring complex sets of variables is crucial to this challenge. The work described here is a step in this direction although it is plain that much more remains to be done.

References

Barrett, B. and Frank, D. A. (1987). *The Effects of Undernutrition on Children's Behavior*. New York: Gordon and Breach.

Brown, K. H. (1991). The importance of dietary quality versus quantity for weanlings in less developed countries: A framework for discussion. *Food and Nutrition Bulletin, 13*, 86–94.

Bundy, D. A. P. and Cooper, E. S. (1989). Trichuris and trichuriasis in humans. *Advances in Parasitology, 28*, 107–173.

Bundy, D. A. P. and Cooper, E. S. (1992). Trichuris and trichuriasis in humans. *Advances in Parasitology, 28*, 107–173.

Butterworth, A. E., Bensted-Smith, R., Capron, A., Capron, M., Dalton, P. R., Dunne, D. W., Grzych, J. M., Kariuki, H. C., Khalife, J., Koech, D., Mugambi, M., Ouma, J. H., Arap, Siongok T. K. and Sturrock, R. F. (1987). Immunity in human schistosomiasis mansoni: Prevention by blocking antibodies of the expression of immunity in young children. *Parasitology, 94*, 281–300.

Callender, J. E. M., Grantham-McGregor, S. M., Walker, S., Cooper, E. S. (1992). Trichuris infection and mental development in children. *Lancet, 339*, 181.

Castle, W. M., Clarke, V. de V. and Hendrikz, E. (1974). The effects of subclinical bilharziasis on mental ability in school children. *South African Medical Journal, 48*, 235–238.

Church, A. T. and Katigbak, M. S. (1988). Imposed etic and emic measures of intelligence as predictors of early school performance of rural Philippine children. *Journal of Cross-Cultural Psychology, 19*, 164–177.

Crompton, D. W. T. (1986). Nutritional aspects of infections. *Transactions of the Royal Society of Tropical Medicine and Hygiene, 80*, 697–705.

Donaldson, M. (1978). *Children's Minds*. London: Fontana.

Edwards, A. L. (1985). *Multiple Regression and the Analysis of Variance and Covariance*. New York: Freeman.

Evans, A. C., Du Preez, L., Maziya, S. P., Van der Merwe, C. A. and Schutte, C. H. J. (1987.) Observations on the helminth infections in black pupils of the Eastern Transvaal Lowveld of South Africa. *South African Journal of Epidemiology and Infection, 2*, 7–14.

Haycock, D. C. and Schutte, C. H. J. (1983). Schistosoma and haematobium infection and scholastic attainment amongst black school children. *South African Journal of Science, 79*, 370–373.

Hetzel, B. (1989). *The Story of Iodine Deficiency*. Oxford: Oxford University Press.

Horowitz, F. D. (1989). Using developmental theory to guide the search for the effects of biological risk factors on the development of children. *American Journal of Clinical Nutrition, 50*, 589–597.

Kvalsvig, J. D. and Schutte, C. H. J. (1986). The role of human water contact patterns in the transmission of schistosomiasis in an informal settlement near a major industrial area. *Annals of Tropical Medicine and Parasitology, 80*, 13–26.

Kvalsvig, J. D. (1988). Selective exposure of active and sociable children to schistosomiasis. *Annals of Tropical Medicine and Parasitology, 82*, 471–474.

Kvalsvig, J. D., Preston-Whyte, E. and Mtsali, T. (1990). Perceptions of common helminth infections in a rural community. *Development Southern Africa*.

Kvalsvig, J. D., Cooppan, R. M. and Connolly, K. J. (1991). The effects of parasite infections on cognitive processes in children. *Annals of Tropical Medicine and Parasitology, 85*, 551–568.

Nokes, C., Cooper, E. S., Robinson, B. A. and Bundy, D. A. P. (1991). Geohelminth infection and academic assessment in Jamaican children. *Transactions of the Royal Society of Tropical Medicine and Hygiene, 85*, 272–273.

Nokes, C., Grantham-McGregor, S. M., Sawyer, A. W., Cooper, E. S. and Bundy, D. A. P.

(1992). Parasitic helminth infection and cognitive function in school children. *Proceedings of the Royal Society, London, 247*, 77–81.

Pollitt, E. and Leibel, M. D. (1982.) *Iron Deficiency: Brain Biochemistry and Behavior*. New York: Raven Press.

Reinthaler, F. F., Mascher, F., Klem, G. and Sixl, W. (1988). A survey of gastrointestinal parasites in Ogum State, southwest Nigeria. *Annals of Tropical Medicine and Parasitology, 82*, 181–184.

Smith, T. A., Lehman, D., Coakley, C., Spooner, V. and Alpers, M. P. (1991). Relationships between growth and acute lower-respiratory infections in children aged < 5 y in a highland population of Papua New Guinea. *American Journal of Clinical Nutrition, 53*, 963–970.

Stephenson, L. S. (1987). *The Impact of Helminth Infections on Human Nutrition*. London: Taylor and Francis.

Stephenson, L. S. (1989). Urinary schistosomiasis and malnutrition. *Clinical Nutrition, 8*, 156–264.

Stephenson, L. S., Latham, M. C., Kurz, K. M., Kinoti, S. N. and Brigham, H. (1989). Treatment with a single dose of Albendazole improves growth of Kenyan school children with hookworm, *Trichuris trichiura*, and *Ascaris lumbricoides* infections. *American Journal of Tropical Medicine and Hygiene, 41*, 78–87.

Tanner, M. (1989). Evaluation of public health impact of schistosomiasis. *Tropical Medicine and Parasitology, 40*, 143–148.

Taylor, N. (1989). *Falling at the First Hurdle: Initial Encounters with the Formal System of African Education in South Africa*. Education Policy Unit Research Report No. 1, University of the Witwatersrand.

Walker, A. R. P., Walker, B. F. and Richardson, B. D. (1970). Studies on schistosomiasis in a South African Bantu schoolchild population. *American Journal of Tropical Medicine and Hygiene, 19*, 792–814.

World Bank (1991). *World Development Report 1991: The Challenge of Development*. Oxford: Oxford University Press.

Young, F. E., Edmonston, B. and Andes, N. (1983). Community level determinants of infant and child mortality in Peru. *Social Indicators Research, 12*, 65–81.

6

Children of the South African Streets
JILL SWART-KRUGER AND DAVID DONALD

[He was] covered in scars from knife fights with other boys in the park where he spent his nights. He worked at a busy traffic intersection, wiping car windscreens to get the cash for his survival – and for gambling with other street boys. In his right hand he held the filthy rag he used. The thumb of his other hand was stuck firmly in his mouth.

One of my boys [observed a newspaper sales representative] sleeps in a dustbin in front of his aunty's house in Elsies River – in a big black dustbin. If it rains he puts the lid on. We pick him up every morning [to sell newspapers]. His ma and pa got eighteen children, like that story about the woman who's got so many children she doesn't know what to do. There's something slightly wrong with him. He was robbed of only 70 cents and cried all day long.

These extracts from observer accounts of street children, the first of an 8-year-old street boy in Jamaica (Ennew 1986) and the second of a boy of unknown age from the Cape Province in South Africa (Altschuler, Christie and Warne 1985), vividly illustrate both the resourcefulness and the vulnerability of street children. Yet how is this apparent contradiction to be understood? The phenomenon of the street child in South Africa is an issue of growing concern. Yet the concern is expressed largely through the media and through both positive and negative public reaction that is often uninformed and emotive in its judgement. Difficult as it is to define just who the street children are and to research their transient lives, this chapter is an attempt to clarify some of the social and psychological factors that appear to be operating. Without such understanding the phenomenon will continue to be seen, and responded to, in emotive terms, and the possibility of meaningful intervention will remain remote.

Estimating the Extent of the Problem

In estimating the numbers of street children, let alone in researching the nature of the phenomenon, a major problem exists in the formulation of an operational definition of the 'street child'. Thus, it is a common misperception that children found working, begging or wandering on the streets during normal school hours or late in the evening have given up home or school and are to be regarded as street children. In the early 1980s, for instance, it was believed that there were 20–30 million street children in Brazil alone. If this had been true almost half of Brazil's children would have been living on the streets. By 1987, however, more careful studies concluded that there were probably only about 10 000 children actually *living* on the streets but that there were also many millions *working* on the streets to help their families (Sanders 1987). The latter situation is common throughout the world. Children are widely involved in income-generating activities in order to help their families survive and may shine shoes, wash cars, beg, sell sweets, flowers, lottery tickets and other goods on the streets, or turn to petty theft to do so. The 'normality' or otherwise of this situation is a complex issue, and relates to cultural norms as well as to structural socio-economic factors in different societies. What is important, however, is the need to separate this from the situation in which children actually live on the streets.

In 1983 the Inter-Non Governmental Organization for Street Children and Street Youth (Inter-NGO) suggested that 'A street child or street youth is any girl or boy who has not reached adulthood for whom the street (in the widest sense of the word, including unoccupied dwellings, wasteland, etc.) has become her or his habitual abode and/or source of livelihood and who is inadequately protected, supervised or directed by responsible adults' (Inter-NGO 1983a). More recently, the terms 'of' and 'on' the streets have become popular as a way of distinguishing between children who actually live on the streets and those who do not. When researchers speak of children 'on' the streets, they mean children who 'still have family connections of a more or less regular nature. Their focus of life is still the home, many attend school, most return home at the end of each working day, and most will have a sense of belonging to the local community in which their home is situated' (Morch 1984). By contrast, children 'of' the streets 'have abandoned (or have been abandoned by) their families, schools and immediate communities, before they are sixteen years of age, and [have] drifted into a nomadic street life' (Richter 1988b).

As Glauser (1990) points out, this distinction is not entirely unproblematic as children may move between living on the street and temporary periods with relatives or acquaintances, in child-care institutions or in jail. However, he concludes that such children may nevertheless be regarded as 'of' the streets since what is common to them is that most eventually return to street life despite temporary variations in this pattern.

A pragmatic solution to the problem of identification is to ask the children themselves. Street children commonly have some term which they use to describe themselves. Thus, in Cape Town they call themselves 'strollers' (Schärf, Powell and Thomas 1986), whereas in Johannesburg they refer to themselves as 'malalapipe' (those who sleep in stormwater, sewerage and other large pipes) or 'malunde' (those of the streets) (Swart 1990a). Once the term used by the children has been discovered, those who do not know it or who strongly refuse to be labelled with it are unlikely to be street children.

Even with some working definition of who street children are, it is extremely difficult to estimate their numbers. Because their very lifestyle demands avoidance of identification or arrest, their movements as well as group composition are fluid. Sleeping venues tend to be somewhat more stable but are generally kept secret. However, with a build-up of trust, the sleeping venue may be disclosed, and in at least one study (Swart 1988) a head count of sleeping children was undertaken to estimate numbers in a particular area. Because street children are commonly arrested for loitering and vagrancy, numbers of arrests have, at times, been used as an indicator of the numbers of street children in a given area – particularly by state agencies. However, street children are involved in a constant cycle of arrest, release or escape from arrest and re-arrest. Since a single child may be arrested several times in the same year, and in different areas, estimates based on arrest are likely to be inflated or confusing.

Despite these uncertainties, it is now widely accepted that there are far fewer children 'of' the street than there are children 'on' the street. Table 1 gives recent estimates of these two categories for Namibia and South Africa – including the 'independent' states. (Estimates are derived from the Ministry of Local Government and Housing, Namibia 1990; Swart 1990c; and Richter, personal communication.) The number of children 'on' the streets in South Africa includes those working on farms and is, at this stage, no more than a gross estimate. It is interesting that the ratios of children 'of' the street to those 'on' the street given in Table 1 are not dissimilar to those given by Espínola, Glauser, Ortiz, and Ortiz de Carrizosa (1987) and Swart (1990c) for two Latin American cities. Milazi (in press) also reports a similar pattern for 'bo-Bashi' (street children) in Bophuthatswana but comparative figures are not available.

Table 1. Incidence estimates for South Africa and Namibia.

	South Africa	Namibia
Children 'of' the street	10 000	100
Children 'on' the street	1 000 000	2 000

The effect of current levels of violence in both townships and rural areas on these figures is, at this stage, not known. However, it is likely that the numbers of street children would have increased as a result of widespread family and community disruption.

Street children throughout the world are mostly boys. In Rio de Janeiro about 87% are boys (Sanders 1987), and in South Africa Richter (1988b) reports about 90%. This difference is not clearly understood. However, many girls who do go to the streets tend to become involved in prostitution networks rather than stay on the streets for long periods of time as boys do. Further, in South Africa at least, it is not unusual for kinsfolk and neighbours to take in girls rather than boys, as girls are seen as a resource to help with household chores and small children.

Aetiological Factors in the Street Child Phenomenon

What causes a child to leave his or her family, school and home community for a life on the streets is a complex issue. Most obviously, answers may be sought in the individual life circumstances of the child. However, such answers would not necessarily reveal the structural factors in the society, which are equally important in creating and maintaining the problem at a social level. Most important, neither of these approaches can, alone, provide answers to the intricately interwoven interaction of social and individual factors that play themselves out in the lives of these children (Williams 1988; Inter-NGO 1983b; Schärf, Powell and Thomas 1986).

Social and Structural Factors

Possibly the most important single factor underlying the street child phenomenon is poverty. Clearly, families that are subjected to poverty are also subject to multiple stressors that affect a range of child-caretaking functions (Richter, Chapter 2; Thomas 1988; Toomey and Christie 1990; Ebigbo 1989). However, although it is an important structural factor, poverty alone is not a sufficient reason to explain why children live on the streets. Examples exist of poor societies where the problem of street children has nevertheless been significantly reduced. Ennew (1986), for instance, points out that vast numbers of street children in Cuba had disappeared by the mid-1980s. This is also known to have happened in Nicaragua, where the number of street children was reduced between 1979 and 1980 from 70 000 to 25 000 because of a move to greater community awareness and solidarity (Inter-NGO 1985).

In South Africa, however, poverty is structurally related to, and has been exacerbated by, the policy of apartheid. Socially constructed and maintained in this way, poverty can be seen as a central factor in the creation of the street child problem in this society. Evidence that large numbers of poor black parents have difficulty in providing for the physical needs of their children is clear (Richter and Griesel, Chapter 4; D'Souza, Mashanini, Pongoma and Mashanini 1987). This is supported in the statements of many street children that their families could not support them and had either sent them out to earn or beg for money or been forced to push them out to look after themselves. It also supports their stories of seeking better lifestyles in the cities than were possible in their home environments. Various street children mention not only the meagre provision of food at home but also the lack of finance to meet the costs of schooling. This has frequently resulted in children being teased or scolded at school, leading them to play truant and eventually to leave school and home. The high rate of unemployment also means that children may be regarded as an essential source of income for hard-pressed families (Swart 1990a, 1990b).

The general inadequacy of education for the underprivileged majority in South Africa is a further structural factor that appears to contribute to the street child phenomenon. Of 31 street children interviewed in the Cape, only 4 said that they had enjoyed their school experience while 27 had failed at least once, several of these being repeated failures (Schärf, Powell and Thomas 1986). Despite its being a small sample, to have 87% of the sample reporting both failure and unhappiness in their short school experience is a telling finding. As Schärf and colleagues point out, there are a number of very concrete reasons, including children experiencing beatings at school, that motivate an 'escape from school' (1986:269). The lack of special educational services (Donald, Chapter 8) as well as the teachers' inability to cope effectively with failing students is another clearly important factor that can be deduced from this sample. Many children also lack access to school at all. About 50% of a sample of street children interviewed in Hillbrow, Johannesburg, appeared never to have attended school (Richter 1988a). This may have been related to difficulties in finding access to a school place or to family factors, including finances, or to a combination of both. Whatever the particular reasons for school not being a positive holding force in the lives of these two samples of children, it is clear that the structural limitations in the society's provision of education interact powerfully with individual factors in both precipitating and maintaining the choice of a street life for these children.

Social factors such as rapid industrialisation and urbanisation are known to disrupt family life and relationships and therefore to contribute, indirectly, to the street child phenomenon (Sanders 1987). In Africa generally, children have traditionally been the concern of the community as a whole, and especially of the patrilineally extended household. Progressive westernisation and urbanisation have, however, led to the loosening of extended family ties and a widespread disintegration of the traditional patriarchal homestead (Hellmann 1971; LeVine and LeVine 1981; Uzoka 1980). In South Africa restrictive legislation has aggravated this situation. The Group Areas Act, migrant labour system and influx control have, amongst other constraints on people's freedom, separated men from their families by preventing them from migrating to the cities together. Amongst the social consequences of this has been widespread illegitimacy – by the 1970s illegitimacy ranged from 26 to 60% in African townships (Hellmann 1971). Thus many street children report that they have never known their fathers and that alternative caretakers such as grandmothers or other extended family members were not available to care for them in the absence of their mothers. Schärf, Powell and Thomas (1986:269), for instance, report that most of the street children they interviewed had had a 'limited support structure to soften their hardships' at home. Equally, in Bophuthatswana Milazi (in press) attributes increasing numbers of street children to destabilised family life and unwanted pregnancies.

Associated with this has been an acute shortage of housing. Consistent with the policy of apartheid and its structural consequences, extensive black townships and informal (squatter) settlements have become established adjacent to every major city as people have migrated to areas in which they have been permitted to live and to seek work. In 1988, for example, when the population of Soweto was calculated at almost 1 500 000 persons, over 130 000 were classed as homeless, while in Alexandra, of 120 000 persons more than 21 000 were categorised as homeless (Mashabela 1988). Although people living in these urban areas might still value extended kinship ties, the shortage of housing has mostly forced them to live in more restricted family units (Venables 1951). This has meant that support structures for both parents and children have been diminished and that the number of adults to whom abused or neglected children might otherwise have turned in any one household has inevitably been restricted by structurally determined constraints.

State welfare structures, such as children's courts, places of safety, reform schools and children's homes, which ostensibly exist to cater for 'the child in need of care', have not dealt with this problem adequately. The conditions are often so poor in these institutions, particularly the places of safety, that many children prefer to abscond to a street existence even though, once they have been committed by the courts, absconding is regarded as a delinquent act and the children may be forcibly returned to the institutions. In the Hillbrow sample (Richter 1988a), 20% of the street children interviewed had originally been committed to a place of safety or reform school. The following case illustrates a typical story:

> Ephraim is an illegitimate child with four siblings. He began street life at the age of 9, his mother having died the year before. His mother's relatives took in his two sisters, and his eldest brother was sent to his maternal grandmother on a farm. He and his brother were sent to a place of safety to await placement in a children's home. Since there were only nine such homes for black children at the time, all privately run, they were already overcrowded and the boys felt they would never be able to leave the place of safety, which had a bad reputation. Ephraim and his brother ran away and lived on the streets because they felt there was no alternative for them.

Interviews with children in places of safety have revealed complaints of insufficient and badly cooked food, of inadequate schooling, of having to do hard manual labour and of being beaten. Despite these conditions, children consistently report that had they felt loved and cared for, they would have stayed and put up with the poor food and schooling (Swart 1988).

Lastly, the Group Areas Act (finally abolished in 1990) has had a very direct effect on the presence of children on the streets. In Johannesburg, for instance, before urban racial segregation became effective in South Africa migrant labourers established a series of temporary dwellings or 'slumyards' in a number of the city's suburbs (Koch 1983). In the 1950s, despite black resistance, people in these suburbs were resettled by the government and, soon after, the first media reports of the presence of street children appeared (Motsisi and Magubane 1957). Some children had apparently not been allowed by the Resettlement Board to move with their families, as it could not be proved that they belonged together, while others had refused to move with their families as they wanted to remain with their friends. Since that time the problem has been aggravated by children being separated from their mothers in cases where the latter have been employed as live-in domestic servants. Where a black woman was permitted to 'live in' as a servant in a white area, she was, in most cases, not permitted to have her family with her. About a quarter of all the street children interviewed in Johannesburg have mentioned this as a factor in their lives.

Individual Factors

In order to establish the individual factors that precipitate the choice of a street existence it is necessary to gather information about children's pre-street lives. However, street children often resist giving information about this period in their lives because they fear reprisal or because revealing this information may be emotionally stressful. It is common for them to be 'repatriated' (returned to their homes of origin) after having been picked up on the streets. For example, in a follow-up of 71 street children arrested in Johannesburg in the first six months of 1984, 68 had simply been returned to their homes of origin without existing problems in the home situation being addressed (Swart 1988). A child sent home in this way simply re-enters the situation which drove him or her from home in the first place. In addition, it is not uncommon for children to be beaten for having brought disgrace on the family through arrest and the involvement of social workers or the police. It is not surprising therefore that such children tend to resist revealing details about their situations of origin and may, under pressure, simply resort to untruths.

Gathering information from family or other adults in the child's pre-street life is also problematic. Incorrect information may be given to social workers or researchers to avoid blame or to cover the guilt that such adults might feel in having neglected their children. Since court records generally rely on the same sources of information, they too tend to be unreliable in establishing the nature of a child's pre-street life.

Nevertheless, through a patient build-up of trust it has been possible to win the confidence of groups of street children and from that position to observe them on the streets and to conduct group and individual interviews: these have revealed much about both the pre-street and the current lives of these children (Swart 1988; Schärf, Powell and Thomas 1986). Group interviews, in particular, may be experienced as supportive, and in this context children will frequently verify each other's information, thus increasing its reliability. Once the essential element of trust has been established, it has also been possible to have children co-operate in the completion of psychological tests and, most usefully, to collect drawings from the children and to use these as a way of discussing personal and social meanings in their lives (Swart 1988, 1990b). All these sources of information will be drawn on in the discussion of factors operating in the children's pre-street lives as well as in the section on coping with street life that follows.

In South Africa, as elsewhere in the world, abuse and neglect in the home are common features in the case histories of street children, as are poor scholastic achievement and punishment for this by parents. Street children typically view their home backgrounds as lacking in support from parents, and as being rejecting, overly punitive, disorganised and hostile. Of the Hillbrow sample almost 50% spoke of pain, hurt, anger, rejection or aggression in family relationships (Richter 1988a). This pattern of family tension and disunity is corroborated in the findings of Schärf, Powell and Thomas (1986).

Nevertheless, not all street children are totally divorced from family members. Many return home from time to time to see how their parents are and to take them money or goods. One child's projective response to a picture (of four people walking along a road) illustrates a need for reassurance that his mother is still about, even if she had rejected him in the past: 'They are thinking about home... They don't know what is happening ... so they must go and see... I don't think that they are happy ... because they don't know where their mother is. Even you too won't be happy if you don't see your mother' (Richter 1988a).

In the Hillbrow study, 40% of street children who had joined non-governmental shelters were found to visit family members at least once a fortnight, 35% saw family members only occasionally and 25% said that they had never seen their families since leaving home. Ironically, children who saw their families regularly showed more signs of emotional disturbance than the others (Richter 1988a).

In general, accounts given by street children themselves as to why they had left home fall into three broad categories. These may be characterised as 'push-outs', 'throw-aways' and 'run-aways'. 'Push-outs' are children who for one reason or another feel that they have been actively driven from their homes.

> Alpheus (aged 12) started street life at the age of 7 years when his mother died. His stepfather who had always neglected him then moved into a hostel and refused to give him food, clothes, shelter or money. Under these circumstances he felt he had no option but to move onto the street in order to survive.

'Throw-aways' are children who have come to believe that their parents no longer want them. Although this is no doubt true in many cases it can also be the result of a misunderstanding, as the following case reveals:

> John (aged 9), an only child, came from Bloemfontein in the Orange Free State. His mother explained that when she found he was playing truant from school she was worried because 'he was taking the wrong stitch'. She consulted a social worker about the matter but did not realise that the papers she was asked to sign would commit John to a reformatory. When he was taken from home she felt powerless to correct the situation. John escaped from the reformatory but did not go home because he believed that his parents did not want him. Johannesburg seemed the best place to go as he had heard that there were good jobs and schools there but he ended up living on the streets with other boys who found him at Park Station. When he went to a shelter for street children his parents were eventually contacted and he returned home.

'Run-aways' are children who, in most instances, have left home through fear or because material or emotional conditions – usually a combination – have become intolerable at home. Street life is quite simply seen as a better alternative. Both of the following cases illustrate the operation of fear, albeit of different orders:

> Michael (aged 11) was arrested by the railway police for taking a train ride without a ticket. They took him to Johannesburg where he was given four 'cuts' and released. Lost and frightened, he wandered about until a group of street children said he should join them. He was afraid to go home as

his father had a quick temper and Michael was afraid he would not believe his story or that he would punish him severely. He joined an educational programme for street children and eventually told the workers there his story. They were able to help him rejoin his family.

Joseph (aged 9) lived in a cramped shack shared by his grandparents and ten other persons. His mother was in domestic service. To keep him out of trouble his grandfather would chain him to a post outside the house and abuse him when he was drunk or angry.

What is clear from the above is that individual emotional factors play a significant role in precipitating the decision to leave home and to take up a life on the streets. What is equally clear, however, is that these emotional factors are not independent of structural factors, which can be seen as creating a context of risk for the breakdown of emotional relationships.

Street Life and Children's Coping Strategies

In South Africa, just as elsewhere in the world, street life presents a range of problems with which a child must cope. These include not only the fulfilment of basic survival needs that are normally met within the family – such as finding shelter, money, food and clothing – but also emotional needs for companionship, protection and support. The following account of the nature of street life and of how children cope with it is based on extended periods of ethnographic research conducted mainly in Johannesburg. The methods of information gathering have been outlined above, and further methodological considerations are dealt with in the final section of this chapter.

Money, a basic necessity for survival in an urban environment, is obtained mainly by offering informal services for which small sums of money are earned. Street children push shopping trolleys, wash cars and guide cars into parking spaces. Semi-formal employment includes selling flowers and newspapers and sweeping pavements for shopkeepers. Money is also obtained by gambling ('tiekie-dice' is a popular gambling game in Johannesburg), from begging, and through providing sex. Goods and money are sometimes also obtained through petty theft, pickpocketing and bagsnatching. In Johannesburg begging is called 'phanda' (a Zulu word which means to scratch up something small, rather like a chicken) and selling sex is called doing 'chip-chop'.

Many children are trapped into providing sexual services through being offered food, money or clothing. Having been solicited, they may be given a bath and food, shown a sex video and told to perform sexual acts similar to those they have seen on the video. Payment for such services is usually quite high. Despite this some children, especially those between the ages of 7 and 14, report being so horrified and scared by these experiences that they subsequently run away from people who they believe are soliciting for sex. However, some, particularly older boys who have become more hardened, say that prostitution is just selling a service like any other. It is difficult to establish what proportion of street children prostitute themselves, as children frequently lie about this because they know that such activities are disapproved of. Nevertheless, the indications are that it is a minority – an estimated 10% in New York (Victim Services Agency 1987). Even if this figure were shown to apply in South Africa, the exposure of street children to the risk of AIDS is of considerable concern, and a national study of this problem is currently in the process of publication (Richter and Swart-Kruger, in press).

It is not uncommon for peer groups on the street to be portrayed as 'quasi-families' because they are seen to provide companionship, protection and support for their members. Although this is partly true, the analogy is misleading as relationships within a street group are by nature erratic, temporary and constituted at a fundamentally different level from those of adults and children within a family. Nevertheless, the peer group does have important functions. One of the most valuable is shared information regarding economic activities and safety. The former includes information about places that are best for begging, for washing cars, for getting left-over food or for soliciting. The latter includes information about unfriendly shopkeepers, dangerous locations (specific alleys, bars, etc.) and, most important, how to avoid the police. If the police are seen on patrol, the word quickly spreads and street children disappear from sight within seconds. This reaction is not surprising for police detention of street children is common, as are allegations of police harassment and maltreatment made by street children themselves (Schärf, Powell and Thomas 1986; Swart 1988, 1990a).

It is as misleading to equate street child groups with gangs as it is to equate them with families. That there is little overlap between gangs and street child groups in either membership or social dynamics has been shown by Schärf, Powell and Thomas (1986) based on their research in Cape Town, and this has been corroborated in work conducted in Johannesburg (Swart 1988). In Johannesburg street groups usually have from five to seven members. Some remain together for as long as a year or two but in most cases membership is erratic. Thus individual members may go off to other suburbs which they feel are safer or which offer more income, to coastal towns in winter, or simply to another preferred group. Generally, territoriality appears to be an important factor in the lives of such groups (Aptekar 1988). In Johannesburg it is related primarily to two things – economic activity and sleeping. If competition for money in a specific area is very fierce, children may stake out territories and defend them against others – although, if the area is a busy commercial district, they seem content to share opportunities. Territoriality is particularly important with regard to sleeping since it is difficult to find 'pozzies' (safe places to sleep). Although some children sleep in rubbish bins and on pavements, most prefer more comfortable and less visible 'pozzies'. Stormwater drains, derelict buildings, parks, vacant lots, alleyways, abandoned cars, driveways, shop entrances and boiler rooms are all commonly used as sleeping places. Flattened cardboard boxes not only keep children warm but also hide them from sight. Sipho (aged 18), who had lived on the streets for seven years, expressed the territorial centrality of the 'pozzie' in the life of the group as follows:

'Malunde [street children] have their own special places to sleep. Other malunde can only take them if the others [original occupants] move away.

This sometimes happens after police raids. Otherwise if a malunde has no place or if a lot of boys need a new place, they can ask another group if they can join. Usually it's OK unless there's a boy who hates another one. Sometimes they won't let new boys in because they don't like to get too big or the police see them easily, then they can maybe have some sport by setting the dogs onto the malunde.' (Translated from Zulu)

Shared activities also have an important function in generating group identity and cohesion. Sharing meals, which may be bought from fast-food outlets or which are prepared in tin cans over open fires, is a common activity. Children also strive to collect enough money to buy clothing that is 'street-fashionable'. As with all children they like to have fun. Groups will often walk long distances to attend carnivals and street entertainments and will spend their money freely on arcade games, cheap movies, cigarettes, special items of clothing and intoxicating substances.

'Smoking glue' is a disturbing but common activity involving the inhalation of fumes from glue, thinners and cleaning fluids, which are relatively cheap and are widely used for this purpose (Swart 1988). Children claim that smoking glue not only generates pleasant feelings but also shuts out cold, hunger, insecurity and loneliness. Apart from this it is clear that, as a shared activity, it acts as a bonding process in groups. The negative effects of this activity, however, have also been clearly demonstrated. Allison and Jerrom (1984) have shown that the cognitive performance of children who chronically inhale solvent fumes is significantly affected, in particular their attention, concentration, memory and visio-spatial capabilities. Visio-spatial disturbances are especially dangerous in street life. Thus, of 52 glue-sniffing children investigated in Johannesburg, 28 had been involved in pedestrian traffic accidents of one form or another, and it was common for intoxicated children to hallucinate that motor cars were driving at them (Swart 1990a). Limited attention span, poor concentration, and impaired memory and visio-spatial functions also have direct implications for cognitive and educational development. On a number of cognitive and scholastic tests, for instance, Richter (1988a) has demonstrated that although the problem-solving capabilities of most of her sample of street children were adequate, they would be likely to experience difficulties on re-entry to school in scholastic tasks requiring spatial orientation and verbal comprehension.

The notion of freedom is consistently reported by street children as both the goal and the highest value in their street existence. Schärf, Powell and Thomas (1986:272) portray this as 'freedom from institutions, freedom of movement, freedom to choose activities and daily rhythms, and freedom from commitments'. How street children actually experience these freedoms is evidenced in their lifestyle. In addition, Richter (1988a) has demonstrated, on a locus-of-control measure, that feelings of autonomy and self-directed choice were high amongst her sample of street children.

Nevertheless, the developmental costs of this 'freedom' are high and are not, in fact, within the children's choice. Most obviously these costs relate to the loss of adult nurturance, protection and support – and in most cases, as has been demonstrated, it is precisely these that have been lacking in the children's pre-street existence. A measure of this cost is the high rate of emotional instability, including enuresis, regressive behaviours, anxiety and depression found amongst street children (Richter 1988a), not to mention the physical and health risks associated with street life.

Profound as they are, these are not the only costs. In terms of their social position, street children are marginalised and frequently victimised by almost all sections of the community. This takes not only obvious forms as in the commonly reported rejection by family and home community, police harassment, sexual exploitation and inadequacy of state welfare intervention. It also takes less commonly recognised forms such as harassment by other more powerful street dwellers, including homeless adults, prostitutes and street gangs. Thus it is not uncommon for street children to recount how their blankets or cash were stolen from them while they were asleep or how protection money was extorted under threat of physical violence. Most subtly, however, street children are characterised and stereotyped as both criminal and morally depraved. This characterisation results in attitudes and acts of victimisation at both a formal (police harassment and arrest) and an informal level in the social structure. In a community survey conducted in Johannesburg, 80% of the respondents believed that street children would become adult criminals or drug addicts and 86% believed that the children had different and inferior moral values to their own (Swart 1988). Acts of rejection, dismissal, and avoidance as well as verbal and even physical abuse follow on such attitudes and are, in fact, frequently reported by street children. The irony of this is that the children see their behaviour as thrust upon them by the adults of their world – they have little other choice if they are to survive. Equally, the characterisation of their immorality is inaccurate as a generalisation and is fundamentally problematic in terms of social values. In a study of the children's drawings it was found that clearly defined moral values were in fact common and that conceptions of right and wrong were remarkably similar to those of school-going children in the British Midlands (Swart 1988). Beyond this, even if street children commonly use deception to survive in a world of hostile adults, there is sufficient evidence from observation and group interactions that morality within and between members of the peer group is a powerful force and may, on occasion, extend beyond the group.

Research Issues

Information on street children has been far too widely based on anecdotal and emotive reporting in the popular media. The few substantive studies of street children which have been done provide no more than a starting point for further research, of which much is still needed. In South Africa the greatest need for further research appears to be around the complex interaction of individual, family-of-origin, social and structural factors that are all involved in the aetiology of the street child phenomenon.

Within this framework, the development of an appropriate methodology for researching street children remains a central issue. Thus far, a number of research approaches to collect and cross-check data have proved to be the most useful. As indicated, these have included ethnographic approaches using extensive participant observation, structured but informally conducted interview sessions, group discussions and discussions around children's drawings as well as more positivist approaches using sample statistics, questionnaires and psychometric and projective testing.

However, each of these approaches has problems when applied to street children. Any form of reliable data collection, whether ethnographic or positivist, is made difficult for a number of reasons which relate to the particular lifestyle and attitudes of street children. These are worth recording for the benefit of future researchers. First, because their lives and location are so fluid it is difficult to define a sample or even individual respondents with any certainty or stability. Street children may simply disappear – as a result of their own volition or because of arrest – before research is complete. Equally, if there is something exciting happening at the other end of town at a scheduled interview time, they are unlikely to put the interview first. Although money and food bribes have been used to encourage attendance at interviews these devices tend to reduce the validity of the information obtained. Thus, children have been overheard discussing, with great glee, the varieties of untruths they had told to a 'short-term' researcher in exchange for payment. As we have emphasised throughout this chapter, the very survival strategies of many of these children depend on their not revealing accurate information about themselves to adults – including casual street contacts as well as police, social workers and others – who may be perceived as seeking to 'repatriate' or otherwise control them. The build-up of a relationship of trust with the children cannot be circumvented and is very important for the collection of reliable information. This process cannot be hurried.

Second, periods of focus for information gathering are limited and transient. Particularly when they have inhaled glue fumes, the children's attention span is very short. They may also not be able to maintain the thread of a specific topic during extended interviews and group discussions and may wander off to more attractive activities, fall asleep or become vague while in the midst of a description of some experience. The most productive approach has been found to be one where information is gathered slowly and informally when and where the situation allows. This, again, cannot be hurried.

Third, as Schärf, Powell and Thomas (1986) have emphasised, information given may not be objectively accurate but may nevertheless represent the way the children themselves make sense of their world. Both sorts of information are important but they should not be confused. A simple example is the length of time that children have lived on the streets. It is common for children to report shorter times than they have in fact spent on the streets because, as they themselves admit when pressed, it is difficult for them to remember and they often do not want to admit that they have been 'living rough' for so long. Thus, unless considerable trust has been built up and the children are given some concrete barometer for establishing a time period – e.g. 'How many Christmases have you eaten on the streets?' (Kramer 1986) – their answers to this question are likely to be little more than random.

In summary, the process of information gathering used with street children is crucial if the information is to be reliable. The time, care and sensitivity that need to go into this cannot be overemphasised. In general, a dialogic process built up through time and trust combined with careful cross-checking of different sources of information has been found to be indispensable.

Conclusion

Ultimately, in assessing the developmental implications of children coping with street life, one must return to the contradiction between vulnerability and resourcefulness posed at the beginning of this chapter. Although the children's apparent resilience and ability to survive through adapting to conditions in the most adverse of environments have been amply illustrated, this should not imply a developmental good. The paradox in this is that children who are forced to survive as if they were adults are nevertheless *not* adults: they have neither the same physical or psychological resources nor the same power in the social structure. It is not surprising therefore that their coping strategies are essentially opportunistic; that lying and deceit are fundamental tools of survival in an adult world which has aligned itself against them; and that escape, whether through running away, endlessly moving on, intoxication or the self-persuasive belief in 'freedom', is a common response to the stresses they face. Adaptive as these strategies might be to the particular circumstances that have been thrust upon street children, they do, in the end, constrain developmental potential.

The developmental costs of street life for many thousands of children – physical, emotional, cognitive and social – that have been mentioned in this chapter are too high to be ignored. Equally, it is not sufficient to understand the phenomenon in individual terms. The role of social and structural factors in creating contexts of risk and in perpetuating the marginalisation and victimisation of street children in South Africa has to form a central part of this understanding and of the solutions that are sought.

References

Allison, W. and Jerrom, D. (1984). Glue sniffing: A pilot study of the cognitive effects of long-term use. *The International Journal of the Addictions, 19,* 453–458.

Altschuler, J., Christie, C. and Warne, P. (1985). Unpublished annotated photographic project. Cape Town: Community Arts Project.

Aptekar, L. (1988). Family structure in Colombia: Its impact on understanding street children. *Journal of Ethnic Studies, 17*(1), 97–108.

D'Souza, F., Mashanini, M., Pongoma, Z. and Mashanini, T. (1987). *First Report on Estimating Vulnerability in Black Rural Communities in South Africa.* Johannesburg: Operation Hunger.

Ebigbo, P. (1989). Situation analysis of child abuse and neglect in Nigeria, making use of Nigerian daily newspapers. *African Journal of Psychology, 1*(2), 95–101

Ennew, J. (1986). Children of the street. *The New Internationalist,* October, 3–4.

Espínola, B., Glauser, B., Ortiz, R. and Ortiz de Carrizosa, S. (1987). *In the Streets: Working Street Children in Asunción.* Bogota: UNICEF.

Glauser, B. (1990). Street children: Deconstructing a construct. In A. James and A. Prout (eds), *Constructing and Reconstructing Childhood: Contemporary Issues in the Sociological Study of Childhood.* London: Falmer Press.

Hellmann, E. (1971). Social change among urban Africans. In H. Adam (ed.), *South Africa: Sociological Perspectives.* London: Oxford University Press.

Inter-NGO Programme on Street Children and Street Youth (1983a). Doc 83/23-SC/35, 18 March. Geneva: International Catholic Child Bureau.

Inter-NGO Programme on Street Children and Street Youth (1983b). Summary of proceedings: Sub-regional seminar for the Mediterranean, Marseilles, 14–17 October. Geneva: International Catholic Child Bureau.

Inter-NGO Programme on Street Children and Street Youth (1985). *The Street Newsletter*, No. 4.

Koch, E. (1983). Without visible means of subsistence: Slumyard culture in Johannesburg 1918–1940. In B. Bozzoli (ed.), *Town and Countryside in the Transvaal: Capitalist Penetration and Popular Response*. Johannesburg: Ravan Press.

Kramer, S. (1986). Street children and education. In Institute for the Study of Man in Africa, *Street Children – Four Perspectives* (ISMA paper no. 40). Johannesburg: University of the Witwatersrand Medical School.

LeVine, S. and LeVine, R. (1981). Child abuse and neglect in sub-Saharan Africa. In J. Korbin (ed.), *Child Abuse and Neglect: Cross-Cultural Perspectives*. Berkeley: University of California Press.

Mashabela, H. (1988). *Townships of the PWV*. Johannesburg: South African Institute of Race Relations.

Milazi, D. (In press). Street children in Botswana and Bophuthatswana: Nature and extent of the problem. *South African Journal of Sociology*.

Ministry of Local Government and Housing, Republic of Namibia (1990). Survey on street children in three urban centres. Windhoek: Ministry of Local Government and Housing.

Morch, J. (1984). Abandoned and street children. *Ideas Forum. United Nations Children's Fund (UNICEF), 18*(3), 1–2.

Motsisi, C. and Magubane, P. (1957). The flame-throwers. *Drum Magazine*, January, 22–25.

Richter, L. (1988a). *A Psychological Study of 'Street Children' in Johannesburg* (IBS report 89–01). Pretoria: Institute for Behavioural Sciences, University of South Africa.

Richter, L. (1988b). Street children: The nature and scope of the problem in southern Africa. *The Child Care Worker, 6*(7), 11–14.

Richter, L. and Swart-Kruger, J. (In press). *Knowledge, Attitudes, Beliefs and Behaviour Patterns of Street Children in South Africa with Regard to AIDS*. Research report. Pretoria: Department of National Health and Population Development.

Sanders, T.G. (1987). *Brazilian Street Children: Who They Are*. Report No. 17. Indianapolis: University Field Study International (UFSI).

Schärf, W., Powell, M., and Thomas, E. (1986). Strollers ≠ Street children of Cape Town. In S. Burman and P. Reynolds (eds), *Growing Up in a Divided Society: The Contexts of Childhood in South Africa*. Johannesburg: Ravan Press.

Swart, J. (1988). An anthropological study of street children in Hillbrow, Johannesburg, with special reference to their moral values. Unpublished MA thesis. Pretoria: University of South Africa.

Swart, J. (1990a). *Malunde: The Street Children of Hillbrow*. Johannesburg: Witwatersrand University Press.

Swart, J. (1990b). Of the streets: A study of black street children in South Africa. In P. Hugo (ed.), *Truth Be in the Field: Social Science Research in Southern Africa*. Pretoria: University of South Africa Press.

Swart, J. (1990c). Street children in Latin America, with special reference to Guatemala. *Latin American Report, 6*(1), 28–41.

Thomas, T. (1988). The psychosocial pathology of the homelands. Paper presented at the Conference of the Organisation for Appropriate Social Services in South Africa. University of the Western Cape.

Toomey, B. and Christie, D. (1990). Social stressors in childhood: Poverty, discrimination and catastrophic events. In L. Arnold (ed.), *Childhood Stress*. New York: John Wiley.

Uzoka, A. (1980). The African child and the dilemma of changing family functions: A psychological perspective. *African Social Research, 30,* December, 851–867.

Venables, L. (1951). The juvenile delinquent. *Journal of Racial Affairs, 2*(3), 12–24.

Victim Services Agency (1987). *The Streetwork Project and AIDS*. New York: Victim Services Agency.

Williams, C. (1988). Street-wise: Research and education amongst South Africa's street children. Unpublished paper presented at the Research in Progress Conference, March. York University, England

7

Disadvantage in South African Education: The Issue of Equality and Equity in Transformative Policy and Research

DAVID GILMOUR AND CRAIN SOUDIEN*

Introduction

The extent and quality of formal educational provision are recognised as having major implications for child development in most contemporary societies. In a society such as South Africa where the degree of educational disadvantage suffered by the majority is not only extensive and acute but directly related to the political policy of apartheid, it is not surprising that educational transformation has come to be seen as a central component in the formation of an egalitarian and democratic society. As South Africa moves towards a period of fundamental socio-political restructuring, the demands and expectations generated by the prospects of educational change are also enormous. This chapter will argue that crucial to the realisation of these hopes will be the ways in which equality and equity in education are understood in both transformative policies and the research that needs to inform such policies.

The history of policies of educational equalisation has reflected two levels of focus, namely the individual and the group, defined usually by some indicator of disadvantage. However, history has also shown how the outcomes of such policies have in general neither matched individual expectations nor promoted major group advancements. An important reason why this has happened has been the ironic omission of an understanding of the significance of schools themselves in the research, analysis and achievement of equality. Consequently this chapter argues, *inter alia,* for a re-insertion of the school and the processes that occur in it into the methodological and policy-making processes.

Prior to this, however, it is important to detail the extent and dimensions of inequality in the South African education system, and also to review the theoretical debates around the concepts of equity and equality.

---

*Editors' Note: The authors of this chapter are educational theorists and not psychologists. Their perspective, however, is crucial to an understanding of the nature of educational disadvantage and of transformative policy issues that are necessarily of concern to developmental psychologists.

Inequality in South African Education

The information and tables below give a somewhat crude indication of the quantitative disparities that exist between the race groups in South Africa. Since there are 18 education departments devised along racial and political lines, it should be noted that there are often difficulties in obtaining complete sets of comparative data.

Table 1 illustrates comparative pupil–teacher and pupil–classroom ratios. While the disparities are obvious, it should be noted that these aggregate figures disguise many regional, particularly rural, variations.

Table 1: Pupil–teacher and pupil–classroom ratios (1990).

	School phase	Pupil–teacher ratio	Pupil–classroom ratio
Africans	Primary	45.0	51.0
	Secondary	30.9	40.7
	Total	40.2	47.8
Whites	Primary	22.0[1]	22.0[1]
	Secondary	16.0[1]	16.0[1]
	Total	17.4	n.a.
Coloureds	Primary	25.5	25.6
	Secondary	18.6	22.6
	Total	23.1	24.7
Indians	Primary	23.9	29.3
	Secondary	16.3	26.8
	Total	20.2	28.3

Source: Du Pisani *et al.* (1991:20)

[1]These are best estimates based on information derived from Assessing Policies for Educational Excellence (APEX 1.03), an information base developed by Edusource/ Education Foundation with the Research Triangle Institute. Note: A number of white schools have suffered closure due to shortages of pupils (94 in 1991 – *Cape Times,* 18 February 1992).

As indicated, there are many regional variations that exist, especially in the so-called homelands. For example, in Gazankulu and KaNgwane the 1988 primary level pupil–classroom ratio was as high as 77:1, while in Lebowa the same ratio for secondary schools was 66:1 (SAIRR 1990:827). If a ratio of 40:1 is taken as acceptable, there was an estimated shortage of 37 000 classrooms in 1989 (Cosser 1991:78). This shortfall is also reflected in the per capita non-salary expenditures. Again, the disparities are enormous. Expenditure per child on white pupils was R514 (R2365) in 1986, compared with an average for all pupils of R195 (R871), and a low of R33 (R384) in KwaNdebele (Cosser 1991:91) – the figures in brackets represent the total spending per pupil.

Similarly, pupil–teacher ratios for primary level were as high as 69:1 in Transkei (SAIRR 1990:826). These different entitlements are reflected in three other common measures of inequality, namely survival rates, examination pass rates and teacher qualifications. These are detailed below.

Table 2. Enrolment and estimated outflow from schools (1985).

African schools				White schools		
Enrolment	Outflow	%	Std	Enrolment	Outflow	%
1 839 600	24 300	4.7	A–B	150 800	–	–
2 980 700	227 900	43.8	1–5	397 900	3 400	4.3
926 700	149 700	28.8	6–8	250 400	14 600	19.0
166 100	117 700	22.6	9–10	245 700	59000	76.6
6 013 400	520 000	100.0	*Total*	927 100	77 000	100.0

Source: Adapted from Donaldson, Table 3 (1989:29)

As this table demonstrates, by the end of the primary level there is a massive wastage of African pupils, with large numbers failing to reach Std 5. Again, imbedded within these data are regional and gender disparities. The reasons for this situation, which leaves 'something in the order of 25% of African children ... growing up to be illiterate' (Taylor 1989:12), are varied. Some commentators relate this lack of ability to retain pupils (by contrast with figures for whites) partly to internal efficiency difficulties (Donaldson 1989:29), while others cite a number of mainly socio–economic factors outside the control of schools as being the main reasons (see Taylor 1989:6-7).

Whatever reasons may prevail, it is evident that disparities in material conditions cannot but affect outcomes. Clear indications of this are seen in the results for the final exit examination.

Table 3. Matriculation examination results (1990).

	African	Coloured	Indian	White
Candidates	253 623	22 315	14 542	68 979
Total passes	93 717	17 721	13 816	66 131
Proportion	36.9%	79.4%	95.0%	95.8%
Passed with exemption[1]	20 999	4 487	6 615	28 615
Proportion	8.3%	20.1%	45.5%	41.5%

[1]A minimum number of passes and grades necessary for entrance to university.
Source: SAIRR (1992:208).

As can be seen from Table 3, the differences in the pass rates for the various education systems are stark, and indeed the African pass rate declined by 4.2% from 1989 (see SAIRR 1990:829). As indicated, this may relate to the quality of the teaching staff available. Comparisons show that teachers in the African education systems[2] are relatively underqualified. In white schools, about 40% of teachers have degrees, compared with about 4% for African schools (Ashley 1991:10). Some 13% were without a professional qualification at all (Du Pisani *et al*. 1991:18).

When the above data are combined, a clear picture of inequality in provision and outcomes becomes apparent. This lack of equality not only begins in the pre-primary phase but is carried right through to post-secondary education (Pillay 1990). Clearly, efforts to rectify the situation must take these factors into account and, as demonstrated below, various actors in the process of reconstruction have indeed concentrated on these obvious areas of disparity in their policy formulations. What will be argued, however, is that while this is necessary it is unlikely to be sufficient.

Equality and Equity

While most of the policy initiatives that are circulating are still in discussion form and as such lacking in detail, a survey of them reveals, if not similar rhetoric, at least similar aims. The Department of National Education's Education Renewal Strategy (ERS) (June 1991), the African National Congress's Discussion Paper on Education Policy (1991) and the National Education Policy Investigation (NEPI) (1991b) all make reference in their aims to 'equality of education'. The ERS refers to 'equal opportunities' and 'equality in expenditure' and links these to justice (1991:20-21); NEPI proposes an 'equalisation of education and the elimination of difference' (1991b:1); and the ANC proposes 'democratic access to education' (1991:21-24) linked to the creation of a 'just society' as key aims.

The reason why these principles are accorded the prominence they have in these widely disparate documents is the belief that egalitarian ends can be realised through structural educational means. Certainly the understandings of what constitutes 'egalitarian' differ in each document relative to varying conceptions, implicit and explicit, of what form society will or should ultimately take. However, although these conceptions often appear opaque, the policy consequences that are detailed convey similar understandings of structural equality. In all three, notions that education should be universal and compulsory up to a point and that equal facilities be provided for all are central.

These understandings of equalisation are all framed in terms of equality of input. In turn this derives from traditional conceptualisations of equality as being concerned with access and opportunity. Both NEPI and the ANC, however, in line with broader societal understandings, go beyond the equality of opportunity argument to establish redress and affirmative action as central aims. This expansion of the concept to include outcomes links theorising to notions of justice and equity, and is bolstered in both documents by reference to the processes of learning and teaching.[3] By contrast, the ERS document is content to argue for

2. These include the Department of Education and Training in 'white' South Africa, and the various 'homeland' departments.
3. The ANC document, for example, notes that 'the way in which knowledge is passed on

equality of input and to leave to 'community' and 'diversity' the workings out of equity principles. In this regard, the ERS sees justice in terms of 'freedom of association' within the context of a unitary structure which will ensure 'greater equality in expenditure on learners' (1991:21-22).

Within these three documents, therefore, appear the key dimensions of equality of education: equality of input, of process and of output. Although Coleman (1975:27) argues that 'equality of educational opportunity ... is not a meaningful term' because equality of input 'is a weak term that offers little constitutional protection' and that equality of output '[if] conceived in terms of results of schooling ... is unachievable', it is a term that appears in most key South African policy documentation, including the Freedom Charter and the De Lange Report. Significantly, however, it is also a term that has increasingly become interchangeable with the concept of equity (Secada 1989:69). The consequences of this conflation will be detailed below.

Firstly, however, it is necessary to outline the policy outcomes of the equality of education thesis. In practical terms, as Secada notes, this thesis is perforce defined in terms of existing inequality between groups. Equality is said to occur when 'parity between groups along some agreed upon index [is achieved]' (1989:69). These indices may include, for example, pupil–teacher ratios, per capita spending and teacher qualifications. Significantly in this situation, parity is usually conceived of as an aggregate measure detailing the elimination of differences between definable groups. These inter-group comparisons have been a predominant focus in British literature on equality (Cosin *et al.* 1989) while, by contrast, American authors have tended 'to write about both equity and equality' (Secada 1989:68), often interchanging the concepts and, what is important, linking them to notions of 'justice'. South African documentation seems to suggest a similar trend.

But, if equity is defined in a qualitative way as the assessment of 'the results of actions directly against standards of justice' (Secada 1989:68), then this should invoke criteria distinct from the largely quantitative measures of equality. If this distinction is allowed, then there follow several important consequences.

As Secada points out, if equality and equity are interchanged there is considerable danger that the resultant discourse will prohibit 'our ability to consider other fundamental issues that should fall under the rubric of educational equity' (1989:74). Thus if one is able to define groups for whom equity is a concern (e.g. women, blacks, etc.), and if one is able to agree upon the yardsticks for measuring opportunity, 'then arguments about justice are in danger of being recast as technical arguments about equality'. It may thus be possible to achieve a measurable equality that nonetheless is unjust in the sense that, firstly, the good that is being distributed (education) may be disadvantaging rather than enabling, and secondly, the good may become an end in itself unrelated to external social and economic realities (see Coleman 1975:28) – both consequences of the loss

and shared must also be shaped by the participation of those who are involved in learning and not by the educator alone' (ANC, 1991:12), while NEPI asks in a more general vein, 'How can an ethos of democracy be fostered amongst existing personnel [teachers and managers] to support and develop the transformation process?' (NEPI, 1991b:1) of a sense of equity. In other words, the content and process of education may become neglected. The significance of this is that it is in the domain of the curriculum that criteria related to equity will have to be worked out and, in so far as educational equity is perceived as being located in the domain of schools, then clearly matters concerned with pedagogic process and organisation will also be of consequence.

Thus, in terms of the good that is being distributed, it may be that the curriculum legitimates only certain forms of knowledge, culture, language or religion (for example), to the disadvantage of those not privy to the dominant mode of discourse. Secondly, in relation to external factors, the curriculum may not articulate with, for instance, home background and labour market or further educational requirements. Thus, while all students may be equally treated, it may only be those with access to different or further knowledge who will be able to succeed. Coleman (1975:29) suggests that 'the school's task is ... [not to commit itself to unrealisable ends, but rather] ... to reduce the unequalizing impact on adult life of ... differential environments'. However, such an injunction could recast current prescriptions into curricular measures – such as variants of multiculturalism – which may, in attempting to address the first problem, paradoxically exacerbate the second.

Serious problems also arise when one attempts to define or establish equality in group terms. In the South African case, if one is seeking justice, are all blacks, women, youth, etc. to be treated as homogeneous entities? Clearly this is problematic, firstly, in terms of reinforcing the in-group versus out-group phenomenon characteristic of apartheid,[4] and secondly, in respect of the logical difficulties that arise in assigning people to groups according to some attribute. This could disguise race, regional, class, gender and other attributes which may, in the context of demands for equity, require as much attention as the assigned attribute. Beyond this, if affirmative action seeks to redress historical inequalities it could be argued, and often is, that groups defined as disadvantaged require *unequal* treatment. But on what attribute should these groups be defined, and how should this be accommodated within the original notion of equality?

Clearly, then, for the protagonists of equality and justice there are considerable philosophical, logical and empirical difficulties to be faced in formulating policy. None of the above suggests that these tasks are not worth while. Indeed, Apple (1989:16) asserts that, in the American context, considerable gains have been made by means of 'aggressive affirmative action programmes ... bilingual programmes and in the development of women's, black, Hispanic and Native American studies in high schools and colleges'.

Nonetheless, it is precisely because equity is not the same as equality and because equity is also significantly related to justice that these gains are in jeopardy. Legal rules and applications, as Secada points out, tend to concern themselves with individual rights (1989:68). This derives from 'a fundamental tenet of classic liberalism: that the individual is the singular unit of society, and that the

4. In terms of research activities, these difficulties are further compounded by what Campbell (1989) notes as systematic bias and stereotyping in comparing groups.

purpose of societal arrangements is to allow the individual the freedom to fulfil his own purposes' (Bell 1977:616). It is this conception, deep-rooted as an ideological form and reinforced by legal interpretations, that has permitted a swing from an acceptance of group rights and claims to justice (as epitomised in the landmark case *Brown* vs *The Board of Education* in the USA, which decreed that separate educational facilities were inherently unequal), to a reformulation of equality in the 1980s as a matter of 'guaranteeing individual choice' (Apple 1989:9). Ironically, it was precisely the often ambiguous formulations about groups and group rights and the often inconsistent policy interpretations of these rights that have permitted the re-insertion of the 'New Right' into educational discourse (Campbell 1989).

The difficulties posed by the individual–group dilemma have been reflected in South Africa by NEPI in its attempt to define and achieve 'a just balance between egalitarian and libertarian demands' (1991a:30). While formal solutions are not yet apparent it is significant that the problem has been posed and acknowledged as central to the educational policy debate by this group.

Wexler goes further in his critique of equality by noting its links to 'the idea of economic opportunity' (1976:11). This idea found fertile soil in the concept of human capital theory, which simultaneously reaffirmed 'the American way of life and [offered] quantitative justification for vast public expenditure on education' (Karabel and Halsey 1977:13). In this view, the individual is able to invest in himself or herself in the form of education, which will provide both private returns in the form of increased income and public returns in the form of greater productivity. The promotion of policies predicated on human capital theory, by international bodies such as the IMF and the World Bank, has produced expectations about the value of education that have, however, resulted in much disenchantment with the efficacy of expansionist policies. As Kelly notes, 'the language [of the 1980s] signifies a growing disillusionment with schools as a vehicle for change ... some have started to ask how much education is enough and how governments might either diminish demand for education or cut back on the provision of educational services' (1987:477). The shift to privatisation of educational provision under Reagan in the USA and Thatcher in Great Britain can be seen as symptomatic of these ideas (Apple 1989; Bennel and Swainson 1990). Significantly, these trends reaffirm the role of the individual in a manner consistent with both the legal and the ideological understandings of equality referred to earlier. The question of group claims to special or different treatment then becomes relegated to the domain of the special pleading of interest groups in a way that denies the linkages of such groups to structural or societal factors (Apple 1989).

Given that there is considerable evidence to support the benefits of educational expansion (Bennel and Swainson 1990; Colclough 1982; Donaldson 1989), one is constrained to ask why the attack both on education *per se* and on progressive groups within education has been so successful? Part of the reason has to do, as Apple (1989) notes, with the success of the New Right in disorganising more progressive groups. It also has to do with difficulties in the very concepts that those concerned with equality and equity have been keen to promote. The intrinsic problems of the concepts have allowed for definitions, usages, research and policies that, while overtly concerned with structurally disadvantaged groups and linkages in education, have nonetheless permitted resolutions which devolve upon the individual.

It will be argued in the second part of this chapter that the aggregation and homogenising of individuals without sufficient reference to the sites of all this educational endeavour – the schools – have prohibited clearer understanding and conceptualisation of what precisely a 'culture of learning' and equity and equality may mean in the contexts of their application.

Central to the problem is untangling the group–individual conundrum. In the South African context, as we argue above, the difficulty manifests itself at several levels. Particularly for research and policy-making purposes, the group concept, given its centrality to the functioning of apartheid, is deeply compromised. While seeking to distance itself from apartheid, however, the reform movement, in appealing to new categories of meaning such as the 'New South Africa', has avoided confronting the process by which disadvantaged groups have come into being. The difficulty with this is that reform measures have outcomes that are meaningful for successfully adapting individuals only. In so doing these measures are in danger of dehistoricising the very process by which blacks, youth or women, as groups, have arrived at their subordinate positions. In facing this issue, the Black Power movement in the United States argued: 'America has asked its Negro citizens to fight for opportunity as *individuals,* whereas at certain points in our history what we have needed most has been opportunity for the *whole group,* not just for selected and approved Negroes. We must not apologise for the existence of this form of group power, for we have been oppressed as a group and not as individuals.' (Quoted in Wexler 1976:18)

The problem of separatist-type struggles for South Africans, as suggested in the extract above, whether they be those of women, blacks or the working class, has a well-known history. Nevertheless, framing universalistic notions such as 'the people' or 'the nation' and appealing to the idea of a new social consensus – the 'New South Africa' – are less than satisfactory, given that deeply oppressive practices are inscribed into those paradigms, which appeal to universal truth claims (Spender 1989).

Directions for addressing this problematic from research and methodological and strategic perspectives are not clear-cut, but are suggested in the interaction of macro and micro frameworks of understanding.

Working Between the Macro and the Micro

There are two widely accepted assumptions made in seeking to account for the failure of black children to make good in the world of work and that of further education. The first is that apartheid as a social system provides a macro framework in which inequality has been inscribed into virtually every facet of South African life. The second, flowing from the first, is that the school has played a key role in socialising black pupils into a specific type of subject and towards specific kinds of jobs.

However, as ethnographic or micro-studies have shown, in particular the work of Willis (1977) in Britain and the initial studies in South Africa of Mpati (1990) on what she calls 'educational survival', this account is by no means sufficient to explain why children do not succeed, or for that matter, why some do. Whether Marxist or liberal in its analysis, the account has found itself locked into *structural* explanations which have obscured the processes at work within institutions. Such attention as is given to describing process amounts to 'strikingly similar explanations of what the school "does" to pupils in terms of *educational differentiation*' (Brown 1987:12, original emphasis). In terms of the Marxist variant of this account, the school functions to serve the needs of society and uses sifting and sorting mechanisms to ensure that pupils arrive at educational and occupational destinations appropriate to their class backgrounds. The school, therefore, is seen as moderating and tailoring the educational and life aspirations of pupils to reproduce the social order. In the liberal account, emphasis is placed on the inevitability of social stratification and the efficacy of education in providing individuals with the means to achieve their own social mobility. Within structural explanations of these kinds, little scope is given to the voices of the subjects themselves, be they working-class, black or women, and their interpretations of their own experience. As Stephen Michelson observed about the famous Jencks study on inequality, 'This book is about numbers. It is not about children, adults, or other kinds of people; it is not about schools, families or other kinds of institutions... The work does not help us understand what structural relationships are hidden behind the numbers' (quoted in Wexler 1976:23). Similarly, in the disintegrating environment of African schools in South Africa, Mpati (1990) urges caution in imputing single causes to the breakdown of schooling.

It is in the light of criticisms such as these that explanations emphasising process take a different direction. In showing that the school itself is a place of conflict and division, process interpretations argue that, in seeking to account for pupil failure or success (or any other social outcome), we have to look much more broadly than simply at what the school does to children. In other words, if schooling is perceived as a complex process through which school children move, then many factors need to be considered, including the social and cultural backgrounds of children, the economic resources at their families' disposal and so on – but most important, their own interpretations of such forces and experiences.

Led by Willis's *Learning to Labour* (1977), these accounts argue that any explanation of underachievement at school has to recognise the active choice of pupils in that process. Analyses of these kinds are based on the assumption that there exist distinctive working-class and middle-class cultural mindsets, and that these have significance in so far as they determine 'objectives ... worthy of pursuit and what qualities entitle a person to the esteem of his fellows' (Turner cited in Brown 1987:18).

While there have been many criticisms of Willis's work, there is agreement that it has exposed the complexity of the school as a site of conflict and resistance – 'a fight between the cultures' (Willis 1977:18). Based on this, a great deal of evidence has been accumulated to show that schools have effects, and that different schools have very different effects. In talking about *Learning to Labour*, Willis explains that the work seeks to 'show something of the *specificity* by which some general themes and discourses are worked up into the particular shape of a "cultural form" in the detail and materiality of its locating institution' (Willis 1983:124, our emphasis).

The strength of this kind of account is its refusal to produce an 'authentic victim', be that person working-class, black or a woman, who is simply a casualty figure. For policy purposes, the reluctance inherent in this analysis to prescribe a general structural 'cure' for education is of crucial importance. In the first instance, it is sensitive to the subjects themselves, to their perceptions of the world and of their institutions, and secondly, it recognises that schools are not all the same.

It is here that a discussion about equity in education could possibly begin. Recognising the specific qualities of each school, and how administrative, religious, political, economic and social forces interact to produce academic results, attitudes and behaviour that are different, is a first step in acknowledging that a uniform reform policy for the 'New South Africa' based on national indices of 'inequality' alone could fail. Further, because such indices are based on aggregated input measures, existing inequalities could be exacerbated since this approach fails to address the specific forms which inequality may take in specific schools.

This point is illustrated in Cynthia Mpati's (1990) account of the complex variety of conditions in African schools in Natal. Drawing on extensive observations of different schools, she noted that while there were many institutions in which very little of educational value is happening, there appear to be many other schools where, despite difficulties, healthy relationships exist between teachers and students and where effective instruction is taking place. Comments such as 'We are proud of our teachers. They make us feel like real people. They work hard and so we work hard too' illustrate the differences between these schools.

Quite clearly, ethnographic work which treats each school as a specific environment shaped by very distinctive forces has much to teach us in developing appropriate strategies for redressing the specific needs of disadvantaged institutions. Already such school-based reports as are available, drawing on student and teacher insights (see Bebb 1991 and Soudien 1992), show that particular schools have substantially different concerns. In Bebb's (1991) view for example, the dominant need in the primary school in which she taught in Khayelitsha, Cape Town, was for a sustained school-feeding programme. By contrast, the most important concern of children interviewed by Kruss (1991), in an area which she described as being 'more stable' (i.e. less prone to socio-economic and political upheaval than in Bebb's school area), was that teachers resorted to physical punishment too frequently.

Substantial difficulties remain, however, in seeking to prove the value of ethnographic work for policy-making. Not the least of these is the invariable silence in micro-studies on the effect of macro, structural factors and on how these are experienced not only by the children in a classroom (who have tended to be the focus of such studies), but also by teachers, parents and administrators. Such attempts as have been made, like Willis's *Learning to Labour,* which focus on the pupils, do not permit a satisfactory reconciliation between the micro and the macro. For example, Willis uses macro-analytic categories like 'penetrations', 'confirmations' and 'dislocations' to explain how concepts such as 'working class' influence his 'lads' either to reject or to accommodate the given order. But he fails to explain how, and on what basis, he is able to import a macro-term, like working class, into his ethnographic analysis. As West (1984:261) complains, 'From where do such concepts derive, *a priori* deductive structuralist theorising about production and reproduction of ideology (Althusser 1971) or *a posteriori* inductive grounded theory...?'

Thus it would seem that, on their own, neither macro-based policies, derived from *a priori* deductions, such as the assumption that being black implies carrying a subordinate status, nor micro policies premissed exclusively on *a posteriori* evidence will permit resolutions of the equality–equity dilemma.

However, David Reynolds's (1984) argument for a 'relative autonomy' approach to social institutions holds promise in permitting the re-insertion of the school into the social structure without reducing it to an epiphenomenon or an after-thought of the macro-system, as the structuralist account would have it, or discussing it in isolation from broader social forces, as the ethnographic explanation would suggest. 'Schools appear to be active participants not merely in the reproduction of existing sets of productive relationships but in actually remaking – utilising their freedom of means – the forces that influence them in a complex interactive relationship between "superstructure" and "base"' (Reynolds 1984:297). Seen thus, the school is at once both determined and free. At play are restraints of an economic and political order, but seldom does the school fit in a manner prescribed for it. What Reynolds's argument does is to make it possible to locate ethnographic research within an epistemological framework. It is possible to show, as Mpati (1990:1) argues, that one can identify distinct factors which facilitate progress within what she calls a broader 'paralysing' framework.

If one argues that the relative autonomy thesis provides a means of holding the micro and macro ends of research in the same place, there are several studies, such as *Fifteen Thousand Hours* (Rutter *et al.* 1979) and *The School Effect* (Smith *et al.* 1989) which could serve as platforms for developing new integrated research directions. The key variables identified in studies such as *Fifteen Thousand Hours* that are understood to determine difference in schools include the head's style of leadership, the type of organisation, the involvement of staff, the curriculum, rewards and punishment used, parental involvement with the school, equal opportunities, school atmosphere and, crucially, the composition of the school in terms of class, age, gender, teacher characteristics and so on. In the context of South Africa, the leadership of principals and the involvement of students in special tuition programmes have shown the importance of taking into account other indices in assessing the nature of educational institutions (Soudien 1992). Needless to say, the use of these takes one beyond the standard South African macro-based indices such as teacher–pupil ratios, per capita expenditure and pupil–classroom ratios. But while they provide important and enhanced yardsticks by which to understand specific institutions and to effect comparisons, at the heart of this approach the subject is still depersonalised, culturally deprived and the victim of unequal resources. Used only in this way, the analysis would continue to focus on individual attainment and the conditions which permit individuals to rise above their contexts.

From a methodological and policy point of view, then, there is a need to transcend the cultural innocence which is manifest in works such as *Schools Matter* and *Fifteen Thousand Hours*. Absent from their account is the agency factor. As Rutter and colleagues put it, 'We may conclude that there is very good evidence that schools vary greatly in rates of attendance, psychiatric referral and delinquency, but that it is uncertain how far these variations are due to differences in the *kinds of children* admitted to each school. Little is known, however, on what makes some schools more "successful" than others in these terms.' (1979:10, our emphasis)

For policy purposes in the South African situation, accounting for the voice of the subjects is central to the reform project. What need to be transcended are both the prevailing conceptions of a dominant culture inherent in macro-analysis, which ignores the variety of voices, *and* the reluctance of micro-analysis to locate itself within a larger social analysis. As West points out, the 'use of social scientific and lay concepts should not just organise data into refutable propositions: they must be thought through as a central part of any analysis, for the data are not self-evident' (1984:271).

For equity and equality to be goals of education policy-making in South Africa, as they must be, it is clear that the means of achieving these are far more complex than may appear at first sight. 'If the notion of the school as both determined and free can be utilised ... to link together apparently disparate phenomena' (Reynolds 1984:300), then it might be possible to avoid the conflation of equality with equity. Therefore, if equality resides perforce in the macro policy and resource domain, then equity may be best achieved by understandings generated at specific sites, in ways which are not prescribed by methodological individualism. It is the resolution of this tension which may capture both the generality and the specificity of the experience of South African schools in a research framework.

If the achievement of equity and equality is to be more than topping up to agreed normative standards, more than Marshall's embourgeoisement of the working class (Halsey 1975), and more than an acceptance of diversity, freedom of association and autonomy, then the way in which we construct these terms must authentically include the voices of those who are defined as problematic. Fundamentally, this calls for developing a research framework which is able to be deeply sensitive to the multiplicity of factors at work in the shaping of specific institutions and their inhabitants. In the South African context, this would call for developing institutional studies which simultaneously recognise the role of apartheid as a macro force that has defined a particular kind of group experience, and other micro forces which give institutions their specific character.

An approach that might be used in designing such a research programme is to look for those processes and events which are small-scale and institution-specific but which have macro implications. Attendance records offer a good example; while it is invariably their aggregated indices which policy-makers would examine, seldom are the micro-processes which cause absenteeism a source of interest. As Cicourel (1981:79) explains, 'the study of micro-events is an essential part of all macro-statements.' In developing policy that is alert to the equality–equity tension we have to draw on a number of dimensions of the schooling experience. These might include:

– standard indices such as class size and teacher–pupil ratios;

– indices such as those developed by Rutter and colleagues (1979) which include teaching styles, school organisation, and parental involvement;

– observations of how children and their teachers experience the environment which they share; for example, what conditions exist which make initiative possible amongst children, and the circumstances present in the successful achievement of children from socially deprived backgrounds;

– and from there draw out the implication of factors such as class, race and gender in determining how each of the above is manifested in the specific institutions.

In this way, maps of requirements sensitive to particular institutions could be developed in a manner and through a process which would be amenable to macro-level policy decisions while simultaneously enabling schools to voice their unique needs. Clearly, problems would emerge in a competition for resources, but such an approach would at least be an advance on the methods which conflate the issues of equality and equity.

References

African National Congress (1955). The Freedom Charter. In R. Suttner and J. Cronin (eds) (1986). *30 Years of the Freedom Charter*. Johannesburg: Ravan Press.

African National Congress (1991). *Discussion Paper for the ANC on Education Policy*.

Althusser, L. (1971). *Lenin and Philosophies and Other Essays*. London: New Left Books.

Apple, M.W. (1989). How equality has been redefined in the conservative restoration. In W.G. Secada (ed.), *Equity in Education*. London: The Falmer Press.

Ashley, M.J. (1991). *South African Education in the 1990s*. Cape Town: Urban Futures Project.

Bebb, S. (1991). Teaching in Khayelitsha. Unpublished B.Ed. assignment, University of Cape Town.

Bell, D. (1977). On meritocracy and equality. In J. Karabel and A.H. Halsey (eds), *Power and Ideology in Education*. New York: Oxford University Press.

Bennel, P. and Swainson, N. (1990). Education and the 'New Right' in South Africa: A critical appraisal of 'The long-term future of education in South Africa' by Elizabeth Dostal. Occasional Paper. Education Policy Unit, University of the Witwatersrand.

Brown, P. (1987). *Schooling Ordinary Kids*. London: Tavistock.

Campbell, P.B. (1989). Educational equity and research paradigms. In W.G. Secada (ed.), *Equity in Education*. London: The Falmer Press.

Cape Times (1992). 94 white schools closed. 18/2/1992.

Cicourel, A.V. (1981). Notes on the integration of micro- and macro-levels of analysis. In K. Knorr-Cetina and A.V. Cicourel (eds), *Advances in Social Theory and Methodology*. Boston: Routledge and Kegan Paul.

Colclough, C. (1982). The impact of primary schooling on economic development: A review of the evidence. *World Development, 10*, 167–185.

Coleman, J.S. (1975). What is meant by 'an equal educational opportunity'. *Oxford Review of Education, 1*, 27–29.

Cosin, B. Flude, M. and Hales, M. (eds) (1989). *School, Work and Equality. A Reader*. London: Open University.

Cosser E. (ed) (1991). *Education for Life: The Challenge of Schooling for All*. Christian Research, Education and Information for Democracy, Johannesburg.

Department of National Education (1991). *Education Renewal Strategy (ERS): Discussion Document*. Pretoria: DNE.

Donaldson, A. (1989). Towards progressive education. Five awkward features of the future. In *Financing of Education*. Workshop Series No. 1. Education Policy Unit, University of the Witwatersrand, Johannesburg.

Du Pisani, T., Plekker, S., Dennis, C. and Strauss, J. (1991). *Education and Manpower Development. No. 11*. Research Institute for Educational Planning. Bloemfontein: University of the Orange Free State.

Human Sciences Research Council (1981). *Report of the Main Committee of the HSRC Investigation into Education (The De Lange Report)*. Pretoria: Human Sciences Research Council.

Halsey, A.H. (1975). Sociology and the equality debate. *Oxford Review of Education, 1*, 9–23.

Karabel, J. and Halsey, A.H. (1977). Educational research : A review and an interpretation. In J. Karabel and A.H. Halsey (eds), *Power and Ideology in Education*. New York: Oxford University Press.

Karabel J. and Halsey A.H. (eds) (1977). *Power and Ideology in Education*. New York: Oxford University Press.

Kelly, G.P. (1987). Comparative education and the problem of change: An agenda for the 1980s. *Comparative Education Review, 31*, 477–489.

Kruss, C. (1991). Four weeks in Khayelitsha. Unpublished B.Ed. assignment, University of Cape Town.

Mpati, C. (1990). Teachers and students locked in turbulence. Paper presented at the Kenton-at-Port St Johns educational conference, October 1990.

National Education Policy Investigation (1991a). *Towards a Framework and a Set of Guiding Principles for NEPI*. A working document prepared by the Principles and Frameworks Committee, April.

National Education Policy Investigation (1991b). *Discussion Document*. June.

Pillay, P.N. (1990). The development and underdevelopment of education in South Africa. In B. Nasson and J. Samuel (eds) *Education: From Poverty to Liberty*. Cape Town: David Philip.

Reynolds, D. (1984). Relative autonomy reconstructed. In L. Barton and S. Walker (eds), *Social Crisis and Educational Research*. London: Croom Helm.

Rutter, M., Maughan, B., Mortimore, P., Ouston, J. and Smith, A. (1979). *Fifteen Thousand Hours*. Shepton Mallet: Open Books.

Secada, W.G. (1989). Educational equity versus equality of education: An alternative conception. In W.G. Secada (ed.), *Equity in Education*. London: The Falmer Press.

Secada, W.G. (ed.) (1989). *Equity in Education*. London: The Falmer Press.

Smith, D.J. and Tomlinson, S. (1989). *The School Effect: A Study of Multi-racial Comprehensives*. London: The Policy Studies Institute.

Soudien, L. (1992). Accomplishments of the 1991 Andover Bread Loaf writing workshop. Unpublished memorandum.

South African Institute of Race Relations (SAIRR) (1990). *Race Relations Survey 1989/90*. Johannesburg: SAIRR.

South African Institute of Race Relations (SAIRR) (1992). *Race Relations Survey 1991/92*. Johannesburg: SAIRR.

Spender, D. (1989). *Invisible Women*. London: The Women's Press.

Taylor, N. (1989). *Falling at the First Hurdle. Initial Encounters with the Formal System of African Education in South Africa*. Research Report No. 1. Education Policy Unit, University of the Witwatersrand, Johannesburg.

West, W.G. (1984). Phenomenon and form in interactionist and neo-Marxist qualitative educational research. In L. Barton and S. Walker (eds), *Social Crisis and Educational Research*. London: Croom Helm.

Wexler, P. (1976). *The Sociology of Education: Beyond Equality*. Indianapolis: The Bobbs-Merrill Company.

Willis, P. (1977). *Learning to Labour*. Farnborough: Saxon House.

Willis, P. (1983). Cultural production and theories of reproduction. In L. Barton and S. Walker (eds), *Social Crisis and Educational Research*. London: Croom Helm.

8
Children with Special Education Needs: The Reproduction of Disadvantage in Poorly Served Communities
DAVID DONALD

Introduction

Concern with special educational need is often considered to be the preserve of a peripheral group of special educationists whose focus is on an equally peripheral group of children with specific and unusual disabilities or educational impairments. This may be true in some contexts. However, this chapter intends to show that consideration of special educational need in a country like South Africa concerns a large and significant proportion of all children. In addition the concern extends well beyond the conventional boundaries of special education since the issues involved cannot be divorced from the concerns of health and of education as a whole.

The focus on special educational need in South Africa has further implications. In one sense conditions experienced by the majority of South African children are no different from those experienced by many other underdeveloped and impoverished communities elsewhere in the world. In this sense the arguments and evidence around special educational need and its reproduction have relevance in other similar contexts. In another sense, however, the focus on South Africa is very particular. The socio-economic and educational disparities and structural inequalities generated by apartheid policy in South Africa have had a particularly devastating impact on the creation and reproduction of special educational need (Donald and Csapo 1989; Donald 1992; Skuy and Partington 1990; Gwalla-Ogisi 1990). This is not merely a problem of individual pathology in South Africa; it is a reflection, in its most acute form, of the distortion of the social formation that has at its core the creation and reproduction of disadvantage.

The notion of 'reproduction' in this context is used, and meant, in two distinct yet inter-related ways. The first is a literal meaning. This refers to the interacting cycles of disadvantage – relating to poverty, health, health-care access, education and employment – that cumulatively entrap the majority of those who have disabilities and special educational need in South Africa. This majority is made up of those who in South Africa happen to be black and poor as well as disabled. The second meaning relates more specifically to social reproduction theory in education – within the tradition of Althusser (1972), Bowles and Gintis (1976) and Bourdieu and Passeron (1977). In this sense it refers to the reproduction, through the very structures and processes of education, of a set of social relationships that act to perpetuate the interests of capital and the dominant power structures of society. The cumulative perpetuation of disadvantage of the group referred to is thus not fortuitous. It is the result of social relationships in a society which has been economically and politically structured to maintain the marginality of this group in terms of its race, its class *and* its disability status.

Special Educational Need

It is important to stress that the very notion of special educational need is itself relative and not absolute. It depends on how 'disability' is perceived and interpreted in a particular social context and on how 'need' is defined in relation to this. Brennan (1985), for instance, has attempted the following definition: 'A special educational need exists when any disability (physical, sensory, intellectual, emotional, social or any combination of these) affects learning *to the extent that* any or all of special access to curriculum, special or modified curriculum, or specially adapted conditions of learning, are necessary if the pupil is to be appropriately and effectively educated' (Brennan, 1985:30; my emphasis).

Such a definition is in line with the current relativist philosophy of special education in developed educational contexts. It is also an appropriate working definition where the resources and facilities exist for making the specialised educational evaluations – and interventions – that it demands. However, in underdeveloped educational contexts, such as those that exist in much of South Africa, these resources are generally not available. Where neither the specialised personnel nor the instruments and facilities are sufficient for assessing the relative nature of special learning needs (Gwalla-Ogisi 1990; Davidson and Dickman 1990), definitions such as Brennan's are problematic.

In South Africa a common alternative has been to define special educational need more absolutely in terms of categories of disability. Thus, within some terminological variation, special educational need is commonly seen as manifesting in the following categories of disability: intellectual impairment, visual or hearing impairment, physical disability, neurological impairment, specific learning disability, speech or language impairment, emotional disability and multiples of these (Anderson 1973; HSRC 1987). However, this formulation is even more problematic. In its categorical assumptions it begs important questions about the relativity of disability itself. Further, it assumes that diagnostic facilities exist – and that people have access to these – for the identification of disabilities. Most important, it operates from the assumption that special educational need arises only from deficits *in* the child and that these deficits, in some positively measurable form, relate to the degree of need (Lea and Foster 1990).

Conceptually these reservations are crucial. At the same time it is unfortunately true that such statistics as are available on the incidence of special educational need in South Africa have been collected in terms of this formulation. Since it is important to have some sense of the extent of the problem these statistics must, on one level, be used. On another level this will be qualified by arguments and evidence that the categorical formulation results, in two important ways, in an underestimate of those who have special educational need.

The first underestimate relates to the lack of diagnostic services, and therefore of reliable epidemiological data, for the very group for whom the reproduction of disadvantage is likely to create the highest rates of disability and special educational need. The second underestimate relates to a large group of children who have no intrinsic deficit as assumed under the disability definition but who are in fact structurally 'handicapped'. As a result of both structural and systemic inadequacies in the South African education system, these children have become educationally disadvantaged to the extent that they also have real special educational needs. This manifests as the need for special educational support in the acquisition of basic skills – especially literacy and numeracy – that have been delayed or denied to learners through lack of access to, or inadequacy of, the existing educational system. It is difficult to determine the precise extent of this group. That the group exists, however, cannot be in question. It is undoubtedly reflected in such indicators as the excessively high drop-out and failure rates in the early grades of African education (Du Pisani *et al.* 1991; Taylor 1989) as well as in the numbers of socially and educationally neglected children generated in this society (Swart-Kruger and Donald, Chapter 6).

The Extent of Educational Disability or Impairment in South Africa

Estimating the incidence of disability in underdeveloped contexts is a notorious problem. Not only are general census statistics unreliable but, as mentioned above, diagnostic services and therefore epidemiological data are frequently just not available (see also Chapter 9). In two relatively recent South African reports for instance, incidence has been estimated on the basis of international figures taken in conjunction with whatever local information is available (Hattingh 1987; HSRC 1987). In both of these reports it is stressed that estimation is intentionally conservative. However, for reasons developed below, the actual extent of the problem is likely to be considerably greater than is given in official estimates. Thus Wiesenger-Ferris (1989), quoting from UNESCO sources, estimates that whereas disability in first world contexts is accepted as being at approximately 10% of population, it is likely to be nearer 20% in third world contexts. Reasons for this are not only based on incomplete statistical information but are quite concretely related to a multiple interaction of socio-economic factors in disadvantaged communities.

Poverty, Health and Disability

People who are poor are inevitably more prone to the health risks associated with malnutrition, disease and infection than those who are not, South Africans being no exception (Olver 1984; White 1980). What is significant here is that many of those health risks associated with poverty commonly result in cognitive or sensory impairments that are likely to create special educational need. Stein and Susser (1984:28) for instance, in a thorough survey of evidence on the epidemiology of mental retardation, conclude that in third world countries 'postnatal damage to the brain is more common than in more developed countries [including] infections such as tuberculosis and acute bacterial meningitis, and the encephalopathies that occur with measles, whooping cough and with electrolyte imbalance and dehydration following gastroenteritis...' The validity and local relevance of this will be reviewed below.

The relationship between malnutrition and cognitive development is perhaps of the most pervasive concern. This has been studied extensively both internationally and in South Africa. Contemporary understandings of the relationship see it not so much as a direct physiological link as a *synergistic* interaction in which a variety of factors related to child nurturance and stimulation under conditions of poverty interact with and reinforce one another to create increased levels of risk for cognitive development (Richter and Griesel, Chapter 4). Clearly, where cognitive development is affected, special educational need is likely to be created. Thus a cycle is generated which, given the extent of poverty and malnutrition in disadvantaged communities in South Africa (Wilson and Ramphele 1989), is likely to produce considerably higher rates of special educational need than in more developed contexts.

The relationship between diseases that are particularly common under conditions of poverty (for example, tuberculosis, pneumonia and measles), secondary cerebral infection and resultant disabilities, such as cerebral palsy and mental retardation, represents another cycle. This has been illustrated in a number of South African studies.

Molteno and colleagues (1990), in a cross-cultural study of the causes of mental handicap, found that 21.7% of the African children in their Cape Town sample, in contrast with 13.6% of the coloured children and only 9.8% of the white children, had become mentally handicapped as a result of *postnatal* causes. As the authors point out, the figure for white children is similar to other findings in developed countries. However, the figures for coloured and African children indicate a relationship between poor socio-economic conditions and health-related causes for postnatally acquired mental handicap. In an earlier study of postnatally acquired cerebral palsy in Cape Town, Arens and Molteno (1989) also found that 24% of the coloured children sampled and 36.1% of the African children had acquired their cerebral palsy *after* birth while only 13.2% of the white children had done so. Again, since this could not be accounted for in ethnic terms the conclusion was that the differences related to the socio-economic circumstances of the communities concerned. Of particular significance was the finding that 11.7% of the coloured children and 22.1% of the African children had acquired cerebral palsy as the result of meningitis while only 5.5% of the white children had done so. Within this again, the specific rates for tuberculous meningitis were 4.8% coloured, 14.8% African and only 1.1% white.

As established by Arens and colleagues (1987), disability associated with this disease is frequently not limited to cerebral palsy alone. They found that 52% of children with cerebral palsy as a result of tuberculous meningitis were also severely to profoundly mentally retarded. With the well-recognised association between tuberculosis and poor living conditions, and the high incidence of this disease in South Africa, it is not difficult to see that a large section of the South

African population is vulnerable to disabilities that create special educational need. The current impact of AIDS on vulnerability to diseases such as tuberculosis and pneumonia is of further and immediate concern in this cycle.

Within the same reproductive pattern, Arens and Molteno also found that, of 14 children whose cerebral palsy was attributable to cerebrovascular accident, 10 had suffered this as the result of dehydration during gastroenteritis. Of these children 8 were African, 2 coloured and none white. As the authors point out, the association between poor living conditions, gastroenteritis, lack of emergency treatment and the resulting permanent disability is all too obvious.

A further example applies particularly to impoverished communities in urban environments. This is the complex relationship between risk factors surrounding pedestrian traffic injury in young children, head injury and the serious neurological sequelae for those who survive. Cumpsty and Theron (1986) have illustrated some of these interrelated factors. Over a two-year prospective sampling period undertaken in the trauma units of two hospitals in Cape Town, 390 children (<14 years) were clinically identified as having suffered head injury. Of these 53% were pedestrians who had suffered from traffic-related accidents. Of this group 68.4% were from the coloured community, 29.4% from the African and 2.2% from the white community. This contrasts with 1980 census ratios of 64% coloured, 11% African, and 25% white for the total <14-year-old population of the greater Cape Town area. Once again ethnicity is not in itself the issue. What would appear to underlie the contrast is the relationship of ethnicity to those socio-economic circumstances that create risks for pedestrian head injury. Looking at this in more detail, the study revealed that 75% of the sample were under 8 years of age, and of these 70% had had no adult custodian present at the time of the accident. Given the vulnerability of this age group, lack of custodial care clearly constitutes a major risk factor. When this in turn is looked at more closely, the study found that of a number of indices of psychosocial adversity, low educational status in the mother correlated most significantly with injury in the child. The association of this with poor socio-economic circumstances, together with the need for parents to be working and the lack of alternative child-minding facilities in poor urban environments, creates a framework of risk that is difficult to ignore. Although this study did not look at the sequelae of these head injuries, it did report that there was a survival rate of 90% for the sample as a whole. The relationship between head injury and various forms of cognitive impairment is well enough established (Kanner 1957) for it to be assumed that many of these children would be found to have special educational needs as a result of their head injuries. This example has been given in some detail as it is a particularly complex yet representative illustration of the reproductive interlocking of factors that relates poverty to the creation of disability and special educational need.

A further extension of the poverty–health cycle affecting the incidence of disability is relative access to health services. It is clear that any of the health risks associated with poverty are exacerbated and the chances of permanent disability are increased where access to health services and appropriate treatment is limited. The provision of such services in South Africa, particularly in rural and underprivileged sectors, is indeed inadequate (Buch 1988). Further, as emphasised by Olver (1984), the services that do exist are mostly based on western models of service delivery that make them culturally and often physically even more inaccessible.

Relative access to prenatal and obstetric services is a good example. As pointed out by a senior consultant at the Child Health Unit of the University of Cape Town (personal communication), inadequate access to such services results in a broad lack of awareness of basic risk factors in pregnancy – such as those related to substance abuse and nutritional requirements. It also results in lack of treatment for prenatal, perinatal and postnatal complications. Disability resulting from such factors not only is common but could be avoided with increased access to relevant health services.

With school-aged children, the inadequacy of basic health screening and relatively simple interventions that could prevent the development of learning-related disabilities again underlines health access as a central factor in the reproduction of educational disadvantage. This is well illustrated in a study by Frets-Van Buuren, Letuma and Daynes (1990). The central question in this study was why so many children in African education (in this case, KwaZulu schools) were failing to progress from the early grades. In 25 schools, 2190 children who were repeating the first year of school (28% of first-year enrolment) were medically screened, and identified ailments were appropriately treated in a local hospital. Altogether 1186 children (54.2% of the repeaters) were found to have identifiable medical problems, almost all of which were readily treatable. This is not to say that these problems were necessarily the direct cause of failure. What is certain is that relatively simple medical screening and treatment can prevent the perpetuation of such problems and avoid whatever effects they are indeed having on learning.

A finding of particular concern in this study was the number of children with 'hearing or ear problems' (202 or 9.2% of the repeaters). The critical relationship of hearing to language development is well recognised (Bloom and Lahey 1978) and is cause for concern with such statistics. Within this, recurrent middle-ear infection (otitis media) has been shown to be related to specific language and scholastic retardation (Rapin 1979; Maritz, Uys and Louw 1988). Although Frets-Van Buuren and colleagues do not report otitis media as a specific condition, it is a common ear problem in children, particularly for those living under poor socio-economic conditions and where recurrent and untreated upper respiratory tract infection occurs (which *was* identified in 138 children or 6.3% of the repeaters). If this risk factor is added to the ear problems identified, then it is possible that untreated otitis media may be a significant factor in early school failure, language retardation and the creation of special educational need in disadvantaged communities.

In summary, there is considerable evidence that, under conditions of poverty and disadvantage such as have been referred to, cycles of reproduction operate to create, exacerbate and perpetuate those disabilities that commonly give rise to special educational need. Although this evidence cannot be converted directly into incidence statistics it is strongly supportive of the claim, articulated by

Table 1. Estimated incidence and number of school-age children affected by disability in South Africa, 1985

Disability	Incidence %	African (6 013 050)	White (971 197)	Coloured (798 782)	Indian (234 469)	Total (8 017 498)★
Hearing impairment (deaf and hard of hearing)	3.50	210 457	33 992	27 957	8 206	280 612
Visual impairment (blind/partially sighted)	0.36	21 647	3 496	2 876	844	28 863
Intellectual impairment (mild/moderate/severe)	3.00	180 391	29 136	23 963	7 034	240 524
Neurological impairment (cerebral palsy and epilepsy)	0.45	27 059	4 370	3 595	1 055	36 079
Physical disability	1.63	98 013	15 830	13 020	3 821	130 685
Speech impairment	2.50	150 326	24 280	19 970	5 861	200 437
Total 1	11.44	687 893	111 104	91 381	26 821	917 200
Total 2 (excluding physical disability)		589 880	95 274	78 361	23 000	786 515

★School enrolments, 1985 (Cooper et al., 1988)

Wiesenger-Ferris (1989), that the extent of disability in such contexts is likely to be substantially greater than it has been shown to be in more advantaged contexts.

Estimates of Incidence

As already mentioned, two relatively recent surveys have attempted to estimate incidence rates for various categories of disability in South Africa (HSRC 1987; Hattingh 1987). The HSRC report is concerned with education for the black disabled and, in the light of the evidence presented above, it is interesting that these incidence rates do not differ significantly from those quoted by Hattingh for the whole South African population. Based on the declared 'conservative' incidence rates as given by Hattingh (1987:15), Table 1 indicates the numbers of school-age children estimated to have special educational need in South Africa with reference to school enrolment figures for 1985 (Cooper *et al.* 1988:431-432). Although more recent enrolment figures are available, those for 1985 are used to make comparison possible with statistics presented in Table 2 reflecting provision of services. (Specific learning disability and emotional disability, two categories where the reliability of incidence estimates is particularly problematic, are not included in the table for lack of consistent information.)

What is apparent is the sheer number of children estimated to suffer disability and therefore the likely extent of special educational need in South Africa. Proportionately the need is greatest for those who are the most disadvantaged: on this reckoning, 75% of children with special educational need are African. What must be borne in mind, however, is that these estimates are incomplete *and* conservative. By definition they also exclude all those who, because of socio-educational disadvantage, experience special educational need. If this and the evidence already presented about the reproduction of disadvantage in impoverished communities are taken into account, then the extent of special educational need, particularly in the African community, becomes even more significant. At least in the initial stages of establishing compulsory primary schooling for all in South Africa, it is estimated that between 30% and 40% of all primary school-age children would need some degree of special educational support (Donald 1992).

Provision of Services for Special Educational Need in South Africa

There are two fundamental issues regarding the provision of services for children with special educational need in South Africa. The first concerns the *numbers* of children with such need who are currently served, or not served, by the facilities and services that exist. This raises the question of the equality of distribution of such services in South Africa. The second relates to the *type of services* that have developed and whether these are appropriate within both international trends in special education and the particular parameters of South African need.

Provision of Existing Services

The provision of services for children with special educational needs is mainly the responsibility of the state's education authorities. In order to appreciate the reproduction of disadvantage in this, it is necessary to understand the structural factors that underlie it.

To date, education in South Africa has been delivered through four essentially separate systems of education with a bureaucratically complex arrangement of departments of education falling within this framework. Within the political policy of separate development, a Department of National Education has governed educational policy under the label of *general affairs*. Under this umbrella four ministries of *own affairs* exist: the Department of Education and Culture (House of Assembly) for whites; the Department of Education and Culture (House of Delegates) for Indians; the Department of Education and Culture (House of Representatives) for coloureds; and the Department of Education and Training for Africans resident outside the national and the 'independent' homelands. All ten of these homelands have their own departments of education. This structurally complicated and divided system has not only created and maintained gross inequalities in the provision of educational services but it has also resulted in bureaucratic rigidity, unnecessary wastage of scarce resources, and lack of communication on common and fundamental educational issues. The development of a rational and effective system of meeting special educational needs in the society as a whole is just one such issue – but one that has been particularly severely affected by the lack of co-ordination and inefficiency in this system.

Particularly as regards equality, the provision of special education services within this divided system has been even more distorted than the inequalities that exist in general education (Gwalla-Ogisi 1990). Most obviously this has been a matter of resources. Those departments operating with the least resources have had to attempt to meet basic needs for classrooms, teachers and books before allocating resources to special education. More subtly, a dominant hegemonic and instrumental policy, as applied particularly to African education (Nkomo 1990), has relegated the meeting of special educational need to a marginal position on the scale of priorities. The results of all this are evident in Table 2, which reflects the numbers of school-age children provided with special educational facilities and services in 1985, as extracted from a report on disability in South Africa of the Department of National Health and Population Development (Hattingh 1987). Each of these is expressed as a percentage of the equivalent incidence estimate given in Table 1. For example, where 1262 hearing-impaired African children were reported as in special educational placements in 1985, there were a conservatively estimated 210 457 African children with special educational need in this category in the same year. In this case 1262 represents 0.6% of the estimated need. Since a more recent set of national statistics with the degree of detail and breakdown given in the Hattingh (1987) report is not available, it is important to take these figures as the best available, although somewhat dated.

Since 1985, the time when the statistics in the Hattingh report were collected, there have been a number of developments in the provision of services, particularly where African education is concerned. The Department of Education and Training, for instance, reported that by 1988, 5436 pupils categorised as severely mentally disabled, aurally disabled, physically disabled, visually disabled

Table 2. Number of children provided with special education in 1985* expressed as a percentage of the estimated number of children affected (Table 1).

Disability/Impairment	African	%	White	%	Coloured	%	Indian	%	Total	%
Hearing impairment (deaf and hard of hearing)	1 262	0.6	2 000	5.9	485	1.7	115	1.4	3 862	1.4
Visual impairment (blind and partially sighted)	710	3.3	626	17.9	123	4.3	117	13.9	1 576	5.5
Intellectual impairment (mild/moderate/severe)	304	0.1	29 813	102.3	8 410	35.1	1 052	15.0	39 579	16.5
Neurological impairment (cerebral palsy and epilepsy)	658	2.4	2 190	50.1	654	18.2	279	26.4	3 781	10.5
Physical disability (numbers not available)	–	–	–	–	–	–	–	–	–	–
Speech impairment	450	0.3	21 000	86.5	450	2.3	200	3.4	22 100	11.0
Total	3 384	0.6+	55 629	58.4	10 122	12.9	1 763	7.7	70 898	9.0

*Special education here refers to special schools, special classes and specialist services offered in mainstream

and cerebral palsied were accommodated in special schools under its jurisdiction (Cooper *et al.* 1990). Further, in Bophuthatswana, where the provision of services for mentally handicapped children has received recent attention, the Annual Report for 1989 gives a figure of 1094 such pupils in special educational placements (Bophuthatswana Department of Education 1989).

Despite these indications, any attempt to gather more current and nationally representative information is bedevilled by inconsistency and unreliability of reporting as well as by the variety of categories used by different departments – including the forms that special education services may take (Partington 1991). More current information, therefore, in the form in which it is available, is neither comparable nor usefully interpretable in any attempt to gain a national picture. However, even if it is accepted that there are now more special educational places for African children – especially in the broad category of intellectual impairment – than are reflected in Table 2, it can still be said with reasonable confidence that the overall, *disproportional* provision of special educational services reflected in the table has not altered significantly from 1985 to 1992. This is further reinforced by the proportional growth rates in school enrolment over this period. Based on 1990 enrolments (Du Pisani *et al.* 1991), the increase was 5.4% per annum between 1985 and 1990 in African education as against an increase of only 1.0% in coloured education and a decline of 0.8% and 0.1% respectively in white and Indian education.

Thus, although both Tables 1 and 2 are somewhat dated and are incomplete owing to the non-availability of information on particular categories of disability, the figures as they stand indicate that the deficit in provision for African children with special educational needs is almost total (only 0.6% provided for), for coloured and Indian children it is severe (12.9% and 7.7% respectively provided for) whereas for white children it is only moderate (58.4% provided for). Put more directly, for every 100 children conservatively estimated to have special educational need, 75 are African, 12 are white, 10 are coloured and 3 are Indian (Table 1: Total 2). By contrast, for every 100 who are being provided for, only 5 are African, 79 are white, 14 are coloured, and 2 are Indian (Table 2). In real, human terms this means that it is mainly those handicapped children from the most disadvantaged communities who are struggling to cope unassisted in already overcrowded and under-resourced classrooms. For many who have not found a place in school or who have dropped out, even this is not an alternative.

Appropriateness of Existing Services

The only really developed model of special educational service delivery in South Africa is that which exists in the more advantaged educational sector. In this model, problems identified by parents, teachers or others are referred, on an individual basis, to educational psychologists for assessment. Following this, recommendations are made for placement in special schools or classes, for professional treatment or for the provision of remedial help within the mainstream. In the light of the overall shortage of special educational facilities and services (Table 2), the severe shortage of educational psychologists (Donald and Csapo 1989) and the extent of the estimated need (Table 1), it is clear that this model is simply not viable, in terms of resources, to meet existing, let alone future, needs. Even were existing resources to be redistributed in a more equitable fashion (De Lange 1981), geographic and linguistic factors and the overall shortfall of special educational facilities and professional services would ensure that these would remain least accessible to *and* least appropriate for the most disadvantaged communities.

Apart from the issue of resources there is the question of whether a model of service delivery that is essentially based on separating those with special educational need from the mainstream is the most appropriate. Opposed to this is the now widely accepted principle of mainstreaming or of educating the child with special educational needs in the 'least restrictive educational environment' (Malloy 1978). The irony in this is that, for the majority of South African children with special educational needs, mainstreaming exists – but by default. Being educated in the mainstream is no advantage where no specialist back-up facilities exist. Understandably therefore, most African teachers and parents who have been denied these facilities tend to see the separate special educational facilities provided in the white education system as desirable. In the African education system as it is, with widespread overcrowding, under-resourcing and inadequate teacher qualification (Cooper *et al.* 1990), this is not unrealistic. Teachers at the moment are simply not in a position to cope with special educational needs in the mainstream without significant back-up support.

A recent and, to this point, largely unsuccessful mainstreaming initiative by the Department of Education and Training illustrates this. The initiative has involved the establishment of Panels for Identification, Diagnosis and Assistance (PIDAs) – composed of selected teachers on the staff of a school – in an attempt to meet special educational needs in the classroom. The idea is that problems should be referred to the PIDA, discussed and resolved through a team process. Intrinsically, this idea is not without merit. Unfortunately, however, the system has been launched in a top-down fashion with insufficient attention to either the needs or the competence of teachers to fulfil the role expected of them. Comments from teachers involved in the system indicate that they feel powerless in the face of problems which they believe they have neither the skills nor the resources to resolve (Donald and Hlongwane 1989a). In particular, the lack of consultative back-up has left teachers feeling inadequate, frustrated and ultimately resentful so that it is not surprising if the solution is seen as the provision of separate special educational facilities.

Nevertheless, in the long term, it may still make more educational and economic sense to deploy future resources in the mainstream rather than attempting to extend the questionable separatist or self-contained model. The principles that have informed the ethical and educational arguments in favour of mainstreaming in developed contexts (Hegarty *et al.* 1981) are equally relevant in underdeveloped contexts. What appears to be necessary is a process of evolution, through consultative negotiation and training, that realistically takes the needs and competencies of those involved into account. Tentative evidence exists, for instance, that with adequate consultative back-up the PIDA system is not unworkable. Under these conditions it has been shown to be effective in

meeting some special educational needs in the mainstream as well as in promoting general teacher competence and confidence in handling such problems
(Donald and Hlongwane 1989a; Green, Donald and Macintosh, 1992).

Certainly the question of what model of service delivery is the most appropriate for meeting special educational needs in South Africa is complex and
requires much more research and debate. What is clear, however, is that the
needs of those who are the most disadvantaged are at the moment being met
neither through the mainstream nor through the model of self-contained special
educational facilities. In addition, the children identified as educationally disadvantaged and in need of special educational support for structural reasons also fall
into this group. The net result is a picture of a very large group of children with
special educational needs whose disadvantage is reproduced in a system that has
an almost total lack of appropriate facilities where they are needed most.

Research Issues and Priorities

Research issues around special educational need in South Africa relate to
both content and process. As regards content, the most fundamental issue is the
historical neglect of research in this area and the fact that what research has been
done has focused almost exclusively on the advantaged educational sector. The
reconceptualisation of both the nature and extent of special educational need
when viewed from the perspective of the disadvantaged sector carries with it the
need to underpin that reconceptualisation with harder evidence than presently
exists. Thus, in order to plan and execute more effective ways of both preventing and meeting special educational needs in South Africa, four major areas of
research appear to be the current priorities.

The first is the need for more extensive and reliable epidemiological data. It
should have become apparent from the arguments presented here that current
information on the extent of disability and special educational need is not only
unreliable but is likely to reflect a severe underestimation in the most disadvantaged communities. No matter how cogent the arguments are, however, this is
still a hypothesis and needs to be verified. No substantive planning to meet these
needs can be undertaken without a clearer indication of the extent and the type
of resources required. This, in turn, cannot be realistically determined and advocated, within a context in which competition for resources is severe, unless the
epidemiological data are more clear and representative of the whole population.
This is, however, more easily said than done. The difficulties, both conceptual
and practical, in gathering such data have been outlined in this chapter and are
further elaborated by Robertson and Berger in Chapter 9. Most important,
special educational need, and indeed disability itself, are not absolutes but are
relative to social and cultural contexts and to the meanings they are given and
the way they are perceived in such contexts. Any attempt to gather epidemiological data, therefore, cannot set out with simple, positivist assumptions. To be
useful such data-gathering must, at the very least, introduce the relativism of an
ecocultural framework as outlined in Chapter 1.

The second area of research is equally problematic. For economic, social and
cultural reasons, models of service delivery that have been developed in western,

first world contexts are not necessarily the most appropriate in the South African context. Thus, the question of whether an optimal and realistic model of service delivery should be based on the principle of mainstreaming has already been raised. Research on this question is needed for it is important that educationally viable, economically realistic and socially acceptable choices are made in relation to meeting special educational need. In order to avoid further blatant, top-down decision-making and the added possibility that special education will be relegated to an insignificant position on the scale of educational priorities, research is needed into what is possible within the given resources, into what models of service delivery work, why they work, and what the recipients, particularly parents and teachers, think of them.

An extension of this is the way the role of the traditional African healer has remained unacknowledged in formal systems of service delivery. Despite this, there is evidence that a significant proportion of parents and teachers, in both rural and urban communities, identify with the beliefs and practices of traditional African healing. Confronted with educational problems, including special educational need, many parents regard traditional healing as an important resource to turn to (Madlala 1990). Certainly the situation is complex and for many there is a conflict between a modern, industrialised lifestyle and traditional African belief systems. However, in precisely this context, a collaborative model of psychological service delivery involving both conventional psychological counselling and consultation with traditional African healers has been shown to be effective (Donald and Hlongwane 1989b). Nevertheless, the relationship is far from unproblematic. What is needed is research that probes both the potential and the dimensions of conflict in this relationship so that all sources of help, regarded as legitimate in the community, can be optimised for the benefit of parents and children with disabilities and special educational need.

The third area of research relates to the whole area of prevention. A major theme of this chapter has been the role that poverty, health and health access play in the cycle of disadvantage where special educational need is concerned. Urgent intervention is required in order to break into this cycle (Gwalla-Ogisi 1990). But intervention for its own sake is unlikely to succeed unless the basis for this intervention has been clearly articulated. For this to be really effective research is required that specifies more exactly not only the relationship between poverty and those health risks that create special educational need but also the interactive processes through which this occurs.

Fourth, special educational need that is created and reinforced in the structural and systemic features of the education system in South Africa has repeatedly been referred to in this chapter. If this is to be substantiated, research is required that specifies the needs, for example, of early drop-outs in the process of reincorporation. Further, the extent to which such basic factors as lack of materials, classroom overcrowding, language medium, teacher underqualification, and rigidly instrumental curricular content and process have both created and exacerbated educational 'retardation' in the classrooms of the most disadvantaged needs to be more clearly specified and analysed. Given the demand on limited resources and the extent of the problem, it is unlikely that the need for special educational support in this area could ever be more than partially met. What is certain, however, is that educational 'retardation' attributable to structural features in the system is preventable. For such prevention to be effective in breaking this most pervasive cycle of reproduction, research is needed to clarify the priorities and the most crucial points of intervention in the curriculum, the classrooms and the process of teaching and learning in an educational system that, as a whole, requires radical, extensive and long-term revision.

Finally, as regards the process of research, it is clear that positivist methodologies have their place in attempting to answer some of these questions. However, it is also clear that answers derived in this way will not necessarily explicate the complex web of factors that underlies such issues as the most appropriate model of service delivery, the priorities of prevention or, for that matter, the very relativism in the conceptualisation and definition of what constitutes 'special educational need' in the historical, cultural, social and ideological context of South Africa. In this context, research methodologies that seek to deal with ecological complexity and with how people give meaning to and understand the nature of disability and special educational need would seem to be essential.

Conclusion

This chapter has attempted to clarify not only the extent of special educational need in South Africa but also the degree to which cycles of reproduction exacerbate and perpetuate this disadvantage under conditions of socio-economic and educational deprivation. The cycles referred to include the multiplicative interaction of poverty, health and health access in the creation of disability and special educational need. This in turn interacts with a lack of sufficient or appropriate special educational resources for those who have the greatest need. Since this lack exists within an educational system that, in itself, creates and reinforces special educational need, the reproduction of disadvantage is disturbingly pervasive and acute.

Most essentially, the significance of all this in the broader context of understanding child development under conditions of adversity would seem to lie in the following. In terms of the notion of developmental vulnerability (Rutter 1985), these children are exposed to multiple and exceptional stressors. They face not only the effects of disability itself but the *multiplicative* effects of this in interaction with a lack of appropriate schooling and, in most cases, severe poverty, increased health risks and family disruption (Berman and Reynolds 1986; Donald 1989). Further, under such circumstances, they have little hope of acquiring even minimal skills for economic survival in a situation in which they are competing against structural economic odds anyway. In other words, and in terms of social reproduction theory, the operation of racially linked capitalism in South African society is such that this group of people is economically marginalised, and their disempowerment is maintained through the cumulative interaction of their racial categorisation, their class and their disability.

Equally, in terms of developmental theory, it is not sufficient to understand such vulnerability within a framework of individual pathology – whether the multiplicative effect of stressors is taken into account or not. The 'pathology' is as much social and structural as it is individual. What needs to be understood is not only the fact that social factors interact with individual factors but how this occurs. The cycles of reproduction outlined above are one attempt to demonstrate this. What is further needed is ecologically sensitive research that clarifies the interactional relationship between various disabilities and their socially and structurally determined contexts. Within this, the ways in which children with special educational needs and their parents develop coping strategies need to be clarified. Thus, how far and in what ways disabled children, subject to the degree of socio-economic and educational adversity described in this context, can display resilience is an important question that at the moment has no clear answers. The implications of this for both general theory and practical intervention in South Africa are significant. For example, with answers that relate to the resilience issue, it is possible that interventions focused on prevention may take on a higher priority in South Africa if only because they might be more effective in breaking into the cycles of reproduction.

Finally, it should be clear that understanding, researching, meeting and preventing special educational need in countries like South Africa is not a peripheral issue. Nor is it unrelated to important theoretical, practical and moral considerations in the overall process of social transformation itself.

References

Althusser, L. (1972). Ideology and ideological state apparatuses. In B. Cosin (ed.), *Education, Structure and Society*. Harmondsworth: Penguin.

Anderson, E. (1973). *The Disabled Schoolchild*. London: Methuen.

Arens, L., Deeny, J., Molteno, C. and Kibel, M. (1987). Tuberculous meningitis in children in the Western Cape: Neurological sequels. *Pediatric Reviews and Communications, 1*, 257–275.

Arens, L. and Molteno, C. (1989). A comparative study of postnatally acquired cerebral palsy in Cape Town. *Developmental Medicine and Child Neurology, 31*, 246–254.

Berman, S. and Reynolds, P. (1986). *Growing Up in a Divided Society*. Johannesburg: Ravan Press.

Bloom, L. and Lahey, M. (1978). *Language Development and Language Disorders*. New York: Wiley.

Bophuthatswana Department of Education (1989). *Annual Report*.

Bourdieu, P. and Passeron, J. (1977). *Reproduction*. London: Sage.

Bowles, S. and Gintis, H. (1976). *Schooling in Capitalist America*. New York: Basic Books.

Brennan, W. (1985). *Curriculum for Special Needs*. Milton Keynes: Open University.

Buch, E. (1988). Current facilities and services in the health sector in South Africa. In C. Owen (ed.), *Towards a National Health Service*. Proceedings of the 1987 National Medical and Dental Association conference. University of the Western Cape.

Cooper, C., Shindler, J., McCaul, C., Brouard, P., Mareka, C., Seimon, J.-M., Markovitz, M., Mashabela, H., Pickard–Cambridge, C. and Hamilton, R. (1988). *Race Relations Survey 1986*. Johannesburg: South African Institute of Race Relations.

Cooper, C., McCaul, C., Hamilton, R., Delvare, I., Moonsamy, J. and Mueller, K. (1990). *Race Relations Survey, 1989-90*. Johannesburg: South African Institute of Race Relations.

Cumpsty, C. and Theron, H. (1986). A sociologically and developmentally oriented analysis of pediatric pedestrian trauma in the Cape Town municipal area. Paper presented at the South African Brain and Behaviour Society 3rd National Neuropsychology Congress, University of Cape Town.

Davidson, J. and Dickman, B. (1990). Issues in the assessment of people regarded as mentally handicapped. In S. Lea and D. Foster (eds), *Perspectives on Mental Handicap in South Africa*. Durban: Butterworths.

De Lange, J. (1981). *Provision of Education in the Republic of South Africa* (Report of the National

Investigation into Education). Pretoria: Human Sciences Research Council.

Donald, D. (1989). *Applied Child Psychology in South African Society: Purposes, Problems and Paradigm Shifts*. Inaugural lecture. Pietermaritzburg: University of Natal Press.

Donald, D. (1992) Estimation of the Incidence of Special Educational Need in South Africa. Unpublished research report. Johannesburg: National Education Policy Investigation.

Donald, D. and Csapo, M. (1989). School psychology in South Africa. In P. Saigh and T. Oakland (eds), *International Perspectives on Psychology in the Schools*. Hillside, N.J.: Lawrence Erlbaum.

Donald, D. and Hlongwane, M. (1989a). Consultative psychological service delivery in the context of black education in South Africa. *International Journal of Special Education, 4,* 119–128.

Donald, D. and Hlongwane, M. (1989b). Issues in the integration of traditional African healing and western counselling in school psychological practice: Three case studies. *School Psychology International, 10,* 243–249.

Du Pisani, T., Plekker, S., Dennis, C. and Strauss, J. (1991). *Education and Manpower Development. No. 11.* Research Institute for Educational Planning. Bloemfontein: University of the Orange Free State.

Frets-Van Buuren, J., Letuma, E. and Daynes, G. (1990). Observations on early school failure in Zulu children. *South African Medical Journal, 77,* 144–146.

Green, L., Donald, D. and Macintosh, I. (1992). Indirect service delivery for special educational needs in South Africa: A comparative study of five consultative interventions. *International Journal of Special Education, 7* (3), 267–278.

Gwalla-Ogisi, N. (1990). Special education in South Africa. In M. Nkomo (ed.), *Pedagogy of Domination: Towards a Democratic Education in South Africa*. Trenton, N.J.: Africa World Press.

Hattingh, J. (ed.) (1987). *Disability in the Republic of South Africa: Main Report*. Pretoria: Department of National Health and Population Development.

Hegarty, S., Pocklington, K. and Lucas, D. (1981). *Educating Pupils with Special Needs in the Ordinary School*. Windsor: NFER-Nelson.

Human Sciences Research Council (1987). *Education for the Black Disabled*. Pretoria: Human Sciences Research Council.

Kanner, L. (1957). *Child Psychiatry*. Springfield: Charles C. Thomas.

Lea, S. and Foster, D. (eds) (1990). *Perspectives on Mental Handicap in South Africa*. Durban: Butterworths.

Madlala, C. (1990). Traditional and western approaches to educational problems. Unpublished M.Ed. dissertation, University of Natal.

Malloy, L. (1978). The changing mandate for special education. In H. Goldstein (ed.), *Readings in Mainstreaming*. Guilford, Conn.: Special Learning Corporation.

Maritz, N., Uys, I. and Louw, B. (1988). Otitis media and language performance in learning disabilities. *South African Journal of Communication Disorders, 35,* 17–23.

Molteno, C., Roux, A., Nelson, M. and Arens, L. (1990). Causes of mental handicap in Cape Town. *South African Medical Journal, 77,* 98–101.

Nkomo, M. (ed.) (1990). *Pedagogy of Domination: Towards a Democratic Education in South Africa*. Trenton, N.J.: Africa World Press.

Olver, G. (1984). Poverty, health and health care in South Africa. Carnegie conference paper no. 166. Second Carnegie Inquiry into Poverty and Development in South Africa. University of Cape Town.

Partington, H. (1991). Specialised education in South Africa – An overview. Unpublished M.Ed. dissertation, University of the Witwatersrand.

Rapin, I. (1979). Conductive hearing loss. Effects on children's language and scholastic skills. A review of literature. *Annals of Otology, Rhinology and Laryngology, 88,* 3–12.

Rutter, M. (1985). Resilience in the face of adversity. *British Journal of Psychiatry, 147,* 598–611.

Skuy, M. and Partington, H. (1990). Special education in South Africa. *International Journal of Disability, Development and Education, 37,* 1–9.

Stein, Z. and Susser, M. (1984). The epidemiology of mental retardation. In *Stress and Disability in Childhood*. Proceedings of the 34th symposium of the Colston Research Society. Bristol: John Wright and Sons.

Taylor, N. (1989). *Falling at the First Hurdle*. Research report No. 1. Education Policy Unit,

University of the Witwatersrand.

Wiesenger-Ferris, R. (1989). Partnership between the developed and developing countries to promote special education and disability prevention. *International Journal of Special Education, 4,* 101–109.

Wilson, F. and Ramphele, M. (1989). *Uprooting Poverty: The South African Challenge*. Cape Town: David Philip.

White, N. (1980). The nutritional status of children in Crossroads and Nqutu. In F. Wilson and G. Westcott (eds), *Hunger, Work and Health*. Johannesburg: Ravan Press.

9

Child Psychopathology in South Africa
BRIAN ROBERTSON AND SHIRLEY BERGER

The concept of psychopathology is a product of the biomedical approach to illness in which health is equated with the absence of illness or pathology. While in many cases physical health may appear indistinguishable from the absence of physical illness, the same cannot be said of mental health, which is notoriously difficult to define. It is perhaps most usefully seen as an all-embracing concept which refers to the psychological functioning of people in relation to their life contexts. This is evident in the following formulation, where a blending of psychological, moral–normative and political constructs is apparent:

> Mental health is the capacity of the individual, the group and the environment to interact with one another in ways that promote subjective well-being, the optimal development and use of mental abilities (cognitive, affective and relational), the achievement of individual and collective goals consistent with justice and the attainment and preservation of conditions of fundamental equality. (Health and Welfare Canada 1989)

Definitions of psychopathology similarly have strong social and normative referents. Psychopathology may be defined as the description and study of disorders of mental functioning, focusing on the psychological aspects of abnormal experience and the meaning of the individual's experience in the context of his or her life history. Psychopathology is categorised in biomedical practice into specific psychiatric disorders, which describe clinically significant forms of behaviour or symptoms that are a source of subjective distress or impairment in functioning. According to the above definition, mental health is not simply the absence of psychiatric disorder and, similarly, having a psychiatric disorder does not imply the absence of elements of healthy functioning.

These provisos also apply to children. A study of child psychopathology examines only a part of the broader phenomenon of child mental health. Nevertheless, accurate information about the nature and prevalence of psychiatric disorder is necessary for the understanding of aetiological processes, and for the planning and provision of preventive and curative services. Obtaining accurate data about child psychopathology is difficult because it is a dynamic phenomenon which makes definition and measurement problematic. Psychopathology, particularly during childhood, is also a very relative and individual phenomenon, and definitions of pathological states should not be generalised across communities, countries and continents without reservation.

Questions about the incidence of child psychopathology in South Africa have to note the particular context within which it arises. As has been noted elsewhere in this volume, there is a range of factors both within the child and in the child's ecocultural system which increases the risk for developing psychological problems. These include not only acute stressors but also ongoing inequalities and structural violence (Swartz and Levett 1989). In situations of poverty, violence and institutionalised racism such as exist in South Africa, the risks are high. It would therefore not be unreasonable to expect these factors to contribute to a heightened incidence of psychological disorders among South Africa's disadvantaged children. This is by no means easy to investigate, and it assumes (incorrectly) that to separate the particular effects of apartheid from those imposed by other forms of disadvantage, such as poverty, is a simple matter. Also, not much is to be gained from attempting to treat apartheid as a research variable as it is far too broad a notion. Thus while it is easy to talk loosely about 'the psychological effects of apartheid', it is another matter to demonstrate this empirically (Swartz and Levett 1989; Swartz, Gibson and Swartz 1990). The issue has to be treated with great conceptual care and has not been investigated in the case of children. However, it has been in the case of adults (Turton and Chalmers 1990). Turton and Chalmers have dealt with these conceptual difficulties by introducing certain assumptions about the way in which apartheid has contributed to disadvantage and stress. They have argued that while South Africa shares many of its economic and social problems with other developing nations, the policy of apartheid has directly amplified them for black people and has produced numerous barriers to advancement that add to the numbers of those who are poor as well as adding to the stresses of poverty. It is this active component of apartheid policy which has increased the stresses and risks for adults and children.

As has been noted by several contributors to this volume, while some children faced with stressful life events develop serious psychological problems, others do not. The concepts of vulnerability and resilience in childhood have become well established in the literature, and underlying these are dynamic processes which may change during the course of a lifetime. Maladaptive outcomes are dependent on whether the early risk experiences are compounded or improved by later circumstances (Garmezy 1983; Luthar and Zigler 1991; Robins and Rutter 1990; Rutter 1985). In understanding these processes consideration has to be given to intervening events, the meaning given to these events by the individual and those around him or her, and their influences on interpersonal interactions (Rutter 1985, 1988). More recently there has been a shift from identifying risk factors to studying protective mechanisms and processes, and from a focus on vulnerability to an emphasis on resilience (Rutter 1987). Longitudinal studies have also been advocated in order to trace developmental processes and the causal relationships underlying the production of psychopathology and resilience (Luthar and Zigler 1991; Rutter 1988; Verhulst and Koot 1991).

Having noted some of these broader conceptual issues, this chapter will proceed to focus on the assessment and prevalence of childhood psychopathology in South Africa. Theoretical and methodological issues in the identification and measurement of psychopathology in a multi-cultural society will be discussed, comparative epidemiological data from the international literature will be presented, and this will be followed by a consideration of the available data on child psychopathology in South Africa. This material has been derived from community and clinic-based studies and other sources. Finally, the implications for future research in this area will be discussed.

ISSUES IN THE ASSESSMENT OF CHILD PSYCHOPATHOLOGY

Measurement of Disorder: Classification and Case Definition

Research into the incidence and prevalence of childhood psychopathology is fraught with difficulties in large part because childhood is a period of rapid growth and change (Rutter 1989; WHO 1987). In assessing and interpreting the child's emotional and behavioural status, it is important to take into account age and developmental level as well as factors relevant to specific developmental time periods. This is because what may appear as psychopathological behaviour can in fact be due to temporary developmental phenomena. Furthermore, childhood problems frequently are not consistent over time and across different situations, and their history is a rapidly changing one.

The identification of children with emotional, behavioural and other problems as 'cases' in epidemiological research is complex. Prevalence figures are greatly affected by the position of the cut-off point, in terms of the number of symptoms and severity required for them to be classified as pathological and therefore as a case (Offord and Fleming 1991). Also, the high co-morbidity of child disorders (disorders of different types presenting in the same child), and the overlap among certain child psychiatric disorders, have put into question the extent to which the currently delineated disorders of childhood are differentiated from each other (Offord and Fleming 1991; Rutter and Tuma 1988). What also contributes to the difficulty of assessing rates of disorder is the fact that there is generally poor agreement on a particular child's behaviour and functioning when different sources (e.g. parents or teachers) are asked to rate the child's behaviour. This indicates that children's 'deviant' or disordered behaviour and difficulties are often a response to specific circumstances and are apparent only in a particular context (Rutter 1989; Verhulst, Akkerhuis and Althaus 1985; WHO 1987). In addition, the perceptions of informants and the contexts in which the assessments occur are central determinants of whether the child will be rated as having a disorder or not (Offord, Boyle and Racine 1989). It is therefore essential in assessing childhood psychopathology to use reports from various sources, including the child, even though discrepancies between sources are inevitable and the issue of how to combine the information is complex (Offord and

Fleming 1991; Rutter 1989; Werry 1992).

There are two approaches to the classification of child psychopathology. The first is the categorical model, where disorders are considered present or absent and are seen as mutually exclusive. The second takes a dimensional approach, where symptoms and phenomena form a continuum at some point along which the individual falls, and the number of symptoms is a measure of the intensity of the disorder (Quay 1986; Volkmar 1991). The two major classification systems currently in use in epidemiological research are the Diagnostic and Statistical Manual of Mental Disorders (Third Edition, Revised: DSM-III-R) of the American Psychiatric Association (APA 1987) and the International Classification of Diseases (ICD-9) of the World Health Organisation (WHO 1977). These official diagnostic systems are based on the categorical model. However, the multiaxial classification system of the DSM-III-R incorporates both to some extent in that it considers not only the clinical syndrome, but also the level of adaptive functioning and the presence of psychosocial stressors.

Most research into child psychopathology is rooted in the biomedical model which is the dominant psychiatric approach. Various critiques of this model have argued that it identifies behaviours and emotions as symptoms, which are distinct disease entities located in individuals independently of context. These entities are considered scientifically established and able to be measured and applied universally (Kleinman 1987; Lock 1987). It has been argued, however (see Dawes and Donald, Chapter 1), that emotional, behavioural and cognitive functioning and expression are socially and culturally constructed, and that the experience, expression and recognition of emotional or behavioural disorder cannot be seen outside of the sociocultural context and of social relations and structures which give it meaning (Kirmayer 1989; Kleinman 1987, 1988; Swartz 1986). Thus definitions of disorder are based on conceptions of normality and deviancy, which may vary with class position and sociocultural context. Assessment involves the differentiation of behaviour that is disordered or deviant from that which is culturally acceptable. In this regard the expectations, values and norms of a particular social grouping will partly shape conceptions of appropriate behaviour and desirable functioning by both child and family (Draguns 1984). For example, aggressiveness may be considered more or less disturbed depending on sociocultural expectations, and in certain contexts it may not be identified as deviance by the community in which the child lives, but may rather be sanctioned by the community. On the other hand, in studies on conduct disorders and juvenile delinquency, bias in the selection of 'cases' may derive from children from particular backgrounds receiving more attention than others. For example, working-class children might be recorded officially more than those from other classes (Farrington 1986). This may also occur when there are inadequacies in the welfare services (as in the South African case), which can also mean that disadvantaged children are particularly likely to be taken up by the penal system and so be recorded as delinquent.

Assessment Instruments

The increase in population studies world-wide has necessitated the development of new assessment instruments for measuring behaviour and for diagnostic purposes. In recent years new screening instruments, structured diagnostic interview schedules and problem checklists have been developed and evaluated for deployment in epidemiological research (Boyle and Jones 1985; Costello 1987; Edelbrock and Costello 1988; Gutterman, O'Brien and Young 1987; Quay 1986; Rutter and Tuma 1988). Structured diagnostic interview schedules allow for standardised data collection and analysis. These are linked to the major classification systems and follow their specific criteria for diagnosing psychiatric disorders.

Structured interview schedules for children and adolescents which employ DSM-III diagnostic criteria include the Diagnostic Interview for Children and Adolescents (DICA), Diagnostic Interview Schedule for Children (DISC), Schedule for Affective Disorders and Schizophrenia for School-Age Children (K-SADS-E), Child Assessment Schedule (CAS) and Interview Schedule for Children (ISC). A further device is the Reporting Questionnaire for Children (RQC), which is a 10-item structured screening questionnaire developed by the World Health Organisation (WHO). It is designed for the purposes of preliminary assessments of the likely presence of a psychiatric disorder, which may then be followed by a fuller assessment. It is administered to the adult accompanying the child and has shown satisfactory sensitivity and specificity (Giel *et al.* 1988). Symptom-rating scales and behavioural checklists have also been developed, for example the Conners' Rating Scales and the Child Behaviour Checklist (CBCL) (Edelbrock 1987). These interview schedules consist of a series of questions in structured or semi-structured form. Information is elicited in order to enable the presence or absence of a symptom to be rated, and further enquiry is made if the symptom is present. Some of the interview schedules must be administered by clinicians. However, others may be used by lay interviewers, which is a particular advantage in a context of limited professional resources, as in southern Africa. The informants are parent or caregiver and child, and in some cases separate interviewers and forms are used for parent and child, while in other cases one interviewer combines and summarises the information provided.

Assessment Instruments in the Cross-Cultural Setting

Problems in the use of standard psychiatric research instruments across various cultural settings have frequently been noted (Gillis, Elk, Ben-Arie and Teggin 1982; Kortmann 1987; Parry 1991; Sen and Mari 1986). In general, there are considerable problems with measuring psychiatric disorders in community studies and then comparing findings with those from different studies. Often, different conceptualisations are employed as to what should be defined as a case, and frequently different diagnostic criteria are used. Assessment tools, data analysis and interpretation may not be standardised and reliable (Links 1983; Costello 1989), and the respondents' (usually the parents') understanding and response to the emotional life and behaviour of their children as well as the ways in which they describe and report it may differ from one community to another even within the same country (Cederblad 1988).

Cross-cultural studies of psychiatric distress usually look at the fit of western diagnostic categories with patterns in other cultures, using structured interview schedules, and cultural variations in the expression of emotional distress are frequently obscured (Kirmayer 1989; Kleinman 1987; Leff 1988). Kleinman (1987) is critical of this tendency to look for universals, and advocates looking at differences in psychiatric disorder across cultures, using what is known as an emic approach. Here the culture's own frame of reference and local conceptualisations of illness are used. This approach has benefited from anthropological methods which explore cultural dimensions and indigenous forms of expression and classification of distress. If one takes this further, in formulating assessment tools for South African use, it may be possible to derive additional categories of child psychological disorder from other sources, for example 'traditional healers', and these indigenous categories may be compared with western psychiatric concepts. In this regard, possible cultural expressions of psychological disturbance in Xhosa-speaking children have begun to be explored (Robertson and Kottler 1993).

The problem of the translation and validation of concepts and assessment instruments derived from the biomedical model is of course of crucial importance (Kleinman 1987). The format, content and language of the instrument are important. For example, it is necessary to establish whether the target grouping expresses subjective states in the way in which they are outlined in the diagnostic instrument. Concepts and terms are not easily translatable, particularly those describing subjective emotional experiences and states (Draguns 1984). In the research setting the respondent will have his or her own understandings, expectations and goals, which may differ from those of the researcher. Therefore, interviewers or interpreters should preferably be drawn from the community under study so as to take account of local understandings. Interpreters should be fluent in both the local languages and English (which underpins the major diagnostic systems of western psychiatry), and have appropriate knowledge and skills within the mental health field (Parry 1991). Researchers who are not part of the community being researched should be aware of the danger of misunderstanding the meaning and significance of actions within that particular cultural context.

There are a limited number of assessment tools and psychometric tests formulated and standardised for the South African population. Most research instruments used in this country are imported from Europe or the United States of America. Parry (1991) has outlined the importance of the process of translation, the need for reliability and validity testing of the instrument, and the significance of cultural issues. Another important factor is the influence of the instrument's format and content on responses and the potential confusion of culturally specific behaviours with psychopathology. Various strategies have been proposed to improve the translation process (Parry 1991; Retief 1988). Drennan, Levett and Swartz (1991) have looked further in examining the broader dynamics involved in the translation of a depression inventory into Xhosa. As they note, the social relationships between instrument user and patient and between researcher and translator parallel larger social dynamics and power structures in South Africa. Thus it is usually the case that the clinician is a white male professional, and both patient and interpreter are working-class black people. The point is that it is not sufficient to simply translate instruments from abroad into local languages with appropriate cultural alteration. The domination of the instrument by bio-medical influences and by white South African psychiatry in particular must be addressed. These power relationships influence and affect both the local valida-tion and adaptation of the instrument and the reliability of epidemiological data derived from its use.

Ultimately, increased clarity on the nature and classification of child psychi-atric disorder is necessary in order to improve the precision of research instru-ments, and in South Africa incorporation of an understanding of the context of the assessment is crucial. This context includes an understanding of the local views on child disorder, as well as the power dynamics which are set up when, for example, white interviewers or professionals interview children or adults from politically and economically oppressed groups.

EPIDEMIOLOGICAL STUDIES OF CHILD PSYCHOPATHOLOGY

International Studies

In their review of major epidemiological studies conducted during the last decade, Brandenburg, Friedman and Silver (1990) comment on the method-ological improvements in studies reported in the 1980s compared with the 25 studies conducted in the United States between 1928 and 1975. These have been reviewed by Gould, Wunsch-Hitzig and Dohrenwend (1980). Half of the eight prevalence studies in the Brandenburg *et al.* review employed the multi-method, multi-stage approach to identify cases in the community. The first stage of this approach involves using screening instruments such as parent and teacher questionnaires to identify likely cases in the study population. In the second stage, these cases and a proportion of the children who were not identified as having problems in stage one (known as screen-negative cases) are interviewed using several diagnostic instruments. The multi-method, multi-stage approach is considered likely to yield a more accurate rate of psychopathology in the study population than the less sophisticated epidemiological methods previously employed. Furthermore, as Brandenburg and colleagues demonstrated, all of the eight multi-stage, multi-method studies achieved greater standardisation of diag-nosis through the use of operational criteria applied to diagnostic interview schedules. These methodological improvements reflect the taxonomic and mea-surement advances made in the study of child psychopathology during the last decade.

A number of important reviews of the epidemiology of child psychiatric dis-orders have appeared recently. Some have focused broadly on community stud-ies (Rutter 1989; Costello 1989; Brandenburg, Friedman and Silver 1990; Links 1983; Verhulst, Akkerhuis and Althaus 1985), and some on paediatric primary-care samples (Costello 1986). Another group of studies has focused on develop-ing countries (Giel *et al.* 1981; Nikapota 1991), while the work of Jegede, Olukayode and Olatawura (1982) and Odejide, Oyewunmi and Ohaeri (1989) has concentrated on the African situation. It is apparent that, despite the methodological improvements referred to by Brandenburg and colleagues, the problems outlined above about the use of assessment instruments across different cultural settings remain evident in these studies. The validity and reliability of the various instruments used have not always been firmly established, and most of them have been developed in the United States of America or the United Kingdom. The likelihood of local variations in semantics and the need for local standardisation, even in the English-speaking developing countries, have not been systematically addressed in this work. There is also the difficulty of deriving a valid translation of the instruments when the language of the country is not English, as well as the possibility of indigenous expressions of illness not being detected by instruments developed in the West. Finally, in developing countries, even should all these obstacles relating to the instruments be addressed, there remains the difficulty of mounting an adequate epidemiological study in the face of inadequate financial and organisational back-up and sensitive or even disruptive sociopolitical circumstances.

Bearing in mind these problems, Brandenburg and colleagues' review, which included eight community studies from North America, Europe, Puerto Rico, Australia and New Zealand, found the range of prevalence estimates of psychiatric disorder among children and adolescents to be between 14 and 20%. The prevalence of severe disorder was roughly 7%; i.e. 7% of the child populations of these countries were likely to be seriously disturbed. Severity was measured by means of rating scales of severity and of impairment of functioning. In her review of paediatric primary-care studies (reports of child psychiatric disorder given by paediatric facilities) in the United States, Costello (1986) reported that the majority of studies found the prevalence rate of psychiatric disorders to be between 4 and 7% – clearly lower than that reported by Brandenburg and colleagues. In a study to investigate the discrepancy between these two rates, it was found that while paediatricians correctly identified 84% of the healthy children, they were very poor at identifying children with psychiatric problems, identifying only 17% of them (Costello, Edelbrock, Costello, Dulcan, Burns and Brent 1988). What this shows is that even in so-called developed contexts, variations in case estimates can arise depending on the qualifications of the personnel involved in the classification process.

Reported prevalence estimates for specific diagnoses vary considerably and must be interpreted with caution. Besides being subject to methodological errors, prevalence rates for specific disorders within a country may vary over time as well as from community to community and even within communities. In Brandenburg's review, the two studies based upon the Diagnostic Interview Schedule for Children (DISC) found that attention deficit disorder, oppositional disorder, conduct disorder, separation anxiety disorder and overanxious disorder accounted for the bulk of the diagnoses made. These studies were carried out in New York State and New Zealand within similar age groups. In Costello and colleagues' (1988) study in the United States, they found anxiety and conduct disorders to be the most prevalent, followed by enuresis, attention deficit disorder, encopresis and depression. Mental retardation and learning disorders were not included in the study. Apart from enuresis and encopresis, which can be expected to present in a medical clinic, the similarity of the other diagnoses to those found in the two community studies may be corroboration of the greater prevalence of these disorders generally. Some of the likely reasons for differences in reported prevalence rates of specific disorders in developed countries are deficiencies in research methodology and variations in the way in which psychopathology is measured. However, another obviously important factor is the impact of particular ecocultural conditions, which may lead to the increase of certain disorders and the reduction of others. Thus in a context of severe poverty and malnutrition, we would expect the incidence of mental handicap to be higher. This is because of the known relationship between prolonged severe undernutrition in infancy and intellectual deficit.

Africa and Other Developing Countries

In their studies of primary care in four developing countries (Colombia, India, Sudan and the Philippines) Giel and colleagues (1981) reported prevalence rates of child psychiatric disorder ranging from 12% to 29%, but found that primary-care health workers identified only 10–20% of actual cases. Goldberg and Blackwell (1970) coined the term 'hidden psychiatric morbidity' to describe the rate of unidentified relative to identified cases. However, Giel's and Costello's studies indicate that this phenomenon not only is confined to developing countries, but also, as we have seen in the case of the paediatric study reported above, occurs in developed countries as well. However, as noted, the factors involved in developing countries are not necessarily the same as those for developed countries. Whereas in the latter, lack of knowledge and training in primary-care workers is seen as an important factor (Costello *et al.* 1988), in the former the deficiencies are more basic. Primary-care workers in poor developing countries usually work with huge case-loads in large areas and can barely cope with the burden of managing the life-threatening physical diseases which are common to such contexts. Also, parents in these settings are frequently preoccupied with their own and their children's basic needs and survival. Superspecialised professionals like child psychiatrists and their services are in short supply, and the level of knowledge and the status of child mental health are correspondingly low among both service-providers and the public (Sartorius and Graham 1984; Nikapota 1991). Child psychiatric disorders are commonly ill understood (or understood in different ways), and their identification is understandably not seen as a priority.

Epidemiological studies in Africa have been reported mainly from the northern half of the continent. Early community-based studies in Sudan and Ethiopia indicated a prevalence rate of psychiatric disorders of between 3 and 11% (Nikapota 1991). The prevalence rates reported by primary-care facilities in the Sudan were 10% (Giel *et al.* 1981) and in Senegal 17% (Odejide *et al.* 1989). Commenting on the marked variation of prevalence rates between developing countries, Nikapota (1991:743) states that 'a major reason for differences in reported rates at the different sites was consultation patterns for children with mental retardation and associated behaviour problems'. Mental retardation forms a significant component of the child psychiatric case-load in developing countries.

Information about the prevalence of specific disorders in developing countries is anecdotal because it is based largely on a few clinic studies. However, what is clear is that a higher rate of mental retardation has been well documented, and these children form a substantial proportion of those seen at paediatric primary-care clinics in developing countries (Nikapota 1991). In large measure, the incidence of mental handicap in developing countries is based on poor nutritional conditions, and the neurological damage which is associated with severe malnutrition and associated diseases in early childhood (see Richter and Griesel, Chapter 4). Nikapota is of the opinion that

> expanding educational services have led also to the identification of children with learning disorders… Children with emotional and neurotic disorders are commonly seen. Hysterical disorders are probably more common than in developed countries, but conduct disorders rarely present. Difficult behaviour is not perceived as requiring help or treatment but rather as a situation requiring advice or discipline… Adolescents with depression and psychosis may present more commonly to adult psychiatric facilities. Available information indicates that schizophreniform psychosis may be more common among adolescents from Asia and Africa than in Western cultures. An emerging problem among adolescents is experimentation with, and addiction to, dependence-producing drugs. (1991:744)

Nikapota concludes that patterns of child psychiatric disorder and prevalence are similar across cultures but concedes that current diagnostic criteria may not always permit identification of disorder in particular cultural contexts. However, it is clear that all of these statements reflect a viewpoint rather than confirmed facts.

The few available reports from southern Africa confirm the general trends suggested by Nikapota. Kundu (1989) states that psychiatrists in Botswana are consulted about a 'good number' of children and adolescents with behaviour problems associated with epilepsy and mental retardation, with alcohol and cannabis abuse, 'delinquency', acute psychosis due to drug abuse, depression and a few cases of attention deficit disorder and autistic disorder. Guinness in Swaziland (1986) described the significant prevalence of a somatoform disorder associated with family pressure to achieve at school. Called 'school anxiety', this condition has been described in other developing countries as 'the brain fag syndrome' (Morakinyo 1980). It seems to affect particularly the children of poor families who are expected to achieve success in the academic sphere so that they will obtain well-paid jobs and be able to provide for the rest of their family. 'School anxiety' is therefore a symptom of a much wider problem caused by the shifting demands imposed by a society in transition. A good education is seen as the way to break out of the past, but the pressures to succeed are increased by the great significance and real potential rewards of doing well.

In another study of children attending primary health clinics in Colombia, India, Sudan and the Philippines, Giel and colleagues (1981) found that 'frequent headaches', 'sleep disturbance' and 'speech disturbance' were relatively common in all four countries. There were, however, also marked differences between the four countries. There are no further studies of significance which have reported on the incidence of specific disorders. Also, very few of the studies (including those reported here) have considered the possible existence of indigenous expressions of illness in children and adolescents. For example, Nikapota (1991:743) states, without commenting on this important issue: 'Case studies done in a number of countries ... illustrated that child psychiatric symptomatology does not differ to a significant extent across cultures. Findings from these studies also demonstrated that culture-specific disorders are very rare among children.'

A recent literature search by the present authors revealed no major reviews of cultural child psychiatry, and the published research consisted mainly of a small number of case studies. However, Ilechukwu (1991) in his overview of psychiatry in Africa discusses a number of 'culture-bound syndromes' which have been described in African children. As culture-specific disorders are by definition constructed by specific cultures, it is not surprising that they may not have any particular meaning for another culture. 'Foreign' researchers or researchers using 'foreign' assessment instruments are likely to reach the conclusion reported by Nikapota above. A recent preliminary study in South Africa, using African traditional healers as informants, has reported what seem to be indigenous categories of childhood disorder. This further suggests the importance of exploring culture-specific forms of disorder in the South African context (Robertson and Kottler 1993).

Child Psychopathology in South Africa

Important epidemiological research into child psychopathology in South Africa has still to be conducted, so a summary of the available data from research studies and other sources of information about child psychopathology will be presented here. There have been many conference papers, academic theses and publications on the psychological effects of political violence on South African children. This matter is dealt with by Dawes in his two chapters in this book on the subject and will not be considered at any length here. The more important studies are included in a bibliography on children, political violence and war (Dawes 1991).

Community Studies

No comprehensive community prevalence studies of child psychopathology have yet been conducted in South Africa (Parry 1991). The largest study, an unpublished thesis conducted by Van Zyl (1990) in randomly selected schools in two magisterial districts in Cape Town, used a two-stage procedure to study the comparative prevalence of psychiatric disorders in 10- and 14-year-old coloured and white children. In the first stage the parent and teacher questionnaires devised by Rutter for the 1965 Isle of Wight study (Rutter, Tizard and Whitmore 1970) and the Self Rating Scale for Depression (Birleson 1981) were administered to approximately a thousand subjects in each of the four categories.

In the second stage 420 children were psychiatrically assessed by the author using a structured interview with the child (Rutter and Graham 1968). These children were randomly selected from the screen-positive and screen-negative cases in each category. The true prevalence rates of psychiatric disorder derived for the whole sample were 31% for coloured and 33% for white 10-year-old children, and 38% for coloured and 15% for white 14-year-old children. No rates for depression are given but deviant scores on the Self Rating Scale for Depression were 25%, 21%, 26% and 16% respectively. It is necessary that these percentages be weighted in relation to the size of the total population from which the sample is drawn, and confidence intervals should be given. Neither of these requirements has been met in Van Zyl's study, which makes the interpretation of the data very problematic.

These prevalence rates for psychiatric disorder are extremely high, being more than four times the rate (6.8%) on the Isle of Wight and approximately twice as high as the community studies in the 1980s reviewed by Brandenburg (1990). This could be due to problems with sampling, the psychiatric interviews or the method of calculation. Van Zyl does not describe how the sample for the second stage of her study was constituted so it is not possible to know whether the children she interviewed were representative of the total sample. For example, how did she calculate the proportion of screen-positives and screen-negatives to interview, given the relatively small number of screen-positives (5%) among the 14-year-old white children compared with 14-year-old coloured children (23%) yielded by the teachers' questionnaire? The problem becomes apparent when one looks separately at her rates of psychiatric disorder in screen-positive and screen-negative children according to the teachers' questionnaire: of the screen-positives 64% of 10-year-old coloured children, 58% of 10-year-old white children, 79% of 14-year-old coloured children and 0% of 14-year-old white children had psychiatric disorders; the respective rates for the screen-negative children were 25%, 31%, 33% and 24%. The absence of any 14-year-old white children with psychiatric disorders among the screen-positives and the unusually high rates among all the screen-negative groups confirm the likelihood of errors in the screening procedure, the sampling for the second stage or the psychiatric assessments. All the psychiatric assessments were conducted by Van Zyl herself using Rutter's diagnostic interview schedule, and she knew to which screening group each child belonged. There does not seem to have been any independent rating of her assessments to evaluate their reliability. The calculation of the final or true prevalence rates of psychiatric disorder does not appear to have taken any of the possible sources of error into account. Finally, Van Zyl presents her findings as valid and reliable without sufficient discussion of the above-mentioned anomalies and limitations. In summary, the results of this study do not appear to be a reliable reflection of the prevalence of psychiatric disorders in the groups of children investigated.

Robertson and Juritz (1988) used Rutter's parent and teacher questionnaires in a school-based study to determine rates of behaviour disorder. The parents' questionnaire consists of 31 items of behaviour on a three-point rating scale and the teachers' scale contains 26 items. Parents and teachers have to state whether the behaviour is absent, present occasionally or to a mild degree, or present frequently or to a marked degree. On this scale, the term 'behaviour disorder' is applied to children scoring above a predetermined cut-off point on the behaviour ratings in the questionnaires. The cut-off point identifies children with behaviour which has been shown in a previous study to bear a statistical association with psychiatric disorder diagnosed by using direct interview techniques. Although a behaviour disorder thus defined cannot be equated with a diagnosed psychiatric disorder, Rutter found that approximately half the children with behaviour disorders in the Isle of Wight study had psychiatric disorders. The cut-off point calibrated by Rutter has not been validated in any South African study.

Robertson and Juritz administered Rutter's behaviour questionnaires to the teachers and parents of 379 10-year-old and 933 13-year-old children in the Cape Peninsula. Of the 10-year-olds 21% and of the 13-year-olds 17.6% met the criteria for behaviour disorder according to the parents, whereas the figures for the teachers were 9.5% and 10.5% respectively. The rates of behaviour disorder in 10–11-year-olds according to the teachers' questionnaires in Rutter's 1969 study on the Isle of Wight and Rutter's 1970 study in London were 10.6% and 19.1% respectively. Parents' questionnaires were not used in this study (Rutter, Cox, Tupling, Berger and Yule 1975).

In Robertson and Juritz's study the frequency of the most common behaviours expressed as a percentage of the total sample of children is given below in the table.

Table 1. Most common behaviours.

10-year-olds	Parents	Teachers
Very restless	12.7%	6.6%
Steals occasionally	11.6%	0.8%
Often worried	11.1%	4.0%
Fearful	4.0%	2.1%
Miserable, unhappy	2.9%	1.0%

Marked differences between parent and teacher ratings have been found in all studies using this method because of the situation specificity of children's behaviour (Rutter 1989). A serious limitation of the South African study is that the schools were not randomly selected (only schools for white English-speaking children were used) and none of the children were personally examined for the presence of psychiatric disorder.

In another South African study, Visser (1990) designed questionnaires for self-completion by 10- and 11-year-old pupils to elicit their emotional experiences and psychological problems. She drew a stratified sample of 2000 children from three of the racially based education departments (civil unrest in schools for black children excluded their education department from consideration). Schools throughout the country were sampled, and sex, language of instruction and urban or rural origin were controlled for; 1739 questionnaires were returned. Some of the combined frequencies are presented below.

Of the sample 10% described themselves as predominantly unhappy and 23% acknowledged depressive symptoms, with 5% indicating that this was to a significant extent. Suicidal ideas were present in 7% of the children. Visser regarded 23% of the children as suffering from marked tension as manifested by continuous headaches (32%), stomachaches (24%), sleeping problems (21%), crying spells (20%) and enuresis (11%). Visser states that the rates were higher among coloured and Indian children than white children. It is not clear whether these combined frequencies are weighted for the different education departments, and confidence intervals are not given. Visser does not comment on the possible limitations of her questionnaire as a research instrument nor is there any mention of validity or reliability studies. A further point which this study illustrates is that it is misleading and indeed racist to employ state-imposed racial categories in studies of this sort without indicating what the theoretical reasons might be for looking at the differences across the so-called racial groupings of these children. Differences due to socio-economic, demographic and other variables are likely to be more important, unless the researcher is attempting to ascertain the effects of apartheid policy in some way by dividing the groups on a racial basis. In this regard, it has been suggested that the focus should fall on comparisons between specific communities as opposed to these 'racial' or so-called cross-cultural comparisons (see Liddell *et al.*, Chapter 3).

In a research project completed as part of a postgraduate thesis in Paediatrics, Broughton (1986) used the Reporting Questionnaire for Children (RQC) to screen black children for the likelihood of psychiatric disorder. Broughton administered the RQC to 179 children aged 5–15 years in a random sample of households in a Durban township and to 185 children in the outpatients department of a large hospital. Of all the children screened 69% scored positive on at least one item and 11% had more than three symptoms. The three most common symptoms were frequent headaches (36%), wetting or soiling (28%) and sleep disturbances (13%). Of the mothers 5% and of the fathers 38% in the total sample admitted to abusing alcohol. Unfortunately, as in the case of the Robertson and Juritz study, these children were not assessed for psychiatric disorder. The usefulness of the study is further limited by the fact that the frequencies from the two samples were combined rather than compared.

Also in the Durban area, Loening (1990) administered the RQC to all children aged 5–18 years in two random samples of 60 black households, one from a settled community and the other from an informal, urbanising settlement. Interpretation of the results is virtually impossible as the number of children in each sample is not given. However, children in the informal settlement showed a higher frequency of symptoms compared with those in the settled community. The frequencies of the three most common symptoms are listed below, with those from the settled community in brackets: frequent headaches 28% (16.7%), wetting or soiling 22% (16%) and being scared 18% (13.1%). Again, these children were not assessed for psychiatric disorder. The studies of both Broughton and Loening produced the same two most frequent symptoms, namely headaches, and wetting and soiling. The extent to which headaches represent psychological distress in this population is not known. Also, headaches can arise for a number of non-psychological reasons, and the cause of the high prevalence of this symptom cannot be established from this study. The frequency of wetting and soiling may reflect the high prevalence of mental retardation in developing countries and not emotional distress (Giel *et al.* 1988).

While the effects of political violence on children are explored elsewhere in this volume, certain observations are appropriate here as they relate to reported incidences of child psychological disorder. Investigating the effects of political violence on symptom presentation in black children, Dawes, Tredoux and Feinstein (1989) interviewed 67 families who were among the survivors of four squatter communities in Cape Town subjected to brutal attacks by political opponents, during the course of which seventy thousand people were rendered homeless and more than 60 killed. They found that 40% of the children aged 2–17 years (n=207) were reported to have had symptoms of emotional stress, and 9% were described as being seriously disturbed enough to warrant a diagnosis of Post-Traumatic Stress Disorder (PTSD). They caution that these results are based on reports and not on mental state examination. Straker, Moosa and the Sanctuaries Treatment Team (1988) reported on the development of PTSD in the majority of a group of 60 youths aged 12-22 years, seen at a community clinic, who had been exposed to a series of traumatic events in Leandra township, Transvaal, including witnessing the political murder of a loved one, condoning the murder of a political opponent and being beaten by police in gaol. Skinner and Swartz (1989) investigated the effects on 19 preschool children of a parent's detention. Primary caregivers were interviewed in this retrospective study, regarding emotional and behavioural problems manifested by the children. A range of problems was noted, including increased dependence on adults, fears, and sleep disorders. Behavioural problems appeared to peak during the detention period and subside over time after release. Considerable individual variation was found, and was linked to the circumstances of the detention, past police contact, and the security of the environment following the detention.

A range of inadequacies has been pointed out about the few larger-scale investigations carried out in this country. The small number of studies is itself an indicator of the pressing need for further work in this area as well as reflective of a situation of neglect.

Clinic Studies

One of the specific limitations of clinic-based studies is that clinic populations tend to be unrepresentative because of referral biases and other selective factors. These studies draw samples only from those children who are brought to the attention of health or mental health professionals. Whether help is sought from medical or psychiatric services depends largely on whether the adult caretaker perceives the need and identifies the situation as illness-related (Verhulst, Akkerhuis and Althaus 1985), whether services are available and accessible, and whether screening procedures and paths of referral lead in this direction.

As in the case of community studies there are many small, unreviewed or descriptive clinic studies in conference papers, academic theses or local publications which will not be discussed. Studies which will not be described here include reports on conduct-disordered children (Holford and Smith 1987; Schlebusch 1979), suicide attempts (Pillay and Schlebusch 1987) and children requiring day or inpatient psychiatric treatment (Moodley and Pillay 1993; Robertson and Pikholz 1987). The largest clinic sample described to date is that discussed by Schoeman, Robertson, Lasich, Bicha and Westaway (1989), who reported on the psychiatric diagnoses of 808 black children and adolescents seen at four major psychiatric units in South Africa. The authors did not attempt to include all clinic attenders or a random sample. Their aim was to conduct an initial exploration into the nature rather than the prevalence of psychiatric disorders in black South African children and adolescents. The methodology employed was a retrospective folder study in which the diagnoses according to the DSM-III-R were noted of all the patients attending during the study period. The sample consisted of both inpatients and outpatients, most of the patients were under 20 years, 86 patients were Indian and the remainder black, and most had presented for treatment during the first nine months of 1988.

The limitations of the study, which are fully described by the authors, include the fact that the diagnosis of psychiatric disorder was based solely on a North American biomedical classification system. Because it is not possible to generalise the findings to the total population, and because the four units themselves differed markedly in the nature of the service offered and therefore the type of patient seen, the qualitative rather than the quantitative aspects of the study will be reported here.

Mental retardation was the single most frequent diagnosis, as has been found in clinic studies of children in other developing countries (Giel *et al.* 1981; Lea and Foster 1990). In line with the trend of previous research in Africa was the absence of autistic disorder among the diagnoses recorded (Lotter 1978). A high frequency of mood disorders was found; this contrasts with earlier research which questioned the occurrence of depression in black people (Oberholzer 1986). Similarly suicide attempts were reported more frequently than expected on the basis of previous publications (German 1987). Conduct disorder, substance abuse and substance-induced organic mental disorders were also relatively common, and a significant number of cases of brief reactive psychosis were found among the adolescent inpatients. Despite the considerable amount of child abuse reported and the prevailing civil unrest in the country at the time, only one centre documented the occurrence of Post-Traumatic Stress Disorder. This could be due to misdiagnosis (Westaway 1991) or to the avoidance of state facilities by the victims of political violence at the time for fear of arrest. Finally, only one centre reported 'culture-specific syndromes' but no details about their nature were supplied.

Other indications of child psychopathology in the South African population have been supplied by two reports. The first, a report of a government committee of inquiry into child mental health care services in South Africa published in 1988, documented the numbers of children treated at various psychiatric facilities over the course of a 12-month period (Department of National Health and

Population Development 1988). However, not all facilitiês are included, no diagnoses are given, and institutionalised mentally retarded children appear to have been included without differentiating them from children with psychiatric disorders.

The second, a report of the Psychological Association of South Africa (PASA 1989), quotes rates of childhood behaviour disorders, learning disorders and suicide rates. However, the rates for behaviour disorders are based on the international literature, not South African studies, while the rates for learning disorders refer to the high failure rate of black pupils rather than the prevalence of learning disorders as such. This report and a number of others underline the aetiological complexity of learning disorders in black children, drawing attention to the significant role of physical factors, including coming to school hungry, chronic malnutrition, and the high rate of visual and hearing defects (Frets-Van Buuren, Letuma and Daynes 1990; Cartwright, Jukes, Wilson and Xaba 1981; Wagstaff, Reinach, Richardson, Mkhasibe and De Fries 1987).

Finally, a recent publication by Flisher, Joubert and Yach (1992) on mortality rates in South African adolescents (10–19 years) indicates that the largest component was due to external causes, of which one-third to one-half were road-related. The mortality rate for suicide per 100 000 Indians, coloured people and whites was respectively 1.3; 0.8; 2.1 (10–14 years) and 12.5; 3.4; 11.4 (15–19 years). The statistics for blacks were regarded as unreliable. In another study of a random sample of Cape Peninsula high school students of all population groups (n = 7340), Flisher reported that 7.8% had said that they had made an attempt to end their lives during the past 12 months (Flisher, Ziervogel, Chalton, Leger and Robertson 1993). However, while suicide attempts clearly do indicate emotional distress, they do not necessarily indicate the presence of psychopathology as we have previously defined the concept. Also, while juvenile delinquency and substance abuse are associated with the sort of urban poverty characteristic of South African cities and townships, and with psychopathology (Greenbaum, Prange, Friedman and Silver 1991; Milin, Halikas, Meller and Morse 1991), no reliable data are available for the South African adolescent population (Du Toit 1991).

Conclusion

Although a fair amount has been written about child psychopathology in South Africa and several studies have been undertaken, no large well-designed epidemiological studies have been completed and there are no major controlled studies investigating aetiological variables. In Chapter 1 of this volume concern was expressed about the small amount of research on South African children, and the field of child psychopathology is no exception. No authoritative data are available on the nature and prevalence of psychopathology in South African children, or on differences between children from different backgrounds who have been exposed to very different life experiences. Although data on the nature and prevalence of child psychopathology would reflect only one aspect of the emotional development and functioning of South African children, it would nevertheless serve as a marker of mental health in the family, the community and the nation. Signs of both healthy and unhealthy functioning in children need to be identified and documented, and their interrelationship understood if a balance in favour of healthy functioning is to be achieved for children.

The difficulty of identifying signs of psychopathology in children has been described, especially in a developing country with a complex cultural and sociopolitical history. What is more, the documentation of the nature and prevalence of psychopathology cannot be divorced from a study of the dynamic aetiological interrelationship between risk and protective factors, and both need to be viewed in a longitudinal or developmental framework. The epidemiology of child psychopathology is a new field even in the international arena, and large-scale studies in developed countries suffer from significant methodological flaws. However, sufficient experience has been gained to enable South African researchers to venture into what is virtually virgin territory. The complexity of South African childhood is both daunting and challenging, and there is a pressing need for data to inform preventive and curative services.

There is a severe shortage of psychiatric, social welfare and special educational services for black children, and general health and mental health services are fragmented by the legacy of apartheid, with gross inequalities in service provision (Freeman 1989, 1992). The psychiatric needs of black children have been largely unacknowledged until recently, and only a small number of the children receiving psychological help are black (PASA 1989). In the field of mental handicap (or mental retardation), the situation is particularly acute. A survey of South African facilities for adults and children found that only 8% of the need for care facilities is met in the black population, while 62% of the need is met in the case of whites (Van der Westhuizen 1990). Moreover, the Human Sciences Research Council (1987) reported that the current provisions for the care of severely intellectually impaired black children reach 3 of every 40 who are estimated to need it. State-funded clinical services for all South African children are very limited, and the situation in poor communities is particularly bad. Thus, as with the special education sector described by Donald in Chapter 8, the structural abuse of apartheid is clearly evident in the under-provision of services to the black mentally handicapped and psychologically troubled child.

Furthermore, there are only 15 practising child psychiatrists in South Africa and the number of psychologists and psychiatrists working in African communities is extremely limited. For the purposes of planning, service provision and training, research on the nature of child mental health problems in South Africa and on the appropriateness of services is essential. Multidisciplinary multi-centre cohort studies in several urban and rural settings need to be mounted to provide comprehensive information about the functioning and development towards maturity of representative groups of South African children. All aspects of the child and of the child's world need to be studied, i.e. the family, the school and the community. Primary academic disciplines that need to be involved in the collaborative fieldwork include health professionals, psychologists, anthropologists, educationists, sociologists, environmentalists and pastoral care workers. Contact with indigenous healers and herbalists is also crucial in order to understand particular cultural presentations of child disorder, and to understand the forms of healing these practitioners employ in their work with troubled children. Of course, before such important and costly research can be conducted, funders need to be convinced of the value of this research to the population of South Africa and the international community. The status of mental health as an area of concern in South Africa, and of child mental health in particular, will need to be elevated before leaders accept child mental health as worthy of study alongside measles and heart and lung diseases.

References

American Psychiatric Association (APA). (1987). *Diagnostic and Statistical Manual of Mental Disorders* (3rd ed. revised). Washington D.C.: APA.

Birleson, P. (1981). The validity of depressive disorder in childhood and the development of a self-rating scale: A research report. *Journal of Child Psychology and Psychiatry, 22,* 73–88.

Boyle, M.H. and Jones, S.C. (1985). Selecting measures of emotional and behavioral disorders of childhood for use in general populations. *Journal of Child Psychology and Psychiatry, 26*(1), 137–159.

Brandenburg, N.A., Friedman, R.M. and Silver, S.E. (1990). The epidemiology of childhood psychiatric disorders: Prevalence findings from recent studies. *Journal of the American Academy of Child and Adolescent Psychiatry, 29*(1), 76–83.

Broughton, M.H. (1986). Psychosocial and mental health problems in black children in and around Durban. Unpublished M.Med. thesis, University of Natal, Durban.

Cartwright, J.D., Jukes, C., Wilson, A. and Xaba, D. (1981). A survey of learning problems in black primary school children. *South African Medical Journal, 59,* 488–490.

Cederblad, M. (1988). Behavioural disorders in children from different cultures. *Acta Psychiatrica Scandinavica, 78,* Suppl. 344, 85–92.

Costello, E.J. (1986). Primary care pediatrics and child psychopathology: A review of diagnostic, treatment and referral practices. *Pediatrics, 78*(6), 1044–1051.

Costello, E.J. (1987). Structured interviewing for the assessment of child psychopathology. In J.D. Noshpitz, J.D. Call, R.L. Cohen, S.I. Harrison, I.N. Berlin, and L.A. Stone (eds), *Basic Handbook of Child Psychiatry,* Vol. 5. New York: Basic Books.

Costello, E.J. (1989). Developments in child psychiatric epidemiology. *Journal of the American Academy of Child and Adolescent Psychiatry, 28,* 836–841.

Costello, E.J., Edelbrock, C., Costello, A.J., Dulcan, M.K., Burns, B.J. and Brent, D. (1988). Psychopathology in pediatric primary care: The new hidden morbidity. *Pediatrics, 82*(2), 415–424.

Dawes, A. (1991). *Children, Political Violence and War – Influences on Emotional, Social and Moral Development: A Bibliography.* Cape Town: University of Cape Town Psychology Department.

Dawes, A., Tredoux, C. and Feinstein, A. (1989). Political violence in South Africa: Some effects on children of the violent destruction of their community. *International Journal of Mental Health, 18*(2), 16–43.

Department of National Health and Population Development (1988). *His Name is Today. Report of an Inquiry into Child Mental Health Care Services for Children.* Pretoria: Department of National Health and Population Development.

Draguns, J.G. (1984). Assessing mental health and disorder across cultures. In P.B. Pedersen, N. Sartorius and A.J. Marsella (eds), *Mental Health Services: The Cross-Cultural Context.* Beverly Hills: Sage Publications.

Drennan, G., Levett, A. and Swartz, L. (1991). Hidden dimensions of power and resistance in the translation process: A South African study. *Culture, Medicine and Psychiatry, 15,* 361–381.

Du Toit, B.M. (1991). *Cannabis, Alcohol, and the South African Student: Adolescent Drug Use, 1974–1985.* Ohio University Center for International Studies. Monographs in International Studies. Africa series, no. 59. Ohio: Ohio University Press.

Edelbrock, C. (1987). Behavioral checklists and rating scales. In J.D. Noshpitz, J. D. Call, R. L. Cohen, S. I. Harrison, I. N. Berlin and L. A. Stone (eds), *Basic Handbook of Child Psychiatry,* Vol. 5. New York: Basic Books.

Edelbrock, C. and Costello, A.J. (1988). A review of diagnostic interview schedules for children. In M. Rutter, A.H. Tuma and I.S. Lann (eds), *Assessment and Diagnosis in Child and Adolescent Psychopathology*. New York: Guilford Press.

Farrington, D.P. (1986). The sociocultural context of childhood disorders. In H.C. Quay and J.S. Werry (eds), *Psychopathological Disorders of Childhood*. New York: John Wiley.

Flisher, A., Joubert, G. and Yach, D. (1992). Mortality from external causes in South African adolescents 1984–1986. *South African Medical Journal, 81,* 77–80.

Flisher, A., Ziervogel, C., Chalton, D., Leger, P. and Robertson, B. (1993). Risk-taking behaviour of Cape Peninsula high-school students: Part II. Suicidal behaviour. *South African Medical Journal, 83,* 474–476.

Freeman, M. (1989). Mental health care in crisis in South Africa. Paper No. 16, Centre for Health Policy, University of the Witwatersrand, Johannesburg.

Freeman, M. (1992). Providing mental health care for all in South Africa – Structure and strategy. Paper No. 24, Centre for Health Policy, University of the Witwatersrand, Johannesburg.

Frets-Van Buuren, J.J., Letuma, E. and Daynes, G. (1990). Observations on early school failure in Zulu children. *South African Medical Journal, 77,* 144–146.

Garmezy, N. (1983). Stressors of childhood. In M. Rutter and N. Garmezy (eds), *Stress, Coping and Development in Children*. New York: McGraw-Hill.

German, G.A. (1987). Mental health in Africa I, II. *British Journal of Psychiatry, 151,* 435–446.

Giel, R., De Arango, M.V., Climent, C.E., Harding, T.W., Ibrahim, H.H.A., Ladrido-Ignacio, L., Murthy, R.S., Salazar, M.C., Wig, N.N. and Younis, Y.O.A. (1981). Childhood mental disorders in primary health care: Results of observations in four developing countries. *Pediatrics, 68*(5), 677–683.

Giel, R., Harding, T.W., Ten Horn, G.H.M.M., Ladrido-Ignacio, L., Murthy, R.S., Sirag, A.O., Suleiman, M.A. and Wig, N.N. (1988). The detection of childhood mental disorders in primary care in some developing countries. In A. S. Henderson and G. D. Burrows (eds), *Handbook of Social Psychiatry*. New York: Elsevier Science Publishers.

Gillis, L.S., Elk, R., Ben-Arie, O. and Teggin, A. (1982). The present state examination: Experiences with Xhosa-speaking psychiatric patients. *British Journal of Psychiatry, 141,* 143–147.

Goldberg, D.P. and Blackwell, B. (1970). Psychiatric illness in general practice. A detailed study using a new method of case identification. *British Medical Journal, 2,* 439–443.

Gould, M.S., Wunsch-Hitzig, R. and Dohrenwend, B.P. (1980). Formulation of hypotheses about the prevalence, treatment and prognostic significance of psychiatric disorders in children in the United States. In B.P. Dohrenwend, B.S. Dohrenwend, M.S. Gould, B. Link, R. Neugebauer and R. Wunsch-Hitzig (eds), *Mental Illness in the United States*. New York: Praeger.

Greenbaum, P.E, Prange, M.E., Friedman, R.M. and Silver, S.E. (1991). Substance abuse prevalence and comorbidity with other psychiatric disorders among adolescents with severe emotional disturbances. *Journal of the American Academy of Child and Adolescent Psychiatry, 30*(4), 575–583.

Guinness, E. (1986). School anxiety. *Forum* (Bulletin of the Ministry of Education, Swaziland), *10,* 12–22.

Gutterman, E.M., O'Brien, J.D. and Young, J.G. (1987). Structured diagnostic interviews for children and adolescents: Current status and future directions. *Journal of the American Academy of Child and Adolescent Psychiatry, 26*(5), 621–630.

Health and Welfare Canada (1989). Mental health for Canadians: Striking a balance. *Dimensions,* Ministry of Supply and Services, Canadian Government.

Holford, L.E. and Smith, C. (1987). Factors which predict the persistence of antisocial behaviour in adolescence. Paper presented at the 6th National Congress of the S.A. Association of Child and Adolescent Psychiatry and Allied Professions, Pretoria, September.

Human Sciences Research Council (HSRC) (1987). *Education for the Black Disabled Child*. Pretoria: HSRC.

Ilechukwu, S.T.C. (1991). Psychiatry in Africa: Special problems and unique features. *Transcultural Psychiatric Research Review, 28,* 169–218.

Jegede, R. Olukayode and Olatawura, M.O. (1982). Child and adolescent psychiatry in Africa: A review. *East African Medical Journal, 59*(7), 435–441.

Kirmayer, L.J. (1989). Cultural variations in the response to psychiatric disorders and emotional distress. *Social Science and Medicine, 29*(3), 327–339.

Kleinman, A. (1987). Anthropology and psychiatry: The role of culture in cross-cultural research on illness. *British Journal of Psychiatry, 151,* 447–454.

Kleinman, A. (1988). *Rethinking Psychiatry: From Cultural Category to Personal Experience*. New York: Free Press.

Kortmann, F. (1987). Problems in communicating in transcultural psychiatry. The self reporting questionnaire in Ethiopia. *Acta Psychiatrica Scandinavica, 75*(6), 563–570.

Kundu, P. (1989). The psychiatric services and common psychological problems for children and adolescents in Botswana. *Southern African Journal of Child and Adolescent Psychiatry, 1*(1), 1–5.

Lea, S. and Foster, D. (eds) (1990). *Perspectives on Mental Handicap in South Africa*. Durban: Butterworths.

Leff, J. (1988). *Psychiatry around the Globe: A Transcultural View*. London: Gaskell.

Links, P.S. (1983). Community surveys of the prevalence of childhood psychiatric disorders: A review. *Child Development, 54,* 531–548.

Lock, M. (1987). DSM-III as a culture-bound construct: Commentary on culture-bound syndromes and international disease classifications. *Culture, Medicine and Psychiatry, 11,* 35–42.

Loening, W. (1990, October). Community mental health project. Paper presented at the Sixth Paediatrics Priorities Conference. Gordons Bay, South Africa.

Lotter, V. (1978). Childhood autism in Africa. *Journal of Child Psychology and Psychiatry, 19,* 231–244.

Luthar, S.S. and Zigler, E. (1991). Vulnerability and competence: A review of research on resilience in childhood. *American Journal of Orthopsychiatry, 61*(1), 6–22.

Milin, R., Halikas, J.H., Meller, J.E. and Morse, C. (1991). Psychopathology among substance abusing juvenile offenders. *Journal of the American Academy of Child and Adolescent Psychiatry, 30*(4), 569–574.

Moodley, S.V. and Pillay, A.L. (1993). Two years of admissions to Natal's first inpatient child mental health centre. *South African Medical Journal, 83,* 209–211.

Morakinyo, O. (1980). A psychophysiological theory of a psychiatric illness (the brain fag syndrome) associated with study among Africans. *Journal of Nervous and Mental Disease, 168,* 84–89.

Nikapota, A.D. (1991). Child psychiatry in developing countries. *British Journal of Psychiatry, 158,* 743–751.

Oberholzer, D.J. (1986). Depression in the eighties: Black population. *Psychotherapeia, 43,* 9–11.

Odejide, A.O., Oyewunmi, L.K. and Ohaeri, J.U. (1989). Psychiatry in Africa: An overview. *American Journal of Psychiatry, 146,* 708–716.

Offord, D.R., Boyle, M.H. and Racine, Y. (1989). Ontario Child Health Study: Correlates of disorder. *Journal of the American Academy of Child and Adolescent Psychiatry, 28*(6), 856–860.

Offord, D.R. and Fleming, J.E. (1991). Epidemiology. In M. Lewis (ed.), *Child and Adolescent Psychiatry: A Comprehensive Textbook*. Baltimore: Williams and Wilkins.

Parry, C.D.H. (1991). Psychiatric epidemiology in South Africa: Future directions. Paper presented at the National Congress of the Psychological Association of South Africa, Pretoria, October.

Pillay, A.L. and Schlebusch, L. (1987). Parasuicide among Indian adolescents. *South African Journal of Psychology, 17,* 107–110.

Psychological Association of South Africa (PASA). (1989). *Mental Health in South Africa*. Report by the Council Committee: Mental Health. Pretoria: PASA.

Quay, H.C. (1986). Classification. In H.C. Quay and J.S. Werry (eds), *Psychopathological Disorders of Childhood*. New York: John Wiley.

Retief, A. (1988). *Method and Theory in Cross-Cultural Psychological Assessment*. Research Report Series 6. Pretoria: Human Sciences Research Council.

Robertson, B.A. and Pikholz, S. (1987). Outcome of treatment at a psycho-educational day unit for young children. *South African Medical Journal, 72,* 552–553.

Robertson, B.A. and Juritz, J.M. (1988). Behavioural screening of 10- and 13-year old pupils in selected schools in the Cape Peninsula. *South African Medical Journal, 73,* 24–25.

Robertson, B.A. and Kottler, A. (1993). Cultural issues in the psychiatric assessment of Xhosa children and adolescents. *South African Medical Journal, 83,* 207–208.

Robins, L.N. and Rutter, M. (eds) (1990). *Straight and Devious Pathways from Childhood to Adulthood*. Cambridge: Cambridge University Press.

Rutter, M. (1985). Resilience in the face of adversity: Protective factors and resistance to psychiatric disorder. *British Journal of Psychiatry, 147,* 598–611.

Rutter, M. (1987). Psychosocial resilience and protective mechanisms. *American Journal of Ortho-psychiatry, 57*(3), 316–331.

Rutter, M. (1988). Longitudinal data in the study of causal processes: Some uses and some pitfalls. In M. Rutter (ed.), *Studies of Psychosocial Risk: The Power of Longitudinal Data.* Cambridge: Cambridge University Press.

Rutter, M. (1989). Isle of Wight revisited: Twenty-five years of child psychiatric epidemiology. *Journal of the American Academy of Child and Adolescent Psychiatry, 28*(5), 633–653.

Rutter, M., Cox, A., Tupling, C., Berger, M. and Yule, W. (1975). Attainment and adjustment in two geographical areas. I. The prevalence of psychiatric disorder. *British Journal of Psychiatry, 126,* 493–509.

Rutter, M. and Graham, P. (1968). The reliability and validity of the psychiatric assessment of the child. *British Journal of Psychiatry, 114,* 563–579.

Rutter, M., Tizard, J. and Whitmore, K. (eds) (1970). *Education, Health and Behaviour.* London: Longman.

Rutter, M. and Tuma, A.H. (1988). Diagnosis and classification: Some outstanding issues. In M. Rutter, A.H. Tuma and I.S. Lann (eds), *Assessment and Diagnosis in Child Psychopathology.* New York: Guilford Press.

Sartorius, N. and Graham, P. (1984). Child mental health: Experience of eight countries. *WHO Chronicle, 38*(5), 208–211.

Schlebusch, L. (1979). *Conduct Disorders in Youth.* Durban: Butterworths.

Schoeman, J.B., Robertson, B.A., Lasich, A.J., Bicha, E. and Westaway, J. (1989). Children and adolescents consulted at four psychiatric units in the Transvaal, Natal and Cape Province. *Southern African Journal of Child and Adolescent Psychiatry, 1*(2), 1–15.

Sen, B. and Mari, J.J. (1986). Psychiatric research instruments in the transcultural setting: Experiences in India and Brazil. *Social Science and Medicine, 23,* 277–281.

Skinner, D. and Swartz, L. (1989). The consequences for preschool children of a parent's detention: A preliminary South African clinical study of caregivers' reports. *Journal of Child Psychology and Psychiatry, 30*(2), 243–259.

Straker, G., Moosa, F. and the Sanctuaries Treatment Team (1988). Post-traumatic stress disorder: A reaction to state-supported child abuse and neglect. *Child Abuse and Neglect, 12,* 383–395.

Swartz, L. (1986). Overview. Transcultural psychiatry in South Africa Part 1. *Transcultural Psychiatric Research Review, 23*(1), 273–303.

Swartz, L., Gibson, K. and Swartz, S. (1990). State violence in South Africa and the development of a progressive psychology. In N.C. Manganyi and A. du Toit (eds), *Political Violence and the Struggle in South Africa.* London: Macmillan.

Swartz, L. and Levett, A. (1989). Political repression and children in South Africa: The social construction of damaging effects. *Social Science and Medicine, 28*(7), 741–750.

Turton, R. and Chalmers, B. (1990). Apartheid, stress and illness: The demographic context of distress reported by South African Africans. *Social Science and Medicine, 31*(11), 1191–1200.

Van der Westhuizen, Y. (1990). Facilities in South Africa – a national survey. In S. Lea and D. Foster (eds), *Perspectives on Mental Handicap in South Africa.* Durban: Butterworths.

Van Zyl, A.M. (1990). The prevalence of psychiatric disorders in children and adolescents. In *The Influence of Violence on Children.* Occasional paper No. 13. Cape Town: Centre for Intergroup Studies.

Verhulst, F.C., Akkerhuis, G.W. and Althaus, M. (1985). Mental health in Dutch children. (I) A cross-cultural comparison. *Acta Psychiatrica Scandinavica,* Suppl. 323, 1–108.

Verhulst, F.C. and Koot, H.M. (1991). Longitudinal research in child and adolescent psychiatry. *Journal of the American Academy of Child and Adolescent Psychiatry, 30*(3), 361–368.

Visser, M.J. (1990). *Geestesgesondheid van die Laerskoolkind.* Human Sciences Research Council Report ED–4. Pretoria: HSRC.

Volkmar, F.R. (1991). Classification in child and adolescent psychiatry: Principles and issues. In M. Lewis (ed.), *Child and Adolescent Psychiatry: A Comprehensive Textbook.* Baltimore: Williams and Wilkins.

Wagstaff, L., Reinach, S.G., Richardson, B.D., Mkhasibe, C. and De Fries, G. (1987). Anthropometrically determined nutritional status and the school performance of black urban primary school children. *Human Nutrition, Clinical Nutrition, 41,* 77–86.

Werry, J.S. (1992). Child psychiatric disorders: Are they classifiable? *British Journal of Psychiatry, 161,* 472–480.

Westaway, J. (1991, September). Post-traumatic stress disorder in sexually abused adolescents at the Masikhule children's home. Paper presented at the 8th National Congress of the S.A. Association of Child and Adolescent Psychiatry and Allied Professions, Johannesburg.

World Health Organisation (WHO). (1977). *Manual of the International Statistical Classification of Diseases, Injuries and Causes of Death* (9th revision). Geneva: WHO.

World Health Organisation (WHO). (1987). *Care for the Mentally Ill.* Geneva: WHO.

10

The Emotional Impact of Political Violence
ANDREW DAWES

Introduction

Growing up under conditions of political instability and violence produces a
particular set of risks and challenges for children. The extent to which exposure
to one or another kind of organised political violence is a common form of
adversity for the world's children is revealed by the fact that in the more than a
hundred conflicts since the end of the Second World War, which have killed 20
million people, civilians (including children) have accounted for 75 per cent of
the casualties (Zwi and Ugalde 1989). It has been the children of the underdeveloped world who have borne the brunt of this carnage.

Concern about the effects of political violence on the psychosocial development of South African children grew during the 1980s. It was towards the middle
of that decade that the pace and scale of resistance to the state increased. This led
to a massive crackdown by the state, whose agents employed various forms of
violence, including torture, murder, and the agency of vigilantes in order to
divide communities and quash resistance to apartheid. During this time, the liberation movements also increased their armed attacks. So as the 1980s progressed,
political violence became an increasingly common feature of the lives of young
black people in particular. Their exposure to violence took many forms. For most
it came through confrontations with the security forces during demonstrations as
schools became major sites of political struggle, through periods of detention
without trial, and through the political activities of their parents and relatives.

During the period since 1990, the pattern of the violence has changed in that
it has been mainly characterised by extremely violent attacks on unarmed civilians in townships, informal settlements and on public transport, sometimes by
identifiable political groups and on other occasions by unknown persons. Over
this period there have been more than 40 massacres in which more than 1200
people have been killed – no one has yet been convicted of these crimes
(*Mayibuye,* August 1992). Many others have been killed and rendered homeless
in various forms of political violence (an average of 7.5 deaths per day in 1991
according to the South African Institute of Race Relations 1992). In a context
like this there are psychological costs which are less obvious than the brutal

deaths and the physical injuries to which South African society has virtually become immune.

The political violence in South and southern Africa has produced a situation in which literally millions of children have to live in high-risk environments. Their normal environments already contain forces which prejudice optimal psychological development, at least from the point of view of the ideals of childhood held in the western industrial world, and political violence adds another dimension to this context. It also occurs against the backdrop of a culture of violence which pervades South African society and takes a number of forms. Moreover, the distinction between political and other violence has tended to become blurred. At the present time it is probably fair to say that in certain parts of South Africa the threat of violence is virtually continuous and is frequently combined with a lack of clarity as to who is perpetrating the violence. These conditions are different from the pre-1990 period, and are producing circumstances of life which are in some ways more stressful than before (Gibson, Mogale and Friedlander 1991).

Since 1986 when the first works appeared (Gibson 1986; Swartz and Swartz 1986; Richman 1986), there have been 48 reports in the South African psychological literature on the effects of political violence on children (reports by lay persons and human rights agencies are not included in this calculation). They include 14 research papers and dissertations (of which only 6 have been published), 20 theoretical contributions, and 14 case descriptions and considerations of the psychological management of affected children. A number of the studies are unpublished postgraduate theses and conference papers, and the only longer-term follow-up study to be published to date is that of Straker, Moosa, Becker and Nkwale (1992), which is a clinical study of 60 youths. The total figure of 48 works is also somewhat misleading as several of the papers based on the same data or argument have appeared in different places (e.g. Dawes, Tredoux and Feinstein 1989; Dawes and Tredoux 1989). If we note this, then the number of specific and separate contributions to our knowledge is reduced. The majority of the contributions focus on emotional reactions, coping and therapeutic intervention. Only 8 specifically consider the socio-moral and attitudinal correlates of living under conditions of political violence (Carrolissen 1987; Lab 1987; Rabinowitz 1988; Pastor 1988; Dawes, Tredoux and Feinstein 1989; Dawes 1992; Straker, Moosa, Becker and Nkwale 1992; Gibson 1991). It is noteworthy that only one unpublished study (Jacobs 1991) has examined the reactions of white children to the political conflict. While the investigative skew towards black children, who have borne the brunt of the violence, is understandable and appropriate, we need to remember that white children have been exposed to the violence as well. Far fewer white children have been victims of actual political violence, and most have experienced it in less direct ways. Because of this, their responses to the violence and political uncertainty are likely to be different from their black compatriots. But it is just as important that their experience is investigated and understood, and that they are also assisted to cope with a stressful situation which is not of their making.

This chapter, then, discusses research and theorisation on the emotional consequences of political violence for children. The principal findings on this issue have been formulated within the psychiatric and biopsychosocial stress paradigms and have to a lesser extent drawn on psychoanalytic thinking. These contributions will be discussed, after which social constructivist formulations (see Chapter 1) will be considered. Although this chapter makes reference to the international literature on the topic, its focus is on southern Africa and it does not seek to provide an exhaustive review, as several are already available (Cairns 1987; Dawes 1990; Gibson 1986).

Problems of Research in This Area

There are five central problems which are frequently not considered carefully enough by investigators. They all influence the quality of the research and the conclusions which can be drawn.

First, political violence is a rather loose term applied to a range of conditions. It refers to organised violence that has political objectives and can take a wide range of forms, which are likely to affect people in different ways (Dawes 1990). Being imprisoned without trial at the age of 14 is unlikely to have the same consequences as being chased and beaten during a demonstration in the streets, or witnessing the death of a parent. It is thus false to speak globally about political violence as though it were a unitary phenomenon with unitary psychological 'effects', and it is thus necessary to specify the form of violence one is investigating.

Second, while it is necessary for those working in this field to draw on evidence collected in other parts of the world, it is very important to consider the differences between the situations in which conflict occurs, and not to make probabilistic statements about one population of children based on findings generated in very different circumstances. Unfortunately this often occurs, for example when South African stone-throwing youths are lumped together with the Cambodian Khmer Rouge and seen as being psychologically similar (Straker 1989).

A third issue concerns definitions of 'childhood' and how this affects our work (see also Chapter 1). First, different communities frequently have different notions of childhood, which influence their behaviour to those called 'children'. Secondly, children of 3 years old are physically and psychologically different from those of 10, regardless of where they grow up – simply because of the limits their level of maturation places on their psychological capacities. There is no point in specifying 'effects on children' without clarifying who the children are that we are talking about.

Gibson (1989), a South African researcher, has devised a formulation to bring these factors together. It bears some similarity to Lerner's epigenetic framework which was discussed in Chapter 1. She suggests that we take into account five interactive levels of analysis when discussing and investigating the effects of political violence. They include the nature of the events themselves, factors internal to the child which promote coping, the quality of family and social support systems, the nature of the political economy, and the material and ideological structure of the society. If we note these points, it is easy to see why it is problematic to generalise the findings of one set of studies conducted in one violent situation to that pertaining in another country in which very different conditions prevail. It is unlikely, for example, that the findings on studies of the moral orientations of Mozambican Renamo child soldiers who have spent some years involved in brutal killings will be predictive of the orientations of children who have thrown stones at the security forces in South Africa. In addition, sites of conflict such as Northern Ireland, the Israeli Occupied Territories and South Africa are very different in terms of their politics and ideological cohesion, their demography, and their levels of economic development and education (see also the ecocultural framework presented in Chapter 1). All these make a difference to the form taken by the violence, the number of people it affects and their response to the violence (Kahn 1978). The tendency to lump psychological studies from these diverse contexts uncritically together probably stems from investigators' focus on the inner psychological level and their belief that the child's behaviour will be adequately explained with reference to a universal set of psychological mechanisms which operate independently of the sociocultural context. Recent developments within the social constructivist orientation suggest that this is problematic: it has been shown that what were once thought to be internally guided universal forms of psychological functioning can be powerfully influenced by the context within which the child is reared.

The fourth problem concerns methodology. Doing research on this topic in countries undergoing conflict is not easy, and the attendant difficulties frequently make access, appropriate sampling, controls and follow-up studies problematic. The central reasons for this include the fact that it is frequently dangerous to enter conflict areas to do the research. The climate of suspicion and fear which is inevitable in conflictual societies often prevents the co-operation of potential subjects. Frequently this can only be gained if the researcher expresses her or his political position before gaining access to subjects. This can render the researcher vulnerable to physical attack, and also to criticism by other academics on grounds of bias in the research. There is also the very genuine problem of the ethics of conducting psychological investigations among people who are already stressed and for whom the relevance and benefits of the work may well be remote. Research is inevitably an intrusive process, and it is an important ethical issue to determine whose interests will best be served by the investigation.

These problems have certainly influenced the type and quality of the research which has been generated from within conflictual societies, and to some extent this explains why studies in the area more often than not do not fulfil the criteria for rigorous research, whatever the framework employed to make such judgements. This is as true of South African research as it is of international studies.

The case-study method is particularly common in studies of political violence, in part because access to large samples is frequently a problem. South African examples include those by Gibson (1990), Gibson, Mogale and Friedlander (1991) and Straker *et al.* (1992). Case studies are often rich and useful accounts of the role of individual life histories and contexts in patterns of coping and pathology in response to organised violence. The South African contributions have tended to draw on the psychoanalytic tradition in accounting for the subject's behaviour and mental state. They can thus address hypotheses about the consequences of political violence for the intrapsychic functioning of particular individuals with particular backgrounds. This is very well illustrated by Straker and colleagues (1992) in the manner in which they link life histories to current functioning in a group of youths who were exposed to police detention, political killings and demonstrations for an extended period.

Of course, from the point of view of positivist science, as indicated in Chapter 1, case studies are not equipped to investigate hypotheses which enable predictions or conclusions to be formulated regarding *populations* of children exposed to violence. Their concern is more with the unique than with the general phenomenon, and both have a place in the development of our understanding. Case studies also tend to rely on theories which embrace the idea of the unitary, largely non-agentic universal psychological individual, although Gibson (1991) has begun to work towards a shift in this position. She combines social constructivist and psychoanalytic, developmentally based object relations formulations in her approach to the child's internalisation of violent experience.

Finally, as is the case in many areas of psychological inquiry, there is a lack of theoretical coherence in the field, as well as a variety of opinions about appropriate research paradigms and method. These reflect several of the tensions within the field which were raised in Chapter 1 – in particular that between the idea of the child as an individual psychological unit, and the idea of the child as a socially constructed subject. Another tension exists between those who argue for the in-depth study of the emotional functioning of individual cases (usually informed by psychoanalytic principles) and those who see large-scale studies as more appropriate for the accumulation of scientific knowledge. The two orientations usually provide contrasting views of the emotional impact of political violence on children, with the case-study approach suggesting more psychological casualties than its experimental counterpart (Quarentelli 1985). But both have a role because they allow different questions to be addressed.

Research Findings

For the most part, research on children's emotional reactions has been framed within a psychiatric, biomedical paradigm (Swartz and Levett 1989). Within this framework, the search is for the mechanisms in the psychological make-up of the child and the context he or she inhabits, which predict various forms of outcome following exposure to violence.

The psychological consequences of political violence and war for children first began to be systematically investigated during the Second World War (e.g. Freud 1973; Strzenecka and Carey Trefzer cited in Leyens and Mahjoub 1992). It is important to remember the scale of that conflict, which produced some 13 million war orphans. In addition, many children had to endure the fear of bombing and removal from parents as a consequence of evacuations from major cities – to say nothing of those who survived the concentration camps. Most of this early work was informed by psychiatric thinking on clinical psychopathology and was largely descriptive. Another important influence was psychoanalysis, and those most central at the time were Anna Freud and John Bowlby. Anna Freud is well known for her work at the Hampstead Nurseries with evacuated children, war orphans and Jewish refugees, while Bowlby's contributions began with his work on the origins of conduct disorders in institutionalised children separated from their parents (Freud 1973; Freud and Burlingham 1943; Bowlby 1953). Bowlby's studies have remained influential, and many decades of research have established that the disruption of early bonding is likely to have negative effects on affectional development.

The results of the psychological studies of children's coping during the Second World War may be summarised as follows. Those who were separated from their families by evacuation did better if they were in the presence of siblings, were older than 5 but younger than 13; the older evacuees were more likely to develop anti-social behaviour patterns, and delinquency was associated with abandonment; other factors that caused more prolonged negative psychological reactions were experiences of being bombed out of one's home, and evacuation immediately following such an experience. These problems were exacerbated by the level of the anxiety of the child's caretakers, and their inability to maintain sufficient control to support the children.

Despite the fact that very large numbers of children were involved in that conflict, there are no studies (apart from those on Holocaust survivors) which indicate that post-war Europe was characterised by many psychologically dysfunctional adults whose difficulties were a consequence of their having grown up during the war. This may in part be a function of the fact that the question was never seriously addressed – possibly because the ideas we currently have about the consequences of childhood experiences for later life had not entered popular discourse about children. This changed after the war, largely as a result of the efforts of John Bowlby and his colleagues. Their studies gave a major stimulus to research during the next 20 years on the consequences of early trauma and parental absence in early childhood. This work stemmed from the concerns raised about evacuated and orphaned children during the war (Rose 1990).

In the clinical descriptive studies of child survivors of concentration camps, very different patterns of adaptation have been observed, from very disturbed to highly adapted ways of coping (Goodyer 1990). The extraordinary degree of war trauma experienced by these children did not predict the psychological outcome in any simple way. As we shall see at a later point, controversy remains about the degree to which the concentration camp experience was transmitted to the next generation. Even Anna Freud commented on the concern that people had at the time that children are 'innocents' in war and that they would automatically be traumatised by it. She did not find this in her intensive studies of children in war-time, particularly when the children had supportive caretakers (Freud 1973). She also noted that it is necessary to distinguish between the normal and adaptive short-term reactions of distress and shock we can expect frightened children to exhibit, and reactions which are more enduring and which are indicative of more serious problems. All people are emotionally affected by war and civil conflict. Children feel fear, excitement and even fascination in war situations. But only a relatively small proportion (usually less than 10%) develop disabling longer-term emotional reactions. Usually these children have witnessed extreme violence to those close to them, or have been exposed to on-going terror without sufficient support.

Thus even before the South African and other post-Second World War conflicts, it was being asserted that the dramatic consequences that we frequently expect after exposure to the violence of war do not eventuate. These points are often forgotten when we discuss the impact of present-day conflicts and express concern for the situation of our 'lost' generations in South Africa (Chikane 1987).

If we look, for example, at the unpublished South African studies of Carrolissen (1987) and Lab (1987), we can note that both produced evidence of the negative effects on emotions of exposure to street battles and security force raids in the township children they investigated. Symptoms of fear and anxiety were common in both studies. However, it would be incorrect to conclude from their work that the children were 'emotionally damaged', as we have no follow-up data. They may well have been showing appropriately fearful reactions to their very frightening situation. Even in a large-scale study of township children's exposure to extreme political violence and displacement during the burning of an informal settlement, less than 10% of the children were seriously disturbed according to parental reports (Dawes *et al.* 1989). Even in this case we only have parental estimates of the children's pre-morbid functioning and no follow-up data or control comparisons with children from non-violent areas. However, it is quite probable that under conditions of continuous violence the findings will be different. Here more extensive negative reactions may be expected (Gibson, Mogale and Friedlander 1991).

International studies of children living in societies characterised by internal repression, civil war and terrorism produced since the Second World War are more germane to the South African case. In these instances children live in societies which are internally polarised (rather than at war with foreigners), and in which they often play some role in the conflict, as has been the case in the South African liberation struggle. Most of this work originates in Northern Ireland (e.g. Cairns 1987, 1992; Wilson and Cairns 1992; Gallagher 1987; Trew 1992). Other important studies have been conducted in the Middle East (e.g. Punamäki 1987; Punamäki and Suleiman 1989; Ayalon 1989), South-east Asia (e.g. Felsman, Leong, Johnson and Crabtree-Felsman 1990; Kinzie, Sack, Angell, Manson and Rath 1986; Eisenbruch 1992), and South and Central America (e.g. Allodi 1989; Zur 1990). It has included the study of children's responses to terror attacks, being a child soldier (Richman 1992), general political repression and situations of civil conflict (Cairns 1987), the detention and torture of the child's family members (Allodi 1989; Montgomery 1992), and long-term exposure to brutality in a civil war, as in Zur's (1990) Guatemalan study.

Studies of children's emotional reactions to these more recent political conflicts have continued to be influenced by the positivist methods and assumptions of the life events framework, diagnostic child psychiatry, and psychodynamically oriented developmental psychology (e.g. Fraser 1974; Straker *et al.* 1992). The

Northern Irish work in particular has drawn on social identity theory in explaining the way in which youth get drawn into the conflict (Gallagher 1987).

The Life Events Framework

Studies from all these sites of violence have recently begun to draw on research which examines the way in which certain negative life circumstances (risks) render children vulnerable for a variety of developmental problems. As this work has progressed it has become evident that certain factors in the child and in the human environment help to build resilience and improve the child's capacity to cope with these risk situations. This is the so-called life events approach, and those who have contributed most to its development in the case of children have been researchers such as Werner and Smith (1983), Rutter (1985), Garmezy (1985), Goodyer, Kolvin and Gatzanis (1987), and Goodyer (1990). The major conclusions of this approach will be outlined here, and links will be made to the political violence literature. The implicit acceptance of the epigenetic framework discussed in the first chapter of this volume will be evident.

The effects of stressors such as political violence depend on a range of intrinsic and extrinsic factors. The events are given a social and an individual meaning and are differential in their effects, depending on the developmental level of the child and the degree of physical danger. This is important to note for it will determine to some degree the extent to which the child can cope actively with the situation, and active engagement is known to be associated with improved coping. Also, events may be of varying duration, and the findings suggest that if a negative event is of chronic duration the outcome is more serious.

Protective Factors and Coping

How the family has coped with past adversity influences how they cope with new problems. Those parents who promote resilience in their children tend to be active rather than passive in their own responses to adversity. The availability of a close individual (he or she need not be an adult) who can provide emotional support for the child and interpret what is occurring in a sensitive manner reduces risk. Also, the availability of a person who can allow the child to express his or her reaction in culturally appropriate ways is helpful and containing – particularly for young children. The resilience of the primary caretakers as a protective factor is well established. A central reason is that these caretakers model coping behaviour for those in their care and provide a sense of control and certainty, which is particularly important for young children. Caretakers who are themselves vulnerable can undermine the coping of the young child. In this regard, the life events literature notes that a distinction must be drawn between focus and amplification. A focused effect refers to the effects of an event which impact directly (e.g. a mother is injured), while amplification occurs through the secondary effects of that injury on those in the family who have not been directly affected. This has been observed in the case of trauma leading to severe psychiatric disturbance in a primary caretaker, which then leads to behaviour that is disturbing to the children – the amplification effect (Goodyer 1990).

The political violence literature confirms the importance of support. Zur's (1990) study of Guatemalan children who experienced severe ongoing terror has demonstrated that the extended family network characteristic of Guatemalan indigenous communities can act as a protective buffer against the loss of parents in civil war. Research by Punamäki (1987) in the Middle East and by Kinzie and colleagues (1986) with Cambodian children has shown that the religious belief system and political ideological commitment of the community and the children help them to cope. However, even in such cases, as Punamäki and Suleiman (1989) have demonstrated empirically, exposure to chronic serious danger eventually decreases coping.

Few studies on protective factors have been conducted in South Africa. Dawes and colleagues (1989) showed that children whose mothers had Post-Traumatic Stress Disorder following political violence were more likely to have symptoms of psychological distress. These mothers were less psychologically available to their children, and their capacity to give support was reduced. Foster, Davis and Sandler (1987) and Foster and Skinner (1990) have produced evidence which supports the work from the Middle East cited above in demonstrating that ideology and political identity have promoted resilience in young South African political detainees.

As noted earlier, only one study has been conducted in South Africa on the emotional reactions of white South African children to political violence (Jacobs, 1991). Her unpublished investigation of 257 children aged 13–14 years, conducted during 1989, tested the hypothesis that their faith in the security forces would act as a protective buffer against stress and thus promote coping. The results of this investigation showed no evidence of heightened anxiety when compared with norms from an American sample, despite the children's knowledge of political instability in the country. There was also no evidence of an association between increased faith in the security forces and lowered anxiety levels. Jacobs concluded (appropriately) that these children did not show the expected levels of anxiety because they are protected by living in areas remote from the violent events, and because their own communities were not particularly threatened by political violence. While Fraser (1974) found that children living on the periphery of violent areas in Belfast were more vulnerable to stress than those at the heart of the 'troubles', the same cannot be said for white children in South Africa. In many ways they are not 'on the periphery' in the same way as their Irish counterparts, for they do not perceive themselves as under threat from the sort of violence which is occurring in black townships. It is probable that a similar study of black children in South Africa who live near violent areas would produce results more similar to those from Belfast. However, if Jacobs's subjects had been assessed in 1993 under conditions of increased insecurity in the white community, the results might have been different.

The idea of protective factors developed within the life events approach has an echo in the psychoanalytic literature. From this point of view, a supportive social context gives the child a sense of being contained by the social objects in the outer world and serves to facilitate the child's mastery over inner terror and turmoil.

Sensitising and Steeling Effects

An experience of violence during childhood may have 'sensitising effects' in that the child remains sensitive to future stress and as a result is rendered more vulnerable. Alternatively, 'steeling effects' may result, in that the child may be rendered more resilient (but not invulnerable) in the face of future struggles. An associated concept is that of the 'sleeper' effect. Some children have been observed to cope well following a crisis and are apparently not overly sensitised in the short-to-medium term, but then they show the effects of their ordeal in adulthood. These phenomena are not well understood and have not been systematically investigated in South Africa.

A central hypothesis regarding steeling is that the presence of early positive family relationships and good early caretaker–child bonding, together with a positive rhythmic temperament under conditions of manageable levels of adversity, will all predict positive coping. Furthermore, it is believed that in a context such as that mentioned above, steeling may be produced by positive coping with early hardship as the child is given support and containment with early difficulties. There is some support for these propositions from Straker and colleagues' (1992) case studies of South African youths who had been active in the struggle during the 1980s. Straker's work showed that the more resilient young leaders in her sample had supportive early childhoods, and they appeared to have had easy temperaments when young (Thomas, Chess and Birch 1970).

While steeling effects are associated with containing environments in which the strength of the caretaker is central, it is clear that the caretakers themselves need support to carry out their functions. Punamäki's studies of Palestinian women have shown that caretakers who have themselves been supported have been able to give better care to their children. In this case their ideological commitment to the Palestinian struggle also acted as a support.

Delayed Effects

An issue which must be raised about much of the recent work on political violence that is framed within the life events model is the question of delayed effects. These refer to effects such as emotional disturbances that appear after a long period during which the individual has apparently coped well.

There are no studies of the delayed effects of South African political violence on emotional development. But there is some case evidence from the Holocaust literature to suggest that recent symbolic events, through association, can trigger psychological problems based on the individual's past experience of violence. Lansen (1990) has described cases of Dutch Jewish survivors showing marked fear and depressive episodes during the period leading up to the reunification of Germany. However, because of the methodology of the life events and clinical psychopathology orientations, their capacity to identify non-pathological forms of reaction is limited. They would not, for example, be able to pick up the form taken by family relationships in adulthood which might be traceable to the traumatic childhood experience of one of the adults. It is the possibility of negative delayed effects on the generations of South African youth who have grown up with political violence that has been of concern to many in this country. As we have no studies on the question as yet, no conclusive statements on the topic can be made.

The Active and the Passive Child

The outcome for the child is not just a function of the severity of the stressors and the availability of social protective factors, but the individual's coping style is also important. If it is passive, the outcome is worse than if it is active, and certain environments encourage passivity in victims while others do not. Thus it is true that older children who are possessed of a positive temperament and an active coping style have been known to obtain resilience from their ability to care for a vulnerable parent (Dawes 1990). Studies by Punamäki and Suleiman (1989) in the Middle East have demonstrated that children who show an active coping style in the face of political violence are rendered more resilient. Active coping has not been systematically investigated in studies in South Africa, but Straker and colleagues (1992) have suggested that this factor, together with a strong group identity, assisted young political activists to cope with their harassments, detentions and exposure to violence.

Transitory or Transitive Events

Goodyer (1990) refers to the 'transitive' quality of some stressful events. These have irrevocable features, such as the death of a parent, and are likely to have more serious effects than events which do not have such a definite effect on life structure. It has been difficult to construct large-scale comparative studies of these features of the child's experience. But there is clear evidence from the work in Northern Ireland and Lebanon that transitory events such as episodic bombing have far less serious consequences than chronic violence. Straker (1987) and her colleagues coined the phrase 'continuous traumatic stress' to denote such conditions in their studies of township youth who were on the run from the police. However, even this chronic stress is usually time-bound. It is not the same as a situation of loss such as the death of a close person, which, not surprisingly, is much more difficult for children to cope with. Straker and colleagues' (1992) study showed that even battle-hardened youngsters were very shaken by the death of a fellow comrade. However, even in these cases, and in the case of the death of a family member, idealisation of the fallen figure can serve to lessen the psychological consequences (Dawes 1990). This is less likely in contexts in which the assailants are unknown and the conflict is ambiguous.

What Have the Life Events and Related Positions Contributed?

Our current understanding is that while many adults and children are highly distressed in the immediate aftermath of a trauma such as political violence, and may suffer distressing memories and hardships for some time, the majority do not develop serious forms of psychopathology (Wilson and Cairns 1992). Those most at risk for more serious problems are those who have minimal support during and following the violence, those who have lost a parent in early childhood and do not have the possibility of supportive relatives to take care of them, and those who have experienced multiple or continuous trauma and loss. The little work done in South Africa confirms this.

Of the long-term reactions of children and adults we do not know a great deal, but there is evidence to suggest that problems can appear many years after the event, which one would not readily have predicted by examining the individual's post-trauma coping style (Lansen 1990). Again it is extremely difficult in these cases to isolate the trauma of political violence itself as the one variable among many others that accounts most for the behaviour (Levett 1989; Widom 1990). It is accepted, though, that the forms of hazard in the life course following trauma and, in particular, the types of personal relationships available can make a major difference to developmental outcome.

It is exceptionally difficult to tease out the effects of the ordinary context of violence which is common to South African children's lives from those produced by political violence. In many ways, being violent to children is legitimised in South Africa. For example, flogging is a common sentence for juvenile criminal offences. Sloth-Nielsen (1990) reports that in excess of 40 000 people (mostly black juveniles) were flogged in South African prisons over the period 1987–8. Corporal punishment of schoolchildren is very common, particularly in black schools. Holdstock (1990) notes that survey data indicate that 30% of black children are beaten on a daily basis by teachers.

A recent study comparing township adolescents' experience of and reactions to political and non-political violence has made an attempt to establish the difference in the contributions of political and civil violence (Turton, Straker and Moosa 1991). These authors observe that 'the startlingly abnormal conditions of open resistance, and reactions to this resistance (commonly called "unrest") may make the usually abnormal conditions of life under apartheid seem normal' (1991:77). Their study shows that against the background of these conditions, their subjects showed high levels of exposure to criminal violence and hardship. Subjects reported raised levels of stress *regardless* of the degree to which they had been exposed to political violence. What this suggests is that if there were no political violence and township life remained otherwise unchanged, there would be little difference in reported stress levels.

In concluding this discussion on the more positivist work, we should note that central to its underlying philosophy is the notion that the factors which determine children's reactions interact in a mechanical fashion. The idea of human agency is often alluded to in such constructs as the 'cognitive appraisal' of stressful events, but the active component of appraisal is not investigated, and cannot be adequately theorised within a mechanistic discourse.

The strengths of this position include its potential to generate predictive statements and to specify the conditions under which a particular developmental outcome is likely to occur. This is what enables us to state that when the caretakers of children exposed to political violence are themselves seriously distressed, the children are also likely to show an adverse reaction. In order to produce such evidence it is necessary to use methods of inquiry such as clinical rating scales or similar instruments and appropriate controls in the design, so as to establish 'real' relationships or predictions. This method has to assume a dichotomy between a passive subject and an external event so that the empirical relationship between the two can be established. This is not to say that the passivity or the dichotomy is real, but that it is necessary to construe them in this way in order to execute one's research in the appropriate positivist manner and so establish lawful relationships. We mostly forget that it is the dictates of this particular view of science and method which produce the passive and separate subject, and that these are not the sum of its inherent qualities.

It is also pertinent to ask (following Quarantelli 1985) whether the methodology of this approach places too shallow a surface grid on the emotional sequelae of violence, and whether our conclusion about the relative lack of 'effects' is warranted. After all, effects of traumatic situations during childhood and youth do not only manifest as symptoms. They appear in a number of more subtle forms. For example, in adults who have experienced repeated traumatic losses in early childhood and have not had adequate ameliorative support, one can anticipate difficulties in forming satisfactory adult attachments. Also, when children have experienced long periods of terror and violence, one would expect their emotional expression to be blunted as has been observed in Mozambican child soldiers (Richman 1992). This issue is highlighted in the differences regarding 'effects' between psychodynamically informed case reports and those informed by the life events or psychiatric models. In the latter, these more subtle effects, which may not even be recognised as having links to exposure to violence in earlier years, may avoid detection. Furthermore, as Richman comments, children and adults can frequently cope quite well with many aspects of daily life despite the presence of symptoms of emotional distress. The fact that they cope does not indicate that they are not affected. As Berkowitz states: 'It is the unusual individual whose character is improved as a result of undergoing painful or merely unpleasant experiences' (quoted in Wilson and Cairns 1992:350).

The Constructivist Contribution

The central weaknesses of the positivist paradigm are its inherent difficulty in dealing with agentic aspects of human behaviour, and the degree to which it posits a mechanistic and dichotomised view of individual–social relations. The social constructivist orientation attempts to grapple with this problem by rejecting this subject–object dualism and proposing that children's understandings develop through a process of social negotiation in a context of discursive practices.

South African authors have been prominent in advancing this position on the effects of political violence. Swartz's contribution (1988) was the first. He challenged the assumptions of childhood innocence and inevitable damage which were prominent in the discourse about the effects of political violence in South Africa. This was followed by Levett (1989), who deconstructed the notion of psychological trauma employed in the literature on child abuse and political violence, and also cautioned against assumptions of inevitable damage, which were based on the decontextualised view of the human subject employed in the paradigms we have discussed above. Swartz and Levett (1989) consolidated their ideas on this theme, and Swartz, Gibson and Swartz (1990) deconstructed the rhetoric of the 'progressive psychology' which has developed in response to apartheid capitalism. These critiques have been informed by developments within the emerging constructivist approach to the conduct of psychological science, by critiques of the stress and biomedical paradigms (Young 1987), and by studies of the role of discourse and language in the structuring of children's consciousness (Wetherell and Potter 1986).

As we have seen, the psychiatric and stress paradigms have continually referred to the key role of the meaning given to events in affecting the child's response to violence and stress. The importance of the social constructivist contribution is that it makes the social construction of meaning its focus, and thus contributes to our awareness of how children's understandings of and responses to violence develop. For this framework, an essential feature of coping, which the stress and related formulations cannot address, is that children are exposed to discourses of coping which are regarded by the society or community as appropriate for their gender and age, and which then become part of their social understanding. It is this understanding in itself which contributes to the outcome for the child exposed to violence. It can render particular forms of violence manageable and others impossible to deal with. It can render some forms more manageable by boys and others by girls. Thus the social constructivist position suggests that many aspects of the child's age–related capacities are a function of social convention and practice, and are crucial to consider when one formulates an understanding of how reactions to political violence come about. Moreover, because notions of danger and trauma are social constructs to which the child is exposed, what is 'stressful' or traumatic also has no status independent of the internalised discourses which give it life.

We have seen how the interpretation the child places on events is related to resilience and how it helps to explain why some children recover from distressing events quickly or do not seem to react in an extreme manner. But from a constructivist point of view, the positivist approach to science is unable to give an adequate account of how these interpretations are internalised or how they may act in a protective manner. Let us take this forward through a brief examination of the idea of trauma and its effects.

Discourse, Psychological Trauma and Power

Swartz and Levett (1989:241) are critical of most psychological research in this area on both adults and children because of its reliance on the 'psychopathological vocabulary of stress and disorder', which reflects its location in biomedical discourse. Drawing on Young (1987), they show that this discourse contains assumptions regarding the nature of persons (as composed of a set of universal natural mechanisms), and of (traumatic) events as having mechanistic 'effects' in the production of the behaviour we call pathological. They indicate how this framework unwittingly constructs all those exposed to political violence as innocent passive victims. Some of them certainly may be: not because they are naturally so, but because they are constructed as such. The reason is that the contexts of the traumatic events may differ, as may the understandings of them that exist in the affected community.

The manner in which questions are framed within the biomedical stress framework does not allow us to take proper account of this formulation. In asking questions such as what sorts of reaction follow particular traumas, and what conditions increase or reduce their impact, it is employing the mechanistic conceptualisation of the person and the environment to which I have referred. Thus, reactions to violence follow from the way in which 'human nature' functions. But in asserting that these discoveries reflect natural relationships between child and traumatic event, the positivist view does not take account of what constructivists would argue is also natural, and that is the fact that the children and the events are constructed in available *discourses* of stress, protection, vulnerability and violence.

Societies also promote certain discourses about emotion and its expression, the nature of self, and gender. These are 'culturally shaped and are embedded in linguistic repertoires' (Levett 1989:22). Once ideas about trauma and reactions to it become established in clinical lore (and in the lay community), they are not easily questioned but become part of received wisdom. An example of this is the ascending currency of the notion of post-traumatic stress disorder (PTSD) as a reference point for the interpretation of reactions to political violence. As Richman (1992) has commented, there is a range of possible reactions to traumatic events, and the current tendency to focus on PTSD often leads to the assumption that if people do not have 'it', then they are not that seriously affected.

This in itself is problematic, but the central concern is that these dominant and naturalised positions on reactions to trauma have the power and authority to perpetuate a certain form of knowledge about psychological development under conditions of political violence. Such knowledge limits our understanding and our ways of intervening. Children do not just react to violence as 'natural' entities, but as social creatures – as individuals with a personal history and as members of groups with a social history. This element of social identity is important in framing the individual's experience of adversity.

In Afghanistan during the war against the Soviet-backed government, young boys answered the call to jihad; in South Africa the 'Young Lions' (a term used for youth activists) rose to resist apartheid. In both instances the youth were constructed as warriors whose task was glorious and whose potential suffering was construed as a necessary component of their role. Having suffered through injury or imprisonment became a mark of true commitment beyond one's individual concerns and was (and still is) worn with pride. Thus it is evident that in contexts of political conflict (like all others), people are constructed as individuals and also as members of groups in opposition, which gives them group as well as individual identities. This factor, and the discourses which are part of the definition of the group, act so as to produce a degree of resilience under extreme conditions like torture. Of course such an identity may equally reduce resilience when the group constructs itself as helpless. In South Africa the rise of the black consciousness movement worked precisely to undermine this perception in the oppressed, reversing it and engendering feelings of pride and power sufficient to bring about the collapse of the apartheid regime (Biko 1978).

South African clinicians have commented that positive group identity factors in young people who have been subjected to torture and solitary confinement and to other forms of violence have rendered the experience meaningful in a positive rather than a negative and helpless sense. This has increased their own sense of coping and resilience even though it has not guaranteed the absence of normal fears, symptoms, and even long-term negative effects (Dawes and De Villiers 1989; Straker *et al.* 1992). These young people were exposed not only to a discourse of vulnerability or fear, but to one of strength given by their place in political struggle.

Hollway (1989) notes that discursive positions have differing individual and social investments or power. Adults and children can thus potentially move between traumatised and other selves – a frightened little boy who can do nothing to stop the enemy bombing and needs his mother's comfort, and the brave brother who takes care of his sister while the bombardment occurs (vulnerable child and gendered subjectivities with differing investments). This formulation allows us to see children subjected to political violence as potentially occupying a range of frequently contradictory positions, as they respond with their own history of internalisations of invested subjectivities which have developed in the context of their learning of social codes and significations of events.

Following from this view, psychological trauma is not analogous to physical trauma, for the 'object' which is subjected to trauma in this case (unlike the physical body) engages with it intelligently and socially. This presents a challenge to conventional uses of the notion of trauma in the biomedical and psychoanalytic paradigms, in which physical (bodily) trauma is often equated with psychological trauma. In these formulations, physical injury as a result of trauma to the body is given the same ontological status as the effect of some environmental stimulus on the psyche – a problematic conflation of different categories (Levett 1989).

It is psychoanalytic theory which has provided the basis for most of our current notions of psychological trauma. In addition it has proposed a genetic stage model of personality and emotional development which it holds to be universal. Regardless of the psychoanalytic school, all would hold that the stages are characterised by different forms of psychological functioning, which in part are based on the level of physical maturation of the child. Thus these forms will determine the type of psychological reality entertained by the child in a politically violent situation, and will place limits on the child's capacity to cope with the extreme stress that is common in war and political violence (Dawes 1990).

Kahn (1963) discusses the various transformations of trauma theory within the psychoanalytic tradition and in particular the contributions of Anna Freud and Melanie Klein. His paper is replete with examples of physical metaphors used to explain the impact of traumas. He quotes Freud: '[traumas are any] excitations from outside which are powerful enough to break through the protective shield [of the defences]' (1963:289). In other sections of the work, the mother is seen as a 'protective shield' who strengthens the ego's resilience under traumatic circumstances. The failure of these protective mechanisms opens the child to potential psychic damage in both the short and long term. While there is clearly an echo here of the ideas already raised regarding the manner in which available discursive practices may be protective, the more traditional psychoanalytic account tends to see protective mechanisms as constituted more fundamentally within the nature of the mechanisms of the psyche and to regard social relations as separate factors rather than as integral components of the structuring of psychic life.

Despite these problems with the more mechanistic elements of the psychoanalytic formulation, there is much to be gained from an incorporation of aspects of the psychoanalytic position within the constructivist framework. As Urwin (1986:276) maintains, we need to 'penetrate the inter-relationships between these socially produced forms of truth and the psychic life of children in order to understand how children may eventually think through, or in terms of, these forms of truth themselves'.

To do this we must have some account of the psychological mechanisms involved (e.g. defensive processes), otherwise our observations of the way in which children assimilate and reconstruct what happens to them would have no possibility of being explained. Thus as indicated in Chapter 1, without the postulation of some forms of psychological universals, we can end up in a crude form of social determinism, which does not account for our observations (Broughton 1981).

So the issue is not whether the psychoanalytic account of psychological functioning is wrong or right, or that the work on risks and resilience is of no relevance. It is the mechanistic physical analogy which is presented as the total truth about children's reactions to stress, and which is common to these accounts, that needs to be rejected. This treatment of trauma reinforces the view of developmental psychological processes as being essentially the same as physical ones – the latter embodying ideas of natural mechanisms, which suggest a view of the child as a passive and helpless entity set upon by traumatic events. It reinforces an ideology of the naturalised ahistorical child whose early psychic history determines its future in a simplistic manner, and fits well within the contemporary images of childhood discussed in the first chapter. It also gives impetus to hypotheses about the long-term inter-generational transmission of the effects of traumatic experience to which I wish finally to turn.

The Social Construction of Long-Term and Delayed Effects

This issue has received particular attention in the case of survivors of the Nazi genocide, where it has been held that the experience of Holocaust survivors will return to influence the psychological development of following generations. The argument is that because of their own trauma, survivors will transmit its effects to their children and even their children's children, through their child-rearing practices (e.g. overly protective parenting) or through the amplification effects we have discussed earlier. As Roseman and Handelsman (1991) have pointed out in their consideration of Prince's (1985) volume on inter-generational effects of the Holocaust, there have been three essential stages which demarcate psychological studies of this type. First, following the Second World War, there was a period in which the psychological effects of the Holocaust were almost too difficult to examine. Then around the 1960s, it became 'permissible' to engage the topic, and psychoanalytic writers began to document and report large-scale psychological damage in survivors. Then towards the end of the decade survivor children began to be investigated within the same tradition and reports of damage in this group began to appear. As Roseman and Handelsman point out, the early literature interpreted any resilience and achievement among the survivors and their children as defensive manoeuvres, and the psychoanalytic discourse made it virtually impossible for these groups to be regarded as psychologically successful and healthy. Finally, during the 1980s reports of controlled studies derived from the positivist tradition contested the conclusion of necessary damage for the second generation, to the extent that 'no symptoms' was sometimes taken to imply 'no effects'. Of course, no symptoms does not mean no effects, and effects of an event such as the Holocaust can show themselves in a variety of ways which may not be clinically pathological. Roseman and Handelsman see the shifts in the 'evidence' as being influenced by changes in the methodologies and theoretical systems employed and, as important, by the shifting discourse about the Holocaust among the survivor and Jewish communities. Thus at the early stages, the material was simply too difficult to 'touch'.

In an extensive review, Van Ijzendoorn (1992) has examined the literature on inter-generational transmission of parenting. As he notes, very little is known about how intergenerational transmission may occur. But it is thought to include genetic factors, which may influence variables such as temperament, as well as psychological factors derived from previous generations' experience of their own childhoods. He suggests that these transmission processes depend on imitation and social learning, parental coaching and symbolic associations between the parent's and the child's history. They are also influenced by the form and content taken by the memories held by individuals and the groups to which they belong. In the case of the Holocaust, the way in which the Jewish communities define the experience and produce discourses that frame that history for their children would be important. Also, the quality of the parents' own attachment to their parents (who in this case may have died in the Holocaust) is believed to affect their responsiveness to their offspring. Van Ijzendoorn's meta-analysis of published work found that few studies (within the positivist mould) were sufficiently well designed to test the inter-generational hypotheses they set out to examine. Global questionnaire methods with large samples are not revealing of effects, but observational studies of interactional style are more promising and do show evidence of cross-generational parenting style.

The attachment thesis is particularly germane for Holocaust survivors and black South Africans who have lost parents or suffered disrupted early caretaking and have not had adequate care thereafter. The mechanistic idea of simple transmission of the trauma residue from the parents to the children is being increasingly rejected (Van Ijzendoorn 1992), in favour of a more complex model, which includes the mediating effects of discourses about the events and the individual's own reworking of early traumatic experience. There is now some evidence that sensitive and intensive measures which employ observational and interview methods that tap parents' internal representations of the parenting styles used on them will be more suited to clarifying inter-generational effects. These more sophisticated methods are of recent origin and have not been applied in the case of Holocaust victims.

Several authors have agreed that despite a degree of popular belief and some support for the inter-generational transmission thesis in this population (Rakoff, Sigal and Epstein 1967; Last 1989; Danielli 1981), 'there is little agreement among studies of children of Holocaust survivors' (Rose and Garske 1987:34). Their own controlled survey comparison of these children with other Jewish children of the same age revealed no differences on a variety of measures, including indices of psychological well-being and autonomy. They conclude with the comment that 'The assumption by clinicians or researchers that children of survivors are maladjusted does a great disservice to them' (1987:342). Interestingly the same point is made by Straker (1989) in her consideration of the manner in which black South African children are portrayed as inevitably damaged and brutalised by political repression.

Thus there would seem to be a variety of truths about the inter-generational transmission of trauma, and there is clearly evidence that it does occur. But the crude idea that of necessity children are psychologically compelled to bring their experiences of abuse and violence to bear on their future social relations in a negative manner is as incorrect as it is common (Widom 1990). This view continues to have a powerful currency, I believe, because it nests well with the ideology of childhood innocence and the notion of the child as a natural mechanism set apart from the social discourses concerning stress and hardship. The fact that positive, negative and neutral transmission effects have been observed in Holocaust families is testimony to the complexity of the process and the important role of the community and the family in the construction of such events. Also, the way in which certain types of survivor reaction are sanctioned and understood at different points in group history is important to understand.

The usefulness of the constructivist formulations which draw on psychoanalytic theory is that they regard children as being positioned and positioning themselves through their own psychological capacities throughout their development. These may also transform earlier damaged subjectivities through the engagement of the subject in more self-affirming discourses – psychotherapy would be one example, but such a change may come about through very different means (the idea of corrective experiences). This helps us to understand why all who are subjected to political violence and war do not carry some unalterable residue of trauma through life nor do they become violent adults.

If we construct the children of Holocaust survivors and the next generation as necessarily showing psychological damage as a consequence of their parents' experience, we run the risk of constructing victims where there may be none. While it may be controversial to suggest this, I believe that the same will be true for the next generation of children in Mozambique and South Africa, despite the frequently atrocious experiences of their parents – the current survivors. The quality of their lives is likely to be as much a function of the quality of the ecocultural settings which they inherit as it will be constructed by their parents' past suffering.

Conclusions

The two approaches we have discussed here have different purposes and give rise to different studies and information. While some would argue for the replacement of positivist studies in their entirety, this does not seem to be a fruitful avenue. It runs the risk of being excessively socially relativist, and of ignoring the reality of the biologically grounded processes of maturation which make certain psychological states possible, and others not, at different points in child development. A developing child is both a mechanism and a social agentic creature, and both lenses are necessary to appreciate the whole.

Scientists are positioned in the popular discourses of their societies as well as part of the creation of scientific discourses. They thus carry the prevailing ideology of childhood (innocence and vulnerability) with them when they enter the research arena. As scientists, they have a particular investment in scientific discourse. The dominant discourse in this field is positivist, and therefore much of the work reflects the methodological requirements and mechanistic assumptions of this orientation.

The social contructivist framework is a disturbing and disruptive alternative. It challenges basic assumptions about psychological functioning and how it develops. In so doing it breaks all sorts of prescriptions about how we study children. It recommends that we spend more time talking to them so as to unravel the sense they make of things. It suggests that we pay more attention to the way in which adults produce forms of truth for children while they talk with them and interact with them in ways which signify what the social world is like. To do this we have to observe them in everyday situations and in situations of violence. Shifting our approach in this way will improve our understanding of the short- and longer-term consequences of violence and displacement for children. It will also assist us to help them overcome their trauma in more appropriate ways. Conventional research will continue to have its place until the conventions change, and because it can answer certain important questions. It can speak an acceptable scientific language, which is important in backing protests against human rights abuses with data. It also speaks a language to which those who offer aid can relate. But in order to improve our understanding of children in traumatic situations we have to recognise the limits of mechanistic formulations. It appears as though constructivist contributions offer a promising way forward.

References

Allodi, F. (1989). The children of victims of persecution and torture: A psychological study of a Latin American refugee community. *International Journal of Mental Health, 18*(2), 3–15.

Ayalon, O. (1989). *C.O.P.E. Community Oriented Preparation for Emergency*. Haifa: University of Haifa Press.

Biko, S. (1978). *I Write What I Like*. London: Heinemann.

Bowlby, J. (1953). *Child Care and the Growth of Love*. Harmondsworth: Penguin.

Broughton, J. (1981). Piaget's structural developmental psychology, IV. Knowledge without a self and without a history. *Human Development, 24*, 320–346.

Cairns, E. (1987). *Caught in crossfire. Children and the Northern Ireland Conflict*. Belfast: Appletree Press.

Cairns, E. (1992). Psychological research in Northern Ireland and the troubles. *The Psychologist, 5*,

341.

Carrolissen R. L. (1987). Children and civil unrest: The Chesterville experience. Unpublished Psychology Honours dissertation, University of Natal, Durban.

Chikane, F. (1987). The effects of township unrest on children. In S. Burman and P. Reynolds (eds), *Growing Up in a Divided Society: The Contexts of Childhood in South Africa.* Johannesburg: Ravan Press.

Danielli, Y. (1981). The group project for Holocaust survivors and their children. *Children Today, 16*(5), 11–33.

Dawes, A. (1990). The effects of political violence on children: A consideration of South African and related studies. *International Journal of Psychology, 25,* 13–31.

Dawes, A., Tredoux, C. and Feinstein, A. (1989). Political violence in South Africa: The effects on children of the violent destruction of their community. *International Journal of Mental Health, 18*(2), 16–43.

Dawes, A. and Tredoux C. (1989). Emotional states of children exposed to political violence in the Crossroads squatter area during 1986/7. *Psychology in Society, 12,* 33–47.

Dawes, A., and De Villiers, C. (1989). Preparing children and their parents for prison. The Wynberg Seven. In J. Mason and J. Rubenstein (eds), *Family Therapy in South Africa Today.* Congella, South Africa: South African Institute of Marital and Family Therapy.

Dawes, A. (1992). Political and moral learning in contexts of political violence. Paper presented to the Refugee Studies Programme Seminar: The Mental Health of Refugee Children Exposed to Violent Environments, Oxford.

Eisenbruch, M. (1992). The use of traditional healing for treating children of war: The case of 'Skan' in Cambodia. Paper presented to the Seminar on the Mental Health of Refugee Children Exposed to Violent Environments. Refugee Studies Programme, Oxford.

Felsman, J.K., Leong, F.T.L., Johnson, M.C. and Crabtree-Felsman. (1990). Estimates of psychological distress among Vietnamese refugees: Adolescents, unaccompanied minors and young adults. *Social Science and Medicine, 31*(11), 1251–1256.

Foster, D., Davis, D. and Sandler, D. (1987). *Detention and Torture in South Africa. Psychological, Legal, and Historical Studies.* Cape Town: David Philip.

Foster, D. and Skinner, D. (1990). Detention and violence: Beyond victimology. In N.C. Manganyi and A. du Toit (eds), *Political Violence and the Struggle in South Africa.* London: Macmillan.

Fraser, M . (1974). *Children in Conflict.* Harmondsworth: Penguin.

Freud, A. (1973). Infants without families. Reports on the Hampstead Nurseries 1939–1945. *The Writings of Anna Freud, Volume 3.* New York: International Universities Press.

Freud, A. and Burlingham, D. T. (1943). *War and Children.* New York: Ernest Willard.

Gallagher, A.M. (1987). Psychological approaches to the Northern Ireland conflict. *Canadian Journal of Irish Studies, 12*(2), 21–32.

Garmezy, N. (1985). Stress-resistant children – The search for protective factors. In J. Stephenson (ed.), *Recent Advances in Child Psychopathology.* Oxford: Pergamon.

Gibson, K. (1986). The effects of civil unrest on children: A guide to research. Unpublished MA (Clinical Psychology) dissertation, University of Cape Town.

Gibson, K. (1989). Children in political violence. *Social Science and Medicine, 28*(7), 659–667.

Gibson, K. (1990). Case studies of children in political violence. In N.C. Manganyi and A. du Toit (eds), *Political Violence and the Struggle in South Africa.* London: Macmillan.

Gibson, K., Mogale, N. and Friedlander, R. (1991). Some preliminary ideas about the meaning of Inkatha political violence for children living in Alexandra. Paper presented to the 8th National Congress of the South African Association of Child and Adolescent Psychiatry and Allied Disciplines, Johannesburg.

Gibson, K. (1991). The indirect effect of political violence on children: Does violence beget violence? Unpublished paper, Project for the Study of Violence, Psychology Department, University of the Witwatersrand, Johannesburg.

Goodyer, I.M., Kolvin, I. and Gatzanis, S. (1987). The impact of recent life events in psychiatric disorders of childhood and adolescence. *British Journal of Psychiatry, 151,* 179–185.

Goodyer, I.M. (1990). *Life Experiences, Development and Childhood Psychopathology.* Chichester: John Wiley.

Holdstock, T. (1990). Violence in schools: Discipline. In B. McKendrick and W. Hoffman (eds), *People and Violence in South Africa. Contemporary Debates*. Cape Town: Oxford University Press.

Hollway, W. (1989). *Subjectivity and Method in Psychology*. London: Sage.

Jacobs, E. (1991). Exposure to manifestations of political instability: Impact on white South African children. Unpublished MA (Clinical Psychology) thesis, University of the Witwatersrand, Johannesburg.

Khan, M.M.R. (1963). The concept of cumulative trauma. *The Psychoanalytic Study of the Child, XVIII*, 286–306.

Kahn, R. (1978). Violence and socio-economic development. *International Social Science Journal, XXX*(4), 834–857.

Kinzie, J. H., Sack, W. H., Angell, R. H., Manson, S. and Rath, B. (1986). The psychiatric effects of massive trauma on Cambodian children: 1. The children. *Journal of the American Academy of Child Psychiatry, 25*, 370–376.

Lab, S. (1987). The psychological effects of violence on black South African children. Unpublished Honours Psychology thesis, University of the Witwatersrand, Johannesburg.

Lansen, J. (1990). Treating the victims: The European experience. Paper presented to the International Conference on the Consequences of Organised Violence in Southern Africa. Harare: Psychiatric Association of Zimbabwe.

Last, U. (1989). The transgenerational impact of Holocaust traumatisation. *International Journal of Mental Health, 17*(4), 72–89.

Levett, A. (1989). Psychological trauma and childhood. *Psychology in Society, 12*, 19–32.

Leyens, P. and Mahjoub, A. (1992). The psycho–social effects of war on children and adolescents. Paper presented to the Refugee Studies Programme Seminar: The Mental Health of Refugee Children Exposed to Violent Environments, Oxford.

Montgomery, E. (1992). Psychological effects of torture on adults, children and family relationships. Paper presented to the Refugee Studies Programme Seminar: The Mental Health of Refugee Children Exposed to Violent Environments, Oxford.

Pastor, C. (1988). Children and attitudes towards violence: Effects of exposure to political violence. Unpublished Psychology Honours thesis, University of Cape Town.

Prince, R. M. (1985). *The Legacy of the Holocaust: Psychohistorical Themes in the Second Generation*. Ann Arbor: University of Michigan Press.

Punamäki, R.L. (1987). Content of and factors affecting coping modes among Palestinian children. *Scandinavian Journal of Development Alternatives, 6*(1), 86–98.

Punamäki, R.L., and Suleiman, R. (1989). Predictors and effectiveness of coping with political violence among Palestinian children. *British Journal of Social Psychology, 29*, 67–77.

Quarentelli, E. L. (1985). An assessment of conflicting views on mental health: The consequences of traumatic events. In C.R. Figley (ed.), *Trauma and Its Wake*. New York: Bruner Mazel.

Rabinowitz, S.R. (1988). The impact of exposure to civil unrest on children's evaluations of violence. Unpublished MA (Clinical Psychology) thesis, University of Cape Town.

Rakoff, V., Sigal, J., and Epstein, N. (1967). Children and families of concentration camp survivors. *Canada's Mental Health, 14*, 24–26.

Richman, A. (1986). Stress and coping mechanisms employed by pre-school teachers in the black townships of South Africa in relation to the South African crisis. Unpublished Psychology Honours thesis, University of Cape Town.

Richman, N. (1992). Annotation: Children in situations of political violence. Under review.

Rose, N. (1990). *Governing the Soul: The Shaping of the Private Self*. London: Routledge.

Rose, S. L. and Garske, J. (1987). Family environment, and coping among children of Holocaust survivors. *American Journal of Orthopsychiatry, 57*(3), 332– 344.

Roseman, S. and Handelsman, I. (1991). The psychohistorian as delegate of a double-binding community. *Journal of Psychohistory, 19*(2), 341–350.

Rutter, M. (1985). Resilience in the face of adversity. Protective factors and resistance to psychological disorder. *British Journal of Psychiatry, 147*, 598–611.

Sloth-Nielsen, J. (1990). Legal violence: Corporal and capital punishment. In B. McKendrick and W. Hoffman (eds), *People and Violence in South Africa. Contemporary Debates*. Cape Town: Oxford University Press.

South African Institute of Race Relations (1992). *Race Relations Survey 1991/92*. Braamfontein: SAIRR.

Straker, G. and the Sanctuaries Treatment Team (1987). The continuous traumatic stress syndrome – The single therapeutic interview. *Psychology in Society, 8*, 48–78.

Straker, G. (1989). From victim to villain: A slight of speech? Media representations of township youth. *South African Journal of Psychology, 19*(1), 20–27.

Straker, G., Moosa, F., Becker, R. and Nkwale, M. (1992). *Faces in the Revolution. The Psychological Effects of Violence on Township Youth*. Cape Town: David Philip

Swartz, S. and Swartz, L. (1986). Negotiation of the role of mental health professionals: Workshops for preschool teachers. Proceedings of the First National Conference of the Organisation for Applied Social Services in South Africa. Johannesburg: OASSSA.

Swartz, L. (1988). The effects of repression on children. A review of some local work and some questions. In C.P. Owen (ed.), *Towards a National Health Service. Proceedings of the National Medical and Dental Association Conference*. Cape Town: NAMDA Publications.

Swartz, L. and Levett, A. (1989). Political repression and children in South Africa. The social construction of damaging effects. *Social Science and Medicine, 28*(7), 741–750.

Swartz, L. Gibson, K. and Swartz, S. (1990). State violence in South Africa and the development of a progressive psychology. In N.C. Manganyi and A. du Toit (eds), *Political Violence and the Struggle in South Africa*. London: Macmillan.

Swartz, L. and Levett, A. (1990). Political oppression and children in South Africa: The social construction of damaging effects. In N.C. Manganyi and A. du Toit (eds), *Political Violence and the Struggle in South Africa*. London: Macmillan.

Thomas, A. S., Chess, S. and Birch, H.G. (1970). The origin of personality. *Scientific American, 223*, 102–109.

Trew, K. (1992). Social psychological research on the conflict. *The Psychologist, 5*, 342–344.

Turton, R., Straker, J. and Moosa, F. (1991). Experiences of violence in the lives of township youths in 'unrest' and 'normal' conditions. *South African Journal of Psychology, 21*(2), 77–84.

Urwin, C. (1986). Developmental psychology and psychoanalysis: Splitting the difference. In M. Richards and P. Light (eds), *Children of Social Worlds. Development in Social Context*. Cambridge: Polity Press.

Van Ijzendoorn, M. H. (1992). Intergenerational transmission of parenting: A review of studies in nonclinical populations. *Developmental Review, 12*, 76–99.

Werner, E. and Smith, R.S. (1983). *Vulnerable But Invincible. A study of Resilient Children*. New York: McGraw Hill.

Wetherell, M. and Potter, J. (1986). Discourse analysis and the social psychology of racism. *Social Psychology Newsletter, 16*, 24–29.

Widom, C. S. (1990). Does violence beget violence? A critical examination of the literature. *Psychological Bulletin, 106*, 3–28.

Wilson, R. and Cairns, E. (1992). Trouble, stress and psychological disorder in Northern Ireland. *The Psychologist, 5*, 347–350.

Young, A. (1980). The discourse on stress and the reproduction of conventional knowledge. *Social Science and Medicine, 14B*, 133–146.

Zur, J. (1990). Children's experience of war. Report on the psycho–social impact of violence on children in Guatemala. Unpublished paper prepared for Unicef.

Zwi, A. and Ugalde, A. (1989). Towards an epidemiology of political violence in the third world. *Social Science and Medicine, 28*, 633–642.

11

The Effects of Political Violence on Socio-Moral Reasoning and Conduct

ANDREW DAWES

Introduction

There has been much concern about whether young South Africans who have been subjected to political violence will have developed a tendency to generalise an acceptance of violent means of conflict resolution in circumstances of political struggle, to other areas of social life. As the violence continues, some believe that more and more young people become candidates for membership of what has come to be called the 'lost generation' of South Africa. This term has been applied to youth who have been exposed to violent conflict in several parts of the world. In the South African context, a member of the 'lost generation' is painted as being black, left-wing, unemployed, potentially violent, ill-educated, and possessed of low moral standards – in short an 'uncivilised' youth. Apart from challenging the racism inherent in this image, it is important for us to examine the psychological evidence which associates exposure to political violence with the production of violent and morally 'deviant' adults.

Therefore it is essential for psychologists to ask whether the violent behaviour observed and learned by young people in political conflict situations will be internalised as normal, and whether this will then lead to the use of such behaviour in other social situations to satisfy personal or group needs and goals. Despite the paucity of research on this problem, there is a general belief expressed in the commercial media that these questions have been answered positively. The task of this chapter will be to assess the research evidence as it pertains to South Africa in particular.

A key feature of this work is that it has frequently been guided by the assumption that a focus on inner psychological processes can provide the answers to the above questions. As I will suggest, this focus is necessary but not sufficient. The literature points to the need to consider several interrelated factors. These include the following:

1. The political–structural and economic contexts within which the political violence occurs, with their associated capacities to satisfy basic needs for survival.

2. The duration and form of the conflict are also important. Societies that have been destroyed by long conflicts offer different sites within which the

young can act, from those which are left functioning fairly intact.

3. The sense in which the members of the society emerging from a conflict share a history of a democratic or repressive culture is likely to be a factor in determining post–conflict behaviour, as these traditions may be mobilised during social reconstruction.

4. The types of political violence in which young people are involved, and the available social identities within which moral conduct is regulated and expressed, are important, as are the forms of moral socialisation available in the society.

5. The individual histories of particular young people must be considered, as some will have grown up in circumstances which are likely to predispose them to finding support and fulfilment in delinquent and violent activities associated with war, and these tendencies are unlikely to disappear once the conflict has ended. Here the individual's internal psychological structure is likely to be of particular significance in determining conduct.

Thus countries undergoing political violence are different in their degree of infrastructural development and modernisation, their sense of a democratic civil culture, and the existence of democratic government. They also differ in their levels of education (and educational culture), their access to basic resources (housing etc.), and the sense of deprivation experienced by sectors of the population. These factors should lead us to be cautious in disregarding the differences between regions and nations undergoing political violence. It is likely that eco-cultural variations between and within societies will be associated with differential outcomes for children, even though elements of the conflict may appear similar.

These factors cannot be ignored when attempting to explain the behaviour of South African township youth in the 1980s. Psychological factors attributable to exposure to political violence are simply not sufficient to explain the rise in violent crime in the past few years. Criminal violence and poverty have been features of urban communities disrupted by apartheid for many years prior to the uprising in the 1980s (Marks and Andersson 1990). And the rise in criminal violence has also paralleled a rise in urban population density in a context of inadequate housing, the absence of a social welfare net for the unemployed, and a reduction in employment opportunities for school-leavers (SAIRR 1992; Bundy 1986).

A further factor in the South African case is of course the availability of dangerous weapons in all communities. There is no doubt that one of the contributions of the period of insurrection has been to equip this arsenal of destructive weaponry, which can be employed for criminal purposes. The same pattern prevails in other African countries such as Mozambique and Somalia where the weapons of war have been turned into weapons of survival or local political control by the former soldiers, warlords and their supporters.

While there are no cross-national studies on the psychological aspects of these particular issues, it does seem that underdeveloped and transitional societies are likely to be more at risk for the production of 'lost generations' than the developed regions. Apart from the differences in the nature of the conflict and the society, it is this factor which distinguishes a region such as Northern Ireland from South Africa, and which makes comparisons between research on the moral orientations of youth in the two contexts problematic.

Main Theoretical Orientations

There are two central theoretical positions which underpin psychological research on moral learning and conduct under conditions of political violence. One draws on the cognitive developmental framework of Kohlberg and his associates, which focuses on moral reasoning, while the other is informed by social learning theory (SLT) and focuses on conduct.

Work on moral reasoning, largely inspired by Piaget (1965) and Kohlberg (Kohlberg, Levine and Hewer 1983), has concentrated on the evolution of the structure of moral thought associated with increasingly sophisticated forms of reasoning, which are a function of cognitive development. Thus children have been shown to pass through stages of moral reasoning ability, which move from pre-moral through conventional to post-conventional forms (although few adults reason consistently at this highest level). Children in different cultures have been shown to exhibit different dominant forms of reasoning, which seem to relate to the available approaches to morality existent in their cultures (Edwards, 1975, 1982; Harkness, Edwards and Super 1981; Rest, Thoma, Moon and Getz 1986) Differences in reasoning have also been found across lines of class (Enright, Enright, Manheim and Harris 1980) and gender (Gilligan 1982). Theorisation about moral development under conditions of political violence tends to suggest that levels of moral reasoning will be lowered to conventional or at worst pre-moral levels, and this will have negative consequences for the moral character of the society. The reasoning behind this proposition is that children in political conflict situations are exposed to a moral discourse which is highly polarised and replete with militaristic rhetoric. Justice is meted out in a violent manner and there is little time for principled discussion. While there have been very few formal studies employing a strictly Kohlbergian approach in studies of political violence (e.g. Fields 1973), this view of moral development is frequently referred to in the literature on the topic.

The relationship between an individual's moral reasoning capacity and behaviour has been a source of debate, and the more precise relationships have yet to be understood. Work on the behavioural aspect has relied more on social learning theory with its important concepts of imitation, identification and cognitive appraisal (Bandura 1973; Hoffman 1970). Here the argument is that children will imitate the violent actions of older actors with whom they identify, and thus engage in aggressive acts. Using the principle of generalisation within learning theory, the theory further proposes that violent conduct learnt in the political arena can generalise to other social settings. It is the social learning perspective which has been most influential in informing actual empirical research.

The influence of psychoanalytic ideas has not been prominent in research on this subject, although theoretical material on the question of whether exposure to violence during childhood has implications for adult behaviour has been generated by this school (e.g. Gibson 1991). This orientation draws on psycho-dynamic views of the failure of appropriate superego development in conditions of violence, as well as on Kleinian object relations formulations. This approach has only been systematically employed in case studies, such as those of Straker and her co-workers (Straker, Moosa, Becker and Nkwale 1992), to which I will refer at a later point. Research based on the Kohlbergian and social learning frameworks will be considered first.

The Research Evidence

While several South African studies note that Kohlberg's theory should pre-dict lower levels of moral reasoning following exposure to political violence, none have utilised the tests of moral reasoning specifically developed by the Kohlbergian school. Research in Northern Ireland has, however, contributed some evidence, which, bearing in mind the differences in the two situations, is instructive for the South African case. As will be seen, much of the work in this area contains methodological problems, which are often ignored when conclu-sions are drawn about the effects of political violence. It is thus essential to high-light some of these difficulties without wishing to deny the problems of con-ducting research in this area.

For example, Garbarino (1992:19) cites Fields's work in Northern Ireland as indicating that 'children [are] stuck at more primitive stages of moral develop-ment when children of the same age in less violently conflictual communities have progressed to more advanced moral reasoning'. However, if we examine Fields's studies a little more closely, we find that the evidence on which Garbarino's conclusion is based is not strong. Nor is it appropriate to use Fields's work as a basis for conclusions about the whole of the Northern Irish research evidence.

What Fields (1973 and 1975) did was to use the Tapp–Kohlberg (Tapp and Kohlberg 1971) moral interview scheme to compare American, Dublin and Belfast children of 6–10 and 11–14 years, during 1971–2 and 1973–4. The year 1972 was particularly violent for Northern Ireland, and the other samples could therefore act as peaceful controls in order to test whether living in the violent context would result in lowered moral reasoning. The American sample was in fact used by Tapp and Kohlberg in their original study. Fields's results indicated that Belfast children showed much lower levels of moral reasoning than the other groups, with the American children being highest.

But, as Cairns (1987) has noted there are several problems with Fields's method which do not allow us to draw the sort of conclusion she and Garbarino have reached. Her Belfast sample was confined to working-class children and was not randomised. Also, we know that working-class children score lower on Kohlberg tests than middle-class children, so uncontrolled class differences could have influenced the direction of the results. Furthermore, the Dublin sample had only 22 children and the Belfast group totalled 78 over the two years of the study, while the size of the American sample was very much greater. Such small and uneven samples render statistical comparisons very problematic. As Cairns observes once more, Fields herself cautions against statistical comparison based on these problems, but she nonetheless goes on to conclude that the violence has been detrimental to the moral development of Ulster children, and that religious authoritarianism is responsible for the generally low levels of reasoning in both the northern and southern regions of Ireland.

While there has never been an exact replication of Fields's method with better controls and larger samples, other studies on the relationship between exposure to violence and moral attitudes, reasoning and behaviour have not supported her conclusions (Cairns 1987). There has been no significant change in children's religious attitudes and behaviour since 1969 despite the rise in sectarian violence. Ulster children have been found to show higher-level moral responses than mainland children in a study of 2000 children (Greer 1980, 1985). Other comparisons between Ulster and Ireland have shown no differences in moral reasoning levels in large sample studies, but they have shown that Irish children as a group tend to reason at lower levels than their American counterparts – thus supporting an aspect of Fields's observation. Finally, to test whether Ulster children exposed to political violence were more likely to accept aggressive behaviour among children as a way of dealing with disputes than children living in peaceful parts of the province, Cairns (1983) tested 600 children on their levels of acceptance of aggressive behaviour in various interpersonal circumstances. There was no evidence that the children from violent areas accepted violence more than those who lived in peaceful areas.

The data from Northern Ireland, a region which has perhaps suffered the longest period of sectarian violence and hostility this century, and from where most of the research has emerged, do not suggest a decline in children's moral standards because of exposure to political violence *per se*. These conclusions can be made fairly confidently, as several of the Northern Irish studies have included careful controls and large samples.

Several South African studies have examined the influence of exposure to political violence on the production of violent fantasy and behaviour. Most are related to work conducted on these issues in Northern Ireland and the Middle East. Liddell, Kvalsvig, Qotyana, and Shabalala (in press) examined the frequency of aggressive behaviour in a well-controlled study of 80 black preschool children living in four communities, which varied in terms of exposure to political violence but which were all very poor. The children were observed in their home settings carrying out their normal activities. The researchers found that the presence of political violence was associated with aggressive behaviour, but the children from the high-violence areas expressed aggression in the same sorts of circumstance as their counterparts from low-violence communities – only at higher rates. There was little evidence of violent fantasy associated with political unrest, unlike that reported in other studies (see below), but unrest together with contact with older boys and men did predict more aggressive behaviour. However, aggressive behaviour was not of high frequency when compared with other social behaviour monitored by the researchers. As Liddell and colleagues note, across the whole sample only 0.51% of the children's time was spent in aggressive conduct, which is clearly extremely low. This study does suggest that aggression in these preschoolers is associated with living in politically violent area, but as the areas studied were also characterised by high rates of criminal violence, it was not possible to attribute the children's responses solely to political violence.

The work of Liddell and colleagues raises a factor of importance in testing the generalisation argument. This is the difficulty of separating out aggressive orientations which might result from exposure to political violence, from other forms of aggression to which the child is exposed at home and in the community. Soweto children's diaries collected by Mtshali (1982) demonstrate fully the degree to which general violence is a common feature of young black children's existence; this might equally account for their aggressive behaviour following political conflict. McWhirter (1983) takes up this point in the case of Northern Ireland, noting that economically depressed areas with higher rates of criminal violence are also those which show the highest incidences of civil conflict.

Lorene and Branthwaite (1986), using a different measure from that of Cairns (1983) and not controlling for the possible interaction of criminal and political violence, attempted to test the generalisation hypothesis by seeing whether exposure to Northern Irish political violence would produce greater acceptance of violence in other interpersonal contexts such as the school and the family. Their study used Piagetian moral stories, and they asked children to rate the acceptability of violence depicted in a series of scenarios (e.g. a teacher and a parent hitting a child; a child throwing a stone at a policeman). They found no relationship between living in politically violent areas and endorsing aggressive and violent conduct in other social settings.

Unpublished South African studies by Rabinowitz (1988) and Pastor (1988) used the same questionnaire. That of Rabinowitz, which had 112 white and 192 African, coloured and Indian subjects, found no differences across class, gender or race on the acceptability of violence. Her study did, however, show that children who had been exposed to certain forms of child–adult violence were more likely to be accepting of it than those who had not. If one looks at her results a little more closely, for those scenarios where there was a significant link between previous exposure and greater acceptance 66% of the exposed respondents still saw it as definitely wrong and only 12% saw it as fairly wrong to not wrong at all. Of those exposed to corporal punishment at school, 65% did not have a problem with this treatment, but even those 42% who had not been exposed to it stated that it was a legitimate punishment. The lack of class differences (which are associated with levels of criminal violence) on orientations to violence in this study is important and contrary to what would be expected by McWhirter's concerns expressed earlier.

Pastor (1988) studied 77 coloured children in two schools, which were selected on the basis that both were situated in similarly poor parts of Cape Town but differed in that in one, political and criminal violence was very high, and in the other both types of violence were low. Thus in contrast to Rabinowitz, class and 'race' were held constant, but levels of criminal and political violence varied. No general relationship was found between exposure and attitudes to violence. As in Rabinowitz's study, exposure to specific scenarios had an effect. Children who lived in the high conflict area were more tolerant of the expression of violence by a child to a policeman, but the direction of the results showed that the majority in both groups judged the act to be wrong. In both groups there was a significant relationship between previous exposure to certain violent acts and the children's tendency to judge these acts less negatively; there was, however, no generalisation effect in that exposure to political violence did not predict a greater acceptance of violence in other settings.

Two other South African studies (both of which are unpublished) have shown (in contrast to Liddell and colleagues' observations) that children who live in politically violent areas do incorporate this violence into their play and fantasy life (Lab 1987; Carolissen 1987). In Lab's study of 52 African urban township children (9–16 years) during a period of high political turmoil, the children were asked to complete several tasks. They included making a drawing of the scene that most worried them about where they lived, an essay, and a list of worries. Of the children's drawings 71% depicted the security forces, and only 23% depicted other forms of violence and problems of poor townships. Games, family and community life were included in 63% of the drawings, all of which were described as very stark. The worry list included common worries about school, but 92% worried about being questioned by police and 100% worried about a family member or friend being detained. The essays also reflected a concern with political violence. Lab's study provides a picture of children preoccupied about the violence around them, and in this regard produced results similar to those from Northern Ireland (Cairns 1987), Mozambique (Mucache and Richman 1990; Richman 1992), and the Occupied Territories of Israel (Punamäki 1987).

A study by Carrolissen (1987) corroborates Lab's work. Her subjects were drawn from Chesterville, an African township near Durban and included 16 children aged 5–12 years and their parents. The adults were interviewed about the situation of violence in the area, their coping modes and the reactions of the children. The children's perspectives on the situation were obtained by drawings elicited by the question: 'What frightens you about living here in Chesterville?' The drawings were replete with pictures of unrest, and the children reported being frightened of the police.

These two studies reflect the considerable initiative of some South African researchers to study issues of public concern, but their small sample sizes and the range of ages covered, as was the case with Fields's work, limit the power of the findings. While children's drawings are most useful ways of accessing their thoughts and feelings, like all projective techniques they are influenced by a range of factors, and reliability is commonly difficult to establish. There are therefore problems with assuming too much from one sample of a child's drawings. No studies have been carried out in this field that have asked for drawings done on several occasions, which might provide a better index of the stability of the children's concerns. Also, in the case of Carolissen's study, asking children to draw things they fear will be likely to produce their most immediate fears, and in a context of ongoing danger it is not surprising that they reproduce this context in their drawings. There is thus the potential for experimenter bias, which would be reduced by asking more open-ended questions.

Whereas these studies produced drawings full of the fear and horror of the violence of that period, drawings collected by Gibson, Mogale and Friedlander (1991) in Alexandra township in Johannesburg show much more variety, a number of the children not depicting any violence at all. Alexandra is an extremely violent area – parts of it are known as 'Beirut'. How does one interpret the lack of violent images in this context? First, it is important to note that Gibson and colleagues asked the children to draw their families and where they lived – a more open-ended request. Gibson and colleagues see the lack of violent imagery as denial and as reflecting the use of this defence as a coping mechanism. From a psychodynamic point of view, this is an entirely plausible explanation. But as these authors are aware, psychodynamic interpretations of drawings need confirmation from other forms of psychoanalytic investigation of the same child before one can confirm that denial is indeed operating. While it is useful for investigators to attempt to make sense of the child's inner world through the use of techniques such as this, their interpretation is a complex matter.

The question therefore is: What do drawings used in such studies mean psychologically? The fact that these children depict violence and fearful imagery does not imply damage nor does it suggest that the children will become violent themselves. Perhaps it says no more than that they are understandably preoccupied with the frightening events in their neighbourhood, as was the case with Anna Freud's war nursery children who became preoccupied (and even intrigued) with the bomb which landed in their garden (Freud and Burlingham 1943). However, when children are unable to be shifted away from an obsessive rumination about violence, then we should be particularly concerned about the possibility that they are seriously troubled.

Gibson and colleagues' work alerts us to another possibility, namely that violence can become so common that either it is not admitted to consciousness (denial) because it is too painful, or it is not expressed in drawings because it has become such a normal backdrop of life that it no longer has particular significance. It is not a simple matter to decide what is occurring here, and further studies are needed if we are to be able to reach more definitive conclusions about how children's fantasy is related to violent behaviour, patterns of coping, and distress.

A rather different strand of work on the effects of growing up with weapons of war and fear has been conducted in the Middle East. No similar studies have emerged from South Africa. Berkowitz (1984, 1990) and Berkowitz and Le Page (1967) have extended social learning theory to produce what has become known as the cognitive neoassociationist model of aggression. The model asserts that outward expressions of aggression as a coping mode are more likely under certain circumstances than others, and the probability that aggression will occur is increased when the means to express it are available. The model predicts a 'weapons effect', in which stimuli that are associated with aggression (e.g. guns) tend to elicit violent behaviour, especially from people who are in a state of negative arousal such as anger or fear (Mahjoub, Leyens and Yzerbyt 1992; Wilson and Cairns 1992). There is experimental evidence to support this claim, but more recent work has shown that the context and meaning surrounding the weapon are more important than its mere presence.

Mahjoub, Leyens and Yzerbyt (1992) examined the weapons effect experimentally among 5–6-year-old Palestinian children living in Damascus, Syria, and in Chatila and Saida in South Lebanon. The Lebanese areas had been under bombardment for six months prior to the experiment, Chatila being the worst affected. A further contrasting sample was drawn from Belgian children, and this makes it the only experimental study of the weapons effect which compares children living in war zones with those in peaceful circumstances. The children were videotaped playing in small groups, some of which were supplied with one plastic rifle, while others had no war toys. Pro-social, anti-social and war-like behaviour was scored. While a complex series of results emerged from this study, some of them are of significance here.

Overall, the children living in the war zones were not significantly more aggressive in their play than those living in peaceful circumstances, and the weapons effect did not operate in the way expected. According to the model, children living in the war zones (high negative arousal plus the weapon) should have been more aggressive and should have used the toy guns to engage in inter-individual conflict. The authors explain the absence of such findings as possibly being related to a lack of arousal in the children (due to the experimental situation). But they also suggest that the more likely reason was that the war-zone children constructed different meanings around the gun from those expected. Thus while there was a lot of military imitation in the groups which had the gun (including those living in Belgium), what was interesting was that it was used by the Palestinian children living in Lebanon as a device which promoted group cohesion rather than interpersonal conflict. They used the gun in play in a co-operative manner to defend themselves as a group (as Palestinian freedom fighters), or as a symbol of resistance, and not to attack each other. For the children in Damascus, the gun actually seemed to have an inhibiting effect on play, producing less aggression than expected. For the Belgian children, the rifle actually produced less co-operative activity than among the Palestinians in Beirut. Clearly there was no simple link between exposure to violent conflict and an increase in the use of interpersonal aggression in an experimental setting among these preschool children. However, they certainly had learned the usefulness of the weapon in dealing with threats to their security.

Punamäki's (1987) studies employing a version of the Rosensweig Picture Frustration Test with Palestinian and Israeli children are also worthy of comment here. She examined the influence of exposure to political violence on children's thought processes and perceptions of an enemy group. Punamäki designed a set of picture stimuli, which are in the form of cartoon drawings of children and adults in both politically sensitive and neutral contexts (see Fig. 1). Her subjects were required to respond projectively to the picture by telling the researcher what the other actors in the picture were saying, thinking and feeling in response to the verbal caption in the picture. As can be seen in her pictures, the protagonists in the Arab–Israeli conflict are identifiable in the pictures, in the

Fig. 1. This picture depicts the recurring violent confrontation between Palestinian children and Israeli soldiers. The soldier has caught a child and says, threatening him with club, 'I'll teach you to throw stones, you devil.' (Reproduced with the permission of the author)

words used, and in their dress. Her results showed high levels of intergroup polarisation, which rose with exposure to political violence. The children commonly displayed aggressive fantasies toward representatives of the enemy, and also brought elements of the political conflict into their responses to pictures which had no obvious political content. However, Punamäki's data do not allow us to conclude anything about the likely transmission of these aggressive orientations to actual social behaviour.

There is one important feature of Punamäki's method that limits the claims which can be made about the data it provides. It seems at face value that the technique has provided a picture of children who are preoccupied by the political conflict and who think of little else. This may be so but we cannot be sure. We need to note that Punamäki's test was specifically designed to contain several politically salient social representations (Moscovici 1984). The children's responses were therefore very likely to have been influenced by these cues, thus giving only a partial picture of their dominant feelings and thoughts. In order to examine this possibility, different versions of Punamäki's picture test would have to be tested.

A South African study by the present author has begun to examine this problem. In this version of the method, pictures which depict South African black children in various situations with and without the presence of figures associated with this conflict are being developed (see Fig 2). The intention is to compare children's responses to pictures with and without the verbal cues used by Punamaki so as to test their effect on children's responses. South African data which have been gathered so far have used pictures without verbal cues, and some of the preliminary results are noted here. Unfortunately an uncued version has not been tested in the original Israeli and Palestinian setting.

Ninety African children (age 10–15 years) from an urban South African squatter settlement which has experienced high rates of both political and crimi-

Fig. 2. South African version of Punamäki's picture test. (Note: no verbal cues.)

nal violence were tested on this device shortly after a period of violence in 1989. They were shown the pictures and were asked to say what they thought was going on, what the people thought and felt, and what was going to happen in the future. They were also given a questionnaire in order to establish their levels of exposure to different forms of political violence.

The levels of exposure to political violence which the children reported was uniformly high. What was most striking was that in this uncued situation the children referred more to general community criminal and domestic violence than to political violence, even when responding to pictures in which there is no conflict depicted and despite the high levels of exposure to political violence in the sample.

Why did they respond like this? It was clear from their responses that these children inhabit worlds in which violence is common in the school playground, the home and on the streets. For this sample, the results suggest that while political violence was recognised, it did not dominate their thinking. The evidence therefore indicates that the sources of their commonly violent or aggressive responses even to the non-violent pictures lay elsewhere in their experience. Alternatively, to follow Gibson and colleagues (1991), it is possible that their lack of politically violent responses was a function of a denial of their situation. But then why were there so many other violent images drawn from other life experiences? Why were these not denied? Once more we do not have enough information to answer these questions.

Some other data collected after the violent destruction of Crossroads informal settlement near Cape Town by vigilantes and security forces can be added to this set of studies (Dawes, Tredoux and Feinstein 1989). A sub-sample of the children in this study (N = 43; aged 7–17) were asked to indicate what they thought should happen to those who were responsible for breaking down their homes and injuring and killing some of the inhabitants. The results showed that despite the horror of the attacks, there was surprisingly little call for violent retribution and there was a great deal of variation in the children's responses. Only

8 subjects said that their attackers should be killed for their actions, and 7 said they should be punished by being beaten. Of the rest of the sample, 24% of the 7–11-year-old group said they should be arrested and taken to court, while 42% of the adolescents chose this option. Of the younger group 28% recommended that they should be forgiven and 'educated' about the wrongfulness of their behaviour, while 21% of the adolescents felt this way. For example, respondents said things like: 'people should not be killed but told what is right or wrong' (age 11). A child (aged 14) with a more punitive orientation, reflecting his political identity as an oppressed person, said: 'They [the black vigilantes] should be killed because they kill blacks for the Boers [police].' In a reference to a practice known as 'necklacing' where a car tyre filled with petrol is placed around a perceived collaborator's neck and set alight, one 10-year-old girl said: 'People should be beaten but not burnt.'

This is again a small sample, from which conclusions should be drawn only tentatively. But it seems fair to comment that in the context of high intergroup polarisation and almost daily exposure to violence, these children did not display significant support for personal revenge against those who contributed to their suffering. Many of their responses reflected an ability to distance themselves from what had occurred by formulating courses of action which showed an understanding of the need for social institutions of the law to take their course. It perhaps reflects a degree of resilience in what they had learnt about such matters at home and in school, which was not overtaken by their exposure to the frequently rough justice of political conflict.

In sum, the South African work and that developed abroad which is based on social learning theory and moral developmental theory point to the complexity of the outcomes for moral and behavioural orientations following political violence. The small scale of the South African work does not allow for definite conclusions to be drawn about the matter.

Individual Abuse as a Factor

All children who have been subjected to forms of political violence and repression can be seen as having been abused. There is work in the area of child abuse which sheds light on the moral orientations of children who have been maltreated in pre-teen years. A study by Smetana, Kelly and Twentyman (1984) provides an example. These researchers studied children who had been subject to abuse and neglect, and compared them with a matched non-abused group. There were few differences in the two groups' judgements of moral and social transgressions. They did, however, find that children who had been subject to more severe abuse were in fact more sensitive to the wrongness of harmful acts towards others. This may be seen to contradict the findings that abused children tend to display more aggressive behaviour than non-abused groups (Burgess and Conger 1978), in suggesting a gap between abstract judgement and action in the real world. However, as Smetana and colleagues note, this may not be the correct interpretation as children's appraisals of situations are related to action. Appraisal is a crucial component of human action, and appraisal includes the social context in which action occurs. The gap between reasoning about the

212 Childhood and Adversity

morality of possible actions and the moral action of subjects in the real world would seem to turn on the individual's construction of the social parameters of the situation, including the social construction of self as a member of a group when group membership becomes salient. Work on children's rule violations in experimental settings shows quite clearly that their appraisal of the situation (e.g. likelihood of punishment, or being observed) influences their actions (Kuczynski 1983). The child's construction of self in such settings has not been examined.

Claims that children exposed to political violence will be violent and aggressive in other contexts and will show lowered moral standards do not take sufficient account of arguments and findings such as those cited above. The observation of aggressive play and aggressiveness to peers following episodes of political violence should not be taken at face value to suggest a shift in the children's moral standards. Apart from these comments on the problematic links between aggressive behaviour and moral reasoning or standards, children frequently engage in aggression as a way of coming to terms with their experience of violence and working through the fears generated by what they have experienced (Dawes 1990).

Regarding adolescents and youth, Straker and colleagues' (1992) psychodynamically informed longitudinal case study of 60 African youth from Leandra in the Transvaal is unique in the South African literature, which contains no similar follow-up studies. It adds support to the caution we should employ in predicting that exposure to political violence and violent conduct within that context will generalise to behaviour in other situations. This work is based on a series of case studies of youth who sought refuge at a sanctuary during 1986 and who had been victims of state and vigilante violence as well as perpetrators of violence themselves. They were followed up in 1989. All these young people had been abused by the apartheid system, and a number had been detained and beaten by the police. One of the specific questions Straker and colleagues attempted to address was the way in which active participation in violence had affected their attitudes to violence and the degree to which violence had become a general response to personal frustration and conflict resolution. They also examined the role of individual historical factors in this process.

Straker's subjects, despite their adverse backgrounds, their militancy and their endorsement of violence as a political tool, did not as a rule see violence as an end in itself. A minority of them saw the value of violence as being to further personal gain and revenge, as was indicated by comments such as 'making the boers [police/army] feel pain too' (1992:101). But only 10% of the sample could be classified in 1989 as gangsters, and it was unlikely that their gang activity was solely due to exposure to political violence. Straker and her colleagues go on to comment on the commonly feared brutalisation of youth during the 1980s:

> In sum there is little evidence of the Leandra youth having become a brutalised generation... There was similarly little to indicate that they would engage in indiscriminate and arbitrary violence, as although there was much to indicate that violence would be their response to particular sets of circumstances ... these experiences still seemed to be contained within

strict boundaries and governed by a system of morality which could be observed and articulated. (1992:105)

There is one case they cite of a youth who had personal problems before 1984 but was not aggressive. After his participation in the political struggle, he did seem to have discovered in violent activity a way of asserting his power and overcoming feelings of inadequacy; this led him to more indiscriminate use of violence.

This stream of inquiry therefore also indicates the complexity of the processes associated with responses to abuse and participation in violence. The final aspect of our discussion will consider the role of social identity, which is not normally addressed in this aspect of the political violence literature.

Social Identity and Violent Conduct

The influence of social identity is not a central element of the previous accounts although Straker's study points to its importance. An alternative to the more traditional formulations we have considered may be developed from the social psychological accounts of group identity in violent situations (Reicher 1987), and of 'reputation' (Emler 1990) in the study of juvenile delinquents. These approaches appear to offer a promising direction for future work precisely because they move beyond the isolated cognitive individual, which is assumed in the forms of psychological inquiry we have discussed. They also provide a way of linking the individual with his or her sociocultural context. Emler's ideas also help to explain why what little research there is on the generalisation of moral learning under conditions of political violence to other contexts of public life has not shown clear evidence of such a generalisation. These formulations also suggest that the socio–political and the moral contexts interlock as group interests become salient, and that this makes possible the existence of seemingly contradictory moralities and forms of moral conduct. The argument is outlined below.

The question whether generalisation of violent conduct following exposure to political violence does occur has much to do with the identity asserted by the actor in question, and this identity is not necessarily fixed but may shift as the context changes. Also, moral conduct is learned in social settings which assign moral rights and duties to persons in terms of a set of socially defined positions – child, adult, male, female, freedom fighter (Hollway 1984; Shweder 1990). Each person can occupy a variety of these positions depending on his or her relationship to the social context. He or she can therefore assert and be subject to different rights and rules of conduct.

Thus in all social contexts, including political violence, children as well as adults occupy social positions as members of groups with particular social identities which embody forms of moral conduct, and when these identities become salient they serve to sanction and prohibit the forms of behaviour which we call moral or immoral. This will be the case regardless of the capacities of the individual members of these groups to reason at certain levels of abstraction about moral problems. Their behaviour as members of a group may suggest either high or low moral standards, which may bear little relation to their performance on tasks of moral reasoning, and will depend more on emerging group norms than on their cognitive capacities.

Emler argues that an individual's reputation (which itself can vary with context) is another important determinant of moral conduct. He notes that reputations are 'prototypes of virtue' (1990:181), which develop in social settings. Different groups may hold different ideas about what constitutes a 'good' or a 'bad' reputation. Delinquent boys promote themselves as villains (a particular moral formation) in a group context which values this quality, but may not promote this image in another context.

Similarly in situations of political violence, young people who identify with one or other group of antagonists have opportunities for the enhancement of their reputations. Thus in order to establish a reputation as a 'good comrade' might require bravery and resilience and acceptance of violent action if necessary. In a context of poverty and few chances for the enhancement of self-esteem, as in poor communities in South Africa, political group identity may provide a particular opportunity for the promotion of one's worth.

When the salience of such group identities becomes high, as in contexts of conflict, group processes govern behaviour in powerful ways (Reicher 1987). Also, one's reputation in the group may lead one to be subject to strong pressures to behave in confirmation of that reputation but contrary to moral principles that one might normally espouse. This has been demonstrated in a collective violence trial in South Africa, in which one of the accused who was found guilty of the gruesome murder of a policeman by 'common purpose' was a respected member of the community who had never engaged in violence (Foster 1991).

One may of course also develop or need to defend a reputation as 'a man'. In a South African study which considered the role of masculine identity and poverty in violent behavior, Campbell (1991) conducted open-ended interviews with young township men and women in Natal, all of whom had been exposed to political violence at some point in their lives. Her results showed that the young men use violence in a number of settings as a way of asserting masculinity in a context within which traditional male authority roles (and thus reputations) have been dislodged by poverty and apartheid. She refers to this as the emergence of a 'macho culture of resistance' (1991:13) to the loss of authority and effectiveness in the world. Campbell notes that 'violence was characterised as the prototypical male activity both in terms of male personality traits, and in terms of physical prowess'. She goes on to observe that while the political context teaches violence to the youth, the family also plays a crucial role. She gives examples of how male interviewees saw themselves as having the right (granted by their identification as male) to control women – violently if necessarily. Campbell quotes one subject: 'I know about disciplining women from watching husbands beat their wives for gossiping' (1991:16). This example illustrates the intersection of economic, ideological and family factors in the production of violence among a group who have experienced political violence. Their orientations are not produced by exposure to political violence *per se*.

This example shows that children and youth are exposed to a range of sources of information about the morality of violence and when it may be legitimated or proscribed in the social contexts they move in. In politically violent situations they are exposed not only to discourses and practices of political violence but also to discourses that limit violence in other social situations, which carry different significations of identity, as Straker's work has shown.

A final example of work on people's courts in South Africa illustrates the role of social identity in regulating moral conduct (Schärf and Ngcokoto 1990) Prototypes of these courts existed prior to the 1980s with the tacit support of the state, and they were run by the senior men of the community (respected elders). Their primary role was to resolve such matters as domestic disputes. Later, as the political struggle intensified, people's courts were transformed into alternatives to state structures and also played an important role in promoting political discipline. At this point they were run by young political activists and were in a sense guardians of appropriate political morality. At a further point in time they became controlled by undisciplined (in the political sense) youths. These courts sentenced both men and women to lashings, fines and other forms of punishment including forms of service to the community. As the undisciplined youth took over in consequence of the detention of the former conveners of the courts, the sentences increased in harshness and lacked the educative function that was characteristic of the courts when they were controlled by disciplined activists.

While the political activists ran these structures, they remained male preserves, but their style of operating reflected the social positioning of the youths as politically disciplined comrades. Their social identity was clearly that of members of the revolutionary struggle, which dictated certain forms of conduct, and their behaviour was characterised by attempts to be reasonable and educative in sentencing. The court was democratically structured, and in many ways could be seen as reflecting forms of moral reasoning which were at least conventional. When the activists and the guiding political structures were removed (by detentions), the undisciplined youth imposed what seems to have been a populist system of retribution which was divorced from the previous political discipline. The identity of political activist was removed, and the identity of gangster or *tsotsi* began to appear in its place.

The point is that while both sets of youthful court officials had been exposed to political violence, the activists' positioning within a rhetoric and practice of democracy and fairness seems to have determined the difference between their form of justice and that which came later. It was not exposure itself which determined the harshness of punishment, but the context within which the rules of the practice were formulated and maintained. Part of this included the clear social identity of being a comrade, which required certain behaviour and accountability to collective decisions. This identity seems to have been responsible for the construction of a form of moral behavior in the people's court situation that was different from that which arose once the politically affiliated youth were removed from the scene.

Conclusion

The theoretical and research evidence presented here suggests that exposure to political violence will not by itself produce lowered moral reasoning or an orientation to violent conduct which generalises beyond the political or military context. We have seen that there are major difficulties with how we interpret some of our research results in this field, and how rather sweeping conclusions have sometimes been reached without much evidence to support them. As in the previous chapter, there is a tension in this area of research between more positivist and individually oriented frames of reference and those which have a more social psychological orientation.

In this regard, a particular argument has been advanced here for seeing morality as a public as well as a private psychological matter. Social positioning, social identity and public reputation have been suggested as being particularly important factors in the production of moral conduct among children and adults. I have employed these constructs in an examination of whether learning about violence in political contexts generalises to other situations, and have indicated that they may provide a more fruitful way forward than the individual-centred research which is characteristic of this field. If at the centre of our investigations, we place the idea that moral conduct occurs within social contexts and is enacted by persons with social identities, our understanding is likely to be advanced.

This chapter has shown that moral thinking and conduct will of course be influenced by exposure to political conflict but not in any simple manner. A range of socio-political, economic and social psychological and individual forces is at play. In order to develop our understanding of the links between political violence and later moral behaviour, it will be important to undertake research which examines the role of certain key factors. We must take care to identify the type and the context of the violence to which children have been exposed. It will be necessary to observe moral conduct across a number of social situations following exposure to political violence in a particular society, so as to look for consistencies and variations. We will have to have an understanding of cultural prescriptions about violence in that society, as well as of common social practices which involve violence and community understandings of who has the right to power and discipline, which predate episodes of political violence. This is the context of socio-moral learning.

Finally, we will have to look particularly at the state of the society following the conflict so as to discern the factors which would be likely to enable the survival of social identities invested in violent reputations. Unfortunately in South Africa today, there are social and economic conditions which make such investments an adaptive survival pathway for many young people. Some youth who have been involved in violent civil conflict will carry an identity forward into the post-conflict situation which is characterised by a particular investment in engaging in violent conduct. There is thus the risk that in the absence of other sources of identity affirmation, and in contexts of socio-economic deprivation, young people with few life chances who have been actively engaged in political violence may carry forward a violent career in order both to survive and to retain a sense of worth.

References

Bandura, A. (1973). *Aggression. A Social Learning Analysis*. Englewood Cliffs, New Jersey: Prentice Hall.

Berkowitz, L. (1984). Some effects of thoughts on anti- and pro-social influences of media events: A cognitive-neoassociational analysis. *Psychological Bulletin, 95*, 410–425.

Berkowitz, L. (1990). On the formation and regulation of anger and angry aggression: A cognitive-neoassociationist analysis. *American Psychologist, 45*, 495–503.

Berkowitz, L. and Le Page, A. (1967). Weapons as aggression-eliciting stimuli. *Journal of Personality and Social Psychology, 7*, 202–207.

Bundy, C. (1986). Street sociology and pavement politics: Some aspects of the 1985 school crisis in the Western Cape. Paper presented to the Conference on Western Cape Roots and Realities. Centre for African Studies, University of Cape Town.

Burgess, R. L. and Conger, R. D. (1978). Family interaction in abusive, neglectful and normal families. *Child Development, 49*, 1163–1173.

Cairns, E. (1983). Children's perceptions of normative and prescriptive interpersonal aggression in low and high areas of violence in Northern Ireland. Unpublished paper, Centre for the Study of Conflict, Coleraine, Northern Ireland.

Cairns, E. (1987). *Caught in Crossfire. Children and the Northern Ireland Conflict*. Belfast: Appletree Press.

Campbell, C. (1991). Learning to kill? Masculinity, the family and the current political violence. Paper presented to the University of Oxford Standing Committee on African Studies and the Journal of African Studies Conference on Political Violence in Southern Africa, St Antony's College, Oxford, June 1991.

Carrolissen R. L. (1987). Children and civil unrest: The Chesterville experience. Unpublished Psychology Honours dissertation, University of Natal, Durban.

Dawes, A. (1990). The effects of political violence on children: A consideration of South African and related studies. *International Journal of Psychology, 25*, 13–31.

Dawes, A., Tredoux, C. and Feinstein, A. (1989). Political violence in South Africa: The effects on children of the violent destruction of their community. *International Journal of Mental Health, 18*(2), 16–43.

Edwards, C. P. (1975). Societal complexity and moral development: A Kenyan study. *Ethnos, 3*, 505–527.

Edwards, C. P. (1982). Moral development in comparative cross-cultural perspective. In D. A. Wagner and H. W. Stephenson (eds), *Cultural Perspectives on Child Development*. San Francisco: W.H. Freeman.

Emler, N. (1990). A social psychology of reputation. In W. Stroebe and M. Hewstone (eds), *European Review of Social Psychology, 1*, 171–193

Enright, R. D., Enright, W. F., Manheim, L. A. and Harris, B. E. (1980). Distributive justice, development and social class. *Developmental Psychology, 16*(6), 555–563.

Fields, R. N. (1973). *Society on the Run: A Psychology for Northern Ireland*. Middlesex: Penguin Books.

Fields, R. N. (1975). Psychological genocide: The children of Northern Ireland. *History of Childhood Quarterly: The Journal of Psychohistory, 3*, 201–204.

Foster, D. 1991. Social influence III: Crowds and collective violence. In D. Foster and J. Louw-Potgieter (eds), *Social Psychology in South Africa*. Isando: Lexicon.

Freud, A. and Burlingham, D.T. (1943). *War and Children*. New York: Ernest Willard.

Garbarino, J. (1992). Developmental consequences of living in dangerous and unstable environments: The situation of refugee children. Paper presented to the Refugee Studies Programme Seminar: The Mental Health of Refugee Children Exposed to Violent Environments, Oxford.

Gibson, K. (1991). The indirect effects of political violence on children: Does violence beget violence? Unpublished paper, Project for the Study of Violence, Psychology Department, University of the Witwatersrand, Johannesburg.

Gibson, K., Mogale, M. and Friedlander, R. (1991). Some preliminary ideas about the meaning of Inkatha violence for children living in Alexandra. Paper presented to the 8th National Congress of the South African Association for Child and Adolescent Psychiatry and Allied Disciplines,

Johannesburg, September.

Gilligan, C. (1982). *In a Different Voice: Psychological Theory and Women's Development*. Cambridge, Mass.: Harvard University Press.

Greer, J. (1980). The persistence of religion: A study of adolescents in Northern Ireland. *Character Potential, 9*, 139–149.

Greer, J. (1985). Viewing the other side in Northern Ireland: Openness and attitudes to religion among Catholic and Protestant adolescents. *Journal of the Scientific Study of Religion. 24*(3), 275–292.

Harkness, S., Edwards, C. P. and Super, C. M. (1981). Social roles and moral reasoning: A case study in a rural African community. *Developmental Psychology, 17*(5), 595–603.

Hoffman, M. L. (1970). Moral development. In P.H. Mussen (ed.), *Carmichael's Manual of Child Psychology* (Vol. 2). New York: John Wiley.

Hollway, W. (1984). Gender differences and the production of subjectivity. In J. Henriques, W. Hollway, C. Urwin, C. Venn and V. Walkerdine (eds), *Changing the Subject: Psychology, Social Regulation and Subjectivity*. London: Methuen.

Kohlberg, L., Levine, C. and Hewer, A. (1983). *Moral Stages: A Current Formulation and a Response to Critics*. Basel: Karger.

Kuczynski, L. (1983). Reasoning, prohibitions, and motivations for compliance. *Developmental Psychology, 19*(1), 126–134.

Lab, S. (1987). The psychological effects of violence on black South African children. Unpublished Honours Psychology thesis, University of the Witwatersrand, Johannesburg.

Leyens, P. and Mahjoub, A. (1992). The psycho-social effects of war on children and adolescents. Paper presented to the Refugee Studies Programme Seminar: The Mental Health of Refugee Children Exposed to Violent Environments, Oxford, January 1992.

Liddell, C., Kvalsvig, J., Qotyana, P., and Shabalala, A. (In press). Community violence and levels of aggression in young South African children. *International Journal of Behavioral Development*.

Lorene, L. and Branthwaite, A. (1986). Evaluations of political violence by English and Northern Irish school children. *British Journal of Social Psychology, 25*, 349–352.

McWhirter, L. (1983). Growing up in Northern Ireland: From aggression to the troubles. In A. P. Goldstein and M. H. Segal (eds), *Aggression in Global Perspective*. New York: Pergamon.

Mahjoub, A., Leyens, J. and Yzerbyt, V. (1992). The weapons effect among children living in an armed conflict environment. Paper presented to the Refugee Studies Programme Seminar: The Mental Health of Refugee Children Exposed to Violent Environments, Oxford, January 1992.

Marks, S. and Andersson, N. (1990). The epidemiology and culture of violence. In N. C. Manganyi and A. du Toit (eds), *Political Violence and the Struggle in South Africa*. London: Macmillan.

Moscovici, S. (1984). The phenomenon of social representations. In R. Farr and S. Moscovici (eds), *Social Representations*. Cambridge: Cambridge University Press.

Mtshali, M. (1982). *Give Us a Break. Diaries of a Group of Soweto Children*. Braamfontein: Skotaville Press.

Mucache, A. A. and Richman, N. (1990). Confronting violence in Mozambique. Paper presented to the International Conference on the Consequences of Organised Violence in Southern Africa, Harare, Zimbabwe, July.

Pastor, C. (1988). Children and attitudes towards violence: Effects of exposure to political violence. Unpublished Psychology Honours thesis, University of Cape Town.

Piaget, J. (1965). *The Moral Judgement of the Child*. New York: The Free Press.

Punamäki, R. (1987). *Childhood under Conflict: The Attitudes and Emotional Life of Israeli and Palestinian Children*. Research Report No. 32. Tampere: Tampere Peace Research Institute.

Rabinowitz, S. R. (1988). The impact of exposure to civil unrest on children's evaluations of violence. Unpublished MA (Clinical Psychology) thesis, University of Cape Town.

Reicher, S. D. (1987). Crowd behaviour as social action. In J.C. Turner (ed.), *Rediscovering the Social Group*. Oxford: Blackwell.

Rest, J., Bebeau, M. and Volker, J. (1986). An overview of the psychology of morality. In J.R. Rest (ed.), *Moral Development. Advances in Research and Theory*. New York: Praeger.

Rest, J. R., Thoma, S. J., Moon, Y. L. and Getz, I. (1986). Different cultures, sexes and religions. In J. R. Rest (ed.), *Moral Development. Advances in Research and Theory*. New York: Praeger.

Richman, N. (1992). Annotation: Children in situations of political violence. Under review.

Schärf, W. and Ngcokoto, B. (1990). Images of punishment from the people's courts of Cape Town, 1985–7: From prefigurative justice to populist violence. In N.C. Manganyi and A. du Toit (eds), *Political Violence and the Struggle in South Africa*. London: Macmillan.

Shweder, R. A. (1990). Culture and moral development. In J. W. Stigler, R. A. Shweder and G. Herdt (eds), *Cultural Psychology: Essays on Comparative Human Development*. Cambridge: Cambridge University Press.

Smetana, J.G., Kelly, M. and Twentyman, C.T. (1984). Abused, neglected, and non-maltreated children's conceptions of moral and social conventional transgressions. *Child Development, 55,* 277–287.

South African Institute of Race Relations (SAIRR) (1992). *Race Relations Survey*. Braamfontein: South African Institute of Race Relations.

Straker, G., Moosa, F., Becker, R. and Nkwale, M. (1992). *Faces in the Revolution. The Psychological Effects of Violence on Township Youth in South Africa*. Cape Town: David Philip.

Tapp, J.L. and Kohlberg, L. (1971). Developing a sense of law and legal justice. *The Journal of Social Issues, 27,* 65–91.

Wilson, R. and Cairns, E. (1992). Trouble, stress and psychological disorder in Northern Ireland. *The Psychologist, 5,* 347–350.

12

Racism and Children's Intergroup Orientations: Their Development and the Question of Psychological Effects on Minority-Group Children

DON FOSTER

Introduction: What is the Question?

This chapter is about the development of children's racial attitudes or, more broadly, their intergroup orientations. It aims to cover the general trends found in international research literature, some theoretical approaches and the somewhat limited South African research on this topic. It also poses some critical questions about this area.

The central question may be derived from statements that have existed as firmly embedded assumptions for some forty or so years and that still surface with regularity. Two recent examples are given by leading North American researchers:

> 'My own opinion is that prejudice is harmful to those who harbour it and to those who are targeted by it.' (Aboud 1988:ix)

> '… it appears that racism negatively affects the mental health functioning of both blacks and whites in American society.' (Landrum-Brown 1990:113)

These assertions are turned into a question. Is it the case that, in particular, black children suffer negative psychological consequences from a racist social system? This question is part of a far broader set of questions about the consequences of minority group status. Minority as used here refers to power relations and not to numerical differences. In the present chapter we restrict the question to children (roughly aged 2–12 years) in particular.

The argument in the chapter takes the following turns. First, a considerable body of evidence exists to suggest that young black children differ from white (or majority-status group) children regarding their racial identity or orientation. Second, it is argued that this phenomenon needs to be understood in the light of three sets of mediating factors: methodological issues, lifespan developmental changes and historical–political changes. Third, we turn to theoretical approaches for some explanation of findings and argue that a number of theories and different levels of analysis need to be considered for a full explanation.

Finally we return to the vexed question about damage or negative consequences, and argue that this is as much a moral and political matter as a psychological one.

Before we proceed it may be as well to clear away a central distinction in order to give direction to the argument as a whole. Although the terminology is not very satisfactory, a distinction may be drawn between direct and indirect consequences of racism. The first concept refers to direct implications of racism on the life opportunities of oppressed children, for instance poor health, nutritional problems, infant mortality rates, poverty, disadvantaged education, limited sporting and recreational training, overcrowding, interpersonal violence and the like. In this case a social system that is oppressive or discriminatory acts directly on the body of the child or on certain abilities, for example to read, write or to play a particular sport. Here, we suggest, there is not much of a debate: racism eventuates in negative consequences. On the other hand, indirect consequences refer to more subtle and less directly observable disabilities such as impaired self-concept, distorted identity, reduced self-esteem, or acceptance of own group (ingroup) members as inferior and other group (outgroup) members as superior. This last notion constitutes the core of this chapter.

A second important distinction needs to be drawn between racism and other ascribed characteristics (such as gender or class), which are also markers of social inequality. Since these effects interact, they should ideally be disentangled before claims can be made for negative consequences of racism. With these distinctions in mind let us examine some of the research.

International Research

Since the early work of Kenneth and Mamie Clark (1940, 1947) in the United States, a fairly consistent finding has been that black children (particularly in younger age groups, say 3–7 years) tend to prefer and identify with white rather than black stimulus figures. These data have been interpreted, perhaps rather loosely, as indications of damage or problems regarding the identity development of black children. Before being over-hasty in confirming this pattern, let us take a more fine-grained look at the research approaches and results.

In the Clarks' (1947) classic study, which set the framework for much subsequent work, they asked 253 Negro children aged 3–7 years to select from four dolls (identical apart from skin and hair colour; two white and two brown) in answering various questions. There were three sets of questions. The first set was aimed to test awareness in terms of questions such as 'Give me the doll that looks like a Negro (or white, or coloured doll)'. Over 90% of all children answered these correctly, but there was a considerable increase in correct answers with age from about 70% at age 3 to 100% at ages 6 or 7.

The second set of questions was aimed to test *preference,* for either the white or the brown doll. Questions and responses are given in Table 1. Taken overall, roughly 60% showed preference for the white doll and about 30% for the brown doll; the remainder were not sure or gave no answer. Age differences were found, with the strongest white preference at ages 4 and 5 years (roughly 75%) declining to about 50% at age 7. Light-skinned children showed stronger preference for white than medium- or dark-skinned children. Children from mixed schools showed stronger preference for white than those from segregated schools in southern states of America.

Table 1.　Preference question and responses: Percent choosing white or brown doll.

	White doll	Brown doll	Don't know
Instructions to the child			
Give me the doll that you like to play with	67	32	1
Give me the doll that is a nice doll	59	38	3
Give me the doll that looks bad	17	59	24
Give me the doll that is a nice colour	60	38	2

Source: Clark and Clark 1947

The final question, 'Give me the doll that looks like you', was designed to assess self-identification. As an overall response, 66% chose the brown doll and 33% chose the white doll. Light-skinned children (80%) were far more likely than darker-skinned to choose white. Here again there were important age trends; younger children being more likely to identify with white while only 13% of 7-year-olds chose the white doll.

In reflecting on this study, and setting the scene for subsequent research, we should note a number of important issues. First, there is not a single result but a number of competing outcomes. There are differences between 'awareness', 'preference' and 'identification'. The significance of the tendency towards white preferences (not identification) emerges in contrast to awareness of difference. Most children were correct in awareness, yet despite this knowledge, tended to prefer white. Second, results also differed across skin colour, age as well as situation and region. So although there was a general tendency towards white *preferences,* it would not be correct to say that there was a general tendency for black children to 'misidentify'. It would be fair to conclude that some black children (mainly those aged 4 and 5 years, with lighter skin colour) in *some* situations, such as northern states and mixed schools, evidenced a tendency to choose the white doll when asked 'Which doll is you?'

However, it is this general pattern of results which has been replicated in many studies over some fifty years. These results have come from a number of countries, in particular the USA and Canada (Porter 1971; Katz 1976; Aboud 1988; Brand, Ruiz and Padilla 1974; Spenser and Markstrom-Adams 1990), England (Davey 1983; Milner 1983; Wilson 1987), New Zealand (Vaughan 1964, 1978) and South Africa (see below) – all countries with varying degrees of white-dominated racial discrimination. Furthermore, these general patterns have emerged from a range of different stimulus materials (line drawings, pictures, dolls, photographs) and techniques (forced choice, multiple item scales, social distance tests, interviews). The work of psychiatrist Robert Coles has shown broadly similar patterns using depth interviews and children's drawings of self and others both in the American South (1967) and in South Africa (1986).

What patterns are we describing? Let us try to be quite clear about this. First, children seem to have knowledge and awareness of racial differentiation from quite early ages, about 4 years, albeit in a manner that is not yet fully developed. Furthermore, even this rudimentary awareness seems to entail some notion of inequality or status differences, and not merely an idea of difference in physical features.

Second, we are *not* saying that black children in general 'misidentify' or have identity problems. Let us look at the data. Williams and Morland (1976) reviewed a wide range of studies which reported identity-type questions, and found that in 27 reports on preschool black children, roughly 45% chose white and 45% chose black, with the remainder not clear. In 9 studies of school-going black children, only about 13% chose white figures. Further literature reviews by Banks (1976) and Aboud and Skerry (1984) both reported that the majority of studies found black children's pro-white choice to be in the region of 50%, that is – as argued by Banks (1976) – not significantly different from chance. For Banks therefore, there was no clear evidence at all for systematic white preference. However, the real significance of these data only emerges in comparison with white children, a comparison that Banks ignored. Williams and Morland (1976) summarised 21 studies showing that young white children's identification with white figures ranged between 75% and 85%. Asher and Allen (1969) found the same. In a review of 16 further studies since 1965, Aboud and Skerry reported virtually 100% own-group preference among white children. So while the evidence for outgroup preference or identification among black children is not that strong, there is a clear picture of a substantial difference between black and white children.

A third characteristic pattern of findings is that there have been historical changes. A number of studies in the USA in the late 1960s and 1970s began to report increased own-group preference and identification among blacks (e.g. Hraba and Grant 1970; Ward and Braun 1972). In New Zealand, Vaughan (1978) also reported positive changes, as did Milner (1983) and Davey (1983) in Britain. There seems to be enough accumulated information to claim that these historical shifts, attributed to the black consciousness movement and political resistance by blacks, are real changes and not artefacts due for instance to the use of different research methods.

Despite evidence of historical shifts, three points need to be made as a cautionary note. First, some studies have in recent years continued to find white preference among black children (e.g. Branch and Newcombe 1986; Spenser and Markstrom-Adams 1990). For instance, Annis and Corenblum (1987) found that 87% of 5- and 6-year Canadian Indian children preferred pictures of white children while 60% identified with white. Furthermore, Aboud and Skerry (1984), reviewing work from 1965 to the early 1980s, reported that only 27% of studies showed strong and unequivocal own-group preference among blacks.

Second, it is important to note that most previous work had been done with black children rather than other minority groups. Aboud and Skerry (1984) found for instance that white preference was stronger among other minority groups such as Chinese Americans, Chicanos and Native American Indians. Only 15% of studies with these groups showed clear own-group preference. If minority-group status rather than being black is the critical issue under consideration, then these recent findings are rather significant.

Third, some British research found a sharp difference between identification and preference patterns. While both decreased historically between the late 1960s and late 1970s, the former dropped to negligible amounts whereas preference for white still remained a majority response (see Table 2). Other research (Williams and Morland 1976; Wilson 1987) has supported the finding that pro-white tendencies are stronger for preference rather than identification. It is almost as if the children are saying something like 'I know who I am, but given the opportunity I would prefer to be in the position that whites are in'. Thus while there have been some historical changes, the pro-white bias, particularly in terms of preference data, and for other American minorities, still apparently persists. This of course mirrors social and political changes, for while there have been some changes, black children and other minorities are still subject to racism and inequality in these societies under discussion.

Table 2. Black children aged 5–10: Historical changes in identification and preferences in England.

Studies:	Percent choosing white figure		
	Milner (1960s)	Milner (1973)	Davey and Norburn (1980)
Identification: 'Which doll looks like you?'			
West Indian	48	27	08
Asian	24	30	15
Preference: 'Which one would you want to be?'			
West Indian	82	78	51
Asian	65	81	55

Source: Milner, 1983, 1984; Davey and Norburn 1980

The fourth general pattern of findings is that there are relatively consistent age-related developments regarding children's ethnic attitudes and identities (Aboud 1988; Katz and Zalk 1976; Vaughan 1987). In general, white children tend to show strong own-group preference between ages 3 to 6 or 7 years; thereafter this tendency decreases from 7 to 12 years. Young black children by contrast evidence strong outgroup preference in the earliest years, 3 to 5 or 6; thereafter this declines, to be replaced by increasing own-group preference through to 12 or so years of age. These trends are shown in terms of an illustrative example in Figure 1. By age 12 there is little difference between black and white children.

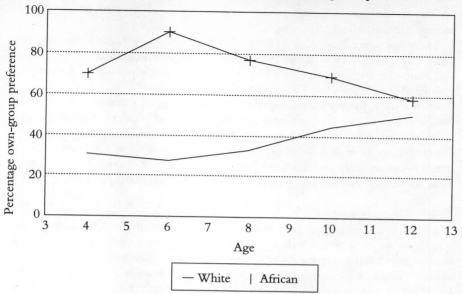

*Fig. 1. Age-related changes in children's own-group preference and identity:
an illustration of trends.*

What are the implications of such age-related trends? Aboud (1988) suggests that the oddities evidenced particularly at the younger ages should not be attributed to real racial orientations at all but rather to particular phases and processes of psychological development. Since it all seems to pan out much the same by age 12 or so anyway, what is the fuss? One can agree with some of what Aboud suggests, particularly the need to explain age-related developmental patterns, but certain major problems remain. We also need to explain the difference between black and white (or minorities and power-related majorities) and in particular the pro-white bias in younger black children. Aboud somewhat despairingly admits that this repeatedly replicated phenomenon is 'a puzzle' (1988:127).

Perhaps if it did pan out more or less evenly by age 12 or thereabouts, there would be little further need for concern. But numerous writings, from Fanon (1952/1967) through Grier and Cobb (1968) and Biko (1978) to intergroup attitudinal research, have suggested that the dual problem – of strong ethnocentrism among whites and black self-disparagement – persists into adulthood.

The final characteristic of these phenomena relates to individual differences. Most of the mainstream evidence has come from group-aggregated data. Aggregated differences between blacks and whites form the focus of conclusions. This obscures the possibility of individual or of additional subgroup differences. But clearly there are individual and subgroup differences. As one example, Wilson (1987) in her study of fifty-one 6–9-year-old natural children of one white and one black parent in England found a range of subgroups in responses. While some children consistently identified with their own group, others con-

226 Childhood and Adversity

sistently evidenced outgroup preferences, and yet others showed a range of inconsistent attitudinal responses.

There are some hints that individual differences may relate to parental attitudes. For instance, Branch and Newcombe (1986) found among 6- and 7-year-olds (but not among younger children) that children's pro-black orientations correlated significantly with parental pro-black attitudes.

In summary, the phenomenon under discussion is not a unitary one. It manifests as different aspects – awareness, identification and preference (or attitude) – and it changes with increasing age and over historical time. Nevertheless, a persistent finding over fifty years is the general tendency of at least some young minority-group children either to identify with or to prefer outgroup symbols in those societies characterised by racial inequality and white domination.

South African Research

Let us begin with the other end of the developmental scale – adults. Over some sixty years of research on racial attitudes a consistent pattern has emerged. Whites in general evidence strong own-group preference but negative attitudes towards blacks. Afrikaans-speakers show this more strongly than English-speakers. Blacks on the other hand, while generally showing own-group preference, also evidence positive attitudes to white English-speakers but negative attitudes to Afrikaans-speakers (Foster and Nel 1991). So to some extent the pattern of young adults' racial attitudes in South Africa shows trends similar to those reported above, with one exception – most studies comprised samples of university students. There is no evidence of identity confusion; repeated studies have shown clear own-group favourability. However, this is usually coupled with a positive and favourable attitude toward white English-speakers, often ranked ahead of other black groupings. In addition the political writings of Biko (1978), the academic work of Manganyi (1973, 1977) and the individual case studies of a few black children by Coles (1986) lend further support to the claim of what Manganyi (1973:29) calls the 'negative sociological schema of the black body'. In careful but elegant wording Manganyi expresses the thesis as follows: 'Thus it is that the self-fulfilling prophecy of the white man, that he is competent and superior while the African is "by nature" inferior and incompetent, tends to take on the semblance of a reality' (1973:29).

Some cautionary notes should be added to these claims, however. Research samples are small, and in the main comprise urban and relatively well-educated blacks. Most of these studies were done before the 1980s, the decade of widespread black resistance. Unfortunately almost no research of a similar nature has been done since the mid-1980s. One study by Howcroft (1990) found no difference in measures of personal self-esteem between black and white university students, similar to American findings. Finally, the volume of research is rather small; we may speak of snippets of research rather than of exhaustive findings.

What of children in South Africa? In general, trends emerging from the handful of studies conducted since the mid-1960s reveal a remarkable similarity with international trends (see Foster 1986, for a review of South African research). Racial awareness, as reported in other countries, increases rapidly

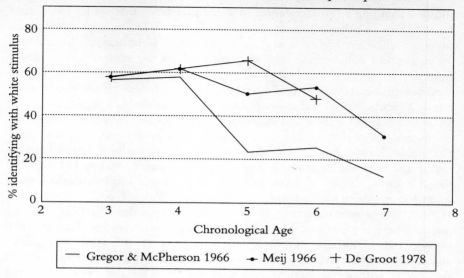

Fig. 2. *Identification with white doll by African children by age:*
summary of three studies.

from age 3 to nearly full accuracy at ages 6–7. A combination of three doll
studies (De Groot 1978; Gregor and McPherson 1966; Meij 1966) among children aged 3–7 years found that about 50% of black children chose the white doll
in response to identification questions, roughly similar to USA data during the
same time period. Like other findings, this black 'misidentification' decreases
from about 60–65% at ages 3 and 4 years to between 15 and 30% at age 7 (see
Figure 2).

A summary of the three South African doll studies – two comprising samples
of African children in the Transvaal and the third, De Groot (1978), a sample of
coloured children in the Western Cape, regarding preference for the white doll –

Table 3. Preference for white stimulus figure in black children: Summary of
South African choice studies.

Questions	Percentage black children choosing white		
	Gregor and McPherson N=139	Meij N=425	De Groot N=196
Which one would you like to play with?	77★	–	–
Which one do you like the best?	76★	77★	67★
Which is a nice doll?	83★	72★	50
Which has a nice colour?	72★	67★	58★
Which one looks bad?	21★	21★	20★

★p = 0.05, following Bank's (1976) criteria.

shows if anything a stronger degree of white preference than either the original Clarks' study or other American studies (see Table 3). In line with international findings, white preference was greater than white identification. In addition, preference did not decrease with increasing age to the same extent as identification.

Other studies, reviewed by Foster (1986), support these trends among black South African children and also suggest that white preference persists to at least 14 years of age (Lambert and Klineberg 1968). Studies of white children by comparison show early and strong degrees of own-group preference and identification, with some indications (Moodie 1980) that this ethnocentrism is maintained and does not decrease through to age 12 years. Certainly Lever (1968) found a strong degree of ethnocentrism and prejudice towards blacks among white Johannesburg adolescents.

As with international research, one should not read these findings as 'all or none'. There are certainly individual and subgroup variations. For example, Gregor and McPherson (1966) found that white identification was greater among urban rather than rural children, perhaps due to a greater contact among the former with white cultural influences, while Geber and Newman (1980) found at least three different clusters of responses among Soweto youth. A general finding is that increased education among black youth is associated with a greater rejection of apartheid.

Unfortunately much of this research, like that with adults, was conducted before the mid-1980s so we have little notion of the potential impact of black consciousness and the black youth revolt of recent years. There is only one substantial study in recent years (conducted in 1989) with over 400 African, coloured and white children in the Western Cape (Aarons 1991). Aarons used

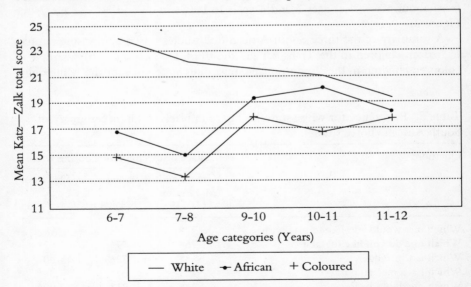

Fig. 3. Mean Katz–Zalk total scores for African, white and coloured children over five age categories (Aarons, 1991).

an improved measure in the form of the multiple-item Katz–Zalk (1976) test, providing photographs as stimulus materials. White children showed a stronger degree of own-group preference and outgroup rejection than did black children, but this difference decreased for both over increasing age, and differences by age 11–12 years were minimal (see Figure 3).

In other words, the ethnocentrism of whites decreases while that of blacks increased between ages 6 and 12 years. Of interest here is that although the rate of decrease was the same, Afrikaans-speaking children remained more ethnocentric and prejudiced than English-speaking children over all ages. Aarons's findings are similar to those obtained by Katz and Zalk (1976) as well as the general research trends reviewed by Aboud (1988).

In summary, the available evidence in South Africa resembles quite closely that of other international trends. It differs, if at all, in suggesting an accentuation of effects, among both black and white South Africans – that is, stronger white ethnocentrism and stronger outgroup preference among young black children – a pattern which would arguably be consistent with the greater intensity of entrenched racism in South Africa contrasted with the USA or UK. However, as already noted, we really have too little recent research evidence to claim anything with confidence. It seems likely that the past decade may have had some impact on inter-racial orientations, particularly in the case of the opening of some white schools since 1991. On the other hand, 'open' schools constitute less than 5% of all schools, and changes in the overall racialised power structure at present evidence more in the way of potential than actuality.

Contextual Considerations and Critique

So far we have simply described the main research findings. Unfortunately, however, research findings are never entirely straightforward or simply factual. They are the product of particular research methods, which in turn are embedded in certain research paradigms and metatheoretical assumptions. Furthermore, research is situated in particular historical, moral and political contexts. Research results are also utilised by some people for certain purposes. For instance the original findings by the Clarks were used as evidence in American legal cases (e.g. the 1954 case of *Brown* vs *Board of Education*) to argue for the desegregation of schools on the grounds that segregation damaged the racial identity of black children. Recently, as reported by Tizard and Phoenix (1989) this line of research was used in the UK by an association of black social workers to argue that black children up for adoption should be placed exclusively with black families. In this section we examine some of these wider contextual issues.

Methodological Problems

Since there is a host of issues, we touch on only a few, beginning with problems pertaining to the original dolls test. What exactly is the meaning of the dolls test? Let us say that white dolls were the only ones normally available at home or in the school. If so, the choice of a white doll by a black child could reflect familiarity rather than attitude. Or, as suggested by Williams and Morland (1976), it could reflect preferences for light rather than dark objects. Alternatively it could reflect aesthetic rather than attitudinal qualities. Certainly there are some doubts regarding the exact meaning of the stimulus materials.

The dolls test, as a 'forced-choice' technique, has a number of disadvantages. It dichotomises responses and has no way of assessing degrees of intensity. Choice of one object implies rejection of the other, which is not necessarily the case. For instance, one may prefer one object or person but not necessarily reject the other. A bipolar (black–white) choice offers no intermediate object, for example a brown doll. Some of these problems have been addressed in recent years by extending the range of choices, using photographs rather than dolls, and including multiple-item tests in order to assess the degree of response, but it should be noted that even recent multiple-item scales such as the Katz–Zalk test (1976) and the PRAM – Preschool Racial Attitude Measure – (Williams and Morland 1976) contain the 'forced-choice' logic as the basis of each separate item.

It is often taken for granted that the various different tests and instruments assess the same underlying construct. A recent study by Nagata (1985) throws some doubt on this assumption. It was found that some instruments did correlate positively (doll test and PRAM $r = 0.41$; PRAM and Katz–Zalk $r = 0.31$) while the doll test and Katz–Zalk showed no correlation. The many different instruments used, the lack of clear psychometric properties of reliability and validity, the varying testing situations, and the varying 'race' of experimenters make it difficult to compare differing results in a precise manner.

This research tradition is embedded in a framework or 'paradigm' guided by positivism, a framework purporting to be objective and neutral. Yet it is also characteristic of this framework that labels or stimulus objects are imposed upon children who merely respond (Foster-Carter 1986). There are few studies – for an exception see Wilson (1987) – that enquire about labels and categories used by children themselves. Because of this paradigmatic dominance there have been few studies that probe the more subjective or qualitative 'culture' of childhood experiences (Troyna and Hatcher 1992).

Finally, the methodological imperative is, in the words of Olivia Foster-Carter (1986), 'colour struck'. It is based on simple and dichotomous colour cues alone, divorced from multiple other possible interacting aspects. In elevating racial or colour cues to a superordinate position it reinforces the very criteria – racially based categorisation – that it is supposed to be questioning.

Wider Contexts

Research occurs in a wider political context that is often left unclear. In this respect Adam (1978) suggested that there have been three politically related phases of black identity research in the USA. The first phase (1950s) was able to use the notion of 'damage' to argue for improved civil rights and desegregation of schools. In other words, this phase, dominated by the 'mark of oppression' thesis, made it respectable to use findings of black damage and inferiorisation as a lever to propose political changes.

The second phase, during the earlier 1960s, shifted emphasis to victim-blaming. Stripped of political interpretations, findings of low self-esteem and identity confusion were seen as deviant and pathological. Blame was pinned on the black family. This was portrayed as disorganised, broken and characterised by matriarchal dominance. The ghetto culture was also held responsible, and special school programmes were advised to cool off the unrealistic ambitions of wounded or 'culturally deprived' black children.

Criticism of the cultural deprivation thesis, along with visible evidence of black militancy and the rise of the black power movements, constituted a shift into a third phase from the late 1960s and 1970s. It became important to undo the image of black persons as damaged or inferior and to emphasise black strength, resilience and pride. Findings of damage or of inferiority became interpreted as reactionary and carrying a taint of racism. Increasingly during this period researchers produced results emphasising 'no difference' between black and white. The worm had turned; it was no longer respectable to find 'damage' among black children. In Britain, Stone (1981) argued strongly against the damaged self-esteem thesis, claiming that it turned teachers into second-rate therapists or social workers when they should be getting on with the business of teaching real skills to black children. Others such as Adam (1978) were critical of the new 'no difference' findings, claiming that it ignored the political context of racial oppression and that 'no difference' was interpreted as 'no further problem'.

This is not to suggest that researchers are hapless victims of political trends, or that they are pulled by the nose to produce appropriate political outcomes. But it does alert us to the notion that researchers do not work in political vacuums. Research questions, instruments, results and interpretations are all actively forged within particular historical, moral and political contexts. Psychological research does not simply produce neutral and objective facts and findings – despite its protestations to the contrary (see also Dawes and Donald, Chapter 1).

Political contexts present considerable implications for the interpretation of results, and this is particularly pertinent for a value-laden area such as racial identity. Put simply, the research described above has seldom produced any direct evidence of 'damage'. That is why the findings in terms of choices of photographs or of dolls have been set out in detail in this chapter. It is one thing to claim that so many people chose this or that doll, in answer to certain questions; it is entirely another thing to interpret this in one phase as indicative of 'damage', in a second phase as representing 'pathology' or 'deviance', and in a third phase in terms of 'resilience' or 'coping' or of 'no difference' under the skin. In these terms, then, it is clear that much of the interpretation and meaning of this line of research has been exaggerated, decontextualised, reified and overgeneralised.

Moral Quandaries of Identity

On the face of it, the issue of identity or of racial attitude seems a straightforward question of neutral psychological investigation. On a deeper probing it becomes an arena fraught with moral and political minefields – matters that mainstream psychology has tried to evade without much success.

The literature on black identity is littered with moral and political bias. First, there is the danger of pathologising. For instance, when some studies have found black self-esteem to be more positive than that of whites it has been interpreted as 'compensatory' or 'inflated' or 'defensively high'. Thus even when positives are reported, interpretation is able to turn them into negatives.

Second, this research tradition has shown a tendency to adopt a white frame of reference. Blacks have been cast as the problem, with negative terms such as 'misidentity', 'identity confusion', 'inferiorisation' or 'self-hatred'. We have a quandary here. Let us say, as shown in the case of South African attitudinal literature, that blacks have favourable views towards English-speaking whites. How should that be interpreted? Is this a mark of positive non-racialism, of a balanced intergroup perspective and of tolerance, or is it indicative of inferiority, low self-esteem or own-group rejection? These questions are not often posed. It is certainly the case, however, that the literature has reported double standards in labelling since whites who show black preference are often described in favourable terms such as 'less ethnocentric' or 'cross-identifying' and not as showing out-group preference and owngroup devaluation! Most damning of all, the steady findings of white ethnocentrism and prejudice are not cast in problematic terms (Foster-Carter 1986).

Foster-Carter (1986) informs us of a further double standard. Working-class children who identify with middle classes are not pathologised to the same extent as blacks. Rather, this is couched in terms of positive aspirations or upward mobility. Underlying this is an assumption of the immutability of racial categorisation.

The concept of identity itself is problematic. Too often it is treated as uni-dimensional and bipolar: positive or negative (Tizard and Phoenix 1989). Positive identity is then held to be ingroup preference, a most dubious moral and psychological claim. A uni-dimensional and bipolar conception of identity ignores the well-grounded distinctions between personal and social identity as well as the notion that we possess multiple identifications such as gender, class, nation and so forth. The bipolar view of identity also obscures the possibility of other identity dimensions such as ambivalence or contradiction, or the relative balance between positive and negative identifications.

The question of positive identity cannot be easily divorced from moral and political questions. If we are striving towards a genuine non-racialism, then different pictures emerge of what is good and proper. One scenario would desire a fusion of identities in which both black and white would shift toward each other and forge new identities. Another scenario would propose different identities as a moral good, on condition that there would be a high degree of mutual acceptance. Both scenarios would suggest outgroup favourability as morally and psychologically sound in contrast to the present equation that ingroup identification is psychologically healthy and morally desirable.

It should be apparent that what starts as a psychological question of racial identity soon becomes embroiled in tricky moral and political dilemmas – too often ignored in the psychological formalism of methods and results.

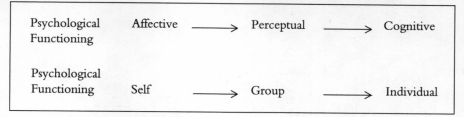

Fig. 4. The social cognitive developmental approach of Frances Aboud (1988)

Theoretical Views

How do we explain the empirical patterns described above? Instead of covering the full range of available theories, we focus instead on two leading theories.

Frances Aboud (1988) has recently proposed a social cognitive developmental theory which has particular advantages in accounting for age-developmental trends found in numerous studies. This involves two overlapping sequences of developmental processes: one set covering psychological functioning, the other set describing changes in focus of attention. It is set out in schematic form in Figure 4.

The two sequences of overlapping processes are seen as operating in combination to produce differing racial orientations in increasing age groups. When affective processes are dominant in the young child (ages roughly 3–5 years), the child is also dominantly egocentric. When perceptual processes begin to emerge, the child will focus on particular external cues, such as colour, and evaluate group differences in terms of such external cues (roughly ages 6–8 years). With the emergence of cognitive dominance, the child will first focus on groups in terms of categories, rather than merely perceptual features, then gradually shift over to a second stage with a focus on individual differences and an increasing capacity for individual differentiation (ages 8–12 years).

According to this view, children have different social and psychological capacities at different ages, which restrict their full understanding of the basis of ethnicity. Therefore, Aboud argues, the surface 'prejudices' evident at different stages are qualitatively different. Prejudice among young children should perhaps not be regarded as proper prejudice at all, but as a bias due to limited (or different) mental capacities.

There is much merit in this approach. It does quite well in tying together a good deal of both empirical evidence and cognitive developmental theorising. In particular it is able to provide a possible account of the striking changes observed broadly around the age of 7 years. However, this approach also has a notable weakness: a failure to explain the black–white (or majority–minority group) differences, i.e. why majority-group children show ingroup preference and minority-group children evidence outgroup preference. As we have seen earlier, Aboud admits that this is 'a puzzle'. This view is woefully short of a social perspective, a characteristic failing of much contemporary cognitive theorising. Fortunately, recent years have also seen the emergence of another approach.

Drawing on the social identity theory developed by Henri Tajfel, various

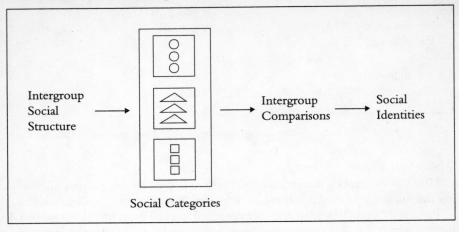

Fig. 5.   The social identity approach

writers (Davey 1983; Milner 1984; Vaughan 1987) have proposed a view which takes seriously the notion that children develop social identities based on existing large-scale social categories. In other words, the processes described by Aboud constitute only one leg of a child's identity – that of personal rather than social identity. Aboud's position needs to be complemented by the social identity approach shown schematically in Figure 5.

Put in other words, children become aware of salient and large-scale social categories, and their own sense of social identity develops in a framework of these categories and comparison between categories. In general, all children should evidence an ingroup bias – an expressed favouritism for their own group – as has been shown in the case of young white children.

However, the existing social order is also hierarchically organised in terms of social status, domination and power. In social orders such as the USA, UK and South Africa where racial criteria feature significantly in the power structure, racial identities become particularly salient. In order to maintain a positive social identity in such a value-ordered world, minority children tend to aspire towards dominant group values, hence the outgroup preference phenomenon. But this can change over historical time. When racially salient group domination, such as in South Africa, is perceived to be illegitimate (as has occurred in recent historical times, and may occur with older children) the outgroup bias for many black children may be discarded.

This theory, by considering social factors such as power, dominance, hierarchies and perceived legitimacy, is able to account for three aspects not well explained by Aboud's approach: (i) black, or minority-group, outgroup preference, (ii) the widespread and shared aspect of certain racial orientations, and (iii) changes over historical time as a result of the perceived legitimacy and stability of the power arrangements in society.

This model suggests that children are not asocial, but are acutely aware, within varying degrees of mental capacities (thus the age-related changes), of the status and power ordering of society. Furthermore, the formation of identity is a dynamic process, constantly in flux. While membership of existing social categories is a powerful initial source of identity, it does not mechanically determine identity. Children (and adults), through interaction with others, through knowledge and experience of the social world, actively construct identities and attitudes. To take merely one example, certain white children may experience their own dominant group status as illegitimate and unfair, and so develop strategies of ambivalence towards, or distancing from, their own group and acceptance of other group members. Other white children, experiencing their situation as legitimate and a source of pride, may remain ethnocentric and prejudiced towards outgroup members. The full theory proposes a range of identity-related strategies and actions for both majority- and minority-group members – which it is beyond the scope of the present chapter to discuss (see Tajfel 1981). In short, this model can also account for individual and subgroup variations in identity strategies.

What are the implications, from these two theoretical views, for the question of 'damage' as posed earlier in this chapter? If we read it correctly, Aboud's cognitive view seems to imply that it 'will all go away' by roughly age 12 years. 'Prejudice' among young children is not really prejudice at all, and with the maturation of psychological development, children evaluate others on the basis of individual merit rather than group characteristics. She does, however, stress that there may be a range of individual variations 'in the extent to which perceptions rather than cognitions and groups rather than individuals dominate their ethnic judgements' (Aboud 1988:125). Her opinion is that ordinary cognitive maturation works towards reducing prejudice, but that forces of social influence (e.g. parents, friends, normative aspects) could pull the child in a more prejudiced direction. Overall, with a concentration on cognitive factors, Aboud seems little concerned with questions of damage or negative consequences.

The social identity model seems to suggest that under certain conditions – when an oppressed group perceives the situation to be legitimate and when no alternatives seem possible – some, but not necessarily all, people may hold self-denigrating views along with positive evaluations of the outgroup. In so far as this may constitute 'damage', then Tajfel's theory would support such a notion. Reporting on his own work which showed self-devaluation among Scottish and Israeli children, Tajfel used these words in conclusion: 'children are highly sensitive to the socially-prevailing evaluations of national and ethnic groups' (Tajfel 1981:205). Furthermore, Tajfel's approach rejects a view of the oppressed as merely passive victims of domination. The theory sketches numerous strategies of resistance and identity retrieval in response to oppression.

Apart from these two theoretical views, which should be treated as complementary rather than as oppositional, a range of recent approaches (Crocker and Major 1989; Jenkins 1982; Rosenberg 1979; Stone 1981) should be added into the equation for a better understanding. These views describe and emphasise the protective, buffering or coping processes of people in the face of oppression and stigmatisation. All of them lay stress on the self as an active agent, rather than a system of response.

Three main factors emerge in this recent phase of writing. The first stresses the active processes of selectivity in self-development. Instead of being over-whelmed by negativity, the self is an active process which employs a whole bat-tery of selective devices to protect against damage. There is selectivity regarding which components or contents of the self are regarded as central or important; selectivity of comparison groups and comparison levels; selectivity of compara-tive others (friends, mentors); and selective processes of self-attribution.

A second factor is the process of system-blaming rather than self-blame. People have the capacity to attribute negative stereotyping to outgroups rather than as a property of real ingroup characteristics. For example blacks may attribute blame to the racist system for their own status in society. Finally, the recent writings lay considerable emphasis on the role of black culture, language and solidarity in providing protective barriers against negative views of the self. All of these factors are relevant to the South African situation and warrant fur-ther investigation.

Concluding Comments

Do black children suffer negative consequences as a result of racist practices? After a tour of some evidence, some of the leading theories and some criticism, both conceptual and methodological, we are left with a more complex but rather equivocal and contradictory picture. Let us try to pull some of the threads together.

Regarding the distinction made at the start of the chapter, there is little doubt that the 'direct' consequences of racism are severe and negative. Racism, which prevents the full flowering of human potentiality, is a form of structural violence and certainly inflicts damage on those at the receiving end. But what exactly is meant by damage when the indirect consequences are considered?

As Spenser and Markstrom-Adams (1990) put it, the pro-white attitude and preference patterns represent cultural-ecological variables (i.e. negative social stereotypes about blacks) and not psychological characteristics. Therefore, 'dam-age' in this respect does not refer to mental health issues or psychopathology. That remains as a separate question, not dealt with in this chapter. Seen in this way, the ecological niche for minority children and youth is different from that of members of the dominant groups.

Regarding evidence, it is clear that despite historical shifts and a greater recognition of age-related changes, there persists a trend of outgroup preference among minority-group children while dominant-group children evidence a greater degree of ethnocentrism and prejudice. By the time one has completed additional methodological and conceptual criticism, these findings remain less clear cut, less powerful and altogether more shaky but nevertheless naggingly still present. We believe that the earlier interpretations in terms of 'self-hatred' and psychopathology are exaggerated. Outgroup preference need not necessarily imply self-rejection. Self-esteem among minority groups seems to remain sur-prisingly unscathed as the result of a host of protective and buffering processes.

To interpret the meaning of these patterns we have to turn to moral and polit-ical considerations. The question of 'damage' cannot be answered in psychologi-cal terms alone. The question of values, in moral and political terms, stands at the core of the whole issue. If, for instance, ingroup chauvinism is treated as the desirable normative standard, then white children constitute the norm and some black children will be evaluated as 'damaged' against this normative criterion. If on the other hand a genuine non-racialism were to be regarded as the moral good, then white (or dominant) children may be held to be 'damaged' and black children evaluated as the norm since they are capable of cross-identification.

Seen from a political perspective, white children, constituting the base for a future ethnocentrism which would stand in the way of mutuality, could be held to be the problem. From another political perspective the phenomenon of outgroup preference among blacks could be seen as fuelling accommodation to the racist system and standing in the way of black resistance and solidarity. That is why certain black political movements have adopted a policy of separatism. But that takes us back to the dilemma of ingroup chauvinism as the normative good. These are thorny matters indeed.

As a minimal conclusion we suggest the following. As long as there is evidence for different ecological niches (Spenser and Markstrom-Adams 1990) for black and white children, there is evidence that racism is still firmly in place. That unfortunately is still the case. Racism is not a desirable form of social organisation for anyone, white or black. The task of striving against racism is to work for the optimal development of all children.

Where to from here? This whole line of research makes it quite clear that young children are highly sensitive to the wider sociopolitical context in which they develop. Children, while active beings, nevertheless are constructed and position themselves in terms of meanings, attitudes and orientations within large-scale intergroup struggles. The study of development of children in complex sociopolitical contexts simply has to be far more sensitive to the multiple contexts ('race', gender, class, youth culture) of development than has hitherto been the case.

We know relatively little of how these multiple contexts position and produce children and youth in South Africa. We need more qualitative research merely describing how children and youth think and feel about gender, class and racial interactions. We need more information on how particular contexts such as schools (e.g. Du Preez 1983; Christie 1990), families, media, politics, churches and youth organisations impact on children's ethnic development. We require greater understanding of how the processes of buffering, selectivity and protection operate in the development of young people's identities. We need a better grasp of how certain contexts 'switch on' or render salient particular types of social indentities such as gender, ethnicity or political identities (e.g. the 'comrades'). It is striking how some of these may vary across historical contexts yet others such as gender and race may retain salience.

Finally, it is remarkable how little we know about the practice of social change. For some while now, practices of social change have been driven by assumptions of assimilation, contact, multiculturalism and the like. It is apparent from western countries that these have not worked particularly well. In South Africa we have hardly started to think about such matters.

If democracy, non-sexism and non-racialism constitute a broad framework of practical ideals, then the business of thinking through the stuff of attitudes, identities and intergroup orientations should be of utmost importance. We do not simply need more research. To adopt a fully social and contextual approach, we also have to consider how research is embedded in moral, political and practical frames as well as the implications of these. In South Africa we have the opportunity. It should not be treated lightly.

References

Aboud, F.E. (1988). *Children and Prejudice*. Oxford: Basil Blackwell.

Aarons, (1991). Race attitude development in black, white and coloured South African children. Unpublished MA thesis, Department of Psychology, University of Cape Town.

Aboud, F.E. and Skerry, S.A. (1984). The development of ethnic attitudes: A critical review. *Journal of Cross-Cultural Psychology, 15*, 3-34.

Adam, B.D. (1978). Inferiorisation and self-esteem. *Social Psychology, 41*, 47-53.

Annis, R.C. and Corenblum, B. (1987). Effect of test language and experimenter race on Canadian Indian children's racial and self-identity. *Journal of Social Psychology, 126*, 761-773.

Asher, S.R. and Allen, V.L. (1969). Racial preference and social comparison processes. *Journal of Social Issues, 25*, 157-166.

Banks, W.C. (1976). White-preference in blacks: A paradigm in search of a phenomenon. *Psychological Bulletin, 83*, 1179-1186.

Biko, S. (1978). *I Write What I Like*. London: Heinemann.

Branch, C.W. and Newcombe, N. (1986). Racial attitude development among young black children as a function of parental attitudes. *Child Development, 57*, 712-721.

Brand, E., Ruiz, R. and Padilla, A. (1974). Ethnic identification and preference: A review. *Psychological Bulletin, 81*, 860-890.

Christie, P. (1990). *Open Schools*. Johannesburg: Ravan Press.

Clark, K.B. and Clark, M.P. (1940). Skin colour as a factor in racial identification of Negro preschool children. *Journal of Social Psychology, 11*, 159.

Clark, K.B. and Clark, M.P. (1947). Racial identification and preference in Negro children. In T. Newcomb and E.L. Hartley (eds), *Readings in Social Psychology*. New York: Holt, Rinehart and Winston.

Coles, R. (1967). *Children of Crisis*. Boston: Atlantic Monthly Press.

Coles, R. (1986). *The Political Life of Children*. Boston: Atlantic Monthly Press.

Crocker, J. and Major, B. (1989). Social stigma and self-esteem. *Psychological Review, 96*, 608-630.

Davey, A. (1983). *Learning to be Prejudiced*. London: Edward Arnold.

Davey, A. G. and Norburn, M. V. (1980). Ethnic awareness and ethnic differentiation amongst primary school children. *New Community, 8*, 206-212

De Groot, W.A. (1978). Kleurbewustheid en groeps-identifikasie onder groepe Kleurlingkinders. Unpublished MA thesis, Rand Afrikaans University.

Du Preez, J.M. (1983). *Africana Afrikaner: Master Symbols in South African School Textbooks*. Alberton: Librarius.

Fanon, F. (1952/1967). *Black Skin, White Masks*. New York: Grove Press.

Foster, D. and Nel, E. (1991). Attitudes and related concepts. In D. Foster and J. Louw-Potgieter (eds), *Social Psychology in South Africa*. Johannesburg: Lexicon.

Foster, D. (1986). The development of racial orientation in children. In S. Burman and P. Reynolds (eds), *Growing Up in a Divided Society*. Johannesburg: Ravan Press.

Foster-Carter, O. (1986). Insiders, outsiders and anomalies: A review of studies of identity. *New Community, 13*(2), 224-234.

Geber, B. and Newman, S. (1980). *Soweto's Children*. London: Academic Press.

Gregor, A.J. and McPherson, D. (1966). Racial preference and ego-identity among white and Bantu children in the Republic of South Africa. *Genetic Psychology Monographs, 73*, 217-253.

Grier, W. and Cobb, P. (1968). *Black Rage*. New York: Basic Books.

Howcroft, G. (1990). The self-esteem of black university students. *South African Journal of Sociology, 21*, 31-36.

Hraba, J. and Grant, G. (1970). Black is beautiful: A re-examination of racial preference and identi-fication. *Journal of Personality and Social Psychology, 16,* 398-402.

Jenkins, A.H. (1982). *The Psychology of the Afro-American.* New York: Pergamon Press.

Katz, P.A. and Zalk, S.R. (1976). The Katz-Zalk prejudice test. *Catalog of Selected Documents in Psychology,* No. 6.

Katz, P.A. (1976). The acquisition of racial attitudes in children. In P.A. Katz (ed.), *Towards the Elimination of Racism.* New York: Pergamon Press.

Lambert, W.E. and Klineberg, O. (1968). *Children's Views of Foreign People: A Cross-National study.* New York: Appleton-Century-Crofts.

Landrum-Brown, J. (1990). Black mental health and racial oppression. In D.S. Ruiz and J.P. Comer (eds), *Handbook of Mental Health and Mental Disorder among Black Americans.* New York: Greenwood Press.

Lever, H. (1968). *Ethnic Attitudes of Johannesburg Youth.* Johannesburg: University of the Witwatersrand Press.

Manganyi, N.C. (1973). *Being-Black-in-the-World.* Johannesburg: Ravan Press.

Manganyi, N.C. (1977). *Mashangu's Reverie and Other Essays.* Johannesburg: Ravan Press.

Meij, L.R. (1966). The Clark dolls test as a measure of children's racial attitudes. *Journal for Social Research, 15,* 25-40.

Milner, D. (1973). Racial identification and preference in black British children. *European Journal of Social Psychology, 3,* 281-295.

Milner, D. (1983). *Children and Race: 10 Years On.* London: Ward Lock International.

Milner, D. (1984). The development of ethnic attitudes. In H. Tajfel (ed.), *The Social Dimension,* Vol. 1. Cambridge: Cambridge University Press.

Moodie, M.A. (1980). The development of national identity in white South African school chil-dren. *Journal of Social Psychology, 3,* 169-180.

Nagata, D.K. (1985). The relationships between ethnic attitude and egocentrism measures. *Journal of Genetic Psychology, 146,* 151-160.

Porter, J. (1971). *Black Child, White Child.* Cambridge, Mass.: Harvard University Press.

Rosenberg, M. (1979). *Conceiving the Self.* Malabar: Krieger.

Spenser, M.B. and Markstrom-Adams, C. (1990). Identity processes among racial and ethnic minority children in America. *Child Development, 61,* 290-310.

Stone, M. (1981). *The Education of the Black Child in Britain.* London: Fontana.

Tajfel, H. (1981). *Human Groups and Social Categories.* Cambridge: Cambridge University Press.

Tizard, B. and Phoenix, A. (1989). Black identity and transracial adoption. *New Community, 15*(3), 427-437.

Troyna, B. and Hatcher, R. (1992). *Racism in Children's Lives.* London: Routledge.

Vaughan, G.M. (1964). The development of ethnic attitudes in New Zealand. *Genetic Psychology Monographs, 70,* 135-175.

Vaughan, G.M. (1978). Social change and intergroup preferences in New Zealand. *European Journal of Social Psychology, 8,* 297-314.

Vaughan, G.M. (1987). A social psychological model of ethnic identity development. In J. Phinney and M. Rotheram (eds), *Children's Ethnic Socialization.* Newbury Park: Sage.

Ward, S.H. and Braun, J. (1972). Self-esteem and racial preference in black children. *American Journal of Orthopsychiatry, 42,* 644-648.

Williams, J. and Morland, J.K. (1976). *Race, Colour and the Young Child.* Chapel Hill: University of North Carolina Press.

Wilson, A. (1987). *Mixed Race Children.* London: Allen and Unwin.

13

Problems of Cultural Imperialism in the Study of Child Sexual Abuse[1]

ANN LEVETT

Introduction

As a site in which to study the workings of power, child sexual abuse assumes a particular significance at this historical moment: many sociopolitical processes are involved, in a range of power structures, in the western world and elsewhere. Despite the widespread publicity and due concern which childhood sexual abuse and its effects have evoked in recent years in western and Anglo–American communities, major conceptual and practical issues have not been seriously addressed. In the late twentieth century, western patriarchal social systems are easily able to take up and accommodate some liberal and feminist demands while giving minimal attention to the workings of power which led to the identification of social phenomena of concern in the first place. Appropriate remedies are not seriously sought. There is selective neglect of important factors. I will briefly address these issues in order to prepare for an examination of the implications for current and imminent attempts to study child sexual abuse in southern Africa, in different speech communities. Patriarchy and other aspects of authority are played out in shared representations of everyday phenomena such as childhood, sexuality, human development and psychological disorder, although these may take distinctive forms in different social and historical contexts. Some dilemmas in current debates over protectionist policies and the abuse of power versus individual rights (and children's rights or needs) will also be briefly mentioned in the discussion which follows.

Hardly mentioned before 1970, child sexual abuse has been the focus of a huge outcry in an increasing range of English-speaking, especially Anglo–American contexts in the past twenty years and is receiving increasing attention in South Africa in the 1990s. Articles and reports are common in the news

[1]My appreciation and thanks are due to Amanda Kottler and to Nomsa Ngqakayi for their comments on some of these ideas, and for saving me from some potentially dangerous claims, although they cannot be held responsible for the arguments or examples set out in this chapter. Amanda also gave me invaluable assistance with editing in the final stages of writing.

media, in weekly magazines and television programmes; parents and teachers are concerned and seek ways to prevent, recognise and deal with sexual abuse.

Clinical and academic research has tended to take three forms. Prevalence studies have been conducted in different communities; but it is interesting that another, larger body of literature concerns the 'damaging' psychological effects of such experience on those subjected to it, and numerous reports on therapeutic interventions. In a third thrust, a handful of recent papers discuss attempts to prevent child sexual abuse; these efforts have been described as largely ineffectual (Reppucci and Haugaard 1989).

There are various reasons why childhood sexual abuse was singled out for attention at a particular socio-historical moment. Effects on children attracted attention first in the 1970s when American feminist and liberal human rights activists took up the issue. Feminist writing around 1970 drew attention to male exploitation of structured power in relation to women, girls and children, particularly in the context of sexuality (Millett 1970; Russell 1975). This writing led to research on child sexual abuse, involving a growing range of professional mental health workers. Nelson (1984) and Hacking (1991) have documented the history of the category 'child abuse'. Nelson provides a fascinating analysis of the association between this preoccupation and the modern emergence of powerful lobbies of medical and legal institutions. The widespread belief that sexual abuse is psychologically damaging arose from these contexts and prompted demands for efforts to identify and redress such damage. All this occurred in the wake of post-Second World War moves to increasing professionalisation, along with the development of social policies highlighting the plight of various groups (the emergence of victimology), and the shaping of public policy and social interventions to improve the situation of such groups. It is conspicuous that there is almost no discussion of child abuse in the non-English literature and very little on this phenomenon in non-English-speaking communities, particularly in Africa.

In the twentieth century children have assumed an increasingly important place in western consciousness and in psychological theory and practice (Kessel and Siegel 1983). Our models of psychology and of psychological development are inherently individualistic and assume that childhood experiences have a great deal of influence on adult behaviour. We have also tended to assume that western studies are universally applicable. I use the term 'assume' advisedly because it has become apparent that much of what has been precious in psychological thinking, when subjected to closer scrutiny, is based on social constructions (Gergen 1985; Arbib and Hesse 1986) and rhetoric (Billig 1987).

Child sexual abuse has assumed a particular significance at this historical moment as a consequence of many sociopolitical processes in a specific set of power structures, and of shifts in the position of women in western societies. The term trauma, associated with child sexual abuse, is used metaphorically to convey various complex ideas and feelings about a set of western, morally based ideologies (exploitation, abuse, the rights of individuals). Such metaphors arise in the context of particular discourses, in this instance those concerning the control of women and women's resistance to being controlled in certain ways. The development of gendered subjectivity occurs in this context in a particular range of semiotic codes (Manning 1987). Cross-cultural study of sexual abuse will have to deal with the problems of eliciting local sets of semiotic codes and counter-discourses in order to understand local circumstances, if we are to compare these with Anglo–American ones and work towards social change.

In the past decade, long-term effects on adults have also been studied (e.g. Beutler and Hill 1992; Wyatt and Powell 1988). All in all, thousands of papers now discuss child sexual abuse, and there are dozens of books on the subject, all published since the late 1970s. The authors are mental health clinicians and academic researchers. Although the issue is still associated with feminist concerns about the abuse of girls and women, probably 95% of this literature is only nominally feminist in the sense of offering an articulated political analysis of sexual abuse. Liz Kelly notes

> a new professional specialisation is emerging – people whose careers (and notice how many of the most 'successful' are men) have been built on the investigation, treatment and 'prevention' of child sexual assault. Within this group there are individuals who are passionately committed to supporting women and children, but very few have a coherent political analysis which would enable them to see just how challenging this issue is and, therefore, how difficult real change is going to be to achieve... The creation of this tier of 'experts' from within the professions means that many of the basic insights feminists developed concerning sexual violence and its impact have been lost, or deliberately ignored. (1989:15).

The inescapables generally glossed over are that it is usually older or adult males who sexually abuse children, mainly girls and women, and that this proclivity is tied in with social constructions of male sexuality, gendered identity and patriarchal power.

How Common Is Child Sexual Abuse?

The study of incidence (the number of new cases in a particular population in a stipulated period of time) has been reported for various populations sampled, almost exclusively in the USA. Studies of prevalence in a range of groups and communities, mainly in North America and in the United Kingdom, commonly suggest up to 54% of women have been subjected to child sexual abuse, the most important difference being related to the definition of sexual abuse used by researchers and to the methods used to collect data. In a sample of women students at a South African university in 1986, the prevalence figure of 44% was regarded as an under-report (Levett 1989a). Although DeMause (1991) steps around difficulties in defining incestuous sexual abuse, he follows the current trend of a broad definition of sexual abuse, including not only cases of rape or attempted sexual intercourse but also genital fondling, and other forms of unwanted and intrusive contact behaviours. In the USA at least 60% of girls (and 45% of boys) are likely to be sexually abused in childhood, 81% before puberty and an equally large number within the family. He notes recent research with children from Berlin, which found an 80% child molestation prevalence, and comments that if children were surveyed in North America the figures are likely to be similar. He states that 'the incidence in countries outside the West is likely to be much higher', attributing this to an 'infanticidal mode of child-rearing' and because, he claims, 'the use of children for the emotional needs of adults is far more accepted, an attitude that fosters widespread incestuous acts along with other child abuse' (1991:142). DeMause is muddled in his use of terms such as incest (see La Fontaine 1987) and in directly comparing human sexual behaviours of different socio-historical periods, with no discussion of the problems involved. However, in all probability the figures he cites for child sexual abuse prevalence in the western world are likely to be true, and there is little reason to argue that prevalence would be lower in Africa.

Given these high prevalence figures, it is difficult to regard child sexual abuse experience as unusual. However, sexual abuse of children is generally studied as if these are uncommon events with specific outcomes even though a very large proportion of girls and women in western society have been sexually abused under the age of 18 years. One would call sexual abuse 'normative' with reluctance because there is a sense of moral indignation associated with such behaviour. It seems absurd then to talk about psychological damage when most women would be involved.

The term 'psychological trauma' widely associated with child sexual abuse has been used metaphorically to convey the idea that, just as the body may be injured or bruised, so might the mind or mental sense of self. Introduced initially in feminist counter-discourse as a critique of male and adult power over girls, the metaphor of damage has shifted. In the context of professional and protectionist discourses of regulation and social control, the damaging effects of child sexual abuse become as factual as a broken bone, and the clinical elicitation of evidence lends itself to this usage. It has become a justification for interventions which are often counterproductive for the child and families involved.

The Relationship to Gendered Subjectivity

For girls, experiences of child sexual abuse contribute to early notions of gendered identity, based on semiotic systems of difference between the sexes. The particular overtones of difference involved in 'trauma' may serve to endorse stigmatised forms of gendered identity (Levett 1992b).

In all sociocultural contexts where men hold most public and economic power, they also dominate the private sphere through their authority over women and children. This is linked with the finding that adolescent boys and men are almost invariably the perpetrators of sexual abuse and that most prevalence research concerns figures and consequences for girls and women. While a recent and growing literature suggests that boys are often sexually abused in contemporary western society, it is not always clearly argued that the implications for boys and girls are different because of the association between gender and power. Boys grow into men and therefore into subjectivities in which coercive sexual relating and the active perpetration of sexual assault, on children and women, become a possibility (even if only in thought and fantasy). The claim that boys who have been sexually abused as children are the ones who become abusers as adults should be rejected as an oversimplification (see Widom 1989). This idea of causation conceals the role of patriarchy: the social production and reproduction of male authority and normative conventions of male promiscuity. These, with the frequently hostile or ambivalent qualities sometimes involved in heterosexual relating, are all implicated in child sexual abuse, sexual assault and rape. Malamuth, Sockloskie and Tanaka (1991:680), in a study of American college men, comment: 'Our findings on sexual aggression suggest that it results from the combination of relatively high levels of hostile masculinity and sexual promiscuity'. They mention elsewhere the significance of adversarial relating between men and a sense of shame and inadequacy involved in sexual coercion and aggression. The details of these aspects of male subjectivities require further, close psychosocial study in different contexts as it is likely that the dynamics which result in some men acting on ideas of sexually abusive behaviours may not be universal.

Although male–female dynamics are profoundly implicated, not all men are abusive; it is inescapable that child sexual abuse is an over-determined phenomenon with complex meanings. Generic factors include socially accepted idealisation of women as well as the degradation of women, both of which objectify women, and the unconscious confusion of women with children and vice versa, all of which are linked with certain forms of patriarchal power (the 'rule of the father').

Socarides discusses psychoanalytic understandings of child sexual abuse and adds that the current epidemic is not a clinical phenomenon but one which is related to 'times of social disequilibrium when there is no "authoritative prohibition by society" against such behaviour' (1991:448). This assumes that such behaviour is 'naturally male' and that men have to learn to inhibit such behaviour through cultural constraints, an essentialist claim (Shotter 1984), although the widespread existence of patriarchal power makes it difficult to debunk. Fuss (1989) argues that the function which an essentialist claim serves should be questioned and, in this case, it seems that it serves to perpetuate the rule of the father.

Girls grow into women with gendered subjectivities in which sexual assault and harassment by males are part of everyday life. Although there has been a trend to research and discuss child sexual abuse as if it were a separate phenomenon (Russell 1984 is a significant exception), experiences of sexual abuse in childhood must be seen as part of the broad processes in which male–female power and authority are epitomised. For both boys and girls who are sexually abused in childhood there is an exploitation of power differences between adults and children, but for girls the dynamics involved in male–female sexual relating also enter the picture, as Ennew (1986) has commented. I will be discussing childhood sexual abuse specifically in relation to girls because of this compounding of power.

Child Sexual Abuse in African Societies

There has been very little 'cross-cultural' study of child abuse and especially of child sexual abuse. The relative absence of research on child abuse and on child sexual abuse in Africa is noteworthy but is also partly understandable in terms of the meagre resources available and because of the scarcity of feminist lobbies (Finkelhor 1989). What exists is mostly an obvious attempt to reproduce western assumptions and ideas, as though they are universal and unquestionable. Ennew (1986) provides a sophisticated commentary on the limitations of such work, and some more conventional difficulties of 'cross-cultural' studies are discussed by Korbin (1987), who also reviews international studies on child neglect and abuse (Korbin 1991). She points out the importance of dealing with infectious disease, diarrhoea and malnutrition as primary problems in third world countries as distinct from child sexual abuse.

Almost all research on sexual abuse initiated in South Africa, a country which is relatively wealthy in the African context, has simply emulated North American research (Levett and Lachman 1991; Levett and Macleod 1992), using a naïvely positivist empiricism. These studies import the assumptions and power structures of the western world which still affect children in those societies (Sullivan 1992). Today great concern is expressed about the sexual abuse of children in South Africa; many (particularly, but not only, those who are literate and educated) know that this occurs mainly within the child's familial environment and involves trusted males. However, 'stranger danger' is given emphasis in the media and in programmes to educate children. As in the USA and England there has been some effort to facilitate assistance for those affected (e.g. in Cape Town there are Child Line and Safeline, neither of which is feminist, and RAPCAN, which is). As with South African social services in general very little help is available, child welfare and social workers feel overwhelmed and helpless, and South African legislation and judicial processes are regarded as almost useless (Levett 1991). The most effective legal procedures involve children who have been molested by strangers (Collings 1989), while newspaper attention is devoted to women and girls who have been raped by intruders or former black employees, or to boys sexually abused by paedophiles (misleadingly depicted as gay men), thus concealing the links between male authority in the family and the most common forms of child sexual abuse beneath myths of stranger danger, racist ideology and heterosexism. In South Africa, as in the UK and North America, the field has been largely co-opted by non-feminist professionals, and the dilemmas are generally depicted as individual or familial problems, psychological and class-related (Kelly 1989). Intervention is shaped by and therefore limited by the dominant ideologies of the medical profession, the state and state-supported welfare services. The implications of patriarchal power in this socio-historical process, the relationship of 'the incest industry' to professionalisation, and the place of current ideas about the effects of childhood sexual abuse in the development of female-gendered subjectivity in contemporary societies demand serious and immediate attention at this significant period of transformation in South Africa.

Although one needs to be cautious in putting forward arguments about 'cultural differences' in the southern African context, for anti-apartheid-related political reasons (Kottler 1990), it may also be necessary to make the socio-cultural context visible in terms of particular forms of patriarchal power in this part of the world. Mejiuni (1991) addresses child abuse in Nigeria and the way that abuse seems to have escalated there, and argues that although particular political and economic factors are implicated in the physical and sexual abuse of children in Africa, these find a fertile base in ideological facets of African patriarchal traditions of family life which facilitate the sexual abuse of women and girls.

There is a great deal of evidence in Bennett (1991) for specific forms of customary treatment of girls and women as male property in African communities. These 'local traditions' were upheld by the imported conventions and laws (introduced by the Dutch and British colonisers or perpetuated up to today) which, in their own ways, are oppressive to women and children. African women have been treated as minors in South African customary law and, generally, in common law as well. Bennett comments: 'On the one hand, the common-law categories of minor and major cannot reflect the nuances and flexibility inherent in customary law, and, on the other, these categories were imposed on women not with a view to protecting them but with a view to restraining them' (1991:323). He adds, 'No country in Africa has legislated with the sole purpose of ameliorating the civil-law status of women' (1991:331).

It is particularly interesting to note that there are no stipulations in customary law to deal with the abuse or neglect of children, the sexual abuse of children or the sexual assault of women, except that there is a requirement of marriage or payment of *lobola* to the girl's father or male relatives if rape is involved, and any child which results from such an assault may then be taken into the paternal household. It is illustrative of the lack of awareness of issues raised by the women's movement that, in an otherwise useful, critical set of interpretative comments, Bennett does not remark on these gaps in his chapters on Children and on Women. However, he notes: 'While [African] governments might have been sympathetic to the feminist cause, they could not afford to estrange the majority of their supporters, who in most cases were the conservative beneficiaries of the patriarchal tradition. Hence, even in countries espousing radical changes to the family structure, improvements to the status of women were incidental benefits, rather than a specific goal.' (1991:331-2).

Physical beatings are widespread and accepted forms of disciplining women and children although in urban areas this may be viewed as a rural and old-fashioned method (Bennett 1991; Straker, Moosa, Becker and Nkwale 1992). Furthermore, the custom that prohibits women from disciplining boys and men once they have gone through initiation rites associated with puberty has general effects, which communicate a set of attitudes to male authority, even though fewer young men go through the initiation rites today.

Given the realities and ramifications of apartheid legislation and its aftermath, and current economic factors, over the last fifty years very large numbers of black men and women have attempted to move to the cities to find work and a range of opportunities to better their lives. For women there are extra benefits in escaping the older traditions of black patriarchy which were so constraining for women. In urban environments they escape more easily from both the customary authority of the father and husband and that of older senior women, often preserve their single status by resisting marriage arrangements, and may live with a number of children fathered by different men with whom they have chosen, in part, to associate. Through direct access to earning their own wages, minimal property rights, small savings and personal initiative, within the constraints of poverty and access to work, the number of women heading single-parent households has increased substantially (Bennett 1991). This may, in some contexts, be a protective factor safeguarding children from sexual abuse.

On the other hand, there is an anecdotal tale I have heard of a black woman in a Cape Town squatter camp who discovered her prepubertal daughter being sexually abused by the woman's current lover and who reported this (and the child's story of previous such abuse) to the police hoping for authoritative assistance. There was insufficient evidence to justify an arrest, and the woman and her daughter were left by the police to deal with the situation themselves, which in itself is not an unusual situation in any part of the city. The accused man, ejected from the woman's home, rallied neighbourhood men to hound the woman and child out of their home and the area, stoning the child.

It is difficult to interpret this anecdote without additional information, which is not available without careful research. Is the men's reaction acceptable behaviour to the men in this community, or was it related to the attempt to involve the police? Was the perpetrator a member of a local criminal circle whose support he could call in, or was he so respected by his peers that the woman's and child's story was disbelieved? How different is this story, in its bare bones, from accounts of child sexual abuse and male responses in other sections of the community?

The difficulty of researching such material in contemporary South Africa is that it will conceivably be understood as a racist commentary, which is neglectful of the role which apartheid has played in the breakdown of family life, communities and social support, the emasculation of black men, the development of an exploited black working class, and the escalation of crime and violence. However, such arguments do not give due consideration to the power of patriarchy and its local forms, essential to analyse in studies that concern women in contemporary Africa. In workshops about child sexual abuse run in different parts of South Africa in recent years, various African women and men have often commented that men who sexually abuse children feel entitled to do so; this is true also of white men, although the excuses and justifications used may differ (Sterling 1990). The analogy of a man who grows and cares for his mealie (maize) patch and feels entitled to savour the crop first, when it is fresh and he chooses to do so, has been introduced by several unconnected African informants. The concurrent notion is that his neighbours have no basis on which to regulate his behaviour and so, although perhaps they feel uneasy about what he is doing, they do nothing to admonish him. The absence of power is similar in white communities in South Africa: people do not feel they are entitled to interfere in a neighbour's family life.

Through informal accounts and small local surveys discussed in conference contexts, the incidence of sexual abuse is described as widespread in the over-crowded and poverty-stricken urban communities which surround the cities of southern Africa. Large numbers of children grow up in a range of conditions varying from impoverished single-parent homes in tin shacks, or with mothers or fathers and occasionally with both parents, or with a single grandparent in urban or rural areas, or with uncles or aunts, often moving from one temporary context to another (Reynolds 1991). Violence is common, and rape and sexual assault are endemic. However, although they are implicated in a range of ways which increase the complexity of the issues, it would be a mistake to take the stand that racism, apartheid, capitalism, class and living in poverty are the main or sole reasons for sexually abusive phenomena. Sexual assault and child sexual abuse occur in all groups and through the entire class structure although the events which involve the wealthiest and the poorest are most invisible. The wealthy conceal these situations to protect the family, perpetrators, or the assaulted woman or child, being aware of the stigmatic effects. Poor people protect their tenuous material circumstances and do not usually expect assistance from the police and social agencies.

However, the power which males feel entitled to exert over females, the ways in which this is institutionalised (particularly through economic resources), and the authority which women accord men in African patriarchy are fundamental and unavoidable aspects of the picture, as they are in western communities, and must not be glossed over. There may be a difference between black and white communities in prevalence rates of child sexual abuse (as some have argued for different social classes) – but this is an empirical question which has not been addressed, is unlikely to be addressed and, in fact, is not really a useful one to ask at all.

Obviously the disruption and dislocation of everyday life in consequence of apartheid labour and social practices has *something* to do with sexual abuse in contemporary South Africa. Any neighbourhood constraints and controls which may have operated within small, familiar community groups have largely been diluted or eliminated; customary African conventions of respect for men and elders have declined (Viljoen 1991) in some ways that are beneficial and in other ways not. South African women have not yet found ways to organise themselves into self-protective groups to deal effectively with the sexual harassment and assault to which they are subjected by adolescent boys and men in their environments; there is very little feminist consciousness in southern Africa in terms of critiques of male–female sexual relating and this is almost as true of the progressive left as it is of nationalist liberation movements, of educated middle-class women and of working-class women. In general, there is tremendous reluctance amongst South African women to 'organise against men' – this has been seen as divisive and undermining of national liberation struggles and class struggles. In a critique of the Malibongwe papers, Charman, De Swardt and Simons (1991:12) say, 'The relationship of gender to colour and of gender to class is of theoretical and empirical importance.' 'The theoretical formulations of these relationships often conceal the central issue, namely the subordination of women to men as a key feature of social organization.' The same authors cite many statements made by the ANC which strongly support the necessity of ensuring the emancipation of women, but note: 'There is no history or tradition within South Africa which recognises gender conflict as potential conflict... The construction of racism and class exploitation by the national liberation movements precludes a gender analysis of both class and race in South Africa' (1991:16).

In a township in a small Karoo town, where living conditions are cramped and privacy is rare, a social worker who had lived and worked in the area told of a widely accepted practice whereby the daughters in the household are frequently involved by older brothers, fathers, cousins and neighbours in sexual activities from the age of 5 or 6 years. These activities are regarded as acceptable. The girls, as young adults, are amazed and indignant to hear this practice described as 'child sexual abuse'. In an environment where this is widely acceptable normative behaviour, girls learn at a young age that sexuality is perhaps one way to negotiate a special status or favours through an older or adult male figure in the household. The loss of the means to do so would be a loss of power to them, however problematic this power may seem to others. The high incidence of early teenage pregnancies and the fact that girls seldom manage to attain much education beyond Standard 4 or 5 in these circumstances are a major cost: the notion of psychological trauma in the ways so widely described in the western literature does not enter the picture at all.

However, Mejiuni (1991:40) notes the high incidence of child sexual abuse (called 'defilement') in Nigeria and comments that in most cases the perpetrator is related to the child and that 'in most Nigerian cultures the extended family tends to cover up such cases so "it won't go to the outside world and spoil the family name."' From my own preliminary data gathered among African and coloured women of little education in South Africa, it emerges that similar constraints operate in South Africa. Stigma, shame and devaluation are implicated for the girl or child involved; thus the perpetrator is protected.

To break with traditions which prohibit talk about relatives and about sex by talking about child sexual abuse will require a major shift in consciousness among South African women. A paradox has been noted by others between South African women's capacity to defiantly resist and bravely act against certain forms of patriarchal power while actively submitting to other forms (Walker 1991; Posel 1991). Posel comments: 'Arguably, the patriarchal "contract" in African societies – pre-capitalist and beyond – has been successively negotiated and redefined in response to a variety of pressures and opportunities – such as arrival of missionaries, insertion into capitalist relations of production, etc. In many cases, the scope of men's authority has been reduced, but in ways which redefine – rather than altogether overthrow – patriarchal norms.' (1991:26)

Although we need to study the detail of male authority in South Africa, the picture is not as different from the Anglo–American world as the foregoing might suggest. For example, commenting on recent changes in Canadian legislation on child sexual abuse (heralded as the most advanced in the world), Sullivan (1992) articulates some provocative questions. He draws attention to the need to think carefully about the notion of children's rights (individual rights to a range of freedoms) in protectionist terms, and cites the following pertinent criticisms made by fellow Canadians regarding the neglect of contextual issues of structural power in the esteemed Badgley Report (1984):

Through the creation of "sexual abuse" as a unified category to be treated as an empirical fact, the Committee precludes the investigation of its social causes or attributes; for example, the patriarchal character of family/ domestic relations in this society, and the question of why in this context, sex-related violence is carried out primarily by heterosexual men. (Brock and Kinsman cited by Sullivan 1992:99)

New institutions must be developed, which embody a single standard of behaviour for all interpersonal and sexual relationships, based on the equality of men and women and their equal shared responsibility for ensuring that all children are given the opportunity to become fully actualized autonomous adults. These changes cannot be effected without facing the fact that patriarchy must be dismantled, and that paternalism must go with it. To fail to see that these problems are deeply rooted in patriarchal institutions related to the distribution and control of sexual property, and in the socialization of male sexuality appropriate to that system, is to mislocate the nature of the problem and the measures necessary to eliminate it. (Clarke cited in Sullivan 1992:100)

If we are to initiate the study of child sexual abuse in the wider communities of southern Africa, the power of patriarchy and paternalism (protectionist policies) must be recognised and highlighted in the assumptions embedded in current western approaches to child sexual abuse, for they have implications for those who have been sexually abused as children.

As argued elsewhere (Levett 1989b, 1992), stigmatic effects associated with difference and damage are produced and reproduced through the naïve empirical study of 'facts' of prevalence and damage and in contexts of professional intervention. It is important to ensure that assumptions which are harboured in such research are not transported, unquestioned, to studies in different sociocultural groups, contributing to the further cultural colonisation of girls and women. In a discussion of the problems of providing Anglo–American forms of therapy for black people whose difficulty may well have to do with patterns of white–black dominance, Littlewood (1992:41) comments: 'the obvious liberal approach is one which simply seeks to offer the European therapeutic model to others on the basis that this is the best we have and that common justice invites us to extend its application'. Of course this might be arguing that therapy is 'only a more insidious variant of European middle-class authority' which transforms 'political' tensions into the less inconvenient form of 'individual' pathology. I will take this point up a little later.

Problems in the Study of Prevalence and Consequences of Child Sexual Abuse

There are major problems of methodology which make it difficult to compare studies of prevalence and the consequences of childhood sexual abuse. At the most obvious level, these have to do with disagreements about definitions of sexual abuse, different conceptions of childhood, and the significance of age differences between perpetrators and victims. The conventions guiding the gathering of data are a further source of difficulty. For example, sampling techniques often rely on volunteer informants or on clinical records, or data have been collected by way of questionnaires, and so on (Levett 1989b; Painter 1986). Completely absent in the literature on child sexual abuse is any understanding or acceptance of children's active sexual life and their interest in adult and taboo behaviours.

As discussed earlier, current research isolates particular events (e.g. child sexual abuse) and attempts to link these to particular patterns of outcome effects. The only relatively consistent findings in western research on child sexual abuse are that experiences of violent sexual abuse, or repeated intercourse involving father and daughter, or situations which involved the child in especially intrusive and insensitive interventions by family or professional agents following such events, appear more likely to be associated with emotional disturbances in children (Browne and Finkelhor 1986), at the time of these events and in the following days or weeks. Since children who are not disturbed have not been identified as sexually abused, and other variables usually confound the picture, the consistencies may be spurious (Briere 1992; Haugaard and Emery 1989).

In an argument which resembles Littlewood's, mentioned above, I am proposing that we need to be careful to avoid researching and dealing with child sexual abuse in South Africa in ways which are not in fact useful for changing the systems of power that operate structurally between males and females and that fundamentally maintain patriarchal power. In a recent paper Russell (1991) criticised my arguments: whereas I am critical of non-reflective, non-feminist and naïvely liberal feminist approaches to the study of child sexual abuse, she felt I had claimed that sexual abuse does not harm children. All forms of sexual abuse are expressions of power; the use of power to coerce, constrain and restrict is problematic and has ramifications which must be examined in research and remedied through other means. However, the danger of adopting a simplistic empirical methodology (following the trends of North American research) is that this is another kind of oppressive behaviour, one which is detrimental in many ways to the interests of women and children (Levett 1992a).

The most useful idea emerging is that a major effect in childhood sexual abuse is the stigma and disruption associated with the aftermath of such experience (Finkelhor and Browne 1985) although two recent reviews of sexual abuse effects (Briere 1992) and of process and outcome research in treatment of adult survivors of sexual abuse (Beutler and Hill 1992) do not mention stigmatic effects at all.

Interventions by welfare and other agencies or the familial discord following identification of child sexual abuse are complicated by a sense of betrayal (by more powerful parental or authority figures), which is exacerbated when there is no retribution through intervention. Therapeutic interventions themselves often involve further abuse (Reppucci and Haugaard 1989).

It is crucial to note that the research never questions whether there are effects following child sexual abuse *per se* (without intervention and familial disruption) but rather what the range of effects may be. The research available represents a style characteristic of a great deal of conventional applied psychology: a type of positivistic empiricism which reflects little awareness of its limitations (Levett

252 Childhood and Adversity

1992a). It is not surprising, then, that the range of 'consequences' which have been documented is vast and that there is much to be criticised in the methods which have been used.

In the first place, the ways in which 'consequences' have been studied have been heavily value-laden with assumptions about normal behaviour. Implicit models of childhood, of development, of appropriate and inappropriate sexual behaviour in relation to age groups, are invoked in an unquestioned way. I call these the dominant discourses of childhood (James and Prout 1990), of development (Shotter 1984) and sexuality, using a model of analysis introduced in Henriques, Hollway, Urwin, Venn and Walkerdine (1984). The term 'discourse' is used as a Foucaultian convention, which draws attention to the significance of language practices in relation to other social practices and of semiotic codes related to power, which are reflected in the ways we talk about and study social phenomena (Levett 1989b).

The psychological consequences of childhood sexual abuse are argued in terms of signs and symptoms, most commonly in a fairly simple sort of causal equation. Particular events occur and the child is examined for evidence of abnormal behaviour; reports of no effects are uncommon. When one seeks abnormal behaviour, it is often 'found'. Furthermore, dominant western models of childhood are themselves contradictory (Levett 1989c). Psychological models of childhood, like lay models, hold for instance that there is a 'natural path' for emotional and cognitive development; children are naïve about sexual matters but can be precipitated into an abnormal route of sexual development; 'proper' socialisation cloaks and harnesses the potential inherent sexuality of children, which otherwise lies dormant; gender development is based on genetic or biological blueprints which can be upset, triggered or deformed by certain kinds of experience; and 'normal' children are rarely anxious or depressed and have no experiences of betrayal.

Ideas about psychiatric disorder (e.g. diagnostic categories derived from the American Psychiatric Association's DSM-III-R), deviance (e.g. promiscuity and truanting), or psychological disorder (e.g. evaluative judgements about self-esteem, how sexual development and relationships should be) are based on implicit models of 'normal' functioning, relative to idealised behaviours, and I term them discourses of psychological trauma.

Because of the power of commonplace ideas prevalent among western middle-class groups perpetuated through the media and through professional writings (the hegemony of science and of tacit knowledge), it is extremely difficult to study childhood sexual abuse *except* in relation to prevalence and expected traumatic effects. Some fifty years ago, Ludwig Fleck discussed the influence of medical knowledge on popular ideas, and vice versa, as social constructions reproduced by 'thought collectives' (Lowy 1988), and we need to take account of the power of social processes which are reproduced through dominant discourses.

Stigma

Stigmatic effects concern personal (and shared) ideas of being 'marked', different or devalued. Viewed within a symbolic interactionist framework, stigma involves people behaving in accordance with what they believe are others' attitudes towards them (Ainlay, Becker and Coleman 1986). Thus stigma depends on dominant discourses about damage, deviance and devaluation: ideas which are widely shared in one's community in association with certain 'social facts' (Mestrovic 1987).

Rules of behaviour have rendered talk about child sexual abuse difficult, constrained or taboo – except in relation to those other than oneself, preferably strangers, reported in newspapers or professional journal articles. The belief that experience of sexual abuse causes psychological damage helps to maintain the taboo (even among feminist researchers) and also makes it difficult to study. Ironically, feminist writing which drew attention to the extent of these phenomena has paradoxically added to the problem. Girls and women are likely to believe that they have been affected by such experiences, and will attribute a range of current problems to these events, while they will not readily disclose or discuss the experience because of the likelihood of stigmatic effects and shame. This makes the study of prevalence and of consequences extraordinarily difficult. Likewise, many parents and families prefer to maintain a silence about these situations, and most commonly will not file reports or seek assistance. This is partly attributable to a sense that they have 'failed' as parents in not providing the child with adequate protection from such damaging exposure, but is also related to the likelihood of stigma for the family and child.

If a woman cannot connect specific current problems with childhood experiences she has come to identify as sexually abusive, she may relabel the experience ('perhaps it was not abuse because I allowed it to happen') or she may wait for the day when the 'delayed effects' widely believed to be inevitable do emerge; alternatively she may doubt her memories ('perhaps I imagined it'). It should be evident that what we are dealing with in this process of focusing on the damaging effects of childhood sexual abuse is a set of discourses which act as a self-fulfilling prophecy. If we label ourselves as damaged, we will find evidence to support this conviction.

Stigma is difficult to study except through spoken discourse, or through careful study of social behaviours, such as otherwise unexplained avoidance, silences or the protection of certain individuals. The way people talk about the significance of certain events or experiences in ordinary, everyday discourse requires a more ethnomethodological approach. We need to talk with girls and women about stigmatic effects and, even better, to find ways to document their talk among themselves about these experiences. The stigmatic associations of child sexual abuse are accessible through the conceptual schemas of adults, who communicate these ideas to children through taboos and silences, and these ideas and social practices need to be studied. Thus it is not essential to study the social representations of child sexual abuse and its effects among *children,* although this would also be highly desirable. In fact, because of the widespread conviction that talking about sexual matters with children is potentially dangerous and thus taboo (McKenna and Kessler 1985) – perhaps as injurious as sexual abuse – it is not readily feasible to carry out such a study with children in general without some risk and considerable difficulty.

Gender Differentiation

While contemporary models of damage after sexual abuse have assumed significance within the current climate of changing relationships between men and women in western society, as metaphorical representations of female distress or dysphoria, it has not generally been recognised that these same models and representations of abuse, victims and exploitation also play an important role in the development of female-gendered subjectivity. The recognition of difference, and the playing out of male–female distinctions in terms of rules and restraints, are part of the social construction of identity and of sexuality during childhood.

From an early age girls in all societies are subjected to codes of behaviour and regulatory prohibitions which relate to the possibility of being sexually abused or molested; boys are not. The exact codes and prohibitions may vary somewhat from one social context to another but for girls and women they have profound implications (1) for the effects of such experience when it does occur, (2) for the shaping of a sense of female subjectivity, whether or not there is an experience of sexual abuse, (3) for the maintenance of socially constructed differences between the sexes, and (4) for the maintenance of male power and authority.

Constructions of female gender development are related to childhood sexual abuse (among other processes), because instances of molestation or abuse – fairly commonplace – are schematised by female children, girls and women within semiotic systems of gender differentiation. The rules of behaviour for girls and women are elaborated around prevention or avoidance of sexual abuse or molestation, partly because of the possibility of pregnancy after the onset of puberty.

The relevance of the study of experiences of all forms of childhood sexual abuse or molestation (and of sexual harassment and rape, the ways in which older girls and women are mostly affected) lies in the close relationship which such experiences, and how they are viewed by the community, are likely to have to the development of female-gendered subjectivity. The point is that even though these experiences may not be daily ones in actuality, *in effect* they are because girls and women have to shape their daily lives around choices which take account of the *possibility* of sexual abuse. Thus sexual abuse plays a role in maintaining existing power structures: female choices and positions from childhood are repeatedly subordinated to those available to men. This contributes to the active participation of girls and women through self-subordination within gendered structures of power (Levett 1989b).

Part of the process involved in the production and reproduction of gender differences today among western women is bound up with ideas about the damaging effects of experiences of childhood sexual abuse. Not only in the Anglo–American psychological literature, but also among the people whose sense of identity (or subjectivity) is formed in a socio-historical context influenced by Anglo–American ideas, there are widespread notions about the traumatic effects of this experience. The folk models of western societies, through the power of professionalisation and the media, have absorbed ideas of damage, which become hegemonic and self-replicating.

In general, ideas of damaging effects have become inseparable from the experience (or the potential experience) of child sexual abuse among English-speaking women: a kind of cultural imperialism. These ideas are perpetuated in everyday talk about sexual abuse and about childhood. In other words they are part of unquestioned tacit knowledge. The consequence of this is that girls are brought up in a highly protective environment, an important aspect of the protection being the avoidance of experiences of sexual molestation.

The study of childhood sexual abuse and ideas about its causes and consequences reflect important dominant discourses about gender development and differentiation in contemporary society. A study of the constraints of discourses concerning child sexual abuse in different sociocultural or linguistic groups may disclose a very similar situation to dominant western discourses, and distinctive differences which relate to local social practices of childrearing, the development of gender-related schemas, attitudes to children's sexuality, and the acceptance or non-acceptance of adult–child sexual relationships. In Africa these will reflect significant aspects of gendered development, since patriarchy prevails, and will have implications for the participation of women in broader social change.

However, it cannot be assumed, firstly, that stigmatic effects will necessarily occur after child sexual abuse in all cases or in all speech communities. This needs to be studied. Secondly, it cannot be assumed that if there are consequences, these will be exactly the same in all cultural groups. This also requires investigation. Thirdly, there is a question which is more fundamental than ideas of damage or pollution; this concerns the part which the sexual abuse of girls and women may play in the development of gendered identity and in the continuing domination of women by men in African societies. It is of great importance that this issue be addressed in its own right.

Studies of Discourse

What is required then is a quite different approach to the study of the phenomena involved and to the range of ideas about them. One route is by collecting common ideas as expressed in ordinary everyday language by ordinary people from different groups. The constraints of dominant ideas and the way these are expressed in everyday spoken language shape emotional responses involved in stigma (Harre 1986). These may be usefully tapped through interpretative analyses of discourses (Potter and Wetherell 1987).

Although dominant discourses about stigma may be extracted, other discourses (which are difficult to predict) may coexist but be muted and confusingly contradictory. These also need to be elicited because they may contain the seeds of alternative paths of resistance. For example, it is rarely noted in the professional literature that there are very large numbers of adult women who were sexually abused or molested as children but who are not psychologically disturbed, delinquent, depressed, abusive and so on. This contradictory discourse emerged in the talk of adult westernised women who expressed confusion and disbelief in the idea of inevitable damage, at the same time as the conventional discourses about damaging effects (Levett 1989b).

The approach which I have used derives from the work of Hollway (1984) and involves the collection of spoken and written talk about childhood sexual abuse and its effects. Material was collected from young English-speaking South African women university students (Levett 1989b) to elicit dominant and anomalous discourses about childhood sexual abuse and its effects. A similar strategy is proposed for the study of these phenomena in other communities – where there may be somewhat differently constructed ideas about individualism, psychopathology, gender development, sexuality, and the effects of adult–child sexual encounters, and where female subjectivity may be socially constructed in different ways – in order to understand the workings of patriarchal power.

The ways in which childhood sexual abuse is depicted in western media and in the talk of these university women, who were not medical or mental health professionals, have been shown to have important links with the study of childhood sexual abuse, as presented in the psychological and psychiatric literature: perpetuating vague ideas about the damaging effects of such experience. There is a process at work of production and reproduction of a certain set of beliefs; these have become a part of tacit knowledge – widely accepted ideas.

A Likely Scenario for the Study of Child Sexual Abuse in South Africa

In an approach which follows the traditions of empirical psychology outlined early in this chapter, the 'cross-cultural' study of child sexual abuse would present no particular problems to the conventional psychological researcher. What I have raised in this chapter are the inadequacies of such an approach in *any* sociocultural context.

What would be the likely scenario? A set of universalist assumptions would be applied: psychological damage follows childhood sexual abuse, and evidence of this would be sought. The first step would be the fairly straightforward collection of 'cases' which come to the attention of medical clinics or social agencies, perhaps because of some related injury or illness, or because of family issues. The children concerned would be described in terms of perceived signs and symptoms of psychiatric distress, developmental disruptions, or other phenomena, in applications of the biomedical model which has evolved in western psychiatric and clinical psychological practice. Subsequent studies of prevalence among various social groups and communities would be conducted to establish the exact range of psychological trauma which the children show, and to justify the provision of certain kinds of welfare and clinical services. It needs to be understood that this would be a disinterested and sympathetic move to monitor and ensure adequate professional (or paraprofessional) services, but would extend authoritative control of family and community life and functioning. Possibly a third step would follow, as has occurred in English-language psychological research: there may be an attempt to elicit information about childhood sexual abuse in the backgrounds of adolescent and adult women (e.g. adult women survivors who volunteer or can be persuaded to engage in interviews), especially those who are regarded as displaying the kinds of problems which have been associated with this history in the western literature (e.g. individualised 'social problems' of delinquency, illegitimate births, neglect or abuse of their own children, or marital breakdowns; or 'psychiatric diagnoses' such as depression, anorexia nervosa, and borderline states; or psychological problems such as low self-esteem or problems of sexual relating). The sample is likely to be biased by self-selection and class.

Little or no account is taken in this sort of research of instructive recent writings in social science which suggest that we all present ourselves, and our histories, in terms of stories or narratives. These narratives are available in each social community as what Bruner (1986) has termed interpretative guides. Geertz (1986) and Howard (1991) also usefully discuss these ways of under-standing human behaviours, and their papers are particularly useful in the study of different speech communities.

In these terms there is a widely accepted way for western women to make sense of a range of social and personal ills through ascribing them to the damag-ing effects of experience of child sexual abuse (undefined); in doing so, they personalise and medicalise a range of human problems, or are subjected to this kind of categorisation by the professional clinicians and researchers whom they encounter. It seems to me that it is an act of resistance to such categorisation that leads to many women not disclosing such a history although, paradoxically, this silence also protects patriarchy.

The importance of developing definitional clarity must relate to a model of child sexual abuse which takes account of existing ideas – what Geertz (1983) has termed local knowledge. These ideas are to be found in the everyday talk and in current social practices of childrearing within a particular language or sociocultural group, and need to be identified in each speech community. Most significant are likely to be dominant discourses concerning:

(1) the nature of childhood, and the kinds of relationship between children and adults seen as feasible and acceptable;

(2) the development of female sexuality, and expressions of sexuality which are viewed as 'natural' for female children;

(3) the development of girls and women, as gendered subjects, in relation to experience of and ideas about sexual abuse;

(4) and, particularly, discourses concerning the consequences of such experi-ence, if such discourses are discerned, and the role of stigmatic effects.

If we accept that there are widespread shared sets of ideas about children in relation to adults and about limits on adult–child (and adolescent–child) sexual-ity, which pervade the everyday social practices of bringing up children in each identifiable community, then it is likely that there will be shared representations of abuse and its effects. While acknowledging that cultural practices are never static and that each subject's sense of self and choices of self-presentation shift from context to context (being related to time, place and person), we still need to study these facets of human life within various language groups and societal contexts, in order to establish the presence and form of stigma constituted – if indeed it is stigma – and to deconstruct how this relates to female subjectivity and deference to male authority, in a range of instances.

At the same time, we need to take seriously the consequences of such research, particularly if it is not interpreted in relation to patriarchal authority and power. For example, in western societies the state has assumed power for regulating the daily life of families, removing responsibility from adults, neighbours and communities, without dismantling patriarchy or carefully considering the rights of children, including their right to sexual knowledge (Sullivan 1992). There is a paradoxical conflict of interest between modern efforts to remedy injustices and eliminate the exploitation of children, including acting 'in their best interest' on the one hand, and the play of middle-class power in the med-icalisation of social issues and extension of professional services on the other. When the capacity of families and communities to find their own remedies for problems such as child sexual abuse is taken away, we find that the law and wel-fare procedures do not generally offer better remedies. An important reason is that structural power accommodates superficially, and no fundamental changes are effected because the ones which are required concern deeply entrenched beliefs and normative systems.

We do not have a clear idea of how young people engage in sexual relation-ships with one another, nor how adults and families in western societies deal with children's sexuality (Sullivan 1992). We have a long way to go in western societies towards understanding exactly how children and adolescents are recruited into discursive positions as sexual and gendered subjects, and how we insert ourselves within familial and local community patterns of gendered behaviours. Alternative solutions for the education of children in the area of sexual relating and in regard to problems of child abuse, including sexual abuse, are long overdue but depend on research on these fundamental questions. Counter-discourses need perhaps to be developed through a collaborative process actively involving women and children within their usual social net-works in the research. Our investigations would be most usefully both research- and education-oriented. 'Solutions' found may turn out to be temporary and makeshift measures, given the constraints of power of cultural colonialism, but our efforts need always to incorporate the re-visioning of alternatives in aware-ness of the subtleties of power. Recognition of strategies of resistance and sur-vival, and building on these, will help, as will the breaking down of stigma through courageous self-examination and open accounts of our own experiences of childhood, including our sexual explorations, sexual abuse and the develop-ment of male and female gendered identities across a range of contexts. Theorising about these matters cannot be done without essential changes in consciousness of researchers, and there will be no change in social practices without changes in the consciousness of large numbers of women and men.

References

Ainlay, S.C., Becker, G. and Coleman, L.M. (1986). *The Dilemma of Difference: A Multidisciplinary View of Stigma*. New York: Plenum Press.

Arbib, M.A. and Hesse, M. (1986). *The Construction of Reality*. Cambridge: Cambridge University Press.

Badgley, R. (1984). *Report of the Committee on Sexual Offenses against Children and Youths*. Ministries of Justice and Attorney General and Supply and Services, Government of Canada.

Bennett, T.W. (1991). *A Sourcebook of African Customary Law for Southern Africa*. Cape Town: Juta.

Beutler, L.E. and Hill, C.E. (1992). Process and outcome research in the treatment of adult victims of childhood sexual abuse: Methodological issues. *Journal of Consulting and Clinical Psychology, 60*(2), 203–212.

Billig, M. (1987). *Arguing and Thinking: A Rhetorical Approach to Social Psychology*. Cambridge:

Cambridge University Press.

Briere, J. (1992). Methodological issues in the study of sexual abuse effects. *Journal of Consulting and Clinical Psychology, 60*(2), 196–203.

Browne, A. and Finkelhor, D. (1986). Impact of childhood sexual abuse: A review of the research. *Psychological Bulletin, 99,* 66–77.

Bruner, E. M. (1986) Ethnography as narrative. In V.W. Turner and E.M. Bruner (eds), *The Anthropology of Experience*. Urbana: University of Illinois Press.

Charman, A., De Swardt, C. and Simons, M. (1991). The politics of gender: A discussion of the Malibongwe Conference Papers and other current papers within the ANC. Paper presented at the Conference on Women and Gender in Southern Africa, University of Natal, Durban.

Collings, S. (1989). Social stereotypes and the likelihood of criminal conviction in cases of child sexual abuse: A research note. *Agenda, 5,* 21–23.

DeMause, L. (1991). The universality of incest. *Journal of Psychohistory, 19*(2), 123–164.

Ennew, J. (1986). *The Sexual Exploitation of Children*. Cambridge: Polity Press.

Finkelhor, D. (1984). *Child Sexual Abuse: New Theory and Research*. New York: Free Press.

Finkelhor, D. and Browne, A. (1985). The traumatic impact of child sexual abuse: A conceptualization. *American Journal of Orthopsychiatry, 55,* 530–541.

Finkelhor, D. (1989). Social and cultural factors in child sexual abuse. Paper presented at the 8th International Congress on Child Abuse and Neglect, Hamburg.

Fuss, D. (1989). *Essentially Speaking: Feminism, Nature and Difference*. New York: Routledge.

Geertz, C. (1983). *Local Knowledge: Further Essays in Interpretive Anthropology*. New York: Basic Books.

Geertz, C. (1986). Making experiences, authoring selves. In V.W. Turner and E.M. Bruner (eds), *The Anthropology of Experience*. Urbana: University of Illinois Press.

Gergen, K.J. (1985). The social constructionist movement in modern psychology. *American Psychologist, 40,* 266–275.

Hacking, I. (1991). The making and molding of child abuse. In M. Douglas and D. Hull (eds), *Coherent Worlds*. (In press, cited by Sullivan, 1992).

Harre, R. (ed.) (1986). *The Social Construction of Emotion*. Oxford: Blackwell.

Haugaard, J.J. and Emery, T.E. (1989). Methodological issues in child sexual abuse research. *Child Abuse and Neglect, 13,* 89–100.

Henriques, J., Hollway, W., Urwin, C., Venn, C. and Walkerdine, V. (1984). *Changing the Subject*. London: Methuen.

Hollway, W. (1984). The power of women in heterosexual sex. *Women's Studies International Forum, 7,* 63–68.

Howard, G.S. (1991). Culture tales: A narrative approach to thinking, cross-cultural psychology and psychotherapy. *American Psychologist, 46*(3), 187–197.

James, A. and Prout, A. (eds) (1990). *Constructing and Reconstructing Childhood: Contemporary Issues in the Sociological Study of Childhood*. London: The Falmer Press.

Kelly, L. (1989). Bitter ironies. *Trouble and Strife, 16* (Summer), 14–21.

Kessell, F.S. and Siegel, A.W. (eds) (1983). *The Child and Other Cultural Inventions*. New York: Praeger Press.

Kottler, A. E. (1990). South Africa: Psychology's dilemma of multiple discourses. *Psychology in Society, 13,* 27–36.

Korbin, J. E. (1987). Child sexual abuse: Implications from the cross-cultural record. In N. Scheper-Hughes (ed.), *Child Survival*. Dordrecht: D. Reidel.

Korbin, J.E. (1991). Cross-cultural perspectives and research directions for the twenty-first century. *Child Abuse and Neglect, 15,* Supp. 1, 67–77.

La Fontaine, J.S. (1987). Child sexual abuse and the incest taboo: Practical problems and theoretical issues. *Man* (N.S.), *23,* 1–18.

Levett, A. (1989a). A study of childhood sexual abuse among South African university women students. *South African Journal of Psychology, 19*(3), 122–129.

Levett, A. (1989b). Psychological trauma: Discourses on childhood sexual abuse. Unpublished doctoral dissertation, University of Cape Town.

Levett, A. (1989c). Children and psychological trauma. *Psychology in Society, 12,* 19–32.

Levett, A. (1991). Contradictions and confusions in child sexual abuse. *South African Journal of Criminal Justice, 4,* 1, 9–20.

Levett, A. (1992a). Regimes of truth: A response to Russell. *Agenda, 12,* 67–74.

Levett, A. (1992b). Stigmatic factors in sexual abuse and the violence of representation. Paper presented at the Domestic Violence Conference, University of South Africa, Pretoria.

Levett, A. and Lachman, P. (1991). *Child Abuse Research Register.* RAPCAN, Child Health Unit, University of Cape Town and Red Cross Children's Hospital, Cape Town.

Levett, A. and Macleod, C. (1992). Child sexual abuse: South African research on incidence, prevalence and intervention (1984–1990). In revision for *South African Journal of Psychology.*

Littlewood, R. (1992). How universal is something we can call therapy? In J. Kareem and R. Littlewood (eds), *Intercultural Therapy: Themes, Interpretations and Practice.* Oxford: Blackwell.

Lowy, I. (1988). Ludwig Fleck on the social construction of medical knowledge. *Sociology of Health and Illness, 10*(2), 133–155.

McKenna, W. and Kessler, S. (1985). Asking taboo questions and doing taboo deeds. In K.J. Gergen and K.E. Davis (eds), *The Social Construction of the Person.* New York: Springer Verlag.

Malamuth, N.M., Sockloskie, R.J., Koss, M.J. and Tanaka, J.S. (1991). Characteristics of aggressors against women: Testing a model using a national sample of college students. *Journal of Consulting and Clinical Psychology, 59* (5), 670–681.

Manning, P. K. (1987). *Semiotics and Fieldwork.* Sage University Paper series: Qualitative Research Methods, Volume 7. Beverly Hills: Sage Publications.

Mejiuni, C.O. (1991). Educating adults against socioculturally induced abuse and neglect of children in Nigeria. *Child Abuse and Neglect, 15,* 139–145.

Mestrovic, S.G. (1987). A sociological conceptualization of trauma. *Social Science and Medicine, 21,* 835–848.

Millett, K. (1970). *Sexual Politics.* New York: Doubleday.

Nelson, B. (1984). *Making an Issue of Child Abuse: Political Agenda Setting for Social Problems.* Chicago: University of Chicago Press.

Painter, S.L. (1986). Research on the prevalence of child sexual abuse: New directions. *Canadian Journal of Behavioral Science, 18,* 323–339.

Posel, D. (1991). Women's powers, men's authority: Rethinking patriarchy. Paper presented at the Women and Gender Conference, University of Natal, Durban.

Potter, J. and Wetherell, M. (1987). *Discourse and Social Psychology.* London: Sage Publications.

Reppucci, N.D. and Haugaard, J.J. (1989). Prevention of child sexual abuse: Myth or reality? *American Psychologist, 44,* 1266–1275.

Reynolds, P. (1991). Paring down the family: The child's point of view. Paper delivered at the Research Seminar on Children and Families, HSRC, Pretoria.

Russell, D.E.H. (1975). *The Politics of Rape.* New York: Stein and Day.

Russell, D.E.H. (1983). The incidence and prevalence of intrafamilial and extrafamilial sexual abuse of female children. *Child Abuse and Neglect, 7,* 133–146.

Russell, D.E.H. (1984). *Sexual Exploitation.* Newbury Park, Calif.: Sage Publications.

Russell, D.E.H. (1991). The damaging effects of discounting damaging effects of child sexual abuse. *Agenda, 11,* 47–56.

Shotter, J. (1984). *Social Accountability and Selfhood.* Oxford: Basil Blackwell.

Socarides, C. (1991). Adult–child sexual pairs: Psychoanalytic findings. *Journal of Psychohistory, 19,* 2, 185–189.

Sterling, C. (1990). Male accounts of child sexual abuse: Excuses and justifications. Unpublished Master's dissertation, University of Cape Town.

Straker, G., Moosa, F., Becker, R. and Nkwale, M. (1992). *Faces in the Revolution. The Psychological Effects of Violence on Township Youth in South Africa.* Cape Town: David Philip.

Sullivan, T. (1992). *Sexual Abuse and the Rights of Children: Reforming Canadian Law.* Toronto: University of Toronto Press.

Viljoen, S. (1991). The nature of parental authority in family lives of black South Africans. Paper delivered at the Conference on the Child and the Family, HSRC, Pretoria.

Walker, C. (1991). *Women and Resistance in South Africa.* Cape Town: David Philip.

Widom, C. (1989). Does violence beget violence? A critical examination of the literature. *Psychological Bulletin, 106,* 3–28.

Wyatt, G.E. and Powell, G.J. (eds) (1988). *The Lasting Effects of Child Sexual Abuse.* Newbury Park, Calif.: Sage.

14

The Way Forward: Developmental Research and Intervention in Contexts of Adversity

DAVID DONALD AND ANDREW DAWES

Transformation in Developmental Research

One constant is present across the diversity of issues that have been presented in this volume. This is the extraordinary and pervasive nature of the adversity suffered by the majority of South African children. This is not to suggest that adversity is not present in the lives of the more economically privileged or children in other societies, but to emphasise that much of the adversity experienced in the South African context has been caused by a racist constitution and social structure which has entrenched disadvantage for the majority. Furthermore, while a highly skewed distribution of wealth is common to developing countries, in South Africa this phenomenon has been exacerbated by the formal restrictions on advancement imposed by apartheid. While progress is being made towards democracy, the legacy of statutory discrimination will probably be with us for generations. A new constitution will not remove adversity from the lives of the majority of South African children and, given current economic circumstances, poverty, racism, gendered power differentials and educational inequities are not going to disappear.

Thus the challenge to developmental psychologists which we raised in Chapter 1 and which was earlier expressed by Liddell and Kvalsvig (1990) will remain important to take up. While it is ideologically problematic and something of a cliché to speak of children as 'the future', there is nonetheless some truth in the idea.

We can claim certain things from within the parameters of current frames of knowledge as long as we remain aware of the historicity of those frames. We do know for example that the broad effects of a poverty environment influence psychological development in a way that reduces the child's social and economic opportunities, power to adapt and adult life chances. This is true regardless of our theoretical orientation. But the value we place on one or other outcome is essentially a moral issue and is tied up with our preference for one sort of human community rather than another.

Modern developmental psychology has been appropriately criticised for its role in ignoring the moral base of ideas of 'optimal' childhoods and for constructing and policing modern childhood (Rose 1990). It has also been criticised for inventing children's needs and for naturalising what are socially determined aspects of development. From this it is evident that the discipline has had considerable power in shaping modern childhood. This power can be used in both positive and negative ways as the discipline enters everyday discourse. The contributions of Rose and others expose this power and the assumptions which underlie much taken-for-granted developmental knowledge and practice.

One can respond to such critiques by retreating from action since all action becomes too tainted or too complex. This would be unfortunate. Whatever system of knowledge we might construct about children's development would be subject to the same problems. We should rather use the power we have as researchers and practitioners to improve our understanding of development under adverse conditions and to advance our ability to intervene so as to prevent and reduce risk in children's lives. However, we should do this informed by the observations of scholars such as Rose and with clarity about the origins of our views of what is psychologically best for children. That is, we should take care not to confuse the psychological and moral bases of our positions.

In our view there is a moral imperative to engage in efforts to transform children's lives, through researching historically neglected issues in the field of child development which are pertinent to the situation of South African children. Working in South Africa is ironically an advantage. Its diversity of class and culture provides the opportunity for the exploration and questioning of basic theoretical and methodological issues. It is through such a critical process that more effective ways of understanding the interrelation of social structures and individual development can be achieved.

The explicit intention of this volume has been to engage with this process. It has presented a variety of research initiatives and perspectives that have in common their concern to advance our understanding of the conditions of adversity prevailing in South Africa and of the effects of these conditions on child development. Underlying the specific issues that have been addressed, however, are a number of broad and recurrent themes. These include the question of how we encourage more research, the appropriateness of current approaches to the study of adversity, and how to produce closer links between these approaches and intervention strategies.

The Insufficiency of Research

In almost every chapter reference is made to either the inadequacy or the insufficiency of existing research on issues that are seen to be crucial to an understanding of the psychological development of disadvantaged children in this society. As discussed in Chapter 1, the reasons for this bias are complex but may be understood as fundamentally derived from the social and political history that has hitherto shaped the development of professional and academic psychology in South Africa. This has led to a broad lack of awareness of the extent, the complexity and the urgency of the issues involved. It constitutes a wide gap in understanding which, until it is filled, will continue to handicap both policy and practice.

Just one typical example of this, as highlighted by Robertson and Berger (Chapter 9) as well as Donald (Chapter 8), is the issue of mental handicap amongst children in disadvantaged communities. There has been a lack of sound epidemiological research with the result that neither the number of children affected is known nor are the causes of mental handicap in impoverished communities properly understood. Most important, we have little understanding of how mental handicap is perceived and dealt with in different communities. A major problem here has been insufficient work on the development of appropriate methods of assessment, although attempts to improve this situation are in progress (Lea and Foster 1990). Without such information it is clear that policy decisions regarding the provision of resources, their extent and type, and even preventive programmes cannot be made with clarity.

The question is how to turn this situation around. On one level it could be argued that the changing political situation will itself have some effect on the issues that are brought to the fore, debated, funded and researched. Certainly, the notion of relevant or appropriate psychology has increasingly been debated in local journals and conferences. Furthermore, there are clear trends in the current situation for funding, from state, private and non-governmental sectors, to be more available for research that is perceived to be socially relevant. Unfortunately funding alone is unlikely to be a sufficient answer to the problem. It is in large measure up to psychologists to pose the right research questions. This would include putting questions posed by members of the community into researchable form and initiating funding proposals. This, in turn, would require a certain set of research interests as well as an increase in the number of researchers committed to this area with appropriate research skills. It would also require appropriate employment opportunities for trained researchers.

Some of these requirements may be enabled by current moves to restructure professional psychology so as to achieve a more widely representative and socially accountable body. The process may also be facilitated by appropriate curricular changes in the teaching of psychology and by the increasing production of graduate psychologists who are not from predominantly white, middle-class backgrounds. As these moves consolidate, we can expect that a more sustained and socially relevant research momentum may be generated.

Theoretical and Methodological Frameworks: The Question of Appropriateness

The question of what is the most appropriate way to study the psychology of childhood adversity has been tackled in various ways in this volume. Perhaps the most central issue that has been confronted is the undeniable and complex relationship between the social context and the developing individual. How to explicate this relationship and its consequences for development is a major challenge. Different philosophical and methodological approaches to the question that have been presented include the more traditional positivist forms of inquiry and those drawn from ethnographic and constructivist orientations. These contributions reflect the current tension within the wider discipline of psychology as to what constitutes psychology's subject and its method. At one pole is the

264 Childhood and Adversity

essentially positivist position which assumes a separation of the psychological subject from her or his context. At the other end are constructivist views which question the idea of an ontologically distinct, unitary psychological subject. As we have seen, the two traditions suggest very different methods of research.

The particular contribution of more positivist formulations is perhaps most apparent in the discussions on the role of poverty and nutritional deficits in development by Richter (Chapter 2) and Richter and Griesel (Chapter 4) respectively. In Chapter 4 the authors develop the notion of synergy, 'which implies that forces at different levels – for example, at the socio-economic and psychological level – may merge to exacerbate, modulate or decrease their combined individual effects on development'. These ideas are echoed in the contributions of Swart-Kruger and Donald (Chapter 6), Donald (Chapter 8) and Robertson and Berger (Chapter 9). They all make the existence of this synergistic, interactional relationship quite concrete in their discussions of such diverse developmental issues as malnutrition, parental stress and depression, the street-child phenomenon, disability and special educational need, and general childhood psychopathology.

Liddell and her colleagues (Chapter 3), and Kvalsvig and Connolly (Chapter 5), provide good examples of the power of the methods suggested by the positivist tradition. In these empirical studies they tease out complex and subtle relationships between variables which contribute to aspects of children's development in adverse circumstances such as have been discussed by Richter in Chapter 2. Liddell's work shows how a complex multivariate research design may be used to investigate, simultaneously, a number of interacting variables associated with sociocultural transformation. In this way the simplistic use of constructs such as cultural identity and socio-economic status as determinants of development is shown to be inadequate, and the interaction of a number of socially determined variables in the process is clarified.

It is this approach that enables us to establish factors associated with children's vulnerabilities and strengths. Its great utility is that it also makes possible certain prescriptions for prevention based on assumptions about the universal nature of psychological development and a knowledge of general risk and protective factors. Therefore if we wish to know the incidence of particular forms of disability or psychopathology under particular social conditions, this is the appropriate research strategy to employ. From there one can plan appropriate facilities. Similarly, if we know that parasite infection constitutes a risk for intellectual development, then this evidence can be added to the public health campaign arguments for better sanitation in poor areas (Chapter 5). These are all important matters, which are most appropriately addressed through the deployment of positivist research methods.

Anglo–American psychology has historically viewed the positivist paradigm as the central guiding force in theorisation and research. In effect a regime of truth has been established which has dictated, until very recently, particular practices for the generation of psychological knowledge. This dominant position is now being questioned and attempts to grapple with other forms of method and understanding are emerging with more force and conviction. As has been noted in several contributions, the paradigm has its limits and is not always the most appropriate way to proceed.

Case study and ethnographic approaches, for instance, place the relativity of context, the perceptions of those who are studied and the interactional framework of human relationships more centrally in their methodology. A significant function of this in developmental research is to reveal the micro-processes involved – whether of resilience, adaptation or vulnerability – more forcefully than is possible through more traditional positivist designs. Thus, Swart-Kruger and Donald (Chapter 6) point out the inappropriateness of using only formal research designs in attempting to research the shifting and complexly determined lives of street children. Their advocacy of an ethnographic approach is appropriate in facilitating a more immediate understanding of both the complexity and the relativity of the developmental effects of children living under such extreme conditions of adversity. Implicitly or explicitly the place of an ethnographic research approach in understanding micro-environments such as classrooms or families is a theme that recurs throughout the volume. More than anything else it relies on an inductive research methodology that involves talking and listening to people as opposed to a deductive process that primarily measures and records predetermined constructs and criteria. In this, it acts more as a foil than as an absolute alternative to positivist methodology.

Yet, ironically, a central challenge to the ethnographic approach is not dissimilar to the equally central challenge facing the positivist approach. Although ethnographic methodology is concerned with context, in practice this is frequently limited to local or micro-contexts. The problem, developed most explicitly by Gilmour and Soudien in Chapter 7, is how, both conceptually and methodologically, to articulate the interaction of macro social–structural forces with the micro-process analysis that is the strength of the ethnographic approach. Gilmour and Soudien talk of the need to work between the 'macro' and the 'micro' (ethnographic, site and person-specific explanations) if the inequity as well as the inequality in education in South Africa is to be understood. This acknowledgement of the simultaneous interaction of the 'macro' and the 'micro' is echoed in different forms by a number of other authors.

The other prominent challenge to positivist research is the constructivist perspective. This challenges the view of the human subject as having an ahistorical and universal psychological nature, and has implications for both how we do research and how we intervene in contexts of adversity.

For example, Levett (Chapter 13) emphasises the centrality of meaning – and the active construal of meaning – in the developmental process of gender socialisation. She points out the complexities in determining the nature of sexual contact between children and their older siblings or adults. Is it always abusive? This is a difficult question to ask, given the emotional nature of the subject and Levett's own concern for the relatively powerless position of girls and women under patriarchy. Similarly, Dawes (Chapter 10) draws attention to the assumptions about childhood which can distort attempts to understand the effects of political violence, and Foster (Chapter 12) asks whether the debate around the effects of racism on children reflects more a moral than a psychological question. Levett's position, in contrast to what the positivist tradition would lead us to expect, is that 'abuse' is socially constructed. Also, one cannot assume that all forms of sexual contact during childhood are necessarily 'damaging' just because they occur at a particular point in the life cycle when, it is assumed, certain psychological forces are operating independently of the social realm. This position has its own implications for research and intervention. For example, one would want to know what sexual conventions exist in the community and in what sense girls are subject to 'abuse' as a 'normal' part of their socialisation as women in a patriarchal community. From this perspective, research is directed to careful observation, understanding and elucidation of meaning, rather than the comparison of distinct variables. However, while Levett's position appropriately critiques the cultural imperialist assumptions which exist in dominant accounts of child sexual abuse, her approach also raises the issue of cultural relativism.

As pointed out by both Dawes and Donald (Chapter 1) and Richter (Chapter 2) cultural relativism is an area that is fraught with conceptual and ideological problems – particularly in South Africa where the policy of apartheid has too often been justified on these grounds. Nevertheless, the issue cannot be buried or ignored simply because it is problematic. As Levett, in discussing gendered power relationships, says: 'Although one needs to be cautious in putting forward arguments about 'cultural difference' in the South African context ... it may also be necessary to make the sociocultural context visible in terms of particular forms of patriarchal power in this part of the world' (Chapter 13). Certainly, if we accept that childhood and many of its associated constructs are indeed socially constructed and not universal, then the cultural context must be subject to examination and form part of our understanding of the emergence of individual psychological capacities.

Cultural practices can be treated as 'variables', the influence of which we can seek to understand in relation to others such as socio-economic status, or they can be examined in a very different manner, as suggested by Levett. Both have their place, although the knowledge generated in each case may not always produce complementary understandings of the child's situation.

At this stage of our understanding, the social constructivist framework offers a challenge to conventional knowledge of development under adverse conditions. In so far as it places the active construction of meaning at its core, constructivism sees the individual as both reflecting the social forces around him or her and construing (creating) them. Methodologically, one powerful way of elucidating this relationship is to analyse the patterning of social activity and discourse in particular social settings. This approach is not easily applied nor will it be easily accepted by traditional developmental psychologists. Ultimately, however, developmental psychologists cannot afford to ignore with this framework and its methodological imperatives.

Finally, in all research contexts, not least the study of psychological development in contexts of adversity, it is essential to make a decision as to what sort of knowledge is needed in a particular instance – what is likely to be most useful in furthering understanding or intervention. One form of knowledge is not inherently superior to the other, and this applies as much to questions of method as it does to theory. It is as well to remember that theories and research models are strategies for apprehending 'reality' rather than fundamental truths. They are also not divorced from history and ideology.

Thus in the South African context we need far more knowledge about development under adversity. To achieve this, we suggest that the way forward is not to dismiss or favour any one approach to epistemology and method. In order to capture the complexity of development under adversity we need a range of lenses, including those we have discussed, through which to construe the child.

The Relationship of Research to Intervention

The problematic distinction between 'pure' and 'applied' research rears its head in developmental psychology as much as it does in any other social science. The difficulty is that the distinction itself obscures the inextricable relationship between the researcher, the research and the social context of its formulation and execution. In a discipline that is as contextually and socially determined as developmental psychology, the possibility of 'pure' research – that is, research which embodies the notions of neutrality, universality and context-independence – is remote, if not a conceptual contradiction (Chapter 1). The importance of this in the present context is that the research and research perspectives presented in this volume are far from being 'applied' in the narrow sense of the word. They are not simply concerned with practical applications and their evaluation. Nor yet can they be considered to be 'pure'. They do reflect a value position – a position that is committed to understanding the impact of adversity and socially entrenched power differentials on child development. Equally they do emerge from the perspective and reality of a particular social context – a context that in the imbalance of its social relationships demands effective intervention in the process of social transformation. Thus, while not narrowly 'applied' in focus, the very nature and origin of the contributions contain the seeds of their application.

More concretely, every chapter has, either directly or indirectly, addressed the issue of intervention. The questions and observations are diverse and in most cases particular to the topic under investigation. What each author has had to say is important as it comes from a depth of observation, research and understanding of the particular issue being addressed. Although there is a danger of losing the impact of particular contributions, broader themes do emerge that have a significance in themselves.

The broadest and perhaps most significant of these is largely unstated but is implied throughout. This is the relationship between the understanding that is generated through theoretical reflection and research and, on the other hand, intervention. In one way or another every contribution has underlined the futility of intervention without an adequate information base or framework of understanding to inform and underpin it. At the centre of this are those fundamental theoretical and methodological issues that have been outlined in the section above. Yet, as Schaffer (1990:15), in a discussion of the relationship between research and its social application, has pointed out, 'In the social science area the gap between research and practice is probably much wider than anywhere else, so that only too often decisions ... are taken in disregard (or, more likely, ignorance) of much useful information that is available.'

As Schaffer indicates, there are many complex and established reasons for this. These include poor lines of communication, different settings and professional constraints, vested interests, the inertia of the system in accepting changes suggested by research and, perhaps most important, the operation of 'financial, political, ideological and organizational factors' (1990:16) in determining what interventions will in fact be applied at any given time.

Thus, for many interventionists research and theory may not only be inaccessible but may be seen as unnecessarily abstract and remote from the practical and immediate demands of action. In the South African context one has sympathy with this position in so far as intervention in the lives of the disadvantaged majority has historically been noticeably absent or ineffective. In other instances interventions have been implemented without consultation – frequently as part of initiatives tainted by apartheid.

However, morally, socially and politically, there are at present intense and justified pressures to take action and to get on with the business of social transformation. But, whatever these pressures, the undeniable reality remains that action motivated by humanitarian or political goals alone may not only be misdirected and ineffective but may also involve a wastage of scarce professional and material resources – something that South Africans are rapidly realising is central to the social and political equation.

Misdirection of this sort, as a result of changing political priorities, may already be happening in two major domains in South Africa. The first is an unprecedented level of spending from the state sector on socially oriented intervention projects (SAIRR 1993). It is not that such spending is not required. The problem is that because it is politically motivated, it appears sometimes to be the most visible action that is taken rather than what is likely to be most effective. Current state spending on education is a case in point. But, as Gilmour and Soudien (Chapter 7) have emphasised, unless the interaction of macrostructural and micro-process factors is taken into account, superficial corrections in equality will not lead to equity in education. Other examples – referred to in several chapters – of misdirection in state-funded policy and initiatives affecting child development can be found, especially in the areas of health and social welfare.

The other domain is the non-governmental (NGO) sector and the degree of intervention activity that has recently arisen from this source. Much of this activity has been more positive in the sense that it has been more community-oriented and democratically negotiated than has been the case with state initiatives. However, even in this sector there is often overlap, duplication and wastage. Also there is frequently a need for co-ordinated critique, from research and theory, of the bases of intervention.

Despite these negative dimensions both the state and the NGO sectors have important roles to play in intervention. The state has the necessary infrastructure as well as the fiscal ability to initiate and sustain widespread structural change, while the NGO sector is less dependent on the direct demands of politics and can afford to be more innovative. Both are necessary players but, equally, both could be more effective in interventions that affect the lives of children if the research findings, theoretical understanding and recommendations of developmentalists could be more integrally incorporated into the planning and execution of intervention programmes.

As Schaffer (1990) has pointed out, the reasons for this lack of integration are complex and well established. Clearly they are not unique to South African society, and simplistic solutions such as 'better communication' are unlikely to have any effect unless the structural and systemic constraints that separate the activities of researchers and interventionists in the real world are taken into account. Nevertheless, one possible way forward is for academic psychologists and research workers to become more involved in those policy-making forums and debates that concern transformational strategies. In such contexts the tensions between political and economic considerations and research or theoretical perspectives have to become explicit, and there is a better chance of their resolution if they can at least be confronted. Recent South African examples of the value of this sort of process have been the National Education Policy Investigation (1993) and initiatives in the area of mental health (e.g. Freeman 1992). On another level, practitioners and interventionists who actively monitor and critique their action, and are prepared to open this to debate through publication, may be powerful in bridging the gap (Stenhouse 1975). Thus action research, which of necessity brings together the demands of practical intervention with the theoretical and systematic constraints of research, constitutes an important challenge to the separating of research and intervention (Flanagan, Breen and Walker 1984).

Another important issue is prevention. Although this has been implicit in a number of contributions, it has been articulated most explicitly by Richter and Griesel (Chapter 4) in relation to malnutrition, Kvalsvig and Connolly (Chapter 5) in relation to health and sanitation, and Donald (Chapter 8) in relation to disability and special educational need. Despite the ease with which the term 'prevention' is used in the rhetoric of intervention, what is common to the notion as it has been developed here is its complexity. Effective prevention is not simple. Certainly any notion of prevention must take aetiology into account – what 'causes' a problem is what must be 'prevented'. However, what recurs thematically is that this relationship cannot be understood in simple, linear terms. The synergistic interaction of factors that in reality constitutes the web of aetiology for the sorts of problem which have been discussed defies linear analyses or solutions. Consistently what has been demonstrated and emphasised is that change at the macro, social-structural level is necessary but not sufficient. Equally, change at the micro, local and psychological level is necessary but not sufficient. The dynamic and constantly shifting relationship between these two levels must be recognised. A further complexity emphasised from the constructivist position is the active, agentic role of both child and adult, interventionist and 'interventionee', in the whole process. It follows that, to be effective, prevention cannot be a linear, single-focus and static process.

Clearly, radical and long-term preventive programmes as opposed to short-term, 'curative' programmes that address only the symptoms of a problem are desirable and central to any process of real change. If a meaningful way forward is to be found here it is in improving our understanding of how preventive intervention can effectively take place in the complex structural, social and interpersonal sets of relationship that constitute the social context of people's real lives.

The final theme relates to children's resilience and their coping strategies. These clearly have implications for intervention. Once again this has been referred to by a number of authors as central to understanding the nature of adversity and the conditions under which resistance to such adversity is possible. More specifically it has been explored by Richter (Chapter 2) in her discussion of the balance between economic stress and social support in the process of effective parenting, by Swart-Kruger and Donald (Chapter 6) in observations of the paradoxical survival strategies of street children, and by Dawes (Chapter 10) in his discussion of the relativity of the impact of political violence on the emotional development of children.

Perhaps the most central thought that emerges is the value of the notion of 'resilience' itself. It changes the way we look at the relationship of development and adversity. In the attempt to understand why and under what conditions some children and not others are able to resist apparently similar adverse circumstances, the focus shifts from broad, and not very useful, generalisations to much more elaborated and powerful formulations of the production of adversity.

In terms of intervention these conceptual shifts are crucial for a number of reasons. First, intervention programmes that have worked in other social contexts to alleviate apparently similar conditions of adversity may not be appropriate in the South African context. As has been emphasised by a number of authors, what is experienced and construed as adversity in one sociocultural context may not be experienced or construed in the same way in another – let alone what people regard as appropriate solutions to their own adversity.

Clearly, to be effective it is those factors promoting vulnerability that intervention should seek to change while those promoting resilience should be fostered. As should be evident, however, a line between these two poles is not easily drawn. In reality, we frequently have to live with ambivalence and relativity in the search for solutions.

In drawing together the major themes that have been developed through this volume, we have focused on some of the central challenges and possible ways of moving forward that we believe face the discipline of developmental psychology in South Africa. In so far as these challenges are common to other contexts – and we suspect that there may well be commonalities particularly with other developing countries – our hope is that the issues raised here will generate debate in the discipline as a whole.

References

Flanagan, W., Breen, C. and Walker, M. (1984). *Action Research – Justified Optimism or Wishful Thinking*. Cape Town: University of Cape Town.

Freeman, M. (1992). Providing mental health care for all in South Africa – Structure and strategy. Paper No. 24, Centre for Health Policy, University of the Witwatersrand, Johannesburg.

Lea, S. and Foster, D. (eds) (1990). *Perspectives on Mental Handicap in South Africa*. Durban: Butterworths.

Liddell, C. and Kvalsvig, J. (1990). Science and social accountability: Issues related to South African developmental psychology. *South African Journal of Psychology, 20,* 1–9.

National Education Policy Investigation (NEPI) (1993). *The Framework Report and Final Report Summaries*. Cape Town: Oxford University Press.

Rose, N. (1990). *Governing the Soul. The Shaping of the Private Self*. London: Routledge.

Schaffer, H. (1990) *Making Decisions about Children. Psychological Questions and Answers*. Oxford: Basil Blackwell.

South African Institute of Race Relations (1993). *Race Relations Survey 1992/93*. Braamfontein: SAIRR.

Stenhouse, L. (1975). *Introduction to Curriculum Research and Development*. London: Heinemann.

Index